OBSERVATIONS

ON THE NATURE OF

CIVIL LIBERTY,

THE PRINCIPLES OF

GOVERNMENT,

AND THE

JUSTICE AND POLICY

OF THE

WAR WITH AMERICA.

Quis furor iste novus? quo nunc, quo tenditis ——
Heu! miseri cives? non Hostem, inimicaque castra,
—— Vestras Spes uritis. VIRG.

By RICHARD PRICE, D.D. F.R.S.

THE EIGHTH EDITION,
With CORRECTIONS and ADDITIONS.

LONDON:
Printed for T. CADELL, in the STRAND.
M.DCC.LXXVIII.

Richard Price and the Ethical Foundations of
the American Revolution

Richard Price and the Ethical Foundations of the American Revolution

Selections from his pamphlets, with appendices, edited and interpreted in an introductory essay by Bernard Peach, with the research assistance of Jon Erik Larson

Duke University Press   Durham, North Carolina   1979

© 1979 Duke University Press
L.C.C. card number 77–91081
I.S.B.N. 0–8223–0400–7
Printed in the United States of
America by Heritage Printers, Inc.

For Amby

Contents

8   Contents

Preface

The three pamphlets written by Richard Price on the American Revolution are well worth reading at any time, but particularly so during the period of the bicentennial of those momentous events. Price was a loyal subject of Great Britain who thought the British were wrong, not only prudentially, financially, economically, militarily, and politically, but, above all, morally wrong. His first pamphlet, its Preface dated February 8, 1776, is entitled *Observations on the Nature of Civil Liberty, the Principles of Government and the Justice and Policy of the War with America.* After an analysis of the concept of liberty he applies the results of that analysis to the war with America, arguing that it is unjust and dishonorable, besides being impolitic, contrary to the British Constitution and, furthermore, likely to fail. *Observations* had an immediate and large sale. Different counts give different numbers of editions, but there were more than a dozen in London in 1776 and upwards of twenty altogether. It sold over a thousand copies in two days, went through five editions within a month and had a sale of over sixty thousand in six months. It was translated into German, French, and Dutch, and circulated widely on the Continent almost as rapidly as it did in the colonies where it was reprinted or published in Philadelphia, New York, Boston, and Charleston. It was widely recognized to be, and frequently referred to as, "the most famous British tract on the war with America." Although it concluded with a plea for the cessation of hostilities by Great Britain and reconciliation, its analyses, arguments, and conclusions, along with the admiration for the colonists and their moral position and qualities, could hardly fail to contribute to their reluctant recognition that there was no real alternative to independence.

Observations raised an extensive and vigorous pamphlet controversy in England, most, though not all, of the pamphlets coming from those who opposed Price's views, many of the writers being in the employ of the government. Finding some of his views not only vilified but misunderstood, Price wrote *Additional Observations on the Nature and Value of Civil Liberty, and the War with America* . . . which appeared early in 1777. He expanded his analysis of liberty, extended its application to the war with America, and greatly expanded his discussion of the economic impact upon Great Britain. It had three editions in London in 1777 and was reprinted in Dublin in 1777 and in Philadelphia in 1778.

In 1778 Price wrote a new, extensive introduction and published *Observations* and *Additional Observations* together under the title of *Two Tracts on Civil Liberty, the War with America, and the Finances of the Kingdom.* . . . It had two editions in London in 1778 and was reprinted in Dublin and Philadelphia in the same year. The *Introduction* is notable for its response to the criticism of Edmund Burke, a prelude to the manifestation of their deep differences over the French Revolution.

Price had many American friends before he wrote in favor of their cause, including Benjamin Franklin. Their correspondence and warm friendship extended over a period of almost thirty years. He corresponded with many Americans on matters of religion, government, finance, education, insurance, and science from the late 1750s or early 1760s until his death. He was well known for his philosophical, mathematical, actuarial, and scientific contributions before his political writings made him more famous on both sides of the Atlantic. His political views were applauded even in England, although by a relatively small group of people, mostly in his same Dissenting tradition, but also by others of liberal views including Lord Shelburne, Lord Chatham, Lord Ashburton, Colonel Isaac Barré, and the Duke of Cumberland. After his political tracts were transmitted to or published in America his name became a household word, certainly among those concerned with government—and at the time that included almost everyone. His honors were numerous, the esteem in which he was held obvious. For example, the Continental Congress on October 6, 1778, passed a motion authorizing Benjamin Franklin, Arthur Lee, or John Adams to invite him to become a citizen and reside in this country. (He found he could not accept.) On April 24, 1781, he and George Washington were voted Doctors of Laws degrees by the Yale Corporation. On January 30, 1782, the American Academy of Arts and Sciences of Boston voted him membership and on January 20, 1785, the American Philosophical Society of Philadelphia did the same.

His third pamphlet was entitled *Observations on the Importance of the American Revolution and the Means of Making it a Benefit to the World*. . . . He offered advice on financial policy and on maintaining peace by increasing the powers of Congress; argued for liberty of thought and discussion; warned of the dangers of debts, internal wars, too great inequalities of property, foreign trade, and oaths; and strongly criticized Negro trade and slavery. First published in 1784, the pamphlet had a second London edition in 1785. Intended by Price for circulation in the United States, it was printed in Boston in 1784, 1812, 1818, and 1820; in Philadelphia, New Haven, and Trenton in 1785; in Dublin and Amsterdam in the same year; and in Charleston in 1786. Jefferson wrote to Price from Paris that he had read it with pleasure and communicated it to others, that its observations were wise and just, and that he expected it to produce much good in America. On the matter of emancipation he suggested that an address from Price to the leading young men of Virginia might be decisive in their future decisions of policy.[1] Washington wrote to Price

---

1. See Appendix 8, Jefferson to Price, August 7, 1785, p. 333.

expressing the wish that "reasoning so sound should take deep root in the minds of the revolutionists."[2]

Price had, in effect, become a concerned citizen of the United States in everything but official status. Certainly to Washington's "revolutionists" he need only speak to be heard. His position had reached the point where anyone who knew him or his writing assumed that everyone else did too.

In the light of these circumstances his writings on the American Revolution should be more readily available. It is relevant and important to listen to what he has to say today as Washington, Jefferson, and Franklin did two hundred years ago. History repeatedly shows us that government cannot be divorced from moral questions. This is true not only in the sense that we must know what is good, in its numerous ramifications, in order to know what is morally good and, more particularly, to know what a good government is. It is true also in the sense that we must know what is right, in its numerous ramifications, in order to know what is morally right and, more particularly, to know when we have officers in government who are characterized by a concern to do what is right. Looking briefly at an analogy used by Price to bring out these relationships we find him saying that civil freedom is the highest value of a civil society as moral freedom is of the individual person. Individual freedom is the power of the individual to do as one pleases when not bound or limited by ignorance, partiality, desire for dominion over others, greed, or the like; in short, to be free is to be able to act in accordance with a knowledge of right and wrong. The autonomy is as essential as the knowledge; the knowledge is as essential as the autonomy. And for a state to be free, Price reminds us, we cannot say simply that it is just individual freedom writ large. The analogy is there, no doubt, as he points out, but the knowledge of right and wrong cannot be the knowledge of the civil society as such but must be the knowledge of its individual members and particularly of its leaders. The autonomy, on the other hand, is more directly analogous to the autonomy of the individual. It is the freedom of the civil society to act through its institutions as its citizens and leaders determine its policies and practices in the light of their knowledge of right and wrong, unencumbered by controls outside of these sources, and within a community of states where no state denies to another the rights and freedoms it claims for itself; that is, where liberty does not destroy itself.

History also will teach us, if we will only learn, that involvement and concerned attention, from the moral point of view, are necessary accompaniments of good government and that the condition of this kind of attention from this point of view is the liberty that Price analyzed under

2. Library of Congress, Washington to Price, November 1785. (Letterbook copy, Series 2, Volume 12, p. 263.)

four headings—physical, religious, moral, and civil; and on the basis of which he argued for maximum freedom of thought and investigation, of expression and communication. We may wish that these lessons did not have to be relearned, at what cost to the good and the right that would otherwise be available to everyone. Since the lessons must not only be learned but apparently relearned, in virtually every age, it is of some satisfaction that we have the writings of Richard Price to contribute their share to the teaching.

In making his pamphlets on the American Revolution available I wish to express my appreciation, first, to the National Endowment for the Humanities, Grant No. RO–6278–72–184. I wish also to thank the Duke Research Council for past and present help and the American Philosophical Society and the John Simon Guggenheim Foundation for help in the past in research on Richard Price and Anglo-American moral philosophy that has made significant contributions to this publication and will contribute to others to come in the future.

The project could not have been completed without the expert assistance of the officers and staff of the British Museum, the Library of Congress, and the Perkins Library at Duke University. I wish to thank in particular at Perkins Library Mary Canada, Janet Vogel, Susan Brinn, and Alice Estes of the Reference Department and Emerson Ford, head of the Interlibrary Loan Department. For excellent and perceptive typing I thank Betsy Godbey, Gwen Kincaid, Hilary Smith, Kristine Larson, and Jon Erik Larson. To the latter, in addition, I extend my thanks for his energy and insight, and his commitment to the often intriguing but sometimes frustrating task of tracking down references. His contributions deserve more than special appreciation.

From the literature on Price I have profited most in preparing this volume from Roland Thomas, *Richard Price, Philosopher and Apostle of Liberty* (London: Oxford University Press, Humphrey Milford, 1924; J. P. Agnew, "Richard Price and the American Revolution" (Ph.D. thesis, University of Illinois, 1949); Carl B. Cone, *Torchbearer of Freedom, The Influence of Richard Price on 18th Century Thought* (Lexington: University of Kentucky Press, 1952); D. O. Thomas, "The Political Philosophy of Richard Price" (Ph.D. thesis, University of Wales, 1956); and Henri Laboucheix, *Richard Price, Théoricien de la Révolution Américaine, Le Philosophe et le Sociologue, Le Pamphlétaire et L'Orateur* (Paris: Didier, 1970). M. Laboucheix makes the interesting claim that in comparison with Franklin, Jefferson, John Adams, Thomas Paine, and Turgot, Price was the best theoretician of the American Revolution from the moral and political points of view.

This book, like me, is dedicated to my wife, Amby.

Introduction

Richard Price was born in 1723 at Tynton in Glamorganshire. He attended various dissenting academies and was ordained to the nonconformist Presbyterian ministry at the age of twenty-one. He became chaplain to the Streatfield family of Stoke Newington, a post he held for twelve years. During this period he also officiated at various Meeting-houses in the vicinity and used the leisure time available in these circumstances to extend his studies in history, mathematics, economic and moral philosophy as well as in religion and theology. Of these studies the result that is most directly relevant to our concern for his views on the ethical foundations of the American Revolution was the publication, in 1758, of *A Review of the Principal Questions and Difficulties in Morals.* A second edition appeared in 1769 and a third in 1787, just four years before his death at Hackney in 1791. My references will be to D. D. Raphael's edition (Oxford: Clarendon Press, 1948), as *Review* followed by the page number.

After leaving the Streatfields in 1756 he served as morning and afternoon preacher at Stoke Newington before accepting a call as evening preacher to the Presbyterian congregation at Poor Jewry Lane in 1762. In 1770 he resigned from Poor Jewry Lane and shifted his service at Stoke Newington to evening in order to accept the pastorate at the Gravel-Pit Meeting House at Hackney, a post he occupied for the remainder of his life, also retaining the post at Newington until 1784.

Problems of moral philosophy and moral epistemology were basic concerns for him throughout his life and are the foundation of many of his views in other fields, particularly his sermons and political views. His ethical theory provides the basis from which I will discuss his three publications supporting the American cause. Before turning to those topics, however, it would be remiss not to mention the range and variety of his accomplishments.

His devotion to the pulpit and the associated practical duties had priority upon his energies throughout his life. It resulted in a series of sermons that are marked by intelligent concern for a variety of matters ranging from civil liberty and love of country to the security and happiness of a virtuous life, questions of immortality, and the relationship between God and truth. His duties were demanding enough that at one point he had to decline an invitation to edit the works of Sir Isaac Newton. But they did not prevent him from writing extensively on mathematical probability and a variety of other topics. In fact it was because of his contribution to the solution of a problem in the doctrine of chances, made as a result of being asked to examine the manuscript remains of his friend and fellow dissenting minister, the Reverend Thomas Bayes, F.R.S., that Price was elected a member of the Royal Society. His extensive actuarial work in numerous pamphlets and his two-volume *Observations on Reversionary Payments* have led more than one commentator to refer to him as the founder of life insurance and the father of old-age pensions. Although these titles may be extravagant, Price was much in demand for actuarial and financial advice. Requests came from as diverse sources as the president of Harvard University, Joseph Willard, about setting up a plan to pay annuities to the widows of Harvard professors and Congregational ministers in Massachusetts, to William Pitt, the Younger, when he was prime minister of Great Britain, about plans for a sinking fund. French statesmen, economists, and financiers, such as Turgot and Necker, sought his advice.

It is therefore not extravagant to refer to Price as philosopher, theologian, mathematician, and economist as well as "apostle of liberty" and "torchbearer of freedom." These phrases are used by two of his biographers who intend to emphasize his deep concern for liberty and freedom of the individual. Such concern is evident throughout his life and works but nowhere more than in his writings in support of the American cause. And these, in turn, are based on his ethical theory.

II

The main doctrines of Price's ethical theory may appropriately be considered in two main categories, epistemological and moral. In conscious opposition to the empiricism of Locke, Hutcheson, and Hume, particularly Hutcheson, Price maintains a rationalism according to which the understanding is a source of new simple ideas. This is of course not a refutation of the empirical theory that any new simple idea must originate in some manner of sensory experience, inner or outer, but an alternative to it. In support of his view Price argues that such ideas as equality, resemblance and difference, space, impenetrability, necessity, causation, and the like, cannot originate in any manner of sensory experience and that the knowledge we have in certain basic principles, for example, that one thing cannot be other than the thing it is, or that every new event must have some cause, cannot be accounted for satisfactorily in empirical terms alone. He maintains that the universality and necessity of these principles cannot be accounted for unless we have *some* ideas that are not derived from particular sensory experiences.

He uses the term "idea" vaguely, however; so the significance of his argument for the question whether the understanding can be a source of new simple ideas is not clear. But he does clearly hold, in the manner of Descartes, although his explicit references are to Plato and Cudworth, that there are certain *principles* that are known by rational intuition in the sense that they are ultimate in certain ways in certain contexts. This is also clear when Price applies his general epistemology to morals.

He argues, using a method later used by G. E. Moore and frequently referred to as "the open question" argument, that the idea of moral rightness is a simple indefinable idea and is original to the understanding in the same way as the ideas of identity, impenetrability, causation, and the like. His emphasis is again, however, on the *ultimacy* of rightness in the moral context. In a typical passage with a typical emphasis he says, ". . . if we will consider why it is right to conform ourselves to the relations in which persons and objects stand to us; we shall find ourselves obliged to terminate our views in a *simple perception,* and *something ultimately* approved, for which no justifying reason can be assigned" (*Review,* 127). In short, rightness is the foundation of morality in the sense that coming to know that an act, situation, or relation is right brings to a conclusion the process of justifying its occurrence or existence. The process of successively answering the question why, from the moral point of view, something should be done, can go no further, Price maintains, than answering truly that it is right that it should be done. This is the role played by the rational intuition of rightness (that is, by the "simple perception of something ultimately approved"). According to Price such an intuition is a moral ultimate; there is nothing more fundamental to appeal to, from the moral point of view, in justifying an act; and rightness cannot be reduced to anything else of a nonethical kind.

This is Price's version of the autonomy of ethics. Rightness is original, irreducible, and fundamental. Obligation and fitness are to be understood as its equivalents in the sense that it is impossible to distinguish between what is right or fit to be done and what ought to be done, although, Price points out, the occasions on which general obligation can be met are subject to differences of time and circumstance. Combining his rationalism and this claimed equivalence, Price concludes that statements asserting that an act is right, fit or obligatory, if true, are necessarily true. In his epistemological language, "right is a species of necessary truth," or, in his ontological language, "right denotes a real character of actions." Another indication of the fundamental role of rightness is that other ethical concepts can be analyzed or explained in its terms, for example, merit or desert. To say that a person deserves happiness is to say that it is right for him to be happy. Thus, for example, if a person does what he thinks are his duties, on the basis of information available, clear understanding, and impartiality, then he deserves happiness. That is, according to Price, the proposition that practical virtue is meritorious is necessarily true, and is known by rational intuition. It is, furthermore, descriptive of the nature of things, not a description or expression of a subjective feeling.

As such a principle it is one of many available to rational intuition. This plurality of principles indicates that considerations of utility or general happiness cannot be the sole criteria in judging what is right. Some acts are right just because of their nature, not because of their consequences for pain or pleasure, despite Priestley. Some acts are right even though not done out of concern for the well-being of others. So benevolence cannot constitute the whole of virtue, despite Hutcheson. Instead, Price maintains, there are several "heads of virtue." He gives a list of six, indicating that he does not consider it complete: (1) duty to God, (2) duty to self, (3) beneficence, (4) gratitude, (5) veracity, (6) justice. That is, one knows by rational intuition, according to Price, that if an act is one which meets a duty to God then it is right—for that reason, by its own nature and "in the nature of things." Similarly for acts that are prudent, benevolent, grateful, veracious, or just.

Although Price is opposed to the view that there is some single principle of morals such as utility or benevolence he is not therefore ready to accept an ultimate pluralism. Although different obligations are often compatible they may, on occasion, conflict. In such cases of conflict, Price says, we must weigh the respective obligations to find which one outweighs, cancels, or takes priority over another. Price recognizes that such a process of "weighing" can be difficult and involves the complicated processes of considering alternatives, taking as many factors as possible into consideration, thinking as carefully as possible, and the like. In the end he believes, however, that the right thing to do can become evident to reason; that is, the process can conclude with a rational intuition. But even if it does not, the truth about which obligation does in fact have priority is not altered, according to Price. "The weakness of our discerning faculties cannot in any case affect the truth" (*Review*, 168n). This leads him to attribute unity to virtue, even though its different "heads" or principles are not reducible to any single principle. He does not explicate the details of this unity but I believe that he would say, if pressed, that the principles are unified in the sense that our knowledge of them and ability to weigh priorities are based on the ability of reason to know what is right. This is one sense, an important one, I believe, in which Price would say that reason and right are the "foundations of morals." I shall refer to these doctrines under the general heading of "The Principle of Plurality and Unity."

To conclude this analytical summary of his ethical views that are basic to his political views we may take note of his distinction between practical and absolute virtue. He identifies as abstract or absolute virtue what is right in itself, right for an agent in such and such circumstances to do and what he would judge he ought to do if he judged truly. He identifies as practical or relative virtue what the agent sincerely believes is right, and what he believes in his heart he ought to do, considering what he knows. In order to do what is practically virtuous, Price says, liberty, intelligence, and a regard for rectitude are *severally* necessary and jointly sufficient. Price means by "liberty" "the power of acting and determining" and says it is self-evident that there are no moral capacities where there is no such power. The concepts of virtue and vice are meaningless without free agency and free choice. Moral praise and blame are significant only if the agent is responsible for his acts. "Ought" implies "can" and the agent can do what he ought only if he is *self*-determined (*Review*, 181). Nor can an agent have any moral capacities unless intelligent enough to know good and evil. Otherwise, according to Price, there would be no point in judging a person's actions from a moral point of view. These capacities, liberty and intelligence, he says, are the *conditions* of virtue but it is a regard for the right, the intention to do what is right, that "gives it actual being in a character" (*Review*, 184). Reason is practical in the sense that knowledge of right and wrong is sufficient to bring about an act. It follows, according to Price, that the degree of virtue is determined according to the degree of concern to do what is understood to be right.

Finally, on the relation of Price's moral philosophy and his theology: He insists that all necessary truths, including those of morality, are a part of God's nature. They constitute God's understanding rather than being something independent that is understood by Him. He therefore *is* truth, and also wisdom, reason, eternity, power, and perfection. In light of the necessary truth that virtue ought to be rewarded and the factual truth that it often is not in this life, Price concludes, on moral grounds, that retributive justices requires ("proves") existence beyond this life—though not unending existence or eternal bliss. Here he turns to the Christian revelation and concludes, with the insertion of some analysis of mathematical probability, in a version of Pascal's wager, "that by such a course as virtue and piety require we can in general lose nothing but may gain infinitely and that, on the contrary, by a careless ill-spent life we can get nothing, or at best, (happen what will) next to nothing, but may lose infinitely" (*Review*, 274)."

There are many controversial points in Price's ethical theory and many issues that deserve critical examination. My concerns are primarily expository and interpretive, however, so I shall proceed to a consideration of some of the relationships between his moral philosophy, his political philosophy, and "the justice and policy of the war with America."

III

The most fundamental relationship is evident in the extension into his political philosophy and his judgments on the justice and policy of the war with America of the roles played in his moral philosophy by the concepts of reason, right, and liberty. In this section I shall be concerned primarily with reason and its fundamental role, in the next with right and liberty and theirs.

In *Observations on Civil Liberty* the knowledge of his leading principle, that civil liberty is the power of a civil society to govern itself, is gained through rational intuition. Its consequences—that a civil society that does not govern itself does not have civil liberty, that in a free state every man is his own legislator, that liberty in its most perfect degree can be enjoyed only in small states or where the will of each individual is represented in the assembly of governors, that no community can have any rightful power over the property or legislation of another without a just and adequate representation, and the like—are known by means of deduction.

This kind of epistemological foundation of the moral foundations of civil society is made even more evident in some of Price's replies to his critics in *Additional Observations on Civil Liberty*. Often clarifying his normative orientation as contrasted with his critics' concentration on descriptive and factual circumstances, he expands without significant substantive changes his earlier account of civil liberty and reaffirms its intuitive and deductive foundations. He proceeds to draw further deductive consequences when he says that it follows from this true account of what a state ought to be that no people can cede their liberty. The context makes clear that he is using descriptive terminology with normative import. His point would be clearer and less open to objection if he had been more explicit that no people who conform to his account of what a state ought to be can cede their liberty. He would be even clearer if he had said no people who conform to his account of what a state ought to be can *consistently* cede their liberty. This normative aspect does become explicit, however, when he asserts that the occurrence of events or the existence of factual circumstances that are incompatible with his account of civil liberty do not constitute arguments against that account. In short, in clarifying and defending his account it has become apparent that his intuitionism and deductivism amount to a claim to knowledge of moral matters that is characterized by *defeasible necessity*.

Put in its simplest, possibly oversimplified, terms a defeasibly necessary principle states what will happen unless something (unusual) prevents it. Defeasible necessity also calls for a distinction between dispositions to do certain things and the occasions on which they are in fact done. For example, there is some basis for interpreting Price in such a way that defeasible necessity characterizes his doctrine that in a free state every person is his own legislator. He would not consider it logically impossible that someone in a free state should fail, on a given occasion, to be his own legislator. And of course he would not consider the principle a generalization derived from empirical evidence. He does not mean by it that in a free state every person probably is his own legislator, or that a certain number are, or even that they legislate for themselves on a certain percentage of their opportunities. This interpretation is supported by his refusal to respond to Adam Ferguson's criticism that such a doctrine gives thieves and pickpockets the right to make laws for themselves. I think Price considered his doctrine to be sufficiently evident that it is "in the nature of things" for a person in a free state to have the right to legislate for himself and to do so, unless there are circumstances that prevent him on some particular occasion. The necessity lies in the nature of people in a free state, in their capacities as morally free agents, to legislate (properly, correctly) for themselves. That they would not appropriately be considered to be members of the population of a free state without such a disposition is my interpretation of Price's claim that the truth of the doctrine is "undeniable." Yet surely, and I take this to be Ferguson's point, there are occasions on which a person does not act rationally, or does not act virtuously, or is not morally free. Thieves and pick-pockets are examples. The principle that every person is (that is, has the right to be) his own legislator may be defeated on particular occasions although it remains undeniably true, as I interpret Price, in its dispositional form.

This interpretation is perhaps even more evident in his response to the criticism that the liberty which he has supported is "a right or power in everyone to act as he likes without any restraint." After denying that this is a fair version of his account he expresses willingness to adopt it if appropriately understood. He is ready to define moral liberty as "a power in everyone to do as he likes." He thinks it unlikely that his opponents will understand or find it acceptable, however, even when explained in a way that is nearly a direct version of my interpretation in terms of defeasible necessity. It means, he says, that every person's will, "if perfectly free from restraint, would carry him invariably to rectitude and virtue."

If this interpretation seems to leave Price with a thin kind of necessity, he makes a more robust claim for religious liberty, although I believe it is correctly interpreted in substantially the same way. "Religious liberty," he says, "is a power of acting as we like in religion." He then makes more explicit the limitation that is implicit in his views on moral liberty: Since everyone has the same inalienable right to this liberty, no one has a right to encroach on the equal liberty of others. This limitation, he says, is self-evident, for if liberty went further there would be a "contradiction in the nature of things," namely, "it would be true that everyone had a right to enjoy what everyone had a right to destroy."

This seems to me to be a perceptive way to defend both liberty and the need for its limitation. It is in the rationalistic tradition with the particular ramifications introduced by the Cambridge Platonists that the contradiction whose denial is a self-evident truth is a contradiction "in the nature of things" and not merely in someone's thought or in language. It is for Price, as for others in his tradition, a contradiction in these senses as well. The nature of the contradiction is of some interest in its own right, however, as well as portraying a part of the epistemological foundations of Price's views on liberty.

"Everyone has a right to enjoy what everyone has a right to destroy" is not in itself a logical contradiction, although it looks more like one than its parent, "Everyone has unlimited liberty." What it shows, I believe, is that if everyone were actively to conform to the principle of unlimited liberty, it would be impossible for everyone to do as he pleased. In terms of a distinction that has not received wide acceptance, this is a pragmatic, rather than a logical, contradiction. In general terms a pragmatic contradiction is one in which something about the uttering or asserting of a proposition is incompatible with some of its practical consequences, that is, its consequences for action. In terms of a classification that, again, has not received wide acceptance, pragmatic contradictions have been distinguished into indicative or imperative, inherent or consequential, performative or conformative, implicit or explicit, and universal or particular. Price's "contradiction in the nature of things" in these terms is an indicative, consequential, conformative, implicit, universal pragmatic contradiction. If everyone conformed his actions to it, the consequence would be the frustration of an attitude implicit in the indicative form of its assertion or acceptance, namely, that everyone should (be free to) do as he pleases.

This kind of interpretation is not limited to Price's views on religious freedom. It is only more obvious here because Price makes his point in a way that makes the interpretation more obvious. For my purpose of pursuing the topic of his extension of the role of reason from his epistemology of morals to his political philosophy, it shows that his conception of the role of reason in morals is considerably broader than the view often attributed to the rational intuitionists, namely, of providing a direct insight into the necessary truth of general and particular moral truths. For in this case although Price appeals to self-evidence, he actually supports the claimed insight with an argument which appeals to consequences that would follow upon the generalization of the practice implicit in the doctrine.

The deductive or inferential role of reason is again indicated by Price when he says that the extension of the general concept of liberty to civil liberty is obvious. A citizen is free when the right to be his own legislator in the sense explained above is secured to him. A government is free when it is structured in such a way that it provides this security. And a community or nation is free when, among communities or nations, it has secured to it the power of legislating for itself in the same sense as the free citizen. There is, then, according to Price, a significant further extension of morality to politics which he offers in the form of an analogy. "It is not . . . then mere possession of liberty that denominates a citizen or a community free, but that security for the possession of it which arises from . . . a free government. . . ." So, also, it is not the mere performance of virtuous actions that "denominates an agent virtuous but the temper and habits from whence they spring. . . ."

Liberty, Price says, is the foundation of all the values of happiness and dignity that people may enjoy as members of civil society and the subjects of civil government. It follows, he claims, that a free government is the only form that is consistent with the basic ends of government, namely, to secure peaceable enjoyment of their citizens' rights and to protect against injustice and violence. Again Price offers a supporting argument in the form of an appeal to the pragmatic contradiction in denying this: "If the benefits of government are sought by establishing a government of men and not of laws made with common consent . . . [this] is . . . the folly of giving up liberty in order to maintain liberty."

A free government, furthermore, is the only kind that is favorable to human improvement. The tumults that often accompany them are due, Price suggests, to failures or inadequacies of detail or application of principle, not to their nature; and in any case, he argues on utilitarian grounds, when such tumults cannot be avoided they will do more good than harm. Finally, free governments are the only governments consistent with the natural and inherent equality with which each person is endowed by God.

Price claims that this is a true acount of what civil government ought to be, no matter what factual circumstances obtain in existing governments. That is, he defends this conception of government by an appeal to defeasible necessity and draws the further inferences that no people can lawfully surrender their liberty and that if they have (unlawfully) done so, they have the right to emancipate themselves. Such a redress of grievances depends upon having the governors responsible to the rest of the people. In large states this requires representation. The degree of security of rights is therefore dependent in part upon the degree of representation. Even an imperfect representation is better than none, and it follows that the most complete security of rights is dependent upon the most complete representation. It follows further, of course, according to Price, that the colonists are quite justified in their insistence upon being represented in the governing bodies of their civil society.

IV

Against this background of Price's conception of the fundamental role of reason in ethics and politics I shall now consider more particularly the extension of his other two basic concepts, namely, liberty and virtue, in some of his more specific applications of them to the American Revolution. In doing this I shall also be continuing my attempt to make more explicit the ways, or senses, in which Price would hold that the American Revolution had ethical foundations.

If my analysis and interpretation are substantially correct up to this point, Price has a much more extensive conception of the role of reason than is usually attributed to an intuitionist. It is a source of new simple ideas, including moral ideas, and has direct insight into general and specific truths, including moral truths. It provides inferential knowledge by deduction from such intuitive knowledge. So much has usually been attributed to rational intuitionism, although the first point was novel in Price's immediate historical context. In fact, it would probably be appropriate to say that he was the first rational intuitionist in this sense. The role of reason extends beyond these functions for Price but perhaps remains within the limits of intuitionism as fairly widely understood, in providing the culminating point of justification of action, belief, or judgment and in providing the basis for the unity of virtue not only in the intuitive knowledge or rightness but also in the role of judging the relative weights of conflicting obligations. This point will be discussed further in Section V as well as another, namely reason's being, or providing, a sufficient motive to conduct—which I interpret in terms of Price's use of imperatives. The first of these points represents a variation on a theme of intuitionism as sometimes understood, the second seems to me to be a definite extension. Finally, reason, according to Price, is both necessary and sufficient for understanding and using general concepts and, thereby, general and particular propositions. Here, again, however, I think Price's conception of the nature and function of reason goes considerably beyond any very widely accepted interpretation of intuitionism. For he not only holds that reason is necessary and sufficient for understanding nonempirical and logically necessary propositions but also empirical and logically contingent propositions, descriptive and normative propositions, and even, I shall claim, imperative propositions. With this range of functions for reason it should not be surprising to find him appealing to quite varied epistemological considerations in his specific applications of the concepts of liberty and virtue to the American Revolution.

In support of his general judgment that the practices and policies of Great Britain with regard to the colonies are unjust, we find him arguing that the act declaring Britain's power and right to make laws and statutes binding the colonies and people of America "in all cases whatever" makes slaves of them. The additional judgment that slavery is morally wrong is clearly implicit and is another, and more specific, instance of his general doctrine that it is appropriate to judge political matters from a moral point of view. Even more specifically, it shows that Price considers it appropriate, in fact mandatory in many cases, to decide a political conflict—whether to abide by this declaratory act or not—in terms of ethical considerations. Recalling the epistemological and ethical considerations mentioned in Section II about the "heads of virtue" it indicates that Price holds, quite generally, that moral and ethical factors carry "greater weight" than political factors.

This receives further support in his evaluation of the claim to the right to control the colonies because they are related to Great Britain as child to parent. Although his response is conditional and raises the interesting, important, controversial, and complex problem of the relationship of "is" to "ought," it also indicates again how ethical considerations are fundamental to political questions for Price. If we take the order of nature in the parent-child relationship as the model for what ought (morally) to be done, Price points out, Britain ought (morally) to have pursued a course in which control over the child was gradually relaxed and, at the appropriate time, relinquished altogether.

I shall not enter into the problem of deriving a conclusion about what ought to be done from a fact or set of facts about what is the case. It is not necessary in this case since Price is rebutting a claim by using an *ad hominem* argument in which he conditionally accepts the framework of his opponent and derives a contrary conclusion. The relevant point is that once again he displays his doctrine that ethical considerations are basic to political considerations: Having insight or understanding of an ethical obligation (however we may gain it epistemologically) determines the particular nature of the associated political obligation.

These cases are perhaps sufficient to indicate the general nature of Price's arguments that the practices and policies of Great Britain toward the colonies are unjust. They may also be sufficient to show that ethical considerations are fundamental to that conclusion, generally and particularly, and some of the ways in which they are. The general nature of his arguments is similar in his subsequent examination of the war with America with regard to the principles of the British constitution, policy and humanity, honor, and success.

Not surprisingly, pragmatic, factual, or tactical considerations play a
greater role in his discussion of policy and success. Even on these topics,
however, ethical considerations are fundamental if the issues are pushed
far enough. For example, in discussing the likelihood of success or failure,
Price points not only to logistical factors but to moral and religious factors.
And his religious appeal is actually a moral one. The colonists are "fighting on their own ground, within sight of their houses and families, and for
that sacred blessing of liberty, without which man is a beast and government a curse." In short, the colonists are doing what is morally right.

In the case of "policy," besides pointing out that there can be no advantage in the war for either side, that it is folly to endeavor to preserve
law and government in America by destroying law and government, that
insisting upon authority reduces it, that preserving America's liberty would
preserve Britain's, he also impugns the motives of Britain's leaders. Their
motives are—in the light of the follies of policy, they can only be—a lust
for power, love of dominion, resentment, and revenge. And when Price
judges such motives to be "infernal," it is clear that he goes beyond judgments of stupidity and ignorance to malice and viciousness. In short, the
motives behind some of the British policies in the war are morally wrong.

In fact, however, we do not need to force Price to push the issue this far
in order to find a moral judgment operating. We noticed in Section II, in
reviewing Price's general ethical theory, his denial that there is some one
basic principle underlying all moral judgments. He rejects Priestley's utilitarian principle as the fundamental moral principle, for example, as well
as Hutcheson's principle of benevolence. Instead, he holds that there are
several different considerations that have, or can have, independent moral
significance, including prudence. While one might question whether pru-
dential concerns are always moral concerns or would always lead to actions
or attitudes that are appropriately to be judged in moral terms, I think
there is a plausible interpretation of Price at this point. In the total context of the American Revolution he considers prudence to be a morally
significant factor in judging Britain's policy in the sense that actions based
upon the rational self-interest of Great Britain would either be morally
right, or would coincide with what is morally right. Thus while he would
deny that rational self-interest can be the one fundamental principle of
morals, despite Hobbes, he would not deny that it can, on occasion, play
a significant moral role even to the point of being a determining factor in
deciding what ought (morally) to be done.

A certain kind of prudence (for example, not wanting harm to befall
one's self) combined with a certain kind of consistency (for example, not
treating others in a way not acceptable to oneself) can actually take Price
quite a long way toward justifying the inclusion of prudence in his list of
the heads of virtue. It seems to me that he has something like this in mind

in his condemnation of inconsistencies in applications of the British constitution and of practices that are inconsistent with former honorable practices. He affirms that the essential characteristic of the British constitution is freedom from being commanded or altered by another civil power, including, in particular, the giving and granting of money. The retention of this right for the population of Great Britain—even though it is not in fact operative it is the *principle* of British government—and the denial of it, in principle, to the colonists is not only a violation of the British constitution. In treating two populations differently where there is no relevant difference in their respective natures or status, it is morally wrong.

There is no doubt that in judging the war with America to be dishonorable Price is making a straightforward moral judgment. It is of some interest, however, to notice that consistency also enters into questions of honor. The war is morally disgraceful not only because it is inconsistent with the feelings of Britons were they to be in a similar situation but also because it is inconsistent with their own former practice of applauding and encouraging the devotion to freedom. This is of course not the consistency of prudence but the consistency of respect for others as for oneself, the consistency of treating alike all those who do not differ in morally relevant ways.

Designed in large part to explain, clarify, or support his views in the original *Observations* against his critics, Price's application of his moral principles to particular cases in *Additional Observatons* does not offer a great deal that is new from the point of view of the ethical foundations of the American Revolution. Besides its extensive reaffirmation of the moral ideal of liberty, however, he argues that the war is unjustified because it is offensive and that the attempt to justify it by claiming the need for revenue from taxes is morally revolting to humanity. He argues against it again on grounds of prudence and self-interest, pointing out its financial folly and the practical contradiction in attempting to keep the colonies by slaughtering their population. At least, he asks, if we cannot be (morally) benevolent, can't we be prudent? In arguing that Britain forced the colonists to change their minds about independence, he again makes an appeal to consistency. He thereby indicates implicitly that the reasons for actions that can be judged to be morally right must apply to humanity generally. We Englishmen have, he points out, treated the colonists not only as if they were not Englishmen, with the feelings and passions of Englishmen, but as if they were not human beings with the reactions which we should expect, given our general knowledge of the principles which govern human nature. And in a mixed appeal to pragmatic and moral considerations he points out that the consequence of such inhumanity has been to bring about unity, self-reliance, military strength, and a just and virtuous government in the colonies.

It is worth mentioning at least one additional aspect of Price's views on the foundations of the American Revolution that appears more explicitly in *Additional Observations* than in the original *Observations*, although it is present there also.

Price had concluded *Observations* by recommending a plan of conciliation suggested by the Earl of Shelburne, who, as presented by Price, urged Britain to "meet the colonies on their own ground . . . suspend all hostilities. Repeal the acts which immediately distress America. . . . All the other acts . . . leave to a temperate revisal. . . ." At the conclusion of his *Additional Observations* Price is apparently more confident of the justification he has offered and he concludes with imperatives of his own.

> Make no longer war against yourselves. Withdraw your armies from your colonies. Offer your power to them as a protecting not a destroying power. Grant the security they desire to their property and charters and renounce those notions of dignity which lead you to prefer the exactions of force to the offerings of gratitude and to hazard everything to gain nothing.

These concluding imperatives, in both *Observations* and *Additional Observations*, raise interesting issues about their relationship to Price's analysis of the nature of liberty, the knowledge and practice of virtue, and his aims in applying his moral principles to the political issues between Britain and the colonies. I shall discuss his imperatives in more detail later. Here I will just say that Price would consider the imperatives *justified* by his moral espistemology and its application to the political issues in the total context of the American Revolution. Speaking generally of this justification, he would consider that the imperatives follow from his moral epistemology, its application to the moral and political issues between Britain and the colonies, and the moral and political aims of practical virtue, reconciliation of differences, avoidance or cessation of hostilities, maximization of liberty and virtue, and the like, which he has set out in *Observations* and *Additional Observations*. It would also be an appropriate interpretation of Price to say, somewhat more specifically, that in his imperatives, and in his appeal to those of Shelburne, he is attempting to move his readers to certain acts in the light of the reasons he has offered. In this sense, they might properly be called "rational imperatives."

Seven years after the publication of *Additional Observations* Price wrote his last book dealing directly with the American Revolution, *Observations on the Importance of the American Revolution and the Means of Making It a Benefit to the World* (first edition, March 1784, second edition, July 1785). The American Revolution had brought victory to the colonists, and the founding fathers were in the early phases of establishing the new republic of the United States of America. Whereas *Observations* and *Addi-*

tional Observations had concluded with imperatives which, according to my interpretation, Price would consider to be justified by analysis and argument within a moral and political context, he stops short of explicit imperatives in *Benefit* although in general it is more hortatory and direc- tive than either *Observations* or *Additional Observations*. He proceeds, rather, to give praise and advice along with some criticism and warning. He offers suggestions about policies and directions of developments, ex- presses hopes both specific and general about attitudes and practices and, in general, proceeds in a way that might be called normative, if the term is taken broadly enough to include advice and directives as well as value judgments of various kinds.

He moves from very sweeping praise of the American Revolution—for example, that its occurrence is next in importance to the advent of Chris- tianity—to quite straightforward and fairly specific pragmatic normatives about finances. Between these two extremes, he offers judgments of the relative good and evil of various practices; for example, in arguing for the liberty of thought, speech, and religion he judges that too little civil au- thority is better than too much, whereas in recommending greater powers for Congress he judges that restraint by civil authority is less evil than anarchy, and the dangers of the abuse of power less evil than the dangers of intestine wars. Not surprisingly he is much more specific on many points than he was in *Observations* or *Additional Observations*; for example, he recommends a regular census as a means of discovering, among other things, the "situations, employments and civil institutions . . . most favor- able to the health and happiness of mankind." There are further specifica- tions of the ethical foundations of the American Revolution, further variations on the themes of *Observations* and *Additional Observations* in terms of knowledge, liberty, and virtue, with the context of ends and means modified by the military victory of those he considered to be morally right. Despite the change of context, the ways in which Price indicates that ethical considerations are fundamental to the American Revolution (and now its consequences or possible consequences) carry over from *Observa- tions* and *Additional Observations* to *Benefit* with only a few variations.

The most general theme that runs through all three is that ethical or moral considerations prevail over others. That is, Price judges political, military, economic, or religious attitudes, practices, or policies from the moral point of view. This is evident in his initial general judgments of the progress and termination of the Revolution. In progress it spread "just sentiments" of the rights of mankind and the nature of legitimate govern- ment. In its termination it has preserved new governments from destruc- tion by Britain, provided a refuge for the oppressed, laid foundations for a country that can become the seat of liberty, science, and virtue. Price is tempted to see the hand of Providence working for the general good.

There is a more specific sense of "foundation" implicit in Price's judgment that acting from a concern to do what is morally right has brought about desirable changes of a political, economic, military, or religious kind. A further, somewhat more specific sense is evident in his suggestion that the political, military, economic, and educational results of the American Revolution can "produce a general diffusion of the principles of humanity, and become the means of setting free mankind from the shackles of super-stition and tyranny by leading them to see and know that nothing is funda-mental but impartial enquiry, an honest mind and virtuous practice." That is, ethical attitudes and practices are shown to be fundamental to political attitudes and practices when the political attitudes and practices aim at, or result in, the ethical attitudes and practices.

As a final point of specification, I think there is a new sense of the fun-damental role of ethics in his moral pragmatism of the middle way. Ac-cording to Price, if we apply the ethical principle of choosing the lesser of two evils we will come to the conclusion that a policy of less rather than more governmental control is advisable with regard to liberty of conduct in civil matters, liberty of discussion in speculative matters, and liberty of conscience in religious matters. On the other hand, applying the same ethical principle, we will come to the conclusion that a policy of more rather than less power in the hands of Congress is advisable when we com-pare the dangers of the possible abuse of that power with the miseries of internal strife. Here the basic nature of ethical factors is indicated by the way in which political practices or policies result from the application of an ethical principle. Another way to put it: political practices and policies ought to be guided by ethical principles.

These are some of the ways in which the ethical foundations of the American Revolution are apparent in Price's evaluation of it and of the means of making it a benefit to the world. His most ubiquitous sense, namely, judging political matters in ethical terms, runs through nearly every topic in *Benefit*. He not only judges the general progress of the American Revolution and the general significance of its conclusion in ethical terms, he also judges the apparent hand of Providence in the whole proceedings in ethical terms, namely as "working for the general good." I should add that this does not at all commit him to utilitarianism but only to the view that a concern for the general good is one of the "heads of virtue." He recognizes that the problem of peace and how to preserve it is in large part a matter of political, economic, and military policies and practices. But he views the whole issue under the aspect of ethics, even in-cluding questions of credit, strength, and respectability abroad and the mundane practice of census-taking at home. Questions of liberty were al-ways for Price ethical questions with the appropriateness of the political and religious practices and policies that affected them always being judged, ultimately, in ethical terms. Even in the case of making what might seem to be a purely pragmatic judgment upon the proper role of civil authorities with regard to the truth or tendencies of doctrines, his pragmatic conclusion is dominated by an ethical concern. Suppose, he says, that civil authority is too late in its actions to suppress the teaching of some doctrine that has brought about overt acts of injustice, violence, or defamation. This is (morally) preferable to the (moral) evil that can result from "making the rulers of states judges of the tendency of doctrines, subjecting freedom of enquiry to the control of their ignorance and perpetuating darkness, intolerance and slavery."

The most general way, then, in which Price shows the ethical foundations of the American Revolution and its consequences is by judging their various aspects in terms of ethical categories. This kind of judgment continues in *Benefit* through his discussion of religion, education, financial and military policies and practices, property and other economic topics, and culminates in his moral denunciation of Negro trade and slavery. This last topic is one of the few on which he censures the United States and praises Great Britain. His denunciation comes in a form that fittingly combines his most ubiquitous sense of foundation, his doctrine of the ultimate moral value of freedom, and his most fundamental appeal to reason. In short, it epitomizes Price's extension of the concepts of reason, liberty, and virtue to politics: After calling the practice "shocking to humanity, cruel, wicked and diabolical" and denying that the Americans deserve the liberty they fought for in the Revolution until they abolish both the trade and the practice, he says, "For it is self-evident that if there are men whom they have a right to hold in slavery there may be others who have had a right to hold them in slavery."

I have indicated that there is one very broad, very inclusive sense in which Price's three pamphlets indicate his conception of the ethical foundations of the American Revolution. But I have also indicated that there are a variety of ways, or senses, in which ethics can be regarded as fundamental—to politics, economics, religion, education, and the like—in Price's essays. I relegate the analysis of these senses to a footnote.[1]

---

1. There is a certain difficulty in attempting to give a reasonably precise and concise version of foundations from my interpretation of the way in which Price deals with the ethical foundations of the American Revolution. I shall use the symbol "E" to refer to a fairly broad spectrum of ethical and moral considerations and the symbol "P" to refer to an even broader spectrum of political, military, economic, educational, religious, financial, or generally "social" considerations. Against the background of Sections III and IV, particularly IV, I offer the following schemata:
1-a If P is judged in terms of E, then E is the foundation of P.
1-b If P is understood in terms of E, then E is the foundation of P.
1-c If P is understood by analogy with E, then E is the foundation of P.
2-a If a P-conclusion is deduced from an E-premise then E is the foundation of P.

I conclude this introductory essay with a consideration of Price's "imperative conclusions" in their context of normative judgments and descriptive background. My aim will be to show by an analysis, interpretation, and evaluation of Price's appeal to reason that it is fundamentally sound, fundamentally humanistic, and is reflected in the opening passages of the Declaration of Independence.

V

It is significant, I think, that Price concludes *Observations* and the section of *Additional Observations* that applies directly to the American war with a number of explicit imperatives or exhortations. It is sometimes thought that the resort to exhortation signals the end of rational thought, deliberation, or argument and constitutes an outright appeal to emotion or, in certain cases, to authority. It would seem odd and inconsistent of Price to make such a shift, considering the fundamental role played by reason throughout all his writings. It seems to me, therefore, not only advisable but necessary to consider whether there is not some plausible interpretation of his use of imperatives that is called for, and consistent with, this extensive appeal to reason.

One such interpretation is that Price considers his concluding imperatives to be based upon reason in a way that is not fundamentally different

---

2-b If a P-conclusion is immediately and necessarily deduced from an E-premise, then E is the foundation of P.

2-c If an E-premise is the major premise and a P-premise is a minor premise and a valid E-P conclusion follows, then E is the foundation of P.

3-a If E circumstances or considerations cause P circumstances or considerations, then E is the foundation of P.

3-b If E circumstances or considerations require P consequences, actions or policies then E is the foundation of P.

3-c If E circumstances or considerations change P circumstances or consequences then E is the foundation of P.

3-d If acting out of E-considerations brings about P-changes, then E is the foundation of P.

3-e If an E-ought requires a P-ought, then E is the foundation of P.

3-f If an E-ought determines a P-ought, then E is the foundation of P.

4-a If we answer a P-question in E-terms, then E is the foundation of P.

4-b If we decide a P-conflict in E-terms, then E is the foundation of P.

5   If P-actions are undertaken to achieve E-results, then E is the foundation of P.

6   If a P-conclusion results from the application of an E-principle, then E is foundation of P.

7   If E circumstances or considerations are common to all P circumstances or considerations, but not conversely, then E is the foundation of P.

These schemata are still uncomfortably vague but somewhat clearer and more precise than in Price's discussion of the American Revolution. Furthermore, I feel fairly confident that he would accept my suggested interpretation according to which at some point or other he has asserted or implied that the American Revolution has ethical foundations in *all* of these senses.

from the way in which he claims to derive consequences from his leading principles. This is consistent with his own statement at the end of *Observations* that such exhortation, even though offered by the Earl of Shelburne, is necessary "to complete his design" and in *Additional Observations* with his aim of bringing about a reconciliation with the colonies. That is, his exhortations come *at* the conclusion of an extensive process of deliberation and argumentation in which he has set forth a variety of relevant factual circumstances, defined his key concepts or terms, set up standards, ideals, aims and goals, elucidated historical sequences, and the like. So I think it is appropriate to say also that they come *as* the conclusion of that process of the use of reason, or at least Price would welcome such an interpretation. If we compress Price's argument in *Observations*, it will have some such structure as the following:

Civil liberty is the power of a civil government to govern itself, as moral liberty is the power of a person to govern one's self.

Civil liberty is the highest value of a civil community as moral liberty is of a person.

Each civil community or person has the inalienable right to these freedoms providing there are no infringements on the equal rights of others.

Many of Britain's policies and acts have removed, infringed, or denied these rightful values to the colonies and the colonists.

This has reduced the colonies to slave-states and the colonists to slavery, a condition of moral degradation.

Such policies and acts are not only foolish, imprudent, constitutionally, pragmatically, and morally inconsistent, but morally wrong.

They ought not to be, or to have been, done.

The war with America is dishonorable, unjustified, and unjustifiable.

All relevant factors being taken into account, including Britain's unjustifiable aggression, hostilities ought to cease.

There is no obligation in this context with greater weight.

Therefore, suspend all hostilities, discuss grievances in a reasonable way, repeal the acts that immediately distress the colonies, leaving others to a temperate revisal.

Detailed analysis of the many facets of such a process of reasoning is inappropriate to this general introduction.[2] It is appropriate to point out as an interpretation, however, that the "therefore" would be accepted by Price as an integral part of the process of reasoning and that he would

2. It would be much illuminated by H. N. Castañeda's *The Structure of Morality* (Springfield, Ill.: C. C. Thomas, 1974).

consider it a logical link from the premises to the conclusion. I think it would also be appropriate to attribute the view to Price that imperatives reached by this or similar processes of reasoning are final or ultimate in the sense that this is the last thing that can be done in the order of reasoning (and may therefore be called "practical reasoning") before action.

Another way in which Price's final use of imperatives is consistent with his emphasis upon reason is that in their role of influencing conduct he would regard them as rational guides of action, not as mere goads or prods. This is so, in my interpretation of Price, not only in the superficial sense that they must be understood in order to be obeyed (or disobeyed) but in the more significant sense that they function against a background of reasons, within a context of facts, definitions, conventions, commitments, and goals which determine their validity and which the agent must come to know, at least to some degree, if his conforming or nonconforming is to have moral significance. In short, some imperatives may be justified and some may be unjustified, and knowledge of their status in this respect can, and sometimes will, serve to guide, orient, or direct the actions of the person who comes to have such knowledge. As I interpret Price, virtually everything preceding them contributes to a justification of the exhortations and his utterance of them in *Observations* and *Additional Observations*. And, perhaps needless to add, the justified status of his imperative-exhortations is ultimately a matter of rational understanding and argument.

In fact, what is often taken as a characteristic, and characteristic weakness, of the type of intuitionism typified by Price may be at work in such cases. Price would not be averse to saying that if we are in circumstances where we understand everything that precedes the "therefore" we can "directly discern" the justification of the imperative to suspend hostilities. This doctrine is in part a psychological description of certain mental processes in certain situations. Price does not deny this but maintains that it is also an epistemological doctrine about a way of coming to acceptable or appropriate conclusions—in practical and moral matters as well as in logic, mathematics, or physics.

As a further interpretation, then, Price holds that we can immediately see that a certain imperative is justified in a certain context just as we can see that a certain proposition is true or follows necessarily from its premises. In both such cases, however, there is a large and complex background which will include the operation of other epistemological processes such as sensing, deducing, and inducing. If my interpretation of the rational status of Price's final imperatives is plausible, intuition comes into play for him as a culmination of these mental processes in the context of his understanding of the extensive complexities relevant to the American Revolution.

This epistemological doctrine of direct discernment of truth, rightness, or justification is perhaps the most widespread interpretation of "intuitionism." And, as I have indicated, with some qualifications, Price is an intuitionist in this sense—in his epistemology generally, in his moral epistemology, and, as I have interpreted the significance of his concluding imperatives, in practical reasoning. There is another aspect of intuitionism, however, which has historical standing in the writings of twentieth-century Anglo-American moralists. According to it intuitionism accepts a number of different fundamental moral principles that may conflict and denies that there is a set of priority rules whose application provides a fixed method of weighing these principles against one another.[3] That Price is also an intuitionist in this sense is indicated in his moral epistemology where he holds that there are several "branches of virtue" or "heads of rectitude and duty," none of which necessarily outweighs the others in every case (*Review*, 138–164). I will conclude by considering these aspects of Price's intuitionism as they relate to his imperatives in terms of his three central categories: reason, liberty, and virtue.

Two problems appear immediately. The first is that these doctrines do not seem to be compatible with my version of a part of his argument in *Observations* and *Additional Observations* in which he seemed to hold as a basic principle that civil liberty is the highest value of a civil state as moral liberty is of a person. The second is that liberty is not on his list of the heads of virtue.

The solution to the first problem is that although there may be conflicts of duty, there need not be. In the context of the American Revolution, as Price sees it, there is no conflict among the most fundamental duties. They all conspire to give an overwhelming weight to civil and personal liberty. This order of priority might not hold in a different context or if the context were changed. We see this when Price returns to the values of personal and civil liberty in *Benefit* after the Revolution had been successfully concluded by the colonists and he was advising them of the values of peace and of the best means of promoting it. Civil and personal liberty retain their status as values, virtues, or duties but, in the new circumstances where they are no longer endangered by coercive external forces, they must be weighed against the disadvantages of anarchy and the risk of the violation of power. I think there is no contradiction, then, between the doctrine of intuitionism, which states that there is no fixed hierarchy of basic principles or ordered priorities of duties, and the ascription of priority to liberty in Price's treatment of the American Revolution. Rather, it is his view, as I interpret it, that different principles may carry, or be given, different weights in different circumstances. The weight such

---

3. See J. O. Urmson, "A Defence of Intuitionism," in *Proceedings of the Aristotelian Society* 75 (1974–75): 111–119.

principles carry will of course, for Price, be found out by reason; or the
weight that any principle is given in its appropriate context will be the
result of the operations of reason in one form or another. The resultant
normative status of the principle and its power to justify its corresponding
imperative will, for Price, also be a result of these same, extended, operations of reason.

The second problem is to be solved in either of two ways: Price did not
claim that his list of the heads of virtue or basic duties was complete. It
might very well be that he could have added liberty to his list if he had
revised that section of the *Review* after writing on the American Revolution. (The fact that he did not make such a revision in the edition of 1787
weakens this solution but of course does not rule it out altogether.) Or, he
could have held that the duty, obligation, virtue, or value of liberty is
contained in or derivative from some listed head of virtue or some combi-
nation of them. There is no passage where Price explicitly offers such a
derivation, but there is a passage in *Additional Observations* that is readily
subject to such an interpretation. Arguing for legislative liberty for the
colonists, freedom to dispose of their property and to alter their governments, he quotes Hutcheson to the effect that there is a right time for this,
namely, "whenever they are so increased in numbers and strength, as to
be sufficient by themselves for all the good ends of a political union."[4] He
also appeals to Montesquieu's recommendation that England ought to
establish and maintain commerce with rather than dominion over the
colonies. From his reference to Hutcheson I elicit the view that Englishmen can know what is right and act in accordance with it by accepting an
imperative to respect the political liberty of the colonists. From his reference to Montesquieu I elicit not only this same view but also the argument
that increase in political dominion is incompatible with the security of
public liberty in general and therefore is morally wrong. The obligation
and imperative to respect and actively implement liberty, then, on this
interpretation, is derivative from a knowledge of what is morally right or
wrong. His own version of the matter could be put as follows: If we cannot
recognize the obligation and imperative to respect liberty out of considerations of benevolence, then at least we can out of considerations of prudence. And benevolence and prudence are, of course, two of his listed
"heads of rectitude and duty."

This interpretation is a consistent extension of my general interpretation of Price on the ethical foundations of the American Revolution. If we
take civil and personal liberty as political values, obligations, or imperatives and if they are derivative from the moral values, obligations, or imperatives listed by Price, then again ethics is shown to be fundamental to

4. Francis Hutcheson, *System of Moral Philosophy*, II:309.

politics in the sense that certain political obligations and imperatives are derived from certain ethical obligations and imperatives. And this fits the general pattern of my analysis of the ways or senses in which ethics is fundamental to politics for Price.[5]

This interpretation also extends to the imperatives of *Benefit* and supports further the interpretation of the contextual-like nature of Price's intuitionism, although there are some significant variations. For example, much of *Benefit* is couched in terms of advice, wishes, optatives, or optative questions. From a logical point of view they belong in the same family as imperatives, so I shall refer to them on occasion as "virtual-imperatives." They may be said to be rational, reasonable, or founded on reason, in much the same sense as the imperatives in the earlier works. There are two general modifications worth noting, however. The first is that their context is modified significantly by the successful outcome of the war of independence for the colonists. The second is that direct imperatives are not so appropriate in this context as they were at the end of *Observations* and *Additional Observations*—where they were almost "desperately appropriate."

Consider, for example, a paraphrased version of his treatment of liberty of discussion:

If some doctrines are too sacred to be discussed, all persecution of expression of opinion is justified.

Judgments of what doctrines are sacred must be made by civil magistrates according to their own opinions.

But civil powers are not proper judges of truth.

They ought to concern themselves with the protection of persons and property.

When they have acted as judges of truth they have hindered the progress of truth and the improvement of the world.

When civil government has performed its duties, and has encouraged rather than restrained discussion, mankind has been improved in knowledge and well-being; instance in Christianity.

Civil magistrates ought to restrict their cognizance to overt acts of injustice, violence, or defamation.

Even if they are too late in these functions, the proper inference is not that freedom of discussion should be limited but that we must choose between this evil and the evil of state control of discussion.

The latter is much more evil than the former.

Therefore, citizens and officials of the United States, let there be maximum liberty of discussion in your country.

---

5. See footnote 1, especially 3b–3f.

Expressing Price's conclusion in the optative rather then the imperative is more consistent with the general tenor of *Benefit* where he is offering suggestions, giving advice, making his wishes known, and the like. Price's imperatives in *Observations* and *Additional Observations* were expressed against a background of what he considered to be unjustifiable attack, following imprudent demands, both of them stemming from immoral motives of domination. Not surprisingly, when he came to his final conclusions, he found that he was "forced to cry out" to British leaders, "Make no longer war against yourselves. Withdraw your armies from your colonies. . . ." His final, urgent, even desperate, imperatives were directed to British leaders who did not agree with his goal of maximizing moral and civil liberty in the colonies. Even with the recognition that his imperatives would almost surely not be effective he found that he had to make them as urgent as he possibly could.

In the changed context of postrevolutionary America the tone is quite different. It is reasonable to assume a considerable agreement about the general goals desired by most of the Americans he is addressing. Logically speaking, his advice, entreaties, urgings, and the like are on a par with direct or explicit commands. Psychologically speaking, they do not have the stridency, urgency, or desperation of his previous imperatives. And, in general, they are closer to normatives because they remain more explicitly based upon reasons for acting than direct commands.

> Would it not be proper to take periodic surveys of the different states, their numbers of both sexes in every stage of life, their condition, occupation, property, etc.? Would not such surveys, in conjunction with accurate registers of births, marriages and deaths at all ages afford much important instruction by showing what laws govern human morality, and what situations, employments, and civil institutions are most favorable to the health and happiness of mankind?

These optative questions are much more appropriate in this context than the direct imperative, "Take censuses!" The optative, "Let censuses be taken for the good ends this will serve" falls between the explicit command to take them and the normative statement that taking them would serve good ends. Optatives are more obviously "rational" than direct imperatives by making the reasons for doing them explicit. They are perhaps "less rational" than normatives in this same respect, although perhaps not in those cases in which the end of the optative is made explicit in the optative itself, for example, "Let good results come from census-taking." In any case, the optative shares the "nonrational" aspect of the command in not being capable of being either true or false. Nevertheless it is appropriate to say that it is justified, and to recognize the role played by reason. As I interpret Price, it follows from the normatives and indicatives that precede it. Understanding this is a function of reason. Acceptance of the optative or its corresponding imperative involves not only an understanding of it in the sense of understanding its meaning but also some understanding of the context from which it emerges. Price epitomizes all this in his dictum that without knowledge nothing can properly be said to be an action.

We have now considered how reason and liberty function in Price's imperatives. It is evident that reason continues to play the most fundamental role in his views of the ethical foundations of the American Revolution. For every interpretation of "foundations" I have found some function of reason is involved, either explicitly or implicitly, in the way in which the ethical factor is fundamental to the political, economic, military, or religious aspect of the American Revolution. Without proceeding through all of Price's imperatives, that is, his optatives, advisements, recommendations, entreaties, urgings, warnings, and the like in *Benefit*, it would not be too much to say that they are all dependent upon the function of reason, more or less directly, guided by the imperative of personal and civil liberty, to the end that virtue prevail. And this brings us to the last of our three basic concepts.

In this context virtuous action, that is, the eighteenth-century "virtuous course," will be action in accordance with the imperative of liberty. As indicated, liberty might be one of Price's heads of virtue although he does not include it in his list, or it might be derivative from some of the heads of virtue explicitly listed. In either case, action in accordance with it as an imperative will be virtuous action and, in the context of his concern with the ethical foundations of the American Revolution, and of its subsequent benefit to humankind, such action will be, in general, the highest virtue. Nevertheless, in accordance with his "Principle of Plurality and Unity," it is not the only virtue nor will it be, without question and without exception, the highest. It might conflict, as Price has indicated, with the ideal of order and stability, so necessary in the early stages of a developing country. Or, just as Price recognizes that the principles of, say, benevolence and prudence may conflict on a given occasion, so both of them might, on a given occasion, conflict with the principle of liberty in one or another of its forms. That is, in a particular personal, moral, religious, or civil context virtuous action will consist in acting in accordance with the ideal obligation or imperative of personal, moral, religious, or civil liberty unless there are interfering factors in that context on that occasion. In short, compatibly with my earlier analysis, the principle of liberty is necessary according to Price, but defeasibly necessary. It will provide the imperative of action, the answer to "what shall I (we) do?" on a given occasion in a particular context, unless some other principle conflicts with it in such a way as to outweigh it. Price indicates one such case, for example, where civil liberty of a state might lead to anarchy and war between the states. In such circumstances the principle of order and stability, supported by the instrumentality of enlarged powers of Congress, outweighs the principle of liberty and provides the imperative of action.

In such circumstances virtuous action will be, as I interpret Price, action in accordance with a weighing up of the relevant factors on both sides. There is no superprinciple for him according to which the principle of liberty *always* will outweigh the principle of order and stability—or of prudence, benevolence, justice, reverence, gratitude or, veracity. It will always be possible that some one head of virtue, or even some derivative principle, will on a given occasion and in a particular context, outweigh any other. It will be the function of reason, as I understand Price, to examine the relevant considerations in these circumstances, to weigh up the factors on one side and the other, and to reach a conclusion through such an examination of facts, circumstances, conventions, and ideals. Such understanding constitutes an imperative or virtual imperative for action.

This, then, is my final interpretation of Price's intuitionism and the fundamental role played by reason in his ethics and thus in the ethical foundations of the American Revolution. As I interpret Price, he holds that there are several different basic moral reasons for action. Where a problem about what to do is complex there is no ready-made order of priority among these heads of virtue; in particular there is no ready-made order of priority where one of these basic moral reasons for action conflicts with another. This requires a rational (intuitive) weighing of the reasons on one side and the other. The study of the nature of people, the analysis of the concepts of liberty, justice, human dignity, and the like all give us some knowledge of some of the most basic relevant principles in these cases. Many principles, functioning as final imperatives of action, have such well-established justifications that they are self-evident to rational understanding in particular contexts. They need no explicit accompaniment by their justifying reasons. Even so, as Price indicates in his Principle of Plurality and Unity, they are not thereby excused from the requirement of having such a justification offered in their behalf if they should be challenged. And this situation is best expressed in its epitome, I believe, by a group of people, far more numerous at his time in the United States than in England, who belong in the same tradition as Richard Price, as followers of John Locke with some modifications. Their spokesman wrote on a given occasion in a particular context, "We *hold* these truths to be self-evident, that all men are created equal, that they are endowed by their Creator with certain inalienable rights, that among these are life, liberty and the pursuit of happiness. . . ."

Price might balk at my emphasis on the "hold" in "We *hold* these truths to be self-evident. . . ." But I think Thomas Jefferson, and the founding fathers, insofar as they accepted his mode of expression, may have expressed John Locke's views, as seen by Richard Price, in a way that does maximum justice to them all.[6] The opening passages of the Declaration of Independence reaffirm, with modifications, Locke's theory that the most fundamental moral values are the foundations of the most fundamental political values; the Declaration retains the basic emphasis on reason that is so characteristic of Price's views of the ethical foundations of the American Revolution, and it manages to convey, in a subtle yet significant and powerful way, the fundamentally humanistic nature of moral and political ultimates expressed by Price in his doctrine of practical virtue and the Principle of Plurality and Unity. In the first Price emphasized that the practically virtuous course open to people will be the course that a person believes he ought to follow in a certain context on a given occasion in the light of what he believes or understands in terms of facts, conventions, and circumstances on the one hand and in terms of hopes, fears, desires, aims, goals, and values on the other. In the end Price gives us a picture of a human being facing his political decisions in terms of his best understanding of these facts and values, in a context where reason provides its insights into the nature of rightness and virtue and their implications for liberty. In the second he emphasized that self-evidence does not in itself provide detailed answers to difficult problems either in ethics or in politics or political action. As I interpret Price, self-evident principles—in ethics or politics—are an essential part of the context of understanding, concluding, and acting. They will often indicate the ends or goals that need to be understood and, if possible, effected by action. And I would suggest that the difference between Price's rational intuitionism and Jefferson's implied rational voluntarism is reconcilable when self-evidence is interpreted in terms of the occasions on which a process of thought has culminated in the acceptance of a principle (or imperative) but the process has become submerged through frequent acceptance and unexceptionable use; in other words, where there is a rationally justified acceptance but the process of eliciting, displaying, or considering the justification is unnecessary or irrelevant.

With his recognition of the fallibility of an individual when he comes to the *application* of the principles of morality I think it is appropriate to suggest that Price would accept a summary interpretation of his views on the ethical foundations of the American Revolution along the following lines. In a certain context on a given occasion it is rationally justified to

---

6. I do not of course mean to suggest that Jefferson was directly influenced by Price in writing the Declaration, only that he explicitly formulated an aspect of their common tradition.

hold that certain truths are self-evident, that people have a right to life, liberty, and justice; that from these rationally justified principles it follows that the colonists have the right to life, liberty, and justice; that it follows, further, that there is a justified imperative applying to Britain to allow them to live under liberty and justice and that if they do not conform to this imperative the colonists have the right to resist by force of arms; and that having prevailed they can make their revolution a benefit to the world by establishing their own security, by establishing and securing liberty of discussion, conscience, and education and extending them by example and by providing a place of refuge for those who want them.

A Note on the Editions

There are two editions of the *General Introduction*, both dated 1778, the second with a supplement on finance and economics. It was published and bound separately from the other tracts. I have used this second edition, omitting the supplement. I have used the edition of *Observations* identified as the eighth and dated 1778, from the first edition of *Two Tracts*, and an edition of *Additional Observations* dated 1777 from this same edition of *Two Tracts*, omitting the sections on finance and economics. It is bound separately and has no edition statement but is almost certainly the first edition. So, in effect, I have used the first edition of *Two Tracts* except for the *General Introduction*. I have used the second edition of *Observations on the Importance of the American Revolution and the Means of Making it a Benefit to the World*, dated 1785, first edition 1784, including the letter to Price from Turgot. In each case I have compared them with the earlier or later editions and have indicated the differences in bracketed footnotes along with other editorial comments or information, using arabic numerals. Brackets elsewhere indicate editorial modifications except in the contents for the second tract where they indicate sections omitted from this edition. Price's footnotes are indicated by lowercase letters. The differences are not extensive or complex in the case of the *General Introduction* or *Benefit*. The case of *Two Tracts* is considerably different.

The important survey of Thomas R. Adams (*American Independence, The Growth of an Idea* [Providence, R.I.: Brown University Press, 1965], 224a–224z) indicates that 1776 saw eighteen (or sixteen) numbered editions of *Observations*, of which three are identified as the eighth, and at least six different printings. To the bibliographer's and editor's delight and dismay, fulfillment, and frustration, however, Price made changes in the eighth edition of *Observations* used as the first tract in the first edition of *Two Tracts* from earlier separate editions which were also identified as the eighth. In the edition of *Two Tracts* identified as the second he used the second edition of the *General Introduction*, dated April 24, 1778, the eighth edition of *Observations* with further, though minor, changes and an edition of *Additional Observations* with no edition number and most of the changes in the financial sections. The two other copies of *Two Tracts* that I have examined, one housed in the British Museum, the other in the Library of Congress, also differ in significant ways. Neither has an edition identification. The copy in the British Museum has a long quote from Hume's *History of England* in the introduction to *Additional Observations*. I shall refer to it as *Two Tracts-H*. The copy in the Library of Congress includes an edition of *Additional Observations* identified as the third, from which Price has deleted the ascription of "want of address" to M. Turgot, minister of finance in France from 1774 to 1776. (See the opening passages of Turgot's letter to Price, and the notes, pp. 215–216.) So this copy of *Additional Observations* would seem to have been published after the other eight copies I have examined, since they all contain the passage, whether they were published separately or as the second tract of *Two Tracts*. There are copies of *Additional Observations* in the British Museum identified as the second and third, but published separately, and an edition of *Two Tracts*, identified as the second, namely, *Two Tracts-H*, which contain the passage even though Price indicates in his footnote to the letter from Turgot that he had removed it after the first edition of *Two Tracts*. Yet the copy of *Two Tracts* which includes this latest variant of *Additional Observations* also includes the earliest edition of the *General Introduction*, dated January 19, 1778. I shall cite it as *Two Tracts-T*.

Needless to say, the bibliographical details can become extremely complex and exquisitely subtle. They deserve special treatment in detail that goes beyond anything appropriate here, and I am preparing such an analysis for publication. For the purposes of this volume I should indicate that I have compared all the copies of the four main texts that are held by the British Museum and the Library of Congress (with the help of Jon Larson), as well as by several libraries in the eastern United States, including a copy of the rare thirteenth edition of *Observations* at Harvard. Mr. Adams could not locate copies of the tenth or twelfth editions of *Observations* and I have had equal success. I believe the evidence is virtually conclusive that they do not exist. When a change originates in the eighth edition of *Observations* in the first edition of *Two Tracts* I will indicate this by a note that it was not in editions 1–13, following Adams's practice of completing the sequence up to the existent and numbered thirteenth edition despite the ghostly nature of the tenth and twelfth.

The collations show that a majority of Price's changes were in the sections dealing with economics and finance, which have not been included in this volume, not being directly relevant to the ethical foundations of the American Revolution. The page-by-page and line-by-line collations revealed differences that were less extensive than they might otherwise have been because of Price's sensible practice of answering his critics in an additional pamphlet rather than revising the original one. In *Additional Observations*, along with other topics, he clarifies, expands, underscores, reaffirms or illustrates points from *Observations* that had been subjected to criticism. Some of these criticisms are contained in the appendices, although the literature of the controversy he aroused is far too extensive and varied to be more than suggested by the selections it has been possible to include in this volume. The criteria for selection have been relevance to the ethical foundations of the American Revolution, the criticism of

Price's views or his replies or, more generally, the significance of Price's views as they relate in a theoretical or practical way to issues or individuals central to the Revolution.

Spelling, punctuation, and italics have been somewhat modernized, but minimally in quotations from official or semiofficial sources. I have favoured the "-our" spelling of English English, however, over the "-or" spelling of American English.

The General Introduction and Supplement to the Two Tracts on Civil Liberty, the War with America, and the Finances of the Kingdom

General Introduction.

The first of the following tracts was published in the beginning of the year 1776 and the second in the beginning of last year. They are now offered to the public in one volume, with corrections and additions. All the calculations in the appendix to the first tract have been transferred to the second and fourth sections in the third part of the second tract.[1]

The section on public loans in the second tract[2] has been revised with care, and a supplement to it, containing additional proposals and some necessary explanations, has been given at the end of the whole. This is a subject to which I have applied (perhaps too unprofitably) much of my attention. I have now done with it and the whole is referred to the candid examination of those who may be better informed, hoping for their indulgence should they find that, in any instance, I have been mistaken. I have not meant, in any thing I have said on this subject, to censure any persons. That accumulation of artificial debt which I have pointed out, and by which the danger of the kingdom from its growing burdens has been so needlessly increased, has, I doubt not, been the effect of inattention in our ministers and the scheme, by which the loan of last year has been procured, gives reason to hope that better plans of borrowing will be adopted for the future.

The principal design of the first part of the second tract was (as I have observed in the introduction to it) to remove the misapprehensions of my sentiments on civil liberty and government into which some had fallen. It gives me concern to find it has not answered that end in the degree I wished. I am still charged with maintaining opinions which tend to subvert all civil authority. I paid little regard to this charge while it was confined to the advocates for the principles which have produced the present war but as it seems lately to have been given the public from the authority of a writer of the first character[a] it is impossible I should not be impressed

---

a. See Mr. Burke's[3] *Letter to the Sheriffs of Bristol* [Appendix 6, pp. 272–274. Edmund Burke, *A Letter from Edmund Burke, Esq.; One of the Representatives in Parliament for the City of Bristol, to John Farr and John Harris, Esqrs., Sheriffs of that City, on the Affairs of America* (London: Printed for J. Dodsley, 1777)].

---

1. The third part of the second tract, i.e., *Additional Observations on Civil Liberty* (hereafter cited as *Additional Observations*), is not included in this volume.

2. The section on public loans in the second tract (Part II, section iii of *Additional Observations*) is not included in this volume.

3. Edmund Burke (1729–1797), statesman, orator, and political theorist; educated at Trinity College, Dublin, and at the Middle Temple; editor and founder of the *Annual Register* (1758); secretary to the Marquess of Rockingham (1765–1782); member of Parlia-

by it, and I find myself under necessity of taking farther notice of it.

There are two accounts, directly opposite to one another, which have been given of the origin of civil government. One of them is that "civil government is an expedient contrived by human prudence for gaining security against oppression and that, consequently, the power of civil governors is a delegation or trust from the people for accomplishing this end."

The other account is that "civil government is an ordinance of the Deity, by which the body of mankind are given up to the will of a few and, consequently, that it is a trust from the Deity, in the exercise of which civil governors are accountable only to him."

The question, "which of these accounts we ought to receive," is important in the highest degree. There is no question which more deeply affects the happiness and dignity of man as a citizen of this world. If the former account is right, the people (that is, the body of independent agents in every community) are their own legislators. All civil authority is properly their authority. Civil governors are only public servants and their power, being delegated, is by its nature limited. On the contrary, if the latter account is right, the people have nothing to do with their own government. They are placed by their Maker in the situation of cattle on an estate which the owner 4may4 dispose of as he pleases. Civil governors are a body of masters, constituted such by inherent rights and their power is a commission from Heaven,5 unbounded in its extent, 6and never to be resisted.6

I have espoused, with some zeal, the first of these accounts and in the following tracts endeavoured to explain and defend it. And this is all I have done to give countenance to the charge I have mentioned. Even the masterly writer who, after a crowd of writers infinitely his inferiors, seems to have taken up this accusation against me, often expresses himself as if he had adopted the same idea of government.*b* Such indeed is my opinion of his good sense, and such has been the zeal which he has discovered for the rights of mankind, that I think it scarcely possible his ideas and mine on this subject should be very different. His language, however, sometimes puzzles me and, particularly, when he intimates that government is an institution of divine authority,*c* when he scouts all discussions of the na-

---

b. "To follow, not to force the public inclination, to give a direction, a form, a technical dress and a specific sanction to the general sense of the community, is the true end of legislature. When it goes beyond this, its authority will be precarious, let its rights be what they will." *Letter to the Sheriffs of Bristol* [Appendix 6, p. 272].

c. [Appendix 6, p. 274.] *Thoughts on the Cause of the Present Discontents,* p. 67 [Edmund Burke, *Thoughts on the Cause of the Present Discontents* (London: Printed for J. Dodsley, 1770)]. "Government certainly is an institution of divine authority, though

---

ment for Bristol (1774–1780) and for Malton (1780–1794); instigator of the impeachment proceedings against Warren Hastings (1787); opponent of the French Revolution.

4. Edition 1 reads "has the right to."

5. Edition 1 inserts "held by divine right."

6. Not in edition 1.

ture of civil liberty, the foundation of civil rights, and the principles of a free government, and when he asserts the competence of our legislature to revive the High Commission Court and Star Chamber, and its boundless authority not only over the people of Britain, but over distant communities who have no voice in it.

---

its forms and the persons who administer it all originate from the people."[7] It is probable that Mr. Burke means only that government is a divine institution in the same sense in which any other expedient of human prudence for gaining protection against injury may be called a divine institution. All that we owe immediately to our own foresight and industry must ultimately be ascribed to God the giver of all our powers and the cause of all causes. It is in this sense that St. Paul in Rom. 13:1–2 calls civil magistracy the ordinance of God and says that there is no power but of God. If any one wants to be convinced of this, he should read the excellent Bishop Hoadly's[8] sermon entitled *The Measures of Submission to the Civil Magistrate*, and the defences of it [Benjamin Hoadly, *The Measures of Submission to the Civil Magistrate, Consider'd. In Defense of the Doctrine Deliver'd in a Sermon Preach'd before the Rt. Hon. the Lord Mayor, Aldermen and Citizens of London, Sept. 29, 1705* (London: Printed for Tim. Childe, 1706)].

It is further probable that when Mr. Burke asserts the omnipotence of parliaments, or their competence to establish any oppressions [Appendix 6, pp. 271–272 and 274], he means mere power abstracted from right, or the same sort of power and competence that trustees have to betray their trust, or that armed ruffians have to rob and murder. Nor should I doubt whether this is his meaning, were it not for the passage I have quoted from him in the last page, the latter part of which seems to imply that a legislature may contradict its end and yet retain its rights. Some of the justest remarks on this subject may be found in the Earl of Abingdon's[9] *Thoughts on Mr. Burke's Letter*, a pamphlet which (on account of the excellent public principles it maintains, and the spirit of liberty it breathes, as well as the rank of the writer) [10]must give particular pleasure to every friend to the true interests of this country[10] [Willoughby Bertie, *Thoughts on the Letter of Edmund Burke, Esq. to the Sheriffs of Bristol, on the Affairs of America* (Oxford: Printed for W. Jackson, 1777)].

In [Appendix 6, p. 270] Mr. Burke says that "if there is one man in the world more zealous than another for the supremacy of parliament and the rights of this imperial crown, it is himself, though many may be more knowing in the extent and the foundation of these rights." He adds that "he has constantly declined such disquisitions, not being qualified for the chair of a professor in metaphysics, and not choosing to put the solid interests of the kingdom on speculative grounds" [Appendix 6, p. 270]. *The less knowledge, the more zeal*, is a maxim which experience has dreadfully verified in religion. But he that, in the present case, should apply this maxim to Mr. Burke, would, whatever he

---

7. The relevant passage reads: "The king is the representative of the people; so are the lords; so are the judges. They all are trustees for the people as well as the commons because no power is given for the sole sake of the holder; and although government certainly is an institution of divine authority, yet its forms, and the persons who administer it, all originate from the people." "Thoughts on the Cause of the Present Discontents," in *The Works of the Right Honourable Edmund Burke*, rev. ed. .Boston: Little, Brown, and Company, 1865), 1:492.

8. Benjamin Hoadly (1675–1761), bishop of Bangor, Hereford, Salisbury, and Winchester.

9. Willoughby Bertie, fourth Earl of Abingdon (1740–1799), politician and political writer; educated at Winchester School under William Markham and at Magdalen College, Oxford; frequent speaker in the House of Lords. Burke felt so keenly attacked by *Thoughts on the Letter of Edmund Burke* that he asked Bertie to suppress it. See *Dictionary of National Biography*, s.v. "Bertie, Willoughby."

10. Edition 1 reads "must give to every friend to the true interest of this country particular pleasure."

But whatever may be Mr. Burke's sentiments on this subject, he cannot possibly think of the former account of government that "it is a speculation which destroys all authority."[13] Both accounts establish an authority. The difference is that one derives it from the people and makes it a limited authority and the other derives it from Heaven and makes it unlimited. I have repeatedly declared my admiration of such a constitution of government as our own would be, were the House of Commons a fair representation of the kingdom and under no undue influence. The sum of all I have meant to maintain is, "that legitimate government, as opposed to oppression and tyranny, consists in the dominion of equal laws made with common consent, or of men over themselves, and not in the dominion of communities over communities, or of any men over other men." (Introduction to the second tract, p. [130]). How then can it be pretended that I have aimed at destroying all authority? Does our own constitution destroy all authority? Is the authority of equal laws made with common consent no authority? Must there be no government in a state that governs itself? Or must an institution, contrived by the united counsels of the members of a community for restraining licentiousness and gaining security against injury and violence, encourage licentiousness and give to every one a power to commit what outrages he pleases.

---

may say of himself, greatly injure him. Though he chooses to decry enquiries into the nature of liberty there are, I am persuaded, few in the world whose zeal for it is more united to extensive knowledge and an exalted understanding. He calls it [Appendix 6, p. 273] "the vital spring and energy of a state, and a blessing of the first order." He cannot, therefore, think that too much pains may be taken to understand it. He must know that nothing but usurpation and error can suffer by enquiry and discussion.

Mr. Wilkes,[11] in an excellent speech which he lately made in moving for the repeal of the declaratory law, observed that this law was a compromise to which the great men, under whose administration it was passed, were forced in order to obtain the repeal of the Stamp Act.[12] I think so highly of that administration and of the service it did the public, that I have little doubt of the truth of this observation. But, at the same time, I cannot help wishing Mr. Burke had given no reason for doubt by defending the principle of that act, a principle which, unquestionably, he and his friends would never have acted upon but which others have since acted upon, with a violence which has brought us to the brink of ruin.

---

11. John Wilkes (1727–1797), journalist, patriot, politician, exile, controversial figure.

12. On December 10, 1777, Wilkes moved the repeal of the Declaratory Act. The relevant passage from Wilkes's speech in support of that motion reads: "I have great reverence, Sir, for the memory of that Whig administration which passed the Declaratory Act. . . . Many excellent regulations of trade and commerce were made by them. But, Sir, I should have thought all their glories sullied by the passing of this Declaratory Act, which pretends to establish a claim of unlimited authority over the colonies, if I did not believe it was a kind of force on that administration, a sort of compromise with the traitors at home for the repeal of the Stamp Act, which had thrown the whole empire into convulsions." T. C. Hansard, ed., *The Parliamentary History of England, from the Earliest Period to the Year 1803* (London: Printed by T. C. Hansard, Peterborough-Court, Fleet Street, for Longman, Hurst, Rees, Orme, & Brown; etc., 1814), 19:570–571. Hereafter cited as *Parliamentary History.*

13. Appendix 6, p. 273.

The Archbishop of York[14] (in a sermon preached before the society for propagating the gospel in foreign parts, Feb. 21, 1777)[15] has taken notice of some loose opinions, as he calls them, which have been lately current on civil liberty, some who mean delinquency having given accounts of it "by which every man's honour is made to be the rule of his obedience, all the bad passions are let loose, and those dear interests abandoned to outrage for the protection of which we trust in law."[16] It is not difficult to guess at one of the delinquents intended in these words. In opposition to the horrid sentiments of liberty which they describe, but which in reality no man in his senses ever entertained, the Archbishop defines it to be simply the supremacy of law, or government by law, without adding to law, as I had done, the words "equal" and "made with common consent,"[d] and without opposing a government by law to a government by men, as others had done. According to him, therefore, the supremacy of law must be liberty, whatever the law is, or whoever makes it. In despotic countries government by law is the same with government by the will of one man, which Hooker[17] has called *the misery of all men*, but, according to this definition, it is liberty. In England formerly the law consigned to the flames all who denied certain established points of faith. Even now it subjects to fines, imprisonment and banishment all teachers of religion who have not subscribed the doctrinal articles of the church of England; and the good Archbishop, not thinking the law in this case sufficiently rigorous, has proposed putting Protestant Dissenters under the same restraints with the Papists.[e] And

d. In [Appendix 5, p. 263] he calls liberty "a freedom from all restraints except such as established law imposes for the good of the community." But this addition can make no difference of any consequence as long as it is not specified where the power is lodged of judging what laws are for the good of the community. In countries where the laws are the edicts of absolute princes the end professed is always the good of the community.

e. "The laws against Papists have been extremely severe. New dangers may arise and if at any time another denomination of men should be equally dangerous to our civil interests it would be justifiable to lay them under similar restraints" [Appendix 5, p. 262]. In another part of this sermon the great men in opposition (some of the first in the kingdom in respect of rank, ability, and virtue) are described as a body of men void of principle who, without regarding the relation in which they stand to the community, have entered into a league for advancing their private interest and "who are held together by the same bond that keeps together the lowest and wickedest combinations" [Appendix 5, p. 264]. Was there ever such a censure delivered from a pulpit? What

14. William Markham (1719–1807), scholar and clergyman; educated at Christ Church, Oxford; headmaster of Winchester School (1753–1765); dean of Rochester (1765–1767); dean of Christ Church, Oxford (1767–1776); bishop of Chester (1771–1776); archbishop of York (1776–1807).

15. William Markham, *A Sermon Preached before the Incorporated Society for the Propagation of the Gospel in Foreign Parts; at their Anniversary Meeting in the Parish Church of St. Mary-le-Bow, on Friday February 21, 1777* (London: Printed by T. Harrison and S. Brooke, 1777). See Appendix 5.

16. Appendix 5, p. 263.

17. Richard Hooker (1554?–1600), theologian and parish priest; author of *Laws of Ecclesiastical Polity*.

should this be done, if done by law, it will be the establishment of liberty.

The truth is that a government by law is or is not liberty just as the laws are just or unjust and as the body of the people do or do not participate in the power of making them. The learned prelate seems to have thought otherwise and therefore has given a definition of liberty which might as well have been given of slavery.

At the conclusion of his sermon the Archbishop adds words which he calls comfortable, addressed to those who had been patient in tribulation,[f] and intimating that they might rejoice in hope, "a ray of brightness then appearing after a prospect which has been long dark." [19] And in an account which follows the sermon, from one of the missionaries in the province of New York, it is said that "the rebellion would undoubtedly be crushed and that then will be the time for taking steps for the increase of the church in America by granting it an episcopate." [20] In conformity to the sentiments of this missionary the Archbishop also expresses his hope that the opportunity which such an event will give for establishing episcopacy among the colonists will not be lost, and advises that measures should be thought

---

wonder is it that the Dissenters should come in for a share in his Grace's abuse? Their political principles, he says, are growing dangerous. On what does he ground this insinuation? He is mistaken if he imagines that they are all such delinquents as the author of the following tracts or that they think universally as he does of the war with America. On this subject they are, like other bodies of men in the kingdom, of different opinions. But I will tell him in what they agree. They agree in detesting the doctrines of passive obedience and non-resistance. They are all whigs, enemies to arbitrary power, and firmly attached to those principles of civil and religious liberty which produced the Glorious Revolution and the Hanoverian Succession. Such principles are the nation's best defence and Protestant Dissenters have hitherto reckoned it their glory to be distinguished by zeal for them and an adherence to them. Once these principles were approved by men in power. No good can be expected if they are now reckoned dangerous.

f. That is, the missionaries of the society in America. The charter of the society declares the end of its incorporation to be "propagating the gospel in foreign parts and making provision for the worship of God in those plantations which wanted the administration of God's word and sacraments and were abandoned to atheism and infidelity." [18] The chief business, on the contrary, of the society has been to provide for the support of episcopalianism in the northern colonies, and particularly New England, where the sacraments are more regularly administered and the people less abandoned to infidelity than perhaps in any country under heaven. The missionaries employed and paid by the society for this purpose have generally been clergymen of the highest principles in church and state. America, having been for some time very hostile to men of such principles, most of them have been obliged to take refuge in this country and here they have, I am afraid, been too successful in propagating their own resentments, in misleading our rulers, and widening the breach which has produced the present war.

---

18. See "The Charter of the Society [for the Propagation of the Gospel in Foreign Parts], June 16, 1701," in Charles F. Pascoe, *Two Hundred Years of the S.P.G.: An Historical Account of the Society for the Propagation of the Gospel in Foreign Parts, 1701–1900* (London: Published at the Society's Office, 1901), 2:932–935.

19. Appendix 5, p. 264.

20. William Markham, *A Sermon* . . . , Appendix, An Abstract of the Proceedings of the Society, February 1776 to February 1777, p. 67.

of for that purpose, and for thereby rescuing the church from the persecution it has long suffered in America.

This is a subject so important, and it has been so much misrepresented, that I cannot help going out of my way to give a brief account of it.

It does not appear that the lay members themselves of the church in America have ever wished for bishops. On the contrary, the assembly of Virginia (the first episcopal colony) some years ago returned thanks to two clergymen in that colony, who had protested against a resolution of the other clergy to petition for bishops.[21] The church here cannot have a right to impose bishops on the church in another country and, therefore, while churchmen in America are averse to bishops it must be persecution to send bishops among them. The Presbyterians, and other religious sects there, are willing, from a sense of the reasonableness of toleration, to admit bishops whenever the body of episcopalian laity shall desire them, provided security is given that they shall be officers merely spiritual, possessed of no other powers than those which are necessary to the full exercise of that mode of religious worship. It is not bishops, as spiritual officers, they have opposed but bishops on a state-establishment, bishops with civil powers, bishops at the head of ecclesiastical courts maintained by taxing other sects and possessed of a pre-eminence which would be incompatible with the equality which has long subsisted among all religious sects in America. In this last respect the colonies have hitherto enjoyed a happiness which is unparalleled but which the introduction of such bishops as would be sent from hence would destroy. In Pennsylvania(one of the happiest countries under heaven before we carried into it desolation and carnage) all sects of Christians have been always perfectly on a level, the legislature taking no part with any one sect against others but protecting all equally as far as they are peaceable. The state of the colonies north of Pennsylvania is much the same and in the province of Massachusetts Bay, in particular, civil authority interposes no farther in religion than by imposing a tax for supporting public worship, leaving to all the power of applying the tax to the support of that mode of public worship which they like best. This

---

21. On July 12, 1771, the House of Burgesses of Virginia passed the following resolution: "Resolved, *nemine contradicente*, that the thanks of this House be given to the Reverend Mr. Henley, the Reverend Mr. Gwatkin, the Reverend Mr. Hewitt, and the Reverend Mr. Bland, for the wise and well timed opposition they have made to the pernicious project of a few mistaken clergymen for introducing an American bishop, a measure by which much disturbance, great anxiety, and apprehension would certainly take place among his Majesty's faithful American subjects, and that Mr. Richard Henry Lee and Mr. Bland do acquaint them therewith." John Pendleton Kennedy, ed., *Journals of the House of Burgesses of Virginia* (Richmond, Va.: The Colonial Press, 1906), 7:122. For a brief account of the events preceeding the acceptance of this resolution, see Arthur Lyon Cross, *The Anglican Episcopate and the American Colonies* (Cambridge, Mass.: Harvard University Press, 1924), pp. 230–236.

tax the episcopalians were, at one time, obliged to pay in common with others but so far did the province carry its indulgence of them that an act was passed on purpose to excuse them.[22] With this let the state of Protestant Dissenters in this country be compared. Not only are they obliged to pay tithes for the support of the established church but their worship is not even tolerated unless their ministers will subscribe the articles of the church. In consequence of having long scrupled this subscription they have lost all legal right to protection and are exposed to the cruelest penalties. Uneasy in such a situation, they not long ago applied twice to parliament for the repeal of the penal laws against them. Bills for that purpose were brought into the House of Commons and passed that House. But in the House of Lords they were rejected in consequence of the opposition of the bishops.[23] There are few I reverence so much as some on the sacred bench but such conduct (and may I not add the alacrity with which most of them support the present measures?) must leave an indelible stain upon them and will probably exclude them for ever from America.

On this occasion I cannot help thinking with concern of the learned prelate's feelings. After a prospect long dark he had discovered a ray of brightness showing him America reduced and the church triumphant. But lately that ray of brightness has vanished and defeat has taken place of victory and conquest. And what do we now see? What a different prospect, mortifying to the learned prelate, presents itself: A great people likely to be formed, in spite of all our efforts, into free communities under governments which have no religious tests and establishments![g] A new era

g. I am sorry to mention one exception to the fact here intimated. The new constitution for Pennsylvania (in other respects wise and liberal) is dishonoured by a religious test. It requires an acknowledgement of the divine inspiration of the Old and New Testament as a condition of being admitted to a seat in the House of Representatives directing however, at the same time, that no other religious test shall for ever hereafter be required of any civil officer.[24] This has been, probably, an accommodation to the prejudices

22. "An act in addition to the several acts or laws of this province for the settlement and support of ministers," Mass. Province Laws, 1742–43, ch. 8. See Daniel Thomas Vose Huntoon, ed., *The Acts and Resolves Public and Private, of the Province of the Massachusetts Bay: to Which are Prefixed the Charters of the Province* (Boston: Printed for the Commonwealth by Albert J. Wright, 1878), 3:25.

23. On April 3, 1772, the Bill for the Relief of Protestant Dissenters was presented to the House of Lords. The bill, if it had been enacted into law, would have removed the requirement that religious teachers subscribe to the thirty-nine articles of faith. A second reading of the bill was approved on April 14 by a vote of 70 to 9; but the bill was defeated on May 19 by a vote of 102 to 29. See *Parliamentary History*, 17:431–446.

24. Penn. Const. art. 2, sec. 10 (1776). The relevant passage reads: "And each member, before he takes his seat, shall make and subscribe the following declaration, viz.:

" 'I do believe in one God, the creator and governor of the universe, the rewarder of the good and the punisher of the wicked. And I do acknowledge the Scriptures of the Old and New Testament to be given by Divine inspiration.'

"And no further or other religious test shall ever hereafter be required of any civil officer or magistrate in this State." See Benjamin Perley Poore, ed., *The Federal and State*

in future annals and a new opening in human affairs beginning among the descendents of Englishmen in a new world. A rising empire extended over an immense continent without bishops, without nobles, and without kings.

O the depth of the riches of the wisdom of God! How unsearchable are his judgments!

But to proceed to another subject.

In the second of the following tracts, page [160]), I have observed that in former times it was the custom of parliament to pass bills for appointing commissioners to take, state, and examine the public accounts. I have lately had it in my power to inform myself more particularly on this subject and I shall here beg leave to give a brief recital of some of the principal facts relating to it.

The first bill for the purpose I have mentioned was passed in the times of the commonwealth and in the year 1653.[26] It was called an "act for accounts and for clearing of public debts and discovering frauds and concealments." Seven commissioners were named in it and the necessary powers given them. In 1667, another act was passed for the same purpose,[27] after which I find no account of any such acts till the beginning of the reign of King William. At this time complaints of mismanagement and embezzlements in the disposition of public money were become so prevalent that the House of Commons thought it necessary to enter into measures

of some of the narrower sects in the province to which the more liberal part have for the present thought fit to yield and, therefore, it may be expected that it will not be of long continuance.

Religious tests and subscriptions in general and all establishments of particular systems of faith with civil emoluments annexed do inconceivable mischief by turning religion into a trade, by engendering strife and persecution, by forming hypocrites, by obstructing the progress of truth, and fettering and perverting the human mind, nor will the world ever grow much wiser or better or happier till, by the abolition of them, truth can gain fair play and reason free scope for exertion. The Archbishop [in Appendix 5, p. 262] speaks of Christianity as "insufficient to rely on its own energies and of the assistances which it is the business of civil authority to provide for gospel truths." A worse slander was never thrown on gospel truths. Christianity disdains such assistances as the corrupted governments of this world are capable of giving it. Politicians and statesmen know little of it. Their enmity has sometimes done it good but their friendship, by supporting [25]superstitions and idolatries[25] carrying its name, has been almost fatal to it.

Constitutions, Colonial Charters, and Other Organic Laws of the United States, pt. 2 (Washington, D.C.: Government Printing Office, 1875), p. 1543. Hereafter cited as *Federal and State Constitutions*.

25. Edition 1 reads "corruptions."

26. "An act for accounts and clearing of public debts; and for discovering frauds or concealments of anything due to the Commonwealth," passed October 7, 1654.

27. "An act for taking the accounts of the several sums of money therein mentioned," 19 Charles 2, ch. 9.

for effectually preventing them by obliging all revenue officers to make up their accounts and bringing defaulters to justice.

With these views six of the acts I have mentioned were passed between the years 1690 and 1701.[28] Another act was passed in the first of Queen Anne and three more in her four last years.[29] In King William's reign they were always passed by the House of Commons without a division. In Queen Anne's reign, not one passed without a division. In 1717 a motion for such an act was rejected without a division[30] and since 1717 only one motion has been made for such a bill and it was rejected by a majority of 136 to 66.[h,31]

The preamble to those acts declares the reason of them to be that "the kingdom may be satisfied and truly informed whether all the monies granted by parliament have been faithfully issued and applied to the end

h. In 1742, after the resignation of Sir Robert Walpole.[32]

---

28. The six acts passed between 1690 and 1701 are: (1) "An act for appointing and enabling commissioners to examine, take, and state the public accounts of the kingdom," 2 William & Mary, sess. 2, ch. 11, passed in 1690; (2) "An act for examining, taking, and stating the public accounts of this kingdom," 4 & 5 William & Mary, ch. 11, passed in 1693; (3) "An act for appointing and enabling commissioners to examine, take, and state the public accounts of the kingdom," 5 & 6 William & Mary, ch. 23, passed in 1694; (4) "An act for appointing and enabling commissioners to examine, take, and state the public accounts," 6 & 7 William 3, ch. 9, passed in 1695; (5) "An act for appointing commissioners to take, examine, and determine the debts due to the army, navy, and for transport service; and also an acount of the prizes taken during the late war," 11 & 12 William 3, ch. 8, passed in 1700; (6) "An act for reviving and continuing an act, entitled, 'An act for appointing commissioners to take . . . the debts due to the army . . . ,' " 13 William 3, ch. 1, passed in 1701.

29. The four acts passed during Queen Anne's reign were: (1) "An act for taking, examining, and stating the public accounts of the kingdom," 1 Anne, ch. 10, passed in 1701 (2) "An act for taking, examining, and stating the public accounts of this kingdom," 9 Anne, ch. 13, passed in 1710; (3) "An act for appointing commissioners to take, examine, and determine the debts due to the army, transport service, and sick and wounded," 10 Anne, ch. 31, passed in 1711; (4) "An act to revive and continue the act for taking . . . the public accounts of the kingdom; and also to continue the act for appointing commissioners to take . . . the debts due to the army, transport service, and sick and wounded," 13 Anne, ch. 3, passed in 1713.

30. Price appears to be mistaken on this point. In 1717 three separate motions for acts to examine the debts due to the army were passed by the House of Commons and sent to the House of Lords for concurrence. Furthermore, at least two more such motions were passed by the House of Commons in the years 1718 and 1721. See *The Journals of the House of Commons* (London: Printed by the order of the House of Commons, n.d.), 18:516f., 592, 618, 619, 621, 622, 684f., 751; 19:119f., 640f. Hereafter cited as *Journals of Commons.*

It should also be noted that this passage, which states that the last motion made before 1741 for an act to examine the debts of the nation was moved in 1717, is inconsistent with a passage on page 160 of *Additional Observations*, which states that the last motion made before 1741 of that kind was moved in 1715.

31. The motion to which Price refers was made on January 20, 1741–1742, and defeated by a vote of 136 to 66 on June 1, 1741–1742. See *Journals of Commons*, 24:51, 268.

32. Robert Walpole, first earl of Orford (1676–1745), politician; advocate of the Hanoverian succession; first lord of the treasury (1721–1742).

for which they had been given and that all loyal subjects may be thereby encouraged more cheerfully to bear the burdens laid upon them."[33] The number of commissioners named in them was generally nine or seven, all members of the House of Commons. It was particularly ordered that they should take an account of all the revenues brought into the receipt of the exchequer, and all arrears thereof, of all monies in the hands of the receivers general of the land tax, customs and excise, of all the public stores, provisions, etc. as well for land as sea service, of all ships of war, and the sums of money provided or paid for the use of the forces by sea and land and the number of them respectively, and of any briberies or corruptions in any persons concerned in the receiving or disposing of the national treasure. And for these purposes they were empowered to call before them, and to examine upon oath, the officers of the exchequer, the secretary at war, paymaster of the forces, commissioners of the navy and ordnance, and all persons whatever employed as commissioners, or otherwise, in or about the Treasury.

The reports, which the commissioners thus appointed delivered from time to time to parliament, contain accounts of a waste of public money arising from the rapacity of contractors and many scandalous abuses and frauds in every part of the public service which must shock every person not grown callous to all the feelings of honesty and honour. In consequence of these reports the House of Commons addressed the throne and remonstrated, several great men were accused and brought to shame, some were dismissed from their places and ordered to be prosecuted, some expelled, and some committed to the Tower. Thus did our representatives in those times discharge their duty as guardians of the public property and it is, in my opinion, only by such means that they are capable of doing this properly and effectually. It must, however, be acknowledged that these commissions of enquiry did not produce all the good effects which might have been expected from them. The influence of the crown and the interest in parliament of many great men entrusted with the disposition of public money rendered the proper execution of them extremely difficult. This led some even of the Tories, at the time of the great change of ministers in 1710, to propose that the receiving and issuing of the public money should be taken from the crown and, in defence of this proposal, it was urged that the issuing of public money, being in some of the most despotic countries left in the hands of the people, it was by no means a necessary part of the royal prerogative. This would indeed have provided a complete remedy

33. The relevant passage reads: ". . . this kingdom may be satisfied and truly informed whether all the same revenues, monies and provisions have been faithfully issued out, disposed, ordered and expended for the ends and purposes aforesaid and that their Majesty's loyal subjects may thereby be encouraged more cheerfully to undergo the like burdens for the support of your Majesties' government. . . ." *Statutes of the Realm* (London: Dawsons of Pall Mall, 1810–1822), 6:243.

and it might have perpetuated the constitution. But, even in these times, it was a reformation too great and too impracticable to engage much attention.

Ever since those times the public accounts have been growing more complicated and the temptations to profusion and embezzlement have been increasing with increasing luxury and dissipation. How astonishing then is it that every idea of such commissions should be now lost and that, at a time when the nation is labouring under expences almost too heavy to be borne, the passing of accounts by the House of Commons is become little more than a matter of form, our representatives scarcely thinking it worth their while to attend on such occasions, and millions of the public treasure being sometimes given away, in a few hours, just as proposed by the Treasury, without debate or enquiry.

I must not forget to mention particularly on this subject that the commissioners named in the acts I have described were always declared incapable of holding any place or office of profit under the crown and directed to take an account "of all pensions, salaries, and sums of money paid or payable to members of parliament out of the revenue or otherwise." Not long before this time the House of Commons would not suffer even the attorney-general[i] to sit and vote in the house because he was the king's servant, and in 1678 a member, as Mr. Trenchard[36] says, was committed to the Tower for only saying in the house that the king might keep guards for his defence if he could pay them. Such once was the House of Commons —so jealous of the power of the crown, and so chaste. Since the reign of Queen Anne and the passing of the Septennial Act[37] a great change has

---

i. Sir Francis Bacon[34] was the second attorney-general who sat in the House of Commons but, to prevent its being drawn into a precedent, the House would not admit him till they had made an order that no attorney-general should for the future be allowed to sit and vote in that house. In conformity to this order, whenever afterwards a member was appointed attorney-general, his place was vacated and a new writ issued. This continued to be the practice till the year 1670, when Sir Heneage Finch,[35] (afterwards Earl of Nottingham) being appointed attorney-general, he was allowed by connivance to preserve his seat, which connivance has been continued ever since. I give these facts not from any enquiry or knowledge of my own but from the authority of a friend who is perhaps better informed than any person in the kingdom on every subject of this kind.

---

34. Francis Bacon, Viscount St. Albans (1561–1626), philosopher, politician; attorney general (1613–1617); lord chancellor (1618–1621).

35. Heneage Finch, first earl of Nottingham (1621–1682), constitutional lawyer and politician; solicitor-general, attorney general, lord keeper of the seals, lord chancellor.

36. John Trenchard (1662–1723), lawyer, political writer; publisher, with Thomas Gordon, of "The Independent Whig" in 1720–1721. Gordon and Finch also coauthored a series of letters from 1720 to 1723 under the pseudonym "Cato."

37. The Septennial Act, 1 George 1, ch. 38, passed in 1714, changed the period for the continuance of parliaments from three to seven years. See Danby Pickering, ed., *Statutes at Large* (Cambridge: Printed for Charles Bathurst, 1762), 13:282. Hereafter cited as *Statutes at Large*.

taken place.*ʲ* A change which is little less than the total ruin of the constitution and which may end in a tyranny the most oppressive and insupportable. It is, therefore, the greatest evil which could have happened to us, and the men by whose abominable policy it has been accomplished ought to be followed with the everlasting execrations of every friend to public virtue and liberty.

j. The following facts will show, in some degree, how this change has been brought about. For ten years ending Aug. 1, 1717 (a period comprehending in it a general war abroad and the demise of the crown, the establishment of a new family, and an open rebellion at home) the money expended in secret services amounted only to £279,444. For ten years ending Feb. 11, 1742, it amounted to no less a sum than 384,600, of which 50,077 was paid to printers of newspapers and writers for government, and a greater sum expended in the last six weeks of these ten years than had been spent in three years before Aug. 1710. See the report of the committee appointed March 23, 1742 to enquire into the conduct of Robert, Earl of Orford, printed in the Journals of the House of Commons, vol. 24, pp. 295, 296, 300. One passage in this report contains remarks so much to my present purpose and so important that I cannot help copying it. "There are no laws particularly adapted to the case of a minister who clandestinely employs the money of the public, and the whole power and profitable employments that attend the collecting and disposing of it, against the people. And, by this profusion, and criminal distribution of offices, in some measure justifies the expence the particular persons are obliged to be at, by making it necessary to the preservation of all that is valuable to a free nation. For in that case, the contest is plain and visible. It is whether the Commons shall retain the third state in their own hands while this whole dispute is carried on at the expence of the people and, on the side of the minister, out of the money granted to support and secure the constitutional independence of the three branches of the legislature. This method of corruption is as sure and, therefore, as criminal a way of subverting the constitution as by an armed force. It is a crime productive of a total destruction of the very being of this government and is so high and unnatural, that nothing but the powers of parliament can reach it; and, as it never can meet with parliamentary animadversion but when it is unsuccessful, it must seek for its security in the extent and efficacy of the michief it produces," p. 395.[38] The obstructions which this committee met with in their enquiry proved that the crime they here describe in such emphatical language had even then obtained that very security in the extent of the mischief it produced which, they observe, it was under a necessity of seeking.

---

38. The relevant passage reads: "Some expences the laws allow by regulating the manner of them and those who engage in illicit expences are subject to heavy penal laws. But there are none particularly adapted to the case of a minister who clandestinely employs the money of the public, and the whole power and profitable employments that attend the collecting and disposing of it, against the people. And, by this profusion and criminal distribution of offices, in some measure justifies the expence that particular persons are obliged to be at, by making it necessary for the preservation of all that is valuable to a free nation. For in that case, the contest is plain and visible. It is whether the Commons shall retain the third state in their own hands whilst this whole dispute is carried on at the expense of the people and, on the side of the minister, out of the money granted to support and secure the constitutional independency of the three branches of the legislature.

"This method of corruption is as sure, and therefore, your committee apprehended as criminal a way of subverting the constitution as by an armed force. It is a crime productive of a total destruction of the very being of this government and is so high and unnatural that nothing but the powers of Parliament can reach it; and, as it can never meet with parliamentary animadverison but when it is unsuccessful, it must seek for its security in the extent and efficacy of the mischief is produces. . . ." *Journals of Commons,* 24:295.

I now withdraw to the situation of an anxious spectator of public events but before I do this I must leave with the public, at this threatening period, the following sentiments.

Not long ago the colonies might have been kept, without bloodshed or trouble, by repealing the acts which have made us the aggressors in the present war but now it would be great folly to expect this. At the same time I think it certain that they may be rendered more useful to us by a pacification on liberal terms which shall bind them to us as friends than by any victories or slaughters (were they possible) which can force them to submit to us as subjects. I think it also certain that should the offer of such terms be delayed till they have formed an alliance with France this country is undone. Such an alliance, we may hope, is not yet settled. Our rulers, therefore, may possibly have still a moment for pausing and retreating and every dictate of prudence and feeling of humanity requires them to be speedy and earnest in improving it. But what am I saying? I know this must not be expected. Too full of ideas of our own dignity, too proud to retract, and too tenacious of dominion, we seem determined to persist. And the consequence must be that the colonies will become the allies of France, that a general war will be kindled and, perhaps, this once happy country be made, in just retribution, the seat of that desolation and misery which it has produced in other countries.

January 19, 1778.[39]

[40] Since the publication of the preceding introduction the event referred to at the end of it has been announced to the public. A memorial from the French court has been delivered to our court, declaring that the former has concluded a treaty of commerce and friendship with the colonies as independent states and acquainting us that, in concert with them, the king of France is determined and prepared to defend his commerce against any interruption we may give it.[41] A new turn, therefore, is now given to our affairs of a nature the most critical and alarming. Would to God there were any concessions by which we could extricate ourselves. But the opportunities for this have been shamefully lost and cannot be now recovered. With a judicial blindness in our councils which has hitherto carried us uniformly from bad to worse, with near half our strength torn from us, and our vaunted dignity in the dust, with our resources failing, our credit tottering, and a debt threatening to overwhelm us of more than a hundred and fifty millions—in these circumstances, we seem to be entering on a war

---

39. Erroneously dated January 19, 1776, in edition 1.
40. This paragraph not in edition 1.
41. The memorial to which Price refers was delivered by the Marquis de Noailles to Lord Viscount Weymouth on March 13, 1778. See *Parliamentary History*, 19:476.

with the united powers of France, Spain and America. This, should it happen, will complete the measure of our troubles and soon bring on that catastrophe which there has been all along reason to expect and dread.

April 24, 1778.[40]

Part I

Our Colonies in North America appear to be now determined to risk and suffer everything, under the persuasion that Great Britain is attempting to rob them of that liberty to which every member of society and all civil communities have a natural and unalienable title. The question, therefore, whether this is a right persuasion, is highly interesting and deserves the careful attention of every Englishman who values liberty, and wishes to avoid staining himself with the guilt of invading it. But it is impossible to judge properly of this question without just ideas of liberty in general and of the nature, limits, and principles of civil liberty in particular. The following observations on this subject appear to me [6]of some importance[6] and I cannot make myself easy without offering them to the public at the present period, big with events of the last consequence to this kingdom. I do this with reluctance and pain, urged by strong feelings, but at the same time checked by the consciousness that I am likely to deliver sentiments not favourable to the present measures of that government under which I live and to which I am a constant and zealous well-wisher. Such, however, are my present sentiments and views, that this is a consideration of inferior moment with me and, as I hope never to go beyond the bounds of decent discussion and expostulation, I flatter myself that I shall be able to avoid giving any person, [7]reason[7] for offence.

The observations with which I shall begin are of a more general and abstracted nature, but being[8] necessary to introduce what I have principally in view, I hope they will be patiently read and considered.

Sect. I. Of the Nature of Liberty in General.

In order to obtain a more distinct view of the nature of liberty as such, it will be useful to consider it under the four following general divisions.

First, *physical* liberty, secondly, *moral* liberty, thirdly, *religious* liberty, and fourthly, *civil* liberty. These heads comprehend all the different kinds of liberty. And I have placed civil liberty last, because I mean to apply to it all I shall say of the other kinds of liberty.

By *physical liberty* I mean that principle of spontaneity or self-determination, which constitutes us agents or which gives us a command over our actions, rendering them properly ours, and not effects of the operation of

---

6. Editions 1–9 read "important as well as just."
7. Editions 1–6 read "cause."
8. Editions 1 and 2 insert "in my opinion of particular consequence and. . . ." Edition 3 inserts "in my opinion."

any foreign cause. *Moral liberty* is the power of following, in all circumstances, our sense of right and wrong or of acting in conformity to our reflecting and moral principles without being controlled by any contrary principles. *Religious liberty* signifies the power of exercising, without molestation, that mode of religion which we think best or of making the decisions of our consciences respecting religious truth the rule of our conduct, and not any of the decisions of [9]our fellow-men.[9] In like manner, *civil liberty* is the power of a civil society or state to govern itself by its own discretion or by laws of its own making without being subject to [10]the impositions of any power in appointing and directing which the collective body of the people have no concern and over which they have no control.[10]

It should be observed that, according to these definitions of the different kinds of liberty, there is one general idea that runs through them all, I mean the idea of self-direction, or self-government. Did our volitions originate not with ourselves but with some cause over which we have no power, or were we under a necessity of always following some will different from our own, we should want physical liberty.

In like manner, he whose perceptions of moral obligation are controlled by his passions has lost his moral liberty, and the most common language applied to him is that he wants self-government.

He likewise who, in religion, cannot govern himself by his convictions of religious duty but is obliged to receive formularies of faith and to practice modes of worship imposed upon him by others, wants religious liberty. And the community also that is governed not by itself but by some will independent of it,[11] wants civil liberty.

In all these cases there is a force which stands opposed to the agent's own will and which, as far as it operates, produces servitude. In the first case this force is incompatible with the very idea of voluntary motion and the subject of it is a mere passive instrument which never acts but is always acted upon. In the second case this force is the influence of passion getting the better of reason, or the brute overpowering and conquering the will of the man. In the third case it is human authority in religion requiring conformity to particular modes of faith and worship and superseding private judgment. And in the last case it is any will distinct from that of the majority of a community, which claims a power of making laws for it and disposing of its property.

That it is, I think, that marks the limit between liberty and slavery. As far as, in any instance, the operation of any cause comes in to restrain the

---

9. Editions 1–13 read "others."
10. Editions 1–9 read "any foreign discretion, or to the impositions of any extraneous will or power."
11. Editions 1–9 insert "and over which it has no control."

power of self government, so far slavery is introduced. Nor do I think that a preciser idea than this of liberty and slavery can be formed.

I cannot help wishing I could here fix my reader's attention and engage him to consider carefully the dignity of that blessing to which we give the name of liberty according to the representation now made of it. There is not a word in the whole compass of language which expresses so much of what is important and excellent. It is, in every view of it, a blessing truly sacred and invaluable. Without physical liberty man would be a machine acted upon by mechanical springs, having no principle of motion in himself or command over events and, therefore, incapable of all merit and demerit. Without moral liberty he is a wicked and detestable being, subject to the tyranny of base lusts and the sport of every vile appetite. And without religious and civil liberty he is a poor and abject animal, without rights, without property, and without a conscience, bending his neck to the yoke and crouching to the will of every silly creature who has the insolence to pretend to authority over him. Nothing, therefore, can be of so much consequence to us as liberty. It is the foundation of all honour and the chief privilege and glory of our nature.

In fixing our ideas on the subject of liberty it is of particular use to take such an enlarged view of it as I have now given. But the immediate object of the present enquiry being civil liberty, I will confine to it all the subsequent observations.

Sect. II. Of Civil Liberty and the Principles of Government.

From what has been said it is obvious that all civil government, as far as it can be denominated *free*, is the creature of the people. It originates with them. It is conducted under their direction and has in view nothing but their happiness. All its different forms are no more than so many different modes in which they choose to direct their affairs and to secure the quiet enjoyment of their rights. In every free state every man is his own legislator.[a][12] All taxes are free-gifts for public services. All laws are particular provisions or regulations established by common consent for gaining protection and safety. And all magistrates are trustees or deputies for carrying these regulations into execution.

Liberty, therefore, is too imperfectly defined when it is said to be "a government by laws, and not by men." If the laws are made by one man,

---

a. See a particular explanation of this assertion in the Second Tract, pages [139–140].[12]

12. Footnote not in editions 1–13.

or a junto of men in a state, and not by common consent, a government by them does not differ from slavery. In this case it would be a contradiction in terms to say that the state governs itself.

From hence it is obvious that civil liberty, in its most perfect degree, can be enjoyed only in small states where every independent agent is capable of giving his suffrage in person and of being chosen into public offices. When a state becomes so numerous or when the different parts of it are removed to such distances from one another as to render this impracticable, a diminution of liberty necessarily arises. There are, however, in these circumstances, methods by which such near approaches may be made to perfect liberty as shall answer all the purposes of government and at the same time secure every right of human nature.

Though all the members of a state should not be capable of giving their suffrages on public measures, individually and personally, they may do this by the appointment of substitutes or representatives. They may entrust the powers of legislation, subject to such restrictions as they shall think necessary, with any number of delegates; and whatever can be done by such delegates within the limits of their trust may be considered as done by the united voice and counsel of the community. In this method a free government may be established in the largest state; and it is conceivable that by regulations of this kind, any number of states might be subjected to a scheme of government that would exclude the desolations of war and produce universal peace and order.

Let us think here of what may be practicable in this way with respect to Europe in particular. While it continues divided, as it is at present, into a great number of independent kingdoms whose interests are continually clashing, it is impossible but that disputes will often arise which end in war and carnage. It would be no remedy to this evil to make one of these states supreme over the rest and to give it an absolute plenitude of power to superintend and control them. This would be to subject all the states to the arbitrary discretion of one and to establish an ignominious slavery not possible to be long endured. It would, therefore, be a remedy worse than the disease, nor is it possible it should be approved by any mind that has not lost every idea of civil liberty. On the contrary, let every state, with respect to all its internal concerns, be continued independent of all the rest; and let a general confederacy be formed by the appointment of a senate consisting of representatives from all the different states. Let this senate possess the power of managing all the common concerns of the united states, and of judging and deciding between them, as a common arbiter or umpire in all disputes, having, at the same time, under its discretion, the common force of the states to support its decisions. In these circumstances, each separate state would be secure against the interference of foreign power in its private concerns and, therefore, would possess liberty;

and at the same time it would be secure against all oppression and insult from every neighbouring state. Thus might the scattered force and abilities of a whole continent be gathered into one point, all litigations settled as they rose, universal peace preserved, and nation prevented from any more lifting up a sword against nation.

I have observed that though, in a great state, all the individuals that compose it cannot be admitted to an immediate participation in the powers of legislation and government, yet they may participate in these powers by a delegation of them to a body of representatives. In this case it is evident that the state will be still free or self governed and that it will be more or less so in proportion as it is more or less fairly and adequately represented. If the persons to whom the trust of government is committed hold their places for short terms, if they are chosen by the unbiassed voices of a majority of the state, and subject to their instructions, liberty will be enjoyed in its highest degree. But if they are chosen for long terms by a part only of the state and if, during that term, they are subject to no control from their constituents, the very idea of liberty will be lost, and the power of choosing representatives becomes nothing but a power lodged in a few to choose, at certain periods, a body of masters for themselves and for the rest of the community. And if a state is so sunk that the majority of its representatives are elected by a handful of the meanest[b] persons in it, whose votes are always paid for, and if, also, there is a higher will on which even these mock representatives themselves depend and that directs their voices, in these circumstances, it will be an abuse of language to say that the state possesses liberty. Private men, indeed, might be allowed the exercise of liberty, as they might also under the most despotic government, but it would be an indulgence or connivance derived from the spirit of the times or from an accidental mildness in the administration. And rather than be governed in such a manner it would perhaps be better to be governed by the will of one man without any representation. For a represen-

b. In Great Britain, consisting of near six millions of inhabitants, 5723 persons, most of them the lowest of the people, elect one half of the House of Commons and 364 votes choose a ninth part. This may be seen distinctly made out in the *Political Disquisitions*, vol. 1, bk. 2, chap. 4, a work full of important and useful instruction [James Burgh,[13] *Political Disquisitions, or An Enquiry into Public Errors, Defects, and Abuses. Illus. by and Established upon Facts and Remarks Extracted from a Variety of Authors, Ancient and Modern. Calculated to Draw the Timely Attention of Government and People to a Due Consideration of the Necessity and the Means of Reforming those Errors, Defects and Abuses of Restoring the Constitution and Saving the State*, 3 vols. (London: E. and C. Dilly, 1774–1775)].

13. James Burgh (1714–1775), teacher, founder of an academy at Stoke Newington (1747), school master at Newington Green, political writer, author of *Political Disquisitions* (London, 1774), life-long friend of Price and fellow-member of the club of Honest Whigs.

tation so degenerated could answer no other end than to mislead and deceive by disguising slavery and keeping up a form of liberty when the reality was lost.

Within the limits now mentioned liberty may be enjoyed in every possible degree, from that which is complete and perfect, to that which is merely nominal, according as the people have more or less of a share in government and of a controlling power over the persons by whom it is administered.

In general, to be free is to be guided by one's own will, and to be guided by the will of another is the characteristic of servitude. This is particularly applicable to political liberty. That state, I have observed, is free, which is guided by its own will or, (which comes to the same) by the will of an assembly of representatives appointed by itself and accountable to itself. And every state that is not so governed, or in which a body of men representing the people make not an essential part of the legislature, is in slavery. In order to form the most perfect constitution of government there may be the best reasons for joining to such a body of representatives an hereditary council consisting of men of the first rank in the state, with a supreme executive Magistrate at the head of all. This will form useful checks in a legislature and contribute to give it vigour, union, and dispatch, without infringing liberty; for, as long as that part of a government which represents the people is a fair representation and also has a negative on all public measures, together with the sole power of imposing taxes and originating supplies, the essentials of liberty will be preserved. We make it our boast in this country that this is our own constitution. I will not say with how much reason.

Of such liberty as I have now described it is impossible there should be an excess. Government is an institution for the benefit of the people governed, which they have power to model as they please; and to say that they can have too much of this power is to say that there ought to be a power in the state superior to that which gives it being and from which all jurisdiction in it is derived. Licentiousness, which has been commonly mentioned, as an extreme of liberty, is indeed its opposite. It is government by the will of rapacious individuals, in opposition to the will of the community, made known and declared in the laws. A free state, at the same time that it is free itself, makes all its members free, by excluding licentiousness and guarding their persons and property and good name against insult. It is the end of all just government, at the same time that it secures the liberty of the public against foreign injury to secure the liberty of the individual against private injury. I do not, therefore, think it strictly just to say that it belongs to the nature of government to entrench on private liberty. It ought never to do this except as far as the exercise of private liberty encroaches on the liberties of others. That is, it is licentiousness it restrains, and liberty itself only when used to destroy liberty.

It appears from hence that licentiousness and despotism are more nearly allied than is commonly imagined. They are both alike inconsistent with liberty and the true end of government, nor is there any other difference between them than that the one is the licentiousness of great men and the other the licentiousness of little men; or that, by the one, the persons and property of a people are subject to outrage and invasion from a king, or a lawless body of grandees, and that, by the other, they are subject to the like outrage from a lawless mob. In avoiding one of these evils mankind have often run into the other. But all well constituted governments guard equally against both. Indeed, of the two, the last is, on several accounts, the least to be dreaded and has done the least mischief. It may be truly said that if licentiousness has destroyed its thousands, despotism has destroyed its millions. The former, having little power, and no system to support it, necessarily finds its own remedy and a people soon get out of the tumult and anarchy attending it. But a despotism, wearing the form of government, and being armed with its force, is an evil not to be conquered without dreadful struggles. It goes on from age to age, debasing the human faculties, levelling all distinctions, and preying on the rights and blessings of society. It deserves to be added that in a state disturbed by licentiousness there is an animation which is favourable to the human mind and which puts it upon exerting its powers. But in a state habituated to a despotism all is still and torpid. A dark and savage tyranny stifles every effort of genius and the mind loses all its spirit and dignity.

Before I proceed to what I have farther in view I will observe that the account now given of the principles of public liberty and the nature of an equal and free government shows what judgment we should form of that omnipotence which, it has been said, must belong to every government as such. Great stress has been laid on this, but most unreasonably. Government, as has been before observed, is, in the very nature of it, a trust; and all its powers a delegation for gaining particular ends. This trust may be misapplied and abused. It may be employed to defeat the very ends for which it was instituted and to subvert the very rights which it ought to protect. A parliament, for instance, consisting of a body of representatives, chosen for a limited period, to make laws and to grant money for public services, would forfeit its authority by making itself perpetual, or even prolonging its own duration, by nominating its own members, by accepting bribes, or subjecting itself to any kind of foreign influence. This would convert a parliament into a conclave or junto of self-created tools; and a state that has lost its regard to its own rights, so far as to submit to such a breach of trust in its rulers, is enslaved. Nothing, therefore, can be more absurd than the doctrine which some have taught with respect to the omnipotence of parliaments. They possess no power beyond the limits of the trust for the execution of which they were formed. If they contradict this trust, they betray their constituents and dissolve themselves. All delegated power must be subordinate and limited. If omnipotence can, with any sense, be ascribed to a legislature, it must be lodged where all legislative authority originates, that is, in the people. For *their* sakes government is instituted and theirs is the only real omnipotence.

I am sensible that all I have been saying would be very absurd were the opinions just which some have maintained concerning the origin of government. According to these opinions, government is not the creature of the people or the result of a convention between them and their rulers, but there are certain men who possess in themselves, independently of the will of the people, a right of governing them, which they derive from the Deity. This doctrine has been abundantly refuted by many[c] excellent writers. It is a doctrine which avowedly subverts civil liberty and which represents mankind as a body of vassals formed to descend like cattle from one set of owners to another who have an absolute dominion over them. It is a wonder that those who view their species in a light so humiliating should ever be able to think of themselves without regret and shame. The intention of these observations is not to oppose such sentiments but, taking for granted the reasonableness of civil liberty, to show wherein it consists and what distinguishes it from its contrary. And in considering this subject, as it has been now treated, it is unavoidable to reflect on the excellency of a free government and its tendency to exalt the nature of man. Every member of a free state, having his property secure, and knowing himself his own governor, possesses a consciousness of dignity in himself and feels incitements to emulation and improvement to which the miserable slaves of arbitrary power must be utter strangers. In such a state all the springs of action have room to operate, and the mind is stimulated to the noblest

c. See among others Dr. Locke on Government [John Locke, *Two Treatises of Government*, 1690], and Dr. Priestley's[14] *Essay on the First Principles of Government* [Joseph Priestley, *An Essay on the First Principles of Government* (London: Printed for J. Johnson, 1768)].

14. Joseph Priestley (1733–1804), clergyman, political theorist, educator, scientist; educated at the Dissenting Academy in Daventry, Northamptonshire; assistant minister to a Presbyterian congregation in Needham Market, Suffolk (1755–1758) and to a congregation in Norwich, Cheshire (1758–1761); tutor at Warrington Academy, Lancashire (1761–1767); elected to the Royal Society of London (1766); minister of Mill Hill Chapel in Leeds, Yorkshire (1767–1773); tutor to the children of William Fitzmaurice-Petty, 2nd earl of Shelburne (1773–1779); minister of the New Meeting congregation in Birmingham (1779–1791); teacher at New College in Hackney (1791–1794); émigré to the United States (1794).

exertions.[d] But to be obliged from our birth to look up to a creature no better than ourselves as the master of our fortunes and to receive his will as our law—What can be more humiliating? What elevated ideas can enter a mind in such a situation? Agreeably to this remark, the subjects of free states have, in all ages, been most distinguished for genius and knowledge. Liberty is the soil where the arts and sciences have flourished and the more free a state has been, the more have the powers of the human mind been drawn forth into action, and the greater number of brave men has it produced. With what lustre do the ancient free states of Greece shine in the annals of the world? How different is that country now, under the great Turk? The difference between a country inhabited by men and by brutes is not greater.

These are reflexions which should be constantly present to every mind in this country. As moral liberty is the prime blessing of man in his private capacity, so is civil liberty in his public capacity. There is nothing that requires more to be watched than power. There is nothing that ought to be opposed with a more determined resolution than its encroachments. Sleep in a state, as Montesquieu[15] says, is always followed by slavery.

The people of this kingdom were once warmed by such sentiments as these. Many a sycophant of power have they sacrificed. Often have they fought and bled in the cause of liberty. But that time seems to be going. The fair inheritance of liberty left us by our ancestors many of us are willing to resign. An abandoned venality, the inseparable companion of dissipation and extravagance, has poisoned the springs of public virtue among us. And should any events ever arise that should render the same opposition necessary that took place in the times of King Charles the First and James the Second, I am afraid all that is valuable to us would be lost. The terror of the standing army, the danger of the public funds, and the all-corrupting influence of the treasury, would deaden all zeal and produce general acquiescence and servility.

Sect. III. Of the Authority of one Country over Another.

From the nature and principles of civil liberty, as they have been now explained, it is an immediate and necessary inference that no one community can have any power over the property or legislation of another community which is not incorporated with it by a just and adequate representation. Then only, it has been shown, is a state free when it is gov-

d. See Dr. Priestley on Government, pp. 68, 69, etc.

15. Charles Louis de Secondat, baron de la Brede et de Montesquieu (1689–1755), lawyer, geographer, philosopher, political theorist.

erned by its own will. But a country that is subject to the legislature of another country in which it has no voice and over which it has no control cannot be said to be governed by its own will. Such a country, therefore, is in a state of slavery. And it deserves to be particularly considered that such a slavery is worse, on several accounts, than any slavery of private men to one another or of kingdoms to despots within themselves. Between one state and another there is none of that fellow-feeling that takes place between persons in private life. Being detached bodies that never see one another and residing perhaps in different quarters of the globe, the state that governs cannot be a witness to the sufferings occasioned by its oppressions or a competent judge of the circumstances and abilities of the people who are governed. They must also have in a great degree separate interests and the more the one is loaded, the more the other may be eased. The infamy likewise of oppression, being in such circumstances shared among a multitude, is not likely to be much felt or regarded. On all these accounts there is, in the case of one country subjected to another, little or nothing to check rapacity and the most flagrant injustice and cruelty may be practised without remorse or pity. I will add that it is particularly difficult to shake off a tyranny of this kind. A single despot, if a people are unanimous and resolute, may be soon subdued. But a despotic state is not easily subdued and a people subject to it cannot emancipate themselves without entering into a dreadful and, perhaps, very unequal contest.

I cannot help observing farther that the slavery of a people to internal despots may be qualified and limited but I don't see what can limit the authority of one state over another. The exercise of power in this case can have no other measure than discretion and, therefore, must be indefinite and absolute.

Once more, it should be considered that the government of one country by another can only be supported by a military force and, without such a support, must be destitute of all weight and efficiency.

This will be best explained by putting the following case. There is, let us suppose, in a province subject to the sovereignty of a distant state, a subordinate legislature consisting of an assembly chosen by the people, a council chosen by that assembly, and a governor appointed by the sovereign state and paid by the province. There are, likewise, judges and other officers, appointed and paid in the same manner, for administering justice agreeably to the laws, by the verdicts of juries fairly chosen. This forms a constitution seemingly free by giving the people a share in their own government and some check on their rulers. But, while there is a higher legislative power, to the control of which such a constitution is subject, it does not itself possess liberty and therefore cannot be of any use as a security to liberty, nor is it possible that it should be of long duration. Laws offensive to the province will be enacted by the sovereign state. The legislature of the province will remonstrate against them. The magistrate will not execute them. Juries will not convict upon them and, consequently, like the Pope's bulls which once governed Europe, they will become nothing but forms and empty sounds to which no regard will be shown. In order to remedy this evil, and to give efficiency to its government, the supreme state will naturally be led to withdraw the governor, the council, and the judges[e] from the control of the province, by making them entirely dependent on itself for their pay and continuance in office, as well as for their appointment. It will also alter the mode of choosing juries on purpose to bring them more under its influence. And in some cases, under the pretence of the impossibility of gaining an impartial trial where government is resisted, it will perhaps ordain that offenders shall be removed from the province to be tried within its own territories. And it may even go so far in this kind of policy as to endeavour to prevent the effects of

e. The independency of the judges we esteem in this country one of our greatest privileges. Before the revolution they generally, I believe, held their places during pleasure. King William gave them their places during good behaviour. At the accession of the present Royal Family their places were given them during good behaviour, in consequence of the Act of Settlement, 12 & 13 William 3, ch. 2. But an opinion having been entertained by some that though their commissions were made under the Act of Settlement to continue during good behaviour, yet that they determined on the demise of the Crown, it was enacted by a statute made in the first year of his present Majesty, ch. 23, "That the commissions of judges for the time being shall be, continue, and remain in full force, during their good behaviour, notwithstanding the demise of his Majesty or of any of his heirs and successors,"[16] with a proviso, "that it may be lawful for his Majesty, his heirs and successors, to remove any judge upon the address of both Houses of Parliament."[17] And by the same statute their salaries are secured to them during the continuance of their commissions. His Majesty, according to the preamble of the statute, having been pleased to declare from the throne to both Houses of Parliament, "That he looked upon the independency and uprightness of judges as essential to the impartial administration of justice, as one of the best securities to the rights and liberties of his loving subjects and as most conducive to the honour of his crown."[18]
A worthy friend and able lawyer has supplied me with this note. It affords, when contrasted with that dependence of the judges which has been thought reasonable in America, a sad specimen of the different manner in which a kingdom may think proper to govern itself and the provinces subject to it.

16. The relevant passage reads: ". . . may it therefore please your Majesty that it may be enacted . . . that the commissions of judges for the time being, shall be, continue and remain, in full force during their good behaviour, notwithstanding the demise of his Majesty (whom God long preserve) or of any of his heirs and successors. . . ." Danby Pickering, ed., *The Statutes at Large* (Cambridge: Printed by Joseph Bentham, printer to the University, for Charles Bathurst, 1766), 23:306. Hereafter cited as *Statutes at Large*.
17. The relevant passage reads: "Provided always, and be it enacted by the authority aforesaid, that it may be lawful for his Majesty, his heirs, and successors, to remove any judge or judges upon the address of both houses of parliament." *Statutes at Large* 23:306.
18. The relevant passage reads: ". . . whereas your Majesty has been graciously pleased to declare from the throne to both houses of parliament that you look upon the independency and uprightness of judges as essential to the impartial administration of justice, as one of the best securities to the rights and liberties of your loving subjects, and as most conducive to the honour of your crown. . . ." *Statutes at Large* 23:306.

discontents by forbidding all meetings and associations of the people except at such times, and for such particular purposes, as shall be permitted them.

Thus will such a province be exactly in the same state that Britain would be in were our first executive magistrate, our House of Lords, and our judges nothing but the instruments of a foreign democratical power, were our judges nominated by that power, or were we liable to be transported to a distant country to be tried for offences committed here and restrained from calling any meetings, consulting about any grievances, or associating for any purposes except when leave should be given us by a lord lieutenant or viceroy.

It is certain that this is a state of oppression which no country could endure and to which it would be vain to expect that any people should submit an hour without an armed force to compel them.

The late transactions in Massachusett's Bay are a perfect exemplification of what I have now said. The government of Great Britain in that province has gone on exactly in the train I have described till at last it became necessary to station troops there not amenable to the civil power and all terminated in a government by the sword. And such, if a people are not sunk below the character of men, will be the issue of all government in similar circumstances.

It may be asked, "Are there not causes by which one state may acquire a rightful authority over another, though not consolidated by an adequate representation?" I answer, that there are no such causes. All the causes to which such an effect can be ascribed are conquest, compact, or obligations conferred.

Much has been said of the right of conquest and history contains little more than accounts of kingdoms reduced by it under the dominion of other kingdoms and of the havoc it has made among mankind. But the authority derived from hence, being founded on violence, is never rightful. The Roman Republic was nothing but a faction against the general liberties of the world and had no more right to give law to the provinces subject to it than thieves have to the property they seize or to the houses into which they break. Even in the case of a just war undertaken by one people to defend itself against the oppressions of another people, conquest gives only a right to an indemnification for the injury which occasioned the war and a reasonable security against future injury.

Neither can any state acquire such an authority over other states in virtue of any *compacts* or *cessions*. This is a case in which compacts are not binding. Civil liberty is, in this respect, on the same footing with religious liberty. As no people can lawfully surrender their religious liberty by giving up their right of judging for themselves in religion, or by allowing any human beings to prescribe to them what faith they shall embrace, or what mode of worship they shall practise, so neither can any civil societies lawfully surrender their civil liberty by giving up to any extraneous juris-diction their power of legislating for themselves and disposing their prop-erty. Such a cession, being inconsistent with the unalienable rights of hu-man nature, would either not bind at all or bind only the individuals who made it. This is a blessing which no one generation of men can give up for another and which, when lost, a people have always a right to resume. Had our ancestors in this country been so mad as to have subjected them-selves to any foreign community we could not have been under any obli-gation to continue in such a state. And all the nations now in the world who, in consequence of the tameness and folly of their predecessors, are subject to arbitrary power have a right to emancipate themselves as soon as they can.

If neither conquest nor compact can give such an authority, much less can any favours received or any services performed by one state for another. Let the favour received be what it will, liberty is too dear a price for it. A state that has been obliged is not, therefore, bound to be enslaved. It ought, if possible, to make an adequate return for the services done to it, but to suppose that it ought to give up the power of governing itself and the disposal of its property would be to suppose that, in order to show its gratitude, it ought to part with the power of ever afterwards exercising gratitude. How much has been done by this kingdom for Hanover? But no one will say that on this account we have a right to make the laws of Hanover or even to draw a single penny from it without its own consent.

After what has been said it will, I am afraid, be trifling to apply the preceding arguments to the case of different communities which are con-sidered as different parts of the same empire. But there are reasons which render it necessary for me to be explicit in making this application.

What I mean here is just to point out the difference of situation between communities forming an empire and particular bodies or classes of men forming different parts of a kingdom. Different communities forming an empire have no connexions which produce a necessary reciprocation of interests between them. They inhabit different districts and are governed by different legislatures. On the contrary, the different classes of men with-in a kingdom are all placed on the same ground. Their concerns and in-terests are the same and what is done to one part must affect all. These are situations totally different and a constitution of government that may be consistent with liberty in one of them may be entirely inconsistent with it in the other. It is, however, certain that even in the last of these situations no one part ought to govern the rest. In order to a fair and equal govern-ment there ought to be a fair and equal representation of all that are governed; and as far as this is wanting in any government it deviates from the principles of liberty and becomes unjust and oppressive. But in the circumstances of different communities all this holds with unspeakably more force. The government of a part in this case becomes complete tyranny and subjection to it becomes complete slavery.

But ought there not, it is asked, to exist somewhere in an empire a supreme legislative authority over the whole or a power to control and bind all the different states of which it consists? This enquiry has been already answered. The truth is that such a supreme controlling power ought to exist nowhere except in such a senate or body of delegates as that described in page [70] and that the authority or supremacy of even this senate ought to be limited to the common concerns of the empire. I think I have proved that the fundamental principles of liberty necessarily require this.

In a word, an empire is a collection of states or communities united by some common bond or tie. If these states have each of them free constitutions of government and, with respect to taxation and internal legislation, are independent of the other states but united by compacts or alliances or subjection to a great council representing the whole, or to one monarch entrusted with the supreme executive power, in these circumstances the empire will be an empire of freemen. If, on the contrary, like the different provinces subject to the Grand Seignior, none of the states possess any independent legislative authority but are all subject to an absolute monarch whose will is their law, then is the empire an empire of slaves. If one of the states is free but governs by its will all the other states, then is the empire, like that of the Roman in the times of the republic, an empire consisting of one state free and the rest in slavery. Nor does it make any more difference in this case that the governing state is itself free than it does in the case of a kingdom subject to a despot, that this despot is himself free. I have before observed that this only makes the slavery worse. There is, in the one case, a chance that in the quick succession of despots a good one will sometimes arise. But bodies of men continue the same and have generally proved the most unrelenting of all tyrants.

A great writer, before[f] quoted, observes of the Roman Empire that while liberty was at the center tyranny prevailed in the distant provinces, that such as were free under it were extremely so, while those who were slaves groaned under the extremity of slavery, and that the same events that destroyed the liberty of the former gave liberty to the latter.

f. Montesquieu's *Spirit of Laws*, vol. 1, bk. 2, chap. 19 [Charles Louis de Secondat, baron de Montesquieu, *L'Esprit de Lois, 1748. The Spirit of Laws. Translated from the French of M. de Secondat, Baron de Montesquieu. With Corrections and Additions Communicated by the Author* . . . , trans. Thomas Nugent (London: J. Nourse and P. Valiant, 1750)].

The liberty of the Romans, therefore, was only an additional calamity to the provinces governed by them and though it might have been said of the citizens of Rome, that they were the "freest members of any civil society in the known world," yet of the subjects of Rome it must have been said that they were the completest slaves in the known world. How remarkable is it that this very people, once the freest of mankind, but at the same time the most proud and tyrannical, should become at last the most contemptible and abject slaves that ever existed?

Part II

In the foregoing disquisitions I have, from one leading principle, deduced a number of consequences that seem to me incapable of being disputed. I have meant that they should be applied to the great question between this kingdom and the Colonies which has occasioned the present war with them.

It is impossible but my readers must have been all along making this application and if they still think that the claims of this kingdom are reconcilable to the principles of true liberty and legitimate government, I am afraid that nothing I shall farther say will have any effect on their judgments. I wish, however, they would have the patience and candour to go with me and grant me a hearing some time longer.

Though clearly decided in my own judgment on this subject, I am inclined to make great allowances for the different judgments of others. We have been so used to speak of the Colonies as *our* Colonies and to think of them as in a state of subordination to us and as holding their existence in America only for our use that it is no wonder the prejudices of many are alarmed when they find a different doctrine maintained. The meanest person among us is disposed to look upon himself as having a body of subjects in America and to be offended at the denial of his right to make laws for them, though perhaps he does not know what colour they are of or what language they talk. Such are the natural prejudices of this country. But the time is coming, I hope, when the unreasonableness of them will be seen and more just sentiments prevail.

Before I proceed I beg it may be attended to that I have chosen to try this question by the general principles of civil liberty and not by the practice of former times or by the charters granted the colonies. The arguments for them, drawn from these last topics, appear to me greatly to outweigh the arguments against them. But I wish to have this question

brought to a higher test and surer issue. The question with all liberal en-
quirers ought to be, not what jurisdiction over them precedents, statutes,
and charters give, but what reason and equity and the rights of humanity
give. This is, in truth, a question which no kingdom has ever before had
occasion to agitate. The case of a free country branching itself out in the
manner Britain has done and sending to a distant world colonies which
have there, from small beginnings and under free legislatures of their own,
increased and formed a body of powerful states likely soon to become
superior to the parent state. This is a case which is new in the history of
mankind and it is extremely improper to judge of it by the rules of any
narrow and partial policy or to consider it on any other ground than the
general one of reason and justice. Those who will be candid enough to
judge on this ground, and who can divest themselves of national prejudices,
will not, I fancy, remain long unsatisfied. But alas! Matters are gone too
far. The dispute probably must be settled another way and the sword
alone, I am afraid, is now to determine what the rights of Britain and
America are. Shocking situation! Detested be the measures which have
brought us into it. And, if we are endeavouring to enforce injustice, cursed
will be the war. A retreat, however, is not yet impracticable. The duty we
owe our gracious sovereign obliges us to rely on his disposition to stay the
sword, and to promote the happiness of all the different parts of the empire
at the head of which he is placed. With some hopes, therefore, that it may
not be too late to reason on this subject I will, in the following sections,
enquire what the war with America is in the following respects.

1. In respect of justice.
2. The principles of the constitution.
3. In respect of policy and humanity.
4. The honour of the kingdom.

And lastly, the probability of succeeding in it.

Sect. I. Of the Justice of the War with America.

The enquiry whether the war with the Colonies is a just war will be
best determined by stating the power over them which it is the end of the
war to maintain. And this cannot be better done than in the words of an
act of parliament, made on purpose to define it. That act, it is well known,
declares, "That this kingdom has power, and of right ought to have power,
to make laws and statutes to bind the Colonies and people of America,
in all cases whatever." [19] Dreadful power indeed! I defy any one to express

---

19. The relevant passage reads: "... the said colonies and plantations in America have
been, are, and of right ought to be, subordinate unto, and dependent upon, the imperial
crown and Parliament of Great Britain; and that the King's Majesty, by and with the

83

slavery in stronger language. It is the same with declaring "that we have a right to do with them what we please." I will not waste my time by applying to such a claim any of the preceding arguments. If my reader does not feel more in this case than words can express, all reasoning must be vain.

But, probably, most persons will be for using milder language and for saying no more than that the united legislatures of England and Scotland have of right power to tax the Colonies and a supremacy of legislation over America. But this comes to the same. If it means anything, it means that the property and the legislations of the Colonies are subject to the absolute discretion of Great Britain and ought of right to be so. The nature of the thing admits of no limitation. The Colonies can never be admitted to be judges how far the authority over them in these cases shall extend. This would be to destroy it entirely. If any part of their property is subject to our discretion, the whole must be so. If we have a right to interfere at all in their internal legislations, we have a right to interfere as far as we think proper. It is self-evident that this leaves them nothing they can call their own. And what is it that can give to any people such a supremacy over another people? I have already examined the principal answers which have been given to this enquiry. But it will not be amiss in this place to go over some of them again.

It has been urged that such a right must be lodged somewhere, "in order to preserve the unity of the British Empire."

Pleas of this sort have, in all ages, been used to justify tyranny. They have in religion given rise to numberless oppressive claims and slavish hierarchies. And in the Romish communion particularly, it is well known that the Pope claims the title and powers of the supreme head on earth of the Christian church, in order to preserve its unity. With respect to the British Empire nothing can be more preposterous than to endeavour to maintain its unity by setting up such a claim. This is a method of establishing unity which, like the similar method in religion, can produce nothng but discord and mischief. The truth is that a common relation to one supreme executive head, an exchange of kind offices, ties of interest and affection, and compacts, are sufficient to give the British Empire all the unity that is necessary. But if not—if, in order to preserve its unity, one half of it must be enslaved to the other half—let it, in the name of God, want unity.

---

advice and consent of the lords spiritual and temporal, and the commons of Great Britain, in Parliament assembled, had, hath, and of right ought to have, full power and authority to make laws and statutes of sufficient force and validity to bind the colonies and people of America, subjects of the crown of Great Britain, in all cases whatsoever." The Declaratory Act (The American Colonies Act), 6 George 3, ch. 12, approved March 18, 1766. See *Statutes at Large*, 27:20.

Much has been said of "the superiority of the British State." But what gives us our superiority? Is it our wealth? This never confers real dignity. On the contrary, its effect is always to debase, intoxicate, and corrupt. Is it the number of our people? The Colonies will soon be equal to us in number. Is it our knowledge and virtue? They are probably equally knowing and more virtuous. There are names among them that will not stoop to any names among the philosophers and politicians of this island.

"But we are the parent state." These are the magic words which have fascinated and misled us. The English came from Germany. Does that give the German states a right to tax us? Children, having no property, and being incapable of guiding themselves, the author of nature has committed the care of them to their parents and subjected them to their absolute authority. But there is a period when, having acquired property and a capacity of judging for themselves, they become independent agents and when, for this reason, the authority of their parents ceases and becomes nothing but the respect and influence due to benefactors. Supposing, therefore, that the order of nature in establishing the relation between parents and children ought to have been the rule of our conduct to the Colonies, we should have been gradually relaxing our authority as they grew up. But, like mad parents, we have done the contrary and, at the very time when our authority should have been most relaxed, we have carried it to the greatest extent and exercised it with the greatest rigour. No wonder, then, that they have turned upon us and obliged us to remember that they are not children.

"But we have," it is said, "protected them and run deeply in debt on their account." The full answer to this has been already given (page [79]). Will any one say that all we have done for them has not been more on our own account,^{g} than on theirs? But suppose the contrary. Have they

---

g. This is particularly true of the bounties granted on some American commodities (as pitch, tar, indigo, etc.) when imported into Britain; for it is well known that the end of granting them was to get those commodities cheaper from the Colonies, and in return for our manufactures, which we used to get from Russia and other foreign countries. And this is expressed in the preambles of the laws which grant these bounties. See the *Appeal to the Justice*, etc., page 21, third edition [Arthur Lee,[20] *An Appeal to the Justice and Interests of the People of Great Britain, in the Present Disputes with America. By* and *Old Member of Parliament*, 3rd ed., corrected (London: Printed for J. Almon, 1775)]. It is, therefore, strange that Doctor Tucker[21] and others should have insisted so much

---

20. Arthur Lee (1740–1792), physician, lawyer, diplomat, friend of John Wilkes; educated at Eton and the University of Edinburgh; author of "The Monitor's Letters" (1768) and of a series of letters addressed to British statesmen under the pseudonym "Junius Americanus" and "Raleigh" (1769); agent of Massachusetts in London (1770); confidential correspondent of the Continental Congress in London (1775); commissioner, together with Silas Deane and Benjamin Franklin, to France (1776); commissioner to Spain (1777); delegate to the Continental Congress from Virginia (1781–1784); opponent of the Constitution.

21. Josiah Tucker (1712–1799), economist and clergyman; educated at St. John's Col-

done nothing for us? Have they made no compensation for the protection they have received? Have they not helped us to pay our taxes, to support our poor, and to bear the burden of our debts, by taking from us, at our own price, all the commodities with which we can supply them? Have they not, for our advantage, submitted to many restraints in acquiring property? Must they likewise resign to us the disposal of that property? Has not their exclusive trade with us been for many years one of the chief sources of our wealth and power? In all our wars have they not fought by our side and contributed much to our success? In the last war, particularly, it is well known, that they ran themselves deeply in debt and that the Parliament thought it necessary to grant them considerable sums annually as compensations for going beyond their abilities in assisting us. And in this course would they have continued for many future years, perhaps for ever. In short, were an accurate account stated, it is by no means certain which side would appear to be most indebted. When asked as freemen they have hitherto seldom discovered any reluctance in giving. But in obedience to a demand and with the bayonet at their breasts they will give us nothing but blood.

It is farther said, "that the land on which they settled was ours." But how came it to be ours? If sailing along a coast can give a right to a country then might the people of Japan become, as soon as they please, the proprietors of Britain. Nothing can be more chimerical than property founded on such a reason. If the land on which the Colonies first settled had any proprietors they are the natives. The greatest part of it they bought of the natives. They have since cleared and cultivated it and, without any help from us, converted a wilderness into fruitful and pleasant fields. It is, therefore, now on a double account their property and no power on earth can have any right to disturb them in the possession of it or to take from them, without their consent, any part of its produce.

But let it be granted that the land was ours. Did they not settle upon it under the faith of charters which promised them the enjoyment of all the

---

upon these bounties as favours and indulgencies to the Colonies [Josiah Tucker, *The True Interest of Great Britain Set Forth in Regard to the Colonies; and the Only Means of Living in Peace and Harmony with Them* (Norfolk, Va., 1774), a reprint of Tract No. IV from *Four Tracts, Together with Two Sermons, On Political and Commercial Subjects* (Gloucester: Printed by R. Raikes, and sold by J. Rivington, 1774)]. But it is still more strange that the same representation should have been made of the compensations granted them for doing more during the last war in assisting us than could have been reasonably expected and also of the sums we have spent in maintaining troops among them without their consent and in opposition to their wishes. See a pamphlet entitled, *The Rights of Great Britain Asserted against the Claims of America* [see footnote 4].

---

lege, Oxford; curate at St. Stephen's Church, Bristol; rector of All Saints' Church, Bristol; chancellor to the rectory at St. Stephen's; dean of Gloucester.

rights of Englishmen and allowed them to tax themselves and to be governed by legislatures of their own similar to ours? These charters were given them by an authority which at the time was thought competent and they have been rendered sacred by an acquiescence on our part for near a century. Can it then be wondered at, that the Colonies should revolt when they found their charters violated and an attempt made to force innovations upon them by famine and the sword? But I lay no stress on charters. They derive their rights from a higher source. It is inconsistent with common sense to imagine that any people would ever think of settling in a distant country on any such condition as that the people from whom they withdrew should for ever be masters of their property and have power to subject them to any modes of government they pleased. And had there been express stipulations to this purpose in all the charters of the colonies they would, in my opinion, be no more bound by them than if it had been stipulated with them that they should go naked or expose themselves to the incursions of wolves and tigers.

The defective state of the representation of this kingdom has been farther pleaded to prove our right to tax America. We submit to a parliament that does not represent us, and therefore they ought. How strange an argument is this? It is saying we want liberty and, therefore, they ought to want it. Suppose it true, that they are indeed contending for a better constitution of government, and more liberty than we enjoy. Ought this to make us angry? Who is there that does not see the danger to which this country is exposed? Is it generous, because we are in a sink, to endeavour to draw them into it? Ought we not rather to wish earnestly that there may at least be one free country left upon earth to which we may fly when venality, luxury, and vice have completed the ruin of liberty here?

It is, however, by no means true that America has no more right to be exempted from taxation by the British Parliament than Britain itself. Here, all freeholders and burgesses in boroughs are represented. *There*, not one freeholder or any other person is represented. Here, the aids granted by the represented part of the kingdom must be proportionably paid by themselves and the laws they make for others, they at the same time make for themselves. There, the aids they would grant would not be paid, but received, by themselves and the laws they made would be made for others only. In short, the relation of one country to another country, whose representatives have the power of taxing it (and of appropriating the money raised by the taxes), is much the same with the relation of a country to a single despot, or a body of despots, within itself, invested with the like power. In both cases, the people taxed and those who tax have separate interests, nor can there be any thing to check oppression besides either the abilities of the people taxed or the humanity of the taxers. But indeed I can never hope to convince that person of any thing who does not see an essential difference[h] between the two cases now mentioned, or between the circumstances of individuals and classes of men making parts of a community imperfectly represented in the legislature that governs it, and the circumstances of a whole community in a distant world not at all represented.

But enough has been said by others on this point, nor is it possible for me to throw any new light upon it. To finish, therefore, what I meant to offer under this head I must beg that the following considerations may be particularly attended to.

The question now between us and the Colonies is whether, in respect of taxation and internal legislation, they are bound to be subject to the jurisdiction of this kingdom; or, in other words, whether the British parliament has or has not, of right, a power to dispose of their property and to model as it pleases their governments? To this supremacy over them we say we are entitled and in order to maintain it we have begun the present war.

Let me here enquire, whether, if we have now this supremacy, we shall not be equally entitled to it in any future time? They are now but little short of half our number. To this number they have grown from a small body of original settlers by a very rapid increase. The probability is that they will go on to increase and that in 50 or 60 years they will be double our number[i] and form a mighty empire, consisting of a variety of states,

h. It is remarkable that even the author of the *Remarks on the Principal Acts of the 13th Parliament of Great Britain*, etc. finds himself obliged to acknowledge this difference [John Lind,[22] *Remarks on the Principal Acts of the Thirteenth Parliament of Great Britain. By the Author of Letters Concerning the Present State of Poland* . . . (London: Printed for T. Payne, 1775)]. There cannot be more detestable principles of government than those which are maintained by this writer. According to him, the properties and rights of a people are only a kind of alms given them by their civil governors. Taxes, therefore, he asserts are not the gifts of the people. See pages 58 and 191.

[In editions 2, 6, 7, 8, and 9 this footnote reads: "It gives me great pleasure to find that the author of the *Remarks on the Principal Acts of the 13th Parliament of Great Britain*, etc. acknowledges this difference. It has, however, been at the same time mortifying to me to find so able a writer adopting such principles of government as are contained in the work. According to him, a people have no right except such as their civil governors are pleased not to take from them. Taxes, therefore, he asserts, are in no sense the gifts, much less the free gifts, of the people. See pp. 58 and 191."

Another edition numbered the 6th and editions numbered the 11th and 13th add, "There is, indeed, one sense in which this may be properly said. Taxes are money levied by the people on themselves, and no one can give to himself. But this is a sense which the author cannot admit."]

i. See *Observations on Reversionary Payments*, pages 207, etc. [Richard Price, *Observations on Reversionary Payments; On Schemes for Providing Annuities for Widows and Persons of Old Age; On the Method of Calculating the Values of Assurances on Lives, and on the National Debt* . . . (London: Printed for T. Cadell, 1771; 2nd ed., 1772; 3rd ed., much enlarged, 1773; 4th ed., enlarged by additional notes and essays, 2 vols., 1783)].

22. John Lind (1737–1781), lawyer, political writer, friend of Jeremy Bentham; employed by Lord Mansfield to advocate his political views.

all equal or superior to ourselves in all the arts and accomplishments which give dignity and happiness to human life. In that period will they be still bound to acknowledge that supremacy over them which we now claim? Can there be any person who will assert this or whose mind does not revolt at the idea of a vast continent holding all that is valuable to it at the discretion of a handful of people on the other side of the Atlantic? But if, at that period, this would be unreasonable, what makes it otherwise now? Draw the line if you can. But there is a still greater difficulty.

Britain is now, I will suppose, the seat of liberty and virtue and its legislature consists of a body of able and independent men who govern with wisdom and justice. The time may come when all will be reversed, when its excellent constitution of government will be subverted, when pressed by debts and taxes, it will be greedy to draw to itself an increase of revenue from every distant province, in order to ease its own burdens, when the influence of the crown, strengthened by luxury and an universal profligacy of manners, will have tainted every heart, broken down every fence of liberty, and rendered us a nation of tame and contented vassals, when a general election will be nothing but a general auction of boroughs, and when the Parliament, the grand council of the nation, and once the faithful guardian of the state and a terror to evil ministers, will be degenerated into a body of sycophants, dependent and venal, always ready to confirm *any* measures, and little more than a public court for registering royal edicts. Such, it is possible, may, some time or other, be the state of Great Britain. What will, at that period, be the duty of the Colonies? Will they be still bound to unconditional submission? Must they always continue an appendage to our government and follow it implicitly through every change that can happen to it? Wretched condition, indeed, of millions of freemen as good as ourselves. Will you say that we now govern equitably and that there is no danger of any such revolution? Would to God this were true. But will you not always say the same? Who shall judge whether we govern equitably or not? Can you give the Colonies any security that such a period will never come?

Once more, if we have indeed that power which we claim over the legislations and internal rights of the Colonies may we not, whenever we please, subject them to the arbitrary power of the crown? I do not mean that this would be a disadvantageous change, for I have before observed that if a people are to be subject to an external power over which they have no command it is better that power should be lodged in the hands of one man than of a multitude. But many persons think otherwise, and such ought to consider that if this would be a calamity the condition of the Colonies must be deplorable. "A government by King, Lords, and Commons, (it has been said) is the perfection of government," and so it is when the Commons are a just representation of the people and when also it is not extended to any distant people or communities not represented. But if this is the best, a government by a king only must be the worst, and every claim implying a right to establish such a government among any people must be unjust and cruel. It is self-evident that by claiming a right to alter the constitutions of the Colonies, according to our discretion, we claim this power. And it is a power that we have thought fit to exercise in one of our Colonies and that we have attempted to exercise in another. Canada, according to the late extension of its limits, is a country almost as large as half Europe and it may possibly come in time to be filled with British subjects. The Quebec Act[23] makes the king of Great Britain a despot over all that country. In the province of *Massachusetts Bay* the same thing has been attempted and begun.

The act for better regulating their government,[24] passed at the same time with the Quebec Act, gives the king the right of appointing and removing at his pleasure the members of one part of the legislature, alters the mode of choosing juries on purpose to bring it more under the influence of the king, and takes away from the province the power of calling any meetings of the people without the king's consent.[j] The judges, likewise, have been made dependent on the king for their nomination and pay and continuance in office. If all this is no more than we have a right to do, may we not go on to abolish the house of representatives, to destroy all trials by juries, and to give up the province absolutely and totally to the will of the king? May we not even establish popery in the province, as has been lately done in Canada, leaving the support of protestantism to the king's discretion? Can there be any Englishman who, were it his own case, would not sooner lose his heart's blood than yield to claims so pregnant with evils and destructive to every thing that can distinguish a freeman from a slave?

I will take this opportunity to add that what I have now said suggests a consideration that demonstrates on how different a footing the Colonies are with respect to our government from particular bodies of men within the kingdom who happen not to be represented. Here, it is impossible that the represented part should subject the unrepresented part to arbitrary power without including themselves. But in the Colonies it is not impossible. We know that it has been done.

j. See pages [77–78].

---

23. The Quebec Act, 14 George 3, ch. 83; approved June 22, 1774; enacted May 1, 1775.
24. The Massachusetts Government Act, 14 George 3, ch. 45; approved May 20, 1774; enacted August 1, 1774.

Sect. II. Whether the War with America is justified by the Principles of the Constitution.

I have proposed, in the next place, to examine the war with the Colonies by the principles of the constitution. I know that it is common to say that we are now maintaining the constitution in America. If this means that we are endeavouring to establish our own constitution of government there, it is by no means true nor, were it true, would it be right. They have chartered governments of their own, with which they are pleased and which, if any power on earth may change without their consent, that power may likewise, if it thinks proper, deliver them over to the Grand Seignior. Suppose the colonies of France had, by compacts, enjoyed for many years free governments open to all the world, under which they had grown and flourished; what should we think of that kingdom, were it to attempt to destroy their governments and to force upon them its own mode of government? Should we not applaud any zeal they discovered in repelling such an injury? But the truth is, in the present instance, that we are not maintaining but violating our own constitution in America. The essence of our constitution consists in its independency. There is in this case no difference between subjection and annihilation. Did, therefore, the Colonies possess governments perfectly the same with ours, the attempt to subject them to ours would be an attempt to ruin them. A free government loses its nature from the moment it becomes liable to be commanded or altered by any superior power.

But I intended here principally to make the following observation. The fundamental principle of our government is "the right of a people to give and grant their own money." It is of no consequence, in this case, whether we enjoy this right in a proper manner or not. Most certainly we do not. It is, however, the principle of which our government, as a free government, is founded. The spirit of the constitution gives it to us and, however imperfectly enjoyed, we glory in it as our first and greatest blessing. It was an attempt to encroach upon this right, in a trifling instance, that produced the civil war in the reign of Charles the First. Ought not our brethren in America to enjoy this right as well as ourselves? Do the principles of the constitution give it to us, but deny it to them? Or can we, with any decency, pretend that when we give to the king their money we give him our own?[k] What difference does it make that in the time of Charles

k. The author of *Taxation No Tyranny* will undoubtedly assert this without hesitation, for in page 69 he compares our present situation with respect to the Colonies to that of the ancient Scythians, who, upon returning from a war, found themselves shut out of their own houses by their slaves [Samuel Johnson,[25] *Taxation No Tyranny; An Answer to the Resolutions and Address of the American Congress* (London: Printed for T. Cadell, 1775)].

---

25. Samuel Johnson (1709–1784), poet, critic, essayist, lexicographer.

the First the attempt to take away this right was made by one man, but that, in the case of America, it is made by a body of men?

In a word, this is a war undertaken not only against the principles of our own constitution but on purpose to destroy other similar constitutions in America and to substitute in their room a military force. See pages [77] and [78]. It is, therefore, a gross and flagrant violation of the constitution.

Sect. III. Of the Policy of the War with America.

In writing the present section I enter upon a subject of the last importance on which much has been said by other writers with great force and in the ablest manner.[1] But I am not willing to omit any topic which I think of great consequence merely because it has already been discussed. And, with respect to this in particular, it will, I believe, be found that some of the observations on which I shall insist have not been sufficiently attended to.

The object of this war has been often enough declared to be "maintaining the supremacy of this country over the colonies." I have already enquired how far reason and justice, the principles of liberty, and the rights of humanity entitle us to this supremacy. Setting aside, therefore, now all considerations of this kind I would observe that this supremacy is to be maintained either merely for its own sake or for the sake of some public interest connected with it and dependent upon it. If for its own sake, the only object of the war is the extension of dominion and its only motive is the lust of power. All government, even within a state, becomes tyrannical

1. See particularly a speech intended to have been spoken on the bill for altering the charter of the Colony of Massachusetts Bay, the *Considerations on the Measures Carrying On with Respect to the British Colonies* [Matthew Robinson-Morris,[26] *Considerations on the Measures Carrying On with Respect to the British Colonies in North-America* (London: Sold by R. Baldwin, 1774)]; the *Two Appeals to the Justice and Interests of the People* [by Arthur Lee; combines his *An Appeal* . . . (see footnote g) and his *A Second Appeal to the Justice and Interests of the People, on the Measures respecting America. By the Author of the First* . . . (London: Printed for J. Almon, 1775)]; [27]and the *Further Examination*, just published, of *Our Present American Measures*, [28]by the author of the *Considerations*, etc.[28],[27] [Matthew Robinson-Morris, *A Further Examination of Our Present American Measures and of the Reasons and the Principles on Which They are Founded. By the Author of Considerations of the Measures Carrying On with Respect to the British Colonies in North-America* (Bath: Printed by R. Crutwell, for R. Baldwin, etc., London, 1776)].

26. Matthew Robinson-Morris, second Baron Rokeby (1713–1800), politician and political writer; educated at Trinity College, Cambridge; elected to Parliament for Canterbury in 1747 and reelected in 1754; critic of British policy towards America.
27. Not in editions 1–3.
28. Not in editions 8–13.

as far as it is a needless and wanton exercise of power or is carried farther than is absolutely necessary to preserve the peace and to secure the safety of the state. This is what an excellent writer calls "governing too much," and its effect must always be weakening government by rendering it contemptible and odious. Nothing can be of more importance in governing distant provinces and adjusting the clashing interests of different societies than attention to this remark. In these circumstances it is particularly necessary to make a sparing use of power in order to preserve power. Happy would it have been for Great Britain had this been remembered by those who have lately conducted its affairs. But our policy has been of another kind. At the period when our authority should have been most concealed it has been brought most in view and by a progression of violent measures, every one of which has increased distress, we have given the world reason to conclude that we are acquainted with no other method of governing than by force. What a shocking mistake! If our object is power we should have known better how to use it and our rulers should have considered that freemen will always revolt at the sight of a naked sword and that the complicated affairs of a great kingdom, holding in subordination to it a multitude of distant communities, all jealous of their rights, and warmed with spirits as high as our own, require not only the most skillful, but the most cautious and tender management. The consequences of a different management we are now feeling. We see ourselves driven among rocks and in danger of being lost.

[29]The following reasons[29] make it too probable that the present contest with America is a contest for power only,[m] abstracted from all the advantages connected with it.

First, there is a love of power inherent in human nature and it cannot be uncharitable to suppose that the nation in general, and the cabinet in particular, are too likely to be influenced by it. What can be more flattering than to look across the Atlantic and to see in the boundless continent of America increasing millions whom we have a right to order as we please, who hold their property at our disposal, and who have no other law than our will. With what complacency have we been used to talk of them as *our* subjects? Is it not the interruption they now give to this pleasure, is it not the opposition they make to our pride, and not any injury they have done us, that is the secret spring of our present animosity against them? I wish all in this kingdom would examine themselves carefully on this point.

m. I have heard it said by a person in one of the first departments of the state, that the present contest is for dominion on the side of the Colonies, as well as on ours. And so it is indeed, but with this essential difference. We are struggling for dominion over others. They are struggling for self-dominion, the noblest of all blessings.

29. Editions 1–13 read "There are the following reasons which seem to. . . ."

Perhaps they might find that they have not known what spirit they are of. Perhaps they would become sensible that it was a spirit of domination more than a regard to the true interest of this country that lately led so many of them, with such savage folly, to address the throne for the slaughter of their brethren in America if they will not submit to them and to make offers of their lives and fortunes for that purpose. Indeed, I am persuaded that, were pride and the lust of dominion exterminated from every heart among us, and the humility of Christians infused in their room, this quarrel would be soon ended.

Second, another reason for believing that this is a contest for power only is that our ministers have frequently declared that their object is not to draw a revenue from America and that many of those who are warmest for continuing it represent the American trade as of no great consequence.

But what deserves particular consideration here is that this is a contest from which no advantages can possibly be derived. Not a revenue, for the provinces of America, when desolated, will afford no revenue or, if they should, the expence of subduing them and keeping them in subjection will much exceed that revenue. Not any of the advantages of trade, for it is a folly, next to insanity, to think trade can be promoted by impoverishing our customers and fixing in their minds an everlasting abhorrence of us. It remains, therefore, that this war can have no other object than the extension of power. Miserable reflection! To sheath our swords in the bowels of our brethren and spread misery and ruin among a happy people for no other end than to oblige them to acknowledge our supremacy—how horrid! This is the cursed ambition that led a Caesar and an Alexander, and many other mad conquerors, to attack peaceful communities and to lay waste the earth.

But a worse principle than even this influences some among us. Pride and the love of dominion are principles hateful enough, but blind resentment and the desire of revenge are infernal principles. And these, I am afraid, have no small share at present in guiding our public conduct. One cannot help indeed being astonished at the virulence with which some speak on the present occasion against the Colonies. For what have they done? Have they crossed the ocean and invaded us? Have they attempted to take from us the fruits of our labour and to overturn that form of government which we hold so sacred? This cannot be pretended. On the contrary, this is what we have done to them. We have transported ourselves to their peaceful retreats and employed our fleets and armies to stop up their ports, to destroy their commerce, to seize their effects, and to burn their towns. Would we but let them alone and suffer them to enjoy in security their property and governments, instead of disturbing us they would thank and bless us. And yet it is we who imagine ourselves ill-used.

The truth is, we expected to find them a cowardly rabble who would lie quietly at our feet, and they have dissappointed us. They have risen in their own defence and repelled force by force. They deny the plentitude of our power over them and insist upon being treated as free communities. It is this that has provoked us and kindled our governors into rage.

I hope I shall not here be understood to intimate that all who promote this war are actuated by these principles. Some, I doubt not, are influenced by no other principle than a regard to what they think the just authority of this country over its colonies and to the unity and indivisibility of the British Empire. I wish such could be engaged to enter thoroughly into the enquiry which has been the subject of the first part of this pamphlet and to consider, particularly, how different a thing maintaining the authority of government within a state is from maintaining the authority of one people over another already happy in the enjoyment of a government of their own. I wish farther they would consider that the desire of maintaining authority is warrantable only as far as it is the means of promoting some end and doing some good and that, before we resolve to spread famine and fire through a country in order to make it acknowledge our authority, we ought to be assured that great advantages will arise not only to ourselves, but to the country we wish to conquer. That from the present contest no advantage to ourselves can arise has been already shown and will presently be shown more at large. That no advantage to the Colonies can arise from it need not, I hope, be shown. It has however been asserted that even their good is intended by this war. Many of us are persuaded that they will be much happier under our government than under any government of their own and that their liberties will be safer when held for them by us than when trusted in their own hands. How kind is it thus to take upon us the trouble of judging for them what is most for their happiness? Nothing can be kinder except the resolution we have formed to exterminate them if they will not submit to our judgment. What strange language have I sometimes heard? By an armed force we are now endeavouring to destroy the laws and governments of America and yet I have heard it said that we are endeavouring to support law and government there. We are insisting upon our right to levy contributions upon them, and to maintain this right we are bringing upon them all the miseries a people can endure, and yet it is asserted that we mean nothing but their security and happiness.

But I have wandered a little from the point I intended principally to insist upon in this section, which is, "the folly, in respect of policy, of the measures which have brought on this contest and its pernicious and fatal tendency."

The following observations will, I believe, abundantly prove this.

First, there are points which are likely always to suffer by discussion.

Of this kind are most points of authority and prerogative and the best policy is to avoid, as much as possible, giving any occasion for calling them into question.

The colonies were at the beginning of this reign in the habit of acknowledging our authority and of allowing us as much power over them as our interest required and more, in some instances, than we could reasonably claim. This habit they would have retained, and had we, instead of imposing new burdens upon them and increasing their restraints, studied to promote their commerce and to grant them new indulgences, they would have been always growing more attached to us. Luxury and, together with it, their dependence upon us and our influence[n] in their assemblies would have increased till in time perhaps they would have become as corrupt as ourselves; and we might have succeeded to our wishes in establishing our authority over them. But, happily for them, we have chosen a different course. By exertions of authority which have alarmed them, they have been put upon examining into the grounds of all our claims and forced to give up their luxuries and to seek all their resources within themselves. And the issue is likely to prove the loss of all our authority over them and of all the advantages connected with it. So little do men in power sometimes know how to preserve power, and so remarkably does the desire of extending dominion sometimes destroy it. Mankind are naturally disposed to continue in subjection to that mode of government, be it what it will, under which they have been born and educated. Nothing rouses them into resistance but gross abuses or some particular oppressions out of the road to which they have been used. And he who will examine the history of the world will find there has generally been more reason for complaining that they have been too patient than that they have been turbulent and rebellious.

Our governors, ever since I can remember, have been jealous that the Colonies, some time or other, would throw off their dependence. This jealousy was not founded on any of their acts or declarations. They have always, while at peace with us, disclaimed any such design; and they have continued to disclaim it since they have been at war with us. I have reason, indeed, to believe, that independency is, even at this moment,[o][30] generally dreaded among them as a calamity to which they are in danger of being driven in order to avoid a greater. The jealousy I have mentioned was, however, natural and betrayed a secret opinion that the subjection in which they were held was more than we could expect them always to

n. This has been our policy with respect to the people of Ireland, and the consequence is that we now see their parliament as obedient as we can wish.

o. It should be remembered that this was written some time before the Declaration of Independence in July 1776. See page [172] of the next tract.[30]

---

30. Footnote not in editions 1–13.

endure. In such circumstances all possible care should have been taken to give them no reason for discontent and to preserve them in subjection by keeping in that line of conduct to which custom had reconciled them, or at least never deviating from it except with great caution and, particularly, by avoiding all direct attacks on their property and legislations. Had we done this, the different interests of so many states scattered over a vast continent, joined to our own prudence and moderation, would have enabled us to maintain them in dependence for ages to come. But instead of this, how have we acted? It is in truth too evident that our whole conduct instead of being directed by that sound policy and foresight which in such circumstances were absolutely necessary, has been nothing (to say the best of it) but a series of the blindest rigour followed by retractation, of violence followed by concession, of mistake, weakness and inconsistency. A recital of a few facts, within every body's recollection, will fully prove this.

In the 6th of George the Second an act was passed for imposing certain duties on all foreign spirits, molasses and sugars imported into the plantations.[31] In this act the duties imposed are said to be *given* and *granted* by the Parliament to the King and this is the first American act in which these words have been used.[32] But notwithstanding this, as the act had the appearance of being only a regulation of trade, the Colonies submitted to it and a small direct revenue was drawn by it from them. In the 4th of the present reign many alterations were made in this act with the declared purpose of making provision for raising a revenue in America.[33] This alarmed the Colonies and produced discontents and remonstrances which might have convinced our rulers this was tender ground on which it became them to tread very gently. There is, however, no reason to doubt but in time they would have sunk into a quiet submission to this revenue act, as being at worst only the exercise of a power which then they seem not to have thought much of contesting, I mean, the power of taxing them externally. But before they had time to cool a worse provocation was given them and the Stamp Act was passed.[34] This being an attempt to tax them internally and a direct attack on their property by a power which would not suffer itself to be questioned, which eased itself by loading them, and to which it was impossible to fix any bounds, they were thrown at once, from one end of the continent to the other, into resistance and rage. Gov-

31. The Molasses Act, 6 George 2, ch. 13; approved May 17, 1733; enacted December 25, 1733.
32. The relevant passage reads: ". . . the commons of Great Britain assembled in parliament have given and granted unto your Majesty the several and respective rates and duties herein after mentioned. . . ." *Statutes at Large*, 16:374.
33. The Sugar Act, 4 George 3, ch. 15; enacted September 29, 1764.
34. The Stamp Act, 5 George 3, ch. 12; approved March 22, 1765; enacted November 1, 1765.

ernment, dreading the consequences, gave way and the Parliament (upon a change of ministry) repealed the Stamp Act,[35] without requiring from them any recognition of its authority or doing any more to preserve its dignity than asserting, by the declaratory law, that it was possessed of full power and authority to make laws to bind them in all cases whatever. Upon this, peace was restored and, had no farther attempts of the same kind been made, they would undoubtedly have suffered us (as the people of Ireland have done) to enjoy quietly our declaratory law. They would have recovered their former habits of subjection and our connexion with them might have continued an increasing source of our wealth and glory. But the spirit of despotism and avarice, always blind and restless, soon broke forth again. The scheme for drawing a revenue from America by parliamentary taxation was resumed and in a little more than a year after the repeal of the Stamp Act, when all was peace, a third act was passed, imposing duties payable in America on tea, paper, glass, painters' colours, etc.[36] This, as might have been expected, revived all the former heats and the Empire was a second time threatened with the most dangerous commotions. Government receded again and the Parliament (under another change of ministry) repealed all the obnoxious duties, except that upon tea.[37] This exception was made in order to maintain a show of dignity. But it was, in reality, sacrificing safety to pride and leaving a splinter in the wound to produce a gangrene. For some time, however, this relaxation answered its intended purposes. Our commercial intercourse with the Colonies was again recovered and they avoided nothing but that tea which we had excepted in our repeal. In this state would things have remained, and even tea would perhaps in time have been gradually admitted, had not the evil genius of Britain stepped forth once more to embroil the Empire.

The East India Company having fallen under difficulties, partly in consequence of the loss of the American market for tea, a scheme was formed

---

35. "An act to repeal an act made in the last session of parliament, entitled, 'An act for granting and applying certain stamp duties, and other duties, in the British colonies and plantations in America . . . ,' " 6 George 3, ch. 11; enacted May 1, 1766.

36. The Townshend Revenue Act, 7 George 3, ch. 46; approved June 29, 1767; enacted November 20, 1767.

37. "An act to repeal so much of an act made in the seventh year of his present Majesty's reign, entitled, 'An act for granting certain duties in the British colonies and plantations in America; for allowing a drawback of the duties of customs upon the exportation from this kingdom of coffee and cocoa nuts of the produce of the said colonies or plantations; for discontinuing the drawbacks payable on china earthenware exported to America; and for more effectually preventing the clandestine running of goods in the said colonies and plantations,' as relates to the duties upon glass, red lead, white lead, painters' colours, paper, paste-boards, mill-boards, and scale-boards, of the produce or manufacture of Great Britain, imported into any of his Majesty's colonies in America; and also to the discontinuing the drawbacks payable on china earthenware, exported to America; and for regulating the exportation thereof," 10 George 3, ch. 17; enacted December 1, 1770.

for assisting them by an attempt to recover that market. With this view an act was passed to enable them to export their tea to America free of all duties here, and subject only to 3d. per pound duty, payable in America.[38] It was to be offered at a low price and it was expected the consequence would prove that the Colonies would be tempted to buy it, a precedent gained for taxing them, and at the same time the company relieved. Ships were, therefore, fitted out and large cargoes sent. The snare was too gross to escape the notice of the Colonies. They saw it and spurned at it. They refused to admit the tea and at Boston some persons in disguise [39]threw it into[39] the sea. Had our governors in this case satisfied themselves with requiring a compensation from the province for the damage done there is no doubt but it would have been granted. Or had they proceeded no farther in the infliction of punishment than stopping up the port and destroying the trade of Boston till compensation was made, the province might possibly have submitted, and a sufficient saving would have been gained for the honour of the nation. But having hitherto proceeded without wisdom they observed now no bounds in their resentment. To the Boston port bill[40] was added a bill which destroyed the chartered government of the province,[41] a bill which withdrew from the jurisdiction of the province persons who in particular cases should commit murder,[42] and the Quebec bill. At the same time a strong body of troops was stationed at Boston to enforce obedience to these bills.

All who knew any thing of the temper of the Colonies saw that the effect of this sudden accumulation of vengeance would probably be not intimidating but exasperating them and driving them into a general revolt.[43] But our ministers had different apprehensions. They believed that

---

38. "An act for granting a drawback of part of the customs upon the exportation of tea to Ireland, and the British dominions in America; . . . ," 12 George 3, ch. 60; enacted July 5, 1772.

39. Editions 1–13 read "buried it in."

40. The Boston Port Act, 14 George 3, ch. 19; approved March 31, 1774; enacted June 1, 1774.

41. The Massachusetts Government Act. See footnote 24.

42. The Administration of Justice Act, 14 George 3, ch. 39; approved May 20, 1774.

43. Editions 1 and 2 have a footnote at the beginning of this sentence, "See the Appendix." The Appendix is primarily financial and is concerned with the amount of the national debt, appropriated revenue, surplus and deficits, taxes, interest on public borrowing, and the like. Price suggests several ways of reducing the national debt; for example, by more efficient but equitable policies of taxation; reduction of the peace establishment, not only the army and navy but also places, pensions and salaries of high officials; and by bringing home the troops: "All the money now spent in maintaining troops in America might be saved. The Colonies are able to defend themselves. They wish to be allowed to do it. Should they ever want the aid of our troops they will certainly be very willing to pay us for them. Indeed I am of opinion they will never be willing to make peace with us without stipulating that we shall withdraw our troops from them. Were there any external power that claimed and exercised a right of stationing troops

the malcontents in the Colony of Massachusetts were a small party, headed by a few factious men, that the majority of the people would take the side of government as soon as they saw a force among them capable of supporting them, that, at worst, the Colonies in general would never make a common cause with this province, and that the issue would prove, in a few months, order, tranquility and submission. Every one of these apprehensions was falsified by the events that followed.

When the bills I have mentioned came to be carried into execution, the whole province was thrown into confusion. The courts of justice were shut up and all government was dissolved. The commander in chief found it necessary to fortify himself in Boston and the other Colonies immediately resolved to make a common cause with this Colony.

[44]Disappointed by these consequences, our ministers took fright. Once more they[44] made an effort to retreat but, indeed, the most ungracious one that can well be imagined. A proposal was sent to the Colonies, called conciliatory, and the substance of which was, that if any of them would raise such sums as should be demanded of them by taxing themselves, the Parliament would forbear to tax them.[45] It will be scarcely believed, hereafter, that such a proposal could be thought conciliatory. It was only telling them, "If you will tax yourselves by our order, we will save ourselves the trouble of taxing you." They received the proposal as an insult and rejected it with disdain.[46]

At the time this concession was transmitted to America open hostilities

---

in this country without our consent we should certainly think ourselves entirely undone. I will estimate this saving at no more than £200,000 per ann."

Editions 1–13 all have this appendix with many variations of detail, and it is much expanded in *Two Tracts.*

44. In editions 1–13 this passage reads: "So strangely misinformed were our ministers that this was all a surprise upon them. They took fright, therefore, and once more. . . ."

45. On February 20, 1775, a resolution containing this proposal was moved by Lord North in the House of Commons. After a heated debate a second reading of the resolution was approved by a vote of 274 to 88. On February 27 the resolution was read a second time. The resolution finally passed following a second intense debate. See *Parliamentary History,* 18:319–358.

46. On May 26, 1775, the resolution of the House of Commons was presented to the Continental Congress. Two months later, on July 31, the Continental Congress adopted a statement rejecting the proposal contained in the resolution. In its statement the Continental Congress asserted:

"We are of opinion that the proposition in this resolution is unreasonable and insidious. Unreasonable because if we declare we accede to it, we declare, without reservation, we will purchase the favor of parliament, not knowing at the same time at what price they will please to estimate their favor. It is insidious because individual colonies, having bid and bidden again till they find the avidity of the seller too great for all their powers to satisfy, are then to return into opposition, divided from their sister colonies whom the minister will have previously detached by a grant of easier terms or by an artful procrastination of a definitive answer." Worthington Chauncey Ford, ed., *Journals of the Continental Congress 1774–1789* (Washington, D.C.: Government Printing Office, 1905), p. 227.

were not begun. In the sword our ministers thought they had still a re-source which would immediately settle all disputes. They considered the people of New England as nothing but a mob, who would be soon routed and forced into obedience. It was even believed that a few thousands of our army might march through all America and make all quiet wherever they went. Under this conviction our ministers did not dread urging the Province of Massachusett's Bay into rebellion by ordering the army to seize their stores and to take up some of their leading men. The attempt was made. The people fled immediately to arms and repelled the attack. A considerable part of the flower of the British army has been destroyed. Some of our best Generals, and the bravest of our troops, are now[p 47] dis-gracefully and miserably imprisoned at Boston. A horrid civil war is com-menced, and the Empire is distracted and convulsed.

Can it be possible to think with patience of the policy that has brought us into these circumstances? Did even Heaven punish the vices of a people more severely by darkening their counsels? How great would be our hap-piness could we now recall former times and return to the policy of the last reigns? But those times are gone. I will, however, beg leave for a few moments to look back to them and to compare the ground we have left with that on which we find ourselves. This must be done with deep regret but it forms a necessary part of my present design.

In those times our Colonies, foregoing every advantage which they might derive from trading with foreign nations, consented to send only to us whatever it was for our interest to receive from them and to receive only from us whatever it was for our interest to send to them. They gave up the power of making sumptuary laws and exposed themselves to all the evils of an increasing and wasteful luxury because we were benefited by vending among them the materials of it. The iron with which providence had blessed their country, they were required by laws, in which they ac-quiesced, to transport hither, that our people might be maintained by working it for them into nails, ploughs, axes, etc. And, in several instances, even one Colony was not allowed to supply any neighbouring Colonies with commodities which could be conveyed to them from hence. But they yielded much farther. They consented that we should have the appoint-ment of one branch of their legislature. By recognizing as their king, a king resident among us and under our influence, they gave us a negative on all their laws. By allowing an appeal to us in their civil disputes, they gave us

p. In February 1776. In a few weeks after this they were driven from Boston and took refuge at Halifax in Nova Scotia from whence, after a strong reinforcement, they in-vaded the Province of New York.[47]

47. Footnote not in editions 1–13.

likewise the ultimate determination of all civil causes among them. In short, they allowed us every power we could desire, except that of taxing them, and interfering in their internal legislations. And they had admitted precedents which, even in these instances, gave us no inconsiderable authority over them. By purchasing our goods they paid our taxes and, by allowing us to regulate their trade in any manner we thought most for our advantage, they enriched our merchants and helped us to bear our growing burdens. They fought our battles with us. They gloried in their relation to us. All their gains centered among us and they always spoke of this country and looked to it as their home.

Such *was* the state of things. What is it now?

Not contented with a degree of power sufficient to satisfy any reasonable ambition we have attempted to extend it. Not contented with drawing from them a large revenue indirectly, we have endeavoured to procure one directly by an authoritative seizure and, in order to gain a pepper-corn in this way, have chosen to hazard millions acquired by the peaceable intercourse of trade. Vile policy! What a scourge is government so conducted? Had we never deserted our old ground, had we nourished and favoured America, with a view to commerce, instead of considering it as a country to be governed, had we, like a liberal and wise people, rejoiced to see a multitude of free states branched forth from ourselves, all enjoying independent legislatures similar to our own, had we aimed at binding them to us only by the ties of affection and interest, and contented ourselves with a moderate power rendered durable by being lenient and friendly, an umpire in their differences, an aid to them in improving their own free governments, and their common bulwark against the assaults of foreign enemies, had this, I say, been our policy and temper, there is nothing so great or happy that we might not have expected. With their increase our strength would have increased. A growing surplus in the revenue might have been gained which, invariably applied to the gradual discharge of the national debt, would have delivered us from the ruin with which it threatens us. The liberty of America might have preserved our liberty and, under the direction of a patriot king or wise minister, proved the means of restoring to us our almost lost constitution. Perhaps, in time, we might also have been brought to see the necessity of carefully watching and restricting our paper credit. And thus we might have regained safety and, in union with our Colonies, have been more than a match for every enemy and risen to a situation of honour and dignity never before known amongst mankind. But I am forgetting myself. Our Colonies are likely to be lost for ever. Their love is turned into hatred and their respect for our government into resentment and abhorrence. We shall see more distinctly what a calamity this is, and the observations I have now made will be confirmed, by attending to the following facts.

Our American Colonies, particularly the northern ones, have been for some time in the happiest state of society or in that middle state of civilization, between its first rude and its last resigned and corrupt state. Old countries consist, generally, of three classes of people, a gentry, a yeomanry, and a peasantry. The Colonies consist only of a body of yeomanry[q] supported by agriculture, and all independent and nearly upon a level; in consequence of which, joined to a boundless extent of country, the means of subsistence are procured without difficulty and the temptations to wickedness are so inconsiderable that executions[r] are seldom known among them. From hence arises an encouragement to population so great that in some of the Colonies they double their own number in fifteen years, in others, in eighteen years, and in all, taken one with another, in twenty-five years. Such an increase was, I believe, never before known. It demonstrates that they must live at their ease and be free from those cares, oppressions, and diseases which depopulate and ravage luxurious states.

With the population of the Colonies has increased their trade, but much faster, on account of the gradual introduction of luxury among them. In 1723 the exports to Pennsylvania were £16,000. In 1742 they were 75,295. In 1757 they were increased to 268,426 and in 1773 to half a million.

The exports to all the Colonies in 1744 were £640,114. In 1758 they were increased to 1,832,948 and in 1773, to three millions.[s] And the probability is that, had it not been for the discontents among the Colonies since the year 1764, our trade with them would have been this year double to what it was in 1773 and that in a few years more it would not have been possible for the whole kingdom, though consisting only of manufacturers, to supply the American demand.

This trade, it should be considered, was not only thus an increasing trade but it was a trade in which we had no rivals, a trade certain, constant, and uninterrupted and which, by the shipping employed in it, and the naval stores supplied by it, contributed greatly to the support of that navy which is our chief national strength. Viewed in these lights it was an object un-

---

q. Except the negroes in the southern Colonies, who probably will now either soon become extinct, or have their condition changed into that of freemen. It is not the fault of the Colonies that they have among them so many of these unhappy people. They have made laws to prohibit the importation of them but these laws have always had a negative put upon them here because of their tendency to hurt our negro trade.

r. In the county of Suffolk, where Boston is, there has not been, I am informed, more than one execution these 18 years.

s. Mr. Burke (in his excellent and admirable speech on moving his resolutions for conciliation with the Colonies, p. 9, etc.) has shown that our trade to the Colonies, including that of Africa and the West Indies, was in 1772 nearly equal to the trade which we carried on with the whole world at the beginning of this century [Edmund Burke, *The Speech of Edmund Burke, Esq.; on Moving his Resolutions for Conciliation with the Colonies, March 22, 1775* (London: Printed for J. Dodsley, 1775)].

speakably important. But it will appear still more so if we view it in its connexions and dependencies. It is well known that our trade with Africa and the West-Indies cannot easily subsist without it. And, upon the whole, it is undeniable that it has been one of the main springs of our opulence and splendour and that we have, in a great measure, been indebted to it for our ability to bear a debt so much heavier than that which, fifty years ago, the wisest men thought would necessarily sink us.

This inestimable prize, and all the advantages connected with America, we are now throwing away. Experience alone can show what calamities must follow. It will indeed be astonishing if this kingdom can bear such a loss without dreadful consequences. These consequences have been amply represented by others and it is needless to enter into any account of them. At the time we shall be feeling them: the Empire dismembered, the blood of thousands shed in an unrighteous quarrel, our strength exhausted, our merchants breaking, our manufacturers starving, our debts increasing, the revenue sinking, the funds tottering, and all the miseries of a public bank-ruptcy impending. At such a crisis should our natural enemies, eager for our ruin, seize the opportunity. The apprehension is too distressing. Let us view this subject in another light.

On this occasion particular attention should be given to the present singular situation of this kingdom. This is a circumstance of the utmost importance and, as I am afraid it is not much considered, I will beg leave to give a distinct account of it.

At the Revolution the specie of the kingdom amounted, according to Davenant's[48] account,[t] to eighteen millions and a half. From the accession to the year 1772 there were coined at the mint near 29 millions of gold and in ten years only of this time, or from January 1759 to January 1769, there were coined eight millions and a half.[u] But it has appeared lately, that the gold specie now left in the kingdom is no more than about twelve millions and a half.[v] Not so much as half a million of silver specie has been coined

t. See Dr. Davenant's *Works*, collected and revised by Sir Charles Whitworth, vol. 1, pages 363, etc.; 443, etc. [Charles Davenant, *The Political and Commercial Works of that Celebrated Writer, Charles D'Avenant, LL.D., Relating to the Trade and Revenue of England, the Plantation Trade, the East India Trade and Africa Trade*, collected and revised by Charles Whitworth (London: Printed for R. Horsfield, 1771)].

u. See *Considerations in Money, Bullion*, etc., pages 2 and 11 [*Considerations on Money, Bullion, and Foreign Exchanges; Being an Enquiry into the Present State of the British Coinage; Particularly with Regard to the Scarcity of Silver Money* . . . (London: Printed for L. Davis, 1772)].

v. The coin deficient between one grain and three grains was not called in at the time this was written. This call was made in the summer of 1776 and it brought in above three millions more than was expected. The quantity of gold coin should therefore have been

48. Charles Davenant (1656–1714), political economist; commissioner of the excise; inspector-general of the exports and imports.

these sixty years and it cannot be supposed that the quantity of it now in circulation exceeds two or three millions. The whole specie of the kingdom, therefore, is probably at this time about fifteen millions. Of this some millions must be hoarded in the Bank. Our circulating specie, therefore, appears to be decreased. But our wealth, or the quantity of money in the kingdom, is greatly increased. This is paper to a vast amount, issued in almost every corner of the kingdom, and, particularly, by the Bank of England. While this paper maintains its credit it answers all the purposes of specie and is in all respects the same with money.

Specie represents some real value in goods and commodities. On the contrary, paper represents immediately nothing but specie. It is a promise or obligation which the emitter brings himself under to pay a given sum in coin, and it owes its currency to the credit of the emitter or to an opinion that he is able to make good his engagement and that the sum specified may be received upon being demanded. Paper, therefore, represents coin and coin represents real value. That is, the one is a sign of wealth. The other is the sign of that sign. But farther, coin is an universal sign of wealth and will procure it every where. It will bear any alarm and stand any shock. On the contrary, paper, owing its currency to opinion, has only a local and imaginary value. It can stand no shock. It is destroyed by the approach of danger or even the suspicion of danger.

In short, coin is the basis of our paper credit and were it either all destroyed, or were only the quantity of it reduced beyond a certain limit, the paper circulation of the kingdom would sink at once. But, were our paper destroyed, the coin would not only remain but rise in value in proportion to the quantity of paper destroyed.

From this account it follows that as far as, in any circumstances, specie is not to be procured in exchange for paper, it represents nothing and is worth nothing. The specie of this kingdom is inconsiderable compared with the amount of the paper circulating in it. This is generally believed and, therefore, it is natural to enquire how its currency is supported. The answer is easy. It is supported in the same manner with all other bubbles. Were all to demand specie in exchange for their notes payment could not be made but, at the same time that this is known every one trusts that no alarm producing such a demand will happen, while he holds the paper he is possessed of, and that if it should happen he will stand a chance for

stated at about sixteen millions and the whole coin of the kingdom at 18 or 19 millions. The evidence from which I have drawn this estimate may be found in the first section of the second part of the next tract.[49]

[In editions 1–13 this footnote reads: "Or nearly the same that it was in Cromwell's time. See Dr. Davenant's *Works*, vol. 1, page 365."]

49. The first section of the second part of *Additional Observations* is not included in this volume.

being first paid; and this makes him easy. And it also makes all with whom he traffics easy. But let any events happen which threaten danger and every one will become dissident. A run will take place and a bankruptcy follow.

This is an account of what has often happened in private credit. And it is also an account of what will (if no change of measures takes place) happen some time or other in public credit. The description I have given of our paper circulation implies that nothing can be more delicate or hazardous. It is an immense fabric with its head in the clouds that is continually trembling with every adverse blast and every fluctuation of trade and which, like the baseless fabric of a vision, may in a moment vanish and leave no wreck behind. The destruction of a few books at the Bank, an improvement in the art of forgery, the landing of a body of French troops on our coasts, insurrections threatening a revolution of government, or any events that should produce a general panic, however groundless, would at once annihilate it, and leave us without any other medium of traffic than a quantity of specie 50not much than50 the money now drawn from the public by the taxes. It would, therefore, become impossible to pay the taxes. The revenue would fail. Near a hundred and forty millions of property would be destroyed. The whole frame of government would fall to pieces and a state of nature would take place. What a dreadful situation? It has never had a parallel among mankind except at one time in France after the establishment there of the Royal Mississippi Bank. In 1720 this bank broke*w* and, after involving for some time the whole kingdom in a golden dream, spread through it in one day desolation and ruin. The distress attending such an event in this free country would be greater than it was in France. Happily for that kingdom they have shot this gulf. Paper credit has never since recovered itself there and their circulating cash consists now all of solid coin amounting, according to the lowest account, to no less a sum than 1500 millions of livres*x* 52 or near 67 millions of pounds sterling. This gives them unspeakable advantages and, joined to that quick reduction of their debts which is inseparable*y* from their nature, places them on a ground of safety which we have reason to admire and envy.

w. See Sir James Steuart's[51] Enquiry into the Principles of Political Economy, vol. 2, bk. 4, chap. 32 [James Steuart Denham, An Enquiry into the Principles of Political Oeconomy: Being an Essay on the Science of Domestic Policy in Free Nations . . . (London: A. Millar and T. Cadell, 1767)].

x. See the Second Tract, p. 65.[52]

y. Their debts consist chiefly of money raised by annuities on lives, short annuities, anticipations of taxes for short terms, etc. During the whole last war they added to their

50. Editions 1–13 read "scarcely equal in amount to."

51. James Steuart Denham (1712–1780), political economist, lawyer, traveler; sympathizer with the exiled Stuarts; prolific writer on economics.

52. Footnote not in editions 1–13. This footnote refers the reader to a page in the first section of the second part of Additional Observations which is not included in this volume.

These are subjects on which I should have chosen to be silent did I not think it necessary that this country should be apprized and warned of the danger which threatens it. This danger is created chiefly by the national debt. High taxes are necessary to support a great public debt and a large supply of cash is necessary to support high taxes. This cash we owe to our paper and, in proportion to our paper, must be the productiveness of our taxes. King William's wars drained the kingdom of its specie. This sunk the revenue and distressed government. In 1694 the Bank was established and the kingdom was provided with a substitute for specie. The taxes became again productive. The revenue rose and government was relieved. Ever since that period our paper and taxes have been increasing together and supporting one another and one reason, undoubtedly, of the late increase in the productiveness of our taxes has been the increase of our paper.

Was there no public debt, there would be no occasion for half the present taxes. Our paper circulation might be reduced. The balance of trade would turn in our favour. Specie would flow in upon us. The quantity of property destroyed by a failure of paper credit (should it in such circumstances happen) would be 140 millions less and, therefore, the shock attending it would be tolerable. But in the present state of things whenever any calamity or panic shall produce such a failure the shock attending it will be intolerable. May heaven soon raise up for us some great statesman who shall see these things and enter into effectual measures, if not now too late, for extricating and preserving us.

Public banks are, undoubtedly, attended with great conveniences. But they also do great harm and, if their emissions are not restrained and conducted with great wisdom, they may prove the most pernicious of all institutions, not only by substituting fictitious for real wealth, by increasing luxury, by raising the prices of provisions, by concealing an unfavourable balance of trade, and by rendering a kingdom incapable of bearing any internal tumults or external attacks, without the danger of a dreadful convulsion, but, particularly, by becoming instruments in the hands of ministers of state to increase their influence, to lessen their dependence on the people, and to keep up a delusive show of public prosperity, when perhaps ruin may be near. There is, in truth, nothing that a government may not do with such a mine at its command as a public bank while it can

---

perpetual annuities only 12 millions sterling, according to Sir James Steuart's account, whereas we added to these annuities near 60 millions. In consequence therefore of the nature of their debts, as well as of the management they are now using for hastening the reduction of them, they must in a few years, if peace continues, be freed from most of their incumbrances, while we probably (if no event comes soon that will unburden us at once) shall continue with them all upon us.

maintain its credit nor, therefore, is there any thing more likely to be improperly and dangerously used. But to return to what may be more applicable to our own state at present.

Among the causes that may produce a failure of paper credit there are two which the present quarrel with America calls upon us particularly to consider. The first is, "an unfavourable balance of trade." This, in proportion to the degree in which it takes place, must turn the course of foreign exchange against us, raise the price of bullion, and carry off our specie. The danger to which this would expose us is obvious and it has been much increased by the new coinage of the gold specie which begun in 1773. Before this coinage, the greatest part of our gold coin being light, but the same in currency as if it had been heavy, always remained in the kingdom. But, being now nearly of full weight, whenever a wrong balance of foreign trade alters the course of exchange, and gold in coin becomes of less value than in bullion, there is reason to fear that it will be melted down in such great quantities and exported so fast as in a little time to leave none behind.[z] The consequence of which must prove that the whole superstructure of paper-credit, now supported by it, will break down. The only remedy, in such circumstances, is an increase of coinage at the mint. But this will operate too slowly and, by raising the price of bullion, will only increase the evil. It is the Bank that at such a time must be the immediate sufferer. For it is from thence that those who want coin for any purpose will always draw it.

For many years before 1773 the price of gold in bullion had been from

z. Mr. Lowndes,[53] in the dispute between him and Mr. Locke, contended for a reduction of the standard of silver. One of his reasons was that it would render the silver coin more commensurate to the wants of the nation and check hazardous paper credit. Mr. Conduitt,[54] Sir Isaac Newton's successor in the mint, has proposed, in direct contradiction to the laws now in being, that all the bullion imported into the kingdom should be carried into the mint to be coined and only coin allowed to be exported. "The height," he says, "of paper credit is the strongest argument for trying this and every other method that is likely to increase the coinage. For whilst paper credit does in a great measure the business of money at home, merchants and bankers are not under a necessity, as they were formerly, of coining a quantity of specie for their home trade; and, as paper credit brings money to the merchants to be exported, the money may go away insensibly and not be missed till it be too late. And where paper credit is large and increasing, if the money be exported and the coinage decrease, that credit may sink at once for want of a proportionable quantity of specie, which alone can support it in a time of distress." See Mr. Conduitt's *Observations on the State of our Gold and Silver Coins in 1730*, pages 36 to 46 [John Conduitt, *Observations upon the Present State of Our Gold and Silver Coins, 1730* (London: Printed for T. Becket, 1774)].

53. William Lowndes (1652–1724), secretary to the treasury, suggested a devaluation of the coinage in 1695. The proposal was opposed by Locke.

54. John Conduitt (1688–1737), soldier, politician; member of Parliament for Whitchurch, Hampshire and for Southampton; master of the mint; biographer of Newton.

2 to 3 or 4 per cent higher than in coin. This was a temptation to melt down and export the coin which could not be resisted. Hence arose a demand for it on the Bank and, consequently, the necessity of purchasing bullion at a loss for a new coinage. But the more coin the Bank procured in this way, the lower its price became in comparison with that of bullion, and the faster it vanished and, consequently, the more necessary it became to coin again and the greater loss fell upon the Bank. Had things continued much longer in this train the consequences might have proved very serious. I am by no means sufficiently informed to be able to assign the causes which have produced the change that happened in 1772. But, without doubt, the state of things which took place before that year must be expected to return. The fluctuations of trade, in its best state, render this unavoidable. But the contest with our Colonies has a tendency to bring it on soon and to increase unspeakably the distress attending it. All know that the balance of trade with them is greatly in our favour[aa] and that this balance is paid partly by direct remittances of bullion and partly by circuitous remittances through Spain, Portugal, Italy, etc. which diminish the balance against us with these countries. During the last year they have been employed in paying their debts, without adding to them, and their exportations and remittances for that purpose have contributed to render the general balance of trade more favourable to us and also (in conjunction with the last operations of the Bank) to keep up our funds. These remittances are now ceased and a few years will determine, it this contest goes on, how far we can sustain such a loss without suffering the consequences I have described.

The second event, ruinous to our paper circulation, which may arise from our rupture with America, is a deficiency in the revenue. As a failure of our paper would destroy the revenue, so a failure of the revenue, or any considerable diminution of it, would destroy our paper. The Bank is the support of our paper and the support of the Bank is the credit of government. Its principal securities are a capital of eleven millions lent to government and money continually advanced to a vast amount on the land tax [55]and malt tax,[55] sinking fund, exchequer bills, navy bills, etc. Should, therefore, deficiencies in the revenue bring government under any difficulties, all these securities would lose their value, and the Bank and Government and all private and public credit would fall together. Let any one here imagine what would probably follow were it but suspected by the public in general that the taxes were so fallen as not to produce enough to pay the interest of the public debts besides bearing the ordinary expences of the nation and that, in order to supply the deficiency and to hide the

aa. According to the accounts of the exports to, and imports from, the North American Colonies laid before Parliament, the balance in our favour appears to have been, for 11 years before 1774, near a million and a half annually.

---

55. Not in editions 1–9.

calamity, it had been necessary in any one year to anticipate the taxes and to borrow of the Bank. In such circumstances I can scarcely doubt but an alarm would spread of the most dangerous tendency. The next foreign war, should it prove half as expensive as the last, will probably occasion such a deficiency and bring our affairs to that crisis towards which they have been long tending. But the war with America has a greater tendency to do this; and the reason is that it affects our resources more and is attended more with the danger of internal disturbances.

Some have made the proportion of our trade depending on North America to be near one half. A moderate computation makes it a third.[bb] Let it, however, be supposed to be only a fourth. I will venture to say this is a proportion of our foreign trade the loss of which, when it comes to be felt, will be found insupportable. In the article of tobacco alone it will cause a deduction from the customs of at least £300,000 *per ann.*[cc] including the duties paid on foreign commodities purchased by the exportation of tobacco. Let the whole deduction from the revenue be supposed to be only half a million. This alone is more than the kingdom can at present bear without having recourse to [57]lotteries and the land tax at 4 shillings[57] in order to defray the common and necessary expences of peace. But to this must be added a deduction from the produce of the excises, in consequence of the increase of the poor, of the difficulties of our merchants and manufacturers, of less national wealth, and a retrenchment of luxury. There is no possibility of knowing to what these deductions may amount. When the

bb. See the substance of the evidence on the petition presented by the West India planters and merchants to the House of Commons as it was introduced at the bar and summed up by Mr. Glover.[56]

cc. The annual average of the payments into the exchequer, on account of the duties on tobacco, was for five years, from 1770 to 1774, 219,117 pounds exclusive of the payments from Scotland. Near one half of the tobacco trade is carried on from Scotland and above four fifths of the tobacco imported is afterwards exported to France, Germany and other countries. From France alone it brings annually into the Kingdom, I am informed, about 150,000 pounds in money.

In 1775, being, alas! the parting year, the duties on tobacco in England brought into the exchequer no less a sum than 298,202.

---

56. Richard Glover (1712–1785) poet, politician; proprietor of the Temple Mills near Marlow; unsuccessful candidate for the office of chamberlain of the city of London (1751); member of Parliament for Weymouth (1761–1768); advisor to Douglas, Heron, & Co. The petition summarized by Glover is probably the "Petition of the West India Planters to the Commons respecting the American Non-Importation Agreement," which was presented to the House of Commons on February 2, 1775. In that petition the planters noted that the North American colonies refused to import molasses, syrups, paneles, and pimento from the British West Indies. They also noted that the North American colonies refused to export any product to the British West Indies. Since such measures severely hurt the planters, they asked the Commons to take whatever measures deemed proper by the Commons to restore the trade between British North America and the British West Indies. See *Parliamentary History*, 18:219–221.

57. Editions 1–13 read "additional taxes."

evils producing them begin they will proceed rapidly and they may end in a general wreck before we are aware of any danger.

In order to give a clearer view of this subject, I will in an appendix,[dd][58] state particularly the national expenditure and income for eleven years, from 1764 to 1774. From that account it will appear that the money drawn every year from the public by the taxes [59]does not fall greatly[59] short of a sum equal to the whole specie of the kingdom and that, notwithstanding the late increase in the productiveness of the taxes, the whole surplus of the national income has not exceeded £338,759[60] *per ann.* [61]See the second tract, p. 160.[61] This is a surplus so inconsiderable as to be scarcely sufficient to guard against the deficiencies arising from the common fluctuation of foreign trade and of home consumption. It is nothing when considered as the only fund we have for paying off a debt of near 140 millions. Had we continued in a state of profound peace, it could not have admitted of any diminution. What then must follow, when one of the most profitable branches of our trade is destroyed, when a third of the Empire is lost, when an addition of many millions is made to the public debt and when, at the same time, perhaps some millions are taken away from the revenue? I shudder at this prospect. A kingdom on an edge so perilous should think of nothing but a retreat.

Sect. IV. Of the Honour of the Nation as Affected by the War with America.

One of the pleas for continuing the contest with America is, "that our honour is engaged and that we cannot now recede without the most humiliating concessions."

With respect to this it is proper to observe that a distinction should be made between the nation and its rulers. It is melancholy that there should be ever any reason for making such a distinction. A government is, or ought to be, nothing but an institution for collecting and for carrying into execution the will of the people. But so far is this from being in general the fact that the measures of government and the sense of the people are sometimes in direct opposition to one another; nor does it often happen that any certain conclusion can be drawn from the one to the other. I will not pretend to determine whether, in the present instance, the dishonour attend-

dd. All the accounts and calculations in the appendix here referred to have been transferred to the 2d and 4th sections of the 3d part of the Second Tract.[58]

58. Footnote not in editions 1–13. The third part of the second tract, i.e., *Additional Observations*, is not included in this volume.

59. Editions 1–13 read "falls but little."

60. Editions 1–13 read "320,000."

61. Not in editions 1–13. This sentence refers the reader to a page in the third part of *Additional Observations* which is not included in this volume.

ing a retreat would belong to the nation at large or only to the persons in power who guide its affairs. [62] Be this as it will, no good argument can be drawn from it against receding. The disgrace which may be implied in making concessions is nothing to that of being the aggressors in an unrighteous quarrel; and dignity, in such circumstances, consists in retracting freely and speedily.[62] For (to adopt on this occasion words which I have heard applied to this very purpose, in a great assembly, by a peer to whom this kingdom has often looked as its deliverer, and whose ill state of health at this awful moment of public danger every friend to Britain must deplore) to adopt, I say, the words of this great man, "Rectitude is dignity. Oppression only is meanness; and justice, honour." [63]

I will add that prudence, no less than true honour, requires us to retract. For the time may come when, if it is not done voluntarily, we may be obliged to do it and find ourselves under a necessity of granting that to our distresses which we now deny to equity and humanity and the prayers of America. The possibility of this appears plainly from the preceding pages; and should it happen, it will bring upon us disgrace indeed, disgrace greater than the worst rancour can wish to see accumulated on a kingdom already too much dishonoured. Let the reader think here what we are doing. A nation, once the protector of liberty in distant countries and the scourge of tyranny, changed into an enemy to liberty and engaged in endeavouring to reduce to servitude its own brethren. A great and enlightened nation, not content with a controlling power over millions of people which gave it every reasonable advantage, insisting upon such a supremacy over them as would leave them nothing they could call their own, and carrying desolation and death among them for disputing it. What can be more ignominious? How have we felt for the brave Corsicans in their struggle with the Genoese and afterwards with the French government? Did Genoa or France want more than an absolute command over their property and legislations or the power of binding them in call cases whatsoever? [64] The Genoese, finding it difficult to keep them in subjection,

---

62. Editions 1–13 read: "Let it be granted, though probably far from true, that the majority of the kingdom favour the present measures. No good argument could be drawn from hence against receding. The disgrace to which a kingdom must submit by making concessions is nothing to that of being the aggressors in an unrighteous quarrel; and dignity, in such circumstances, consists in retracting freely, speedily and magnanimously."

63. William Pitt, the elder, first earl of Chatham. Sentiments of this kind are expressed in Pitt's many speeches in Parliament in support of the American cause, but I have been unable to locate this exact passage. He might have said it, however, in supporting the Bill for the Relief of Protestant Dissenters on May 19, 1772. This bill was strongly supported by Price, who may have been present at the debate. See footnote 23 to the *General Introduction*.

64. Editions 1–11 read: "The Corsicans had been subject to the Genoese but, finding it difficult to keep them in subjection, they ceded them to the French." Edition 13 reads: "The Corsicans had been subject to Genoa but that republic finding it difficult to keep them in subjection, ceded them to the French."

ceded them to the French.[64] All such cessions of one people by another are disgraceful to human nature. But if our claims are just, may not we also, if we please, cede the Colonies to France? There is, in truth, no other difference between these two cases than that the Corsicans were not descended from the people who governed them but that the Americans are.

There are some who seem to be sensible that the authority of one country over another cannot be distinguished from the servitude of one country to another and that unless different communities, as well as different parts of the same community, are united by an equal representation, all such authority is inconsistent with the principles of civil liberty. But they except the case of the Colonies and Great Britain because the Colonies are communities which have branched forth from and which, therefore, as they think, belong to Britain. Had the Colonies been communities of foreigners over whom we wanted to acquire dominion, or even to extend a dominion before acquired, they are ready to admit that their resistance would have been just. In my opinion this is the same with saying that the Colonies ought to be worse off than the rest of mankind because they are our own brethren.

Again, the United Provinces of Holland were once subject to the Spanish monarchy but, provoked by the violation of their charters by levies of money without their consent, by the introduction of Spanish troops among them, by innovations in their ancient modes of government, and the rejection of their petitions, they were driven to that resistance which we and all the world have ever since admired and which has given birth to one of the greatest and happiest republics that ever existed. Let any one read also the history of the war which the Athenians, from a thirst of empire, made on the Syracusans in Sicily, a people derived from the same origin with them, and let him, if he can, avoid rejoicing in the defeat of the Athenians.

Let him, likewise, read the account of the social war among the Romans. The allied states of Italy had fought the battles of Rome and contributed by their valour and treasure to its conquests and grandeur. They claimed, therefore, the rights of Roman citizens and a share with them in legislation. The Romans, disdaining to make those their fellow citizens whom they had always looked upon as their subjects, would not comply and a war followed, the most horrible in the annals of mankind, which ended in the ruin of the Roman Republic. The feelings of every Briton in this case must force him to approve the conduct of the Allies and to condemn the proud and ungrateful Romans.

But not only is the present contest with America thus disgraceful to us, because inconsistent with our own feelings in similar cases, but also because condemned by our own practice in former times. The colonies are persuaded that they are fighting for liberty. We see them sacrificing to this persuasion every private advantage. If mistaken, and though guilty of irregularities, they should be pardoned by a people whose ancestors have given them so many examples of similar conduct. England should venerate the attachment to liberty amidst all its excesses and, instead of indignation or scorn, it would be most becoming them, in the present instance, to declare their applause and to say to the Colonies, "We excuse your mistakes. We admire your spirit. It is the spirit that has more than once saved ourselves. We aspire to no dominion over you. We understand the rights of men too well to think of taking from you the inestimable privilege of governing yourselves and, instead of employing our power for any such purpose, we offer it to you as a friendly and guardian power, to be a mediator in your quarrels, a protection against your enemies, and an aid to you in establishing a plan of liberty that shall make you great and happy. In return, we ask nothing but your gratitude and your commerce."

This would be a language worthy of a brave and enlightened nation. But alas! it often happens in the political world as it does in religion, that the people who cry out most vehemently for liberty to themselves are the most unwilling to grant it to others.[65]

But farther, this war is disgraceful on account of the persuasion which led to it and under which it has been undertaken. The general cry was last winter that the people of New England were a body of cowards who would at once be reduced to submission by a hostile look from our troops. In this light were they held up to public derision in both Houses of Parliament and it was this persuasion that, probably, induced a nobleman of the first weight in the state to recommend, at the passing of the Boston Port Bill, coercive measures, hinting at the same time that the appearance of hostilities would be sufficient, and that all would be soon over, *Sine clade*.[66] Indeed no one can doubt but that had it been believed some time ago that the people of America were brave, more care would have been taken not to provoke them.

Again, the manner in which this war has been hitherto conducted renders it still more disgraceful. English valour being thought insufficient to subdue the Colonies, the laws and religion of France were established in Canada on purpose to obtain the power of bringing upon them from thence an army of French papists. The wild Indians and their own slaves have been instigated to attack them and attempts have been made to gain

---

65. Editions 1–13 add the paragraph:
"One of the most violent enemies of the colonies has pronounced them 'All Mr. Locke's disciples.' Glorious title! How shameful is it to make war against them for that reason."
66. In March and April 1774 the House of Commons debated three bills moved by Lord North. These bills, when passed into law, were known as the Boston Port Act, the Massachusetts Government Act, and the Administration of Justice Act. These acts, together with the Quebec Act, came to be known as the Coercive (or Intolerable) Acts. The hint to which Price refers was probably made by North in his speech on moving the Massachusetts Government Bill on March 28. See *Parliamentary History*, 17:1192–1193.

the assistance of a large body of Russians. With like views, German troops have been hired and the defence of our forts and garrisons trusted in their hands.

These are measures which need no comment. The last of them, in particular, having been carried into execution without the consent of Parliament, threatens us with imminent danger and shows that we are in the way to lose even the forms of the constitution. If, indeed, our ministers can at any time, without leave, not only send away the national troops but introduce foreign troops in their room we lie entirely at mercy; and we have every thing to dread.

Sect. V. Of the Probability of Succeeding in the War with America.

Let us next consider how far there is a possibility of succeeding in the present war.

Our own people, being unwilling to enlist, and the attempts to procure armies of Russians, Indians and Canadians having miscarried, the utmost force we can employ, including foreigners, does not exceed, if I am rightly informed, 40,000[67] effective men.[68] This is the force that is to conquer half a million at least *ee* of determined men fighting on their own ground, within sight of their houses and families and for that sacred blessing of liberty without which man is a beast and government a curse. All history proves that in such a situation a handful is a match for millions.

In the Netherlands a few states, thus circumstanced, withstood for [69]a long course of [69] years the whole force of the Spanish monarchy when at its zenith and at last humbled its pride and emancipated themselves from its tyranny. The citizens of Syracuse also, thus circumstanced, withstood the whole power of the Athenians and almost ruined them. The same happened in the contest between the house of Austria and the cantons*ff* of

ee. A quarter of the inhabitants of every country are fighting men. If, therefore, the Colonies consist only of two millions of inhabitants, the number of fighting men in them will be half a million.

ff. See the Appendix to Dr. Zubly's[70] *Sermon Preached at the Opening of the Provincial Congress of Georgia* [John Joachim Zubly, *The Law of Liberty. A Sermon on American Affairs, Preached at the Opening of the Provincial Congress of Georgia. Addressed to the Right Honourable the Earl of Dartmouth. With an Appendix, Giving a Concise Account of the Struggles of Swisserland to Recover their Liberty* (Philadelphia: Printed and sold by Henry Miller, 1775)].

67. Editions 1–13 read "30,000."
68. Editions 1–13 insert: "Let it, however, be called 40,000."
69. Editions 1–13 read "thirty."
70. John Joachim Zubly (1724–1781), born in St. Gall, Switzerland; ordained a Presbyterian minister in London (1744); pastor in Charlestown and Wando Neck, South Carolina, before 1760; first pastor of the Independent Presbyterian Church of Savannah, Georgia (1760–1781); delegate to the Georgia Provincial Congress (1775); delegate to the Continental Congress (1775–1776); opponent of independence.

Switzerland. There is in this case an infinite difference between attacking and being attacked, between fighting to destroy and fighting to preserve or acquire liberty. Were we, therefore, capable of employing a land force against America equal to its own there would be little probability of success. But to think of conquering that whole continent with 30,000 or 40,000 men to be transported across the Atlantic and fed from hence and incapable of being recruited after any defeat—this is indeed a folly so great that language does not afford a name for it.

With respect to our naval force, could it sail at land as it does at sea, much might be done with it but as that is impossible, little or nothing can be done with it which will not hurt ourselves more than the Colonists. Such of their maritime towns as they cannot guard against our fleets, and have not been already destroyed, they are determined either to give up to our resentment or[gg][71] destroy themselves. The consequence of which will be that these towns will be rebuilt in safer situations and that we shall lose some of the principal pledges by which we have hitherto held them in subjection. As to their trade, having all the necessaries and the chief conveniences of life within themselves they have no dependence upon it and the loss of it will do them unspeakable good, by preserving them from the evils of luxury and the temptations of wealth and keeping them in that state of virtuous simplicity which is the greatest happiness. I know that I am now speaking the sense of some of the wisest men in America. It has been long their wish that Britain would shut up all their ports. They will rejoice, particularly, in the last restraining act.[72] It might have happened that the people would have grown weary of their agreements not to export or import. But this act will oblige them to keep these agreements and confirm their unanimity and zeal. It will also furnish them with a reason for confiscating the estates of all the friends of our government among them and for employing their sailors, who would have been otherwise idle, in making reprisals on British property. Their ships, before useless, and consisting of many hundreds, will be turned into ships of war and that attention, which they have hitherto confined to trade, will be employed in fitting out a naval force for their own defence and thus the way will be prepared for their becoming, much sooner than they would otherwise have been, a great maritime power. This act of parliament,

gg. [Editions 1–13 include the footnote: "New York has long been deserted by the greatest part of the inhabitants and they are determined to burn it themselves rather than suffer us to burn it."][71]

71. The text of this eighth edition in the first edition of *Two Tracts* calls for the footnote but it was not included. It was included in editions 1–13 and was reinserted in the second edition of *Two Tracts*.

72. The American Prohibitory Act, 16 George 3, ch. 5; probably approved in December 1775; enacted January 1, 1776. This act forbade all trade with the thirteen American colonies while the rebellion continued. See *Statutes at Large*, 31:135–154.

therefore, crowns the folly of all our late measures.[hh][73] None who know me can believe me to be disposed to superstition. Perhaps, however, I am not in the present instance free from this weakness. I fancy I see in these measures something that cannot be accounted for merely by human ignorance. I am inclined to think that the hand of Providence is in them working to bring about some great ends. But this leads me to one consideration more which I cannot help offering to the public and which appears to me in the highest degree important.

In this hour of tremendous danger it would become us to turn our thoughts to Heaven. This is what our brethren in the Colonies are doing. From one end of North America to the other they are fasting and praying. But what are we doing?[74] We are ridiculing them as fanatics and scoffing at religion. We are running wild after pleasure and forgetting every thing serious and decent at masquerades. We are[75] trafficking for boroughs, perjuring ourselves at elections, and selling ourselves for places. Which side then is Providence likely to favour?

In America we see a number of rising states in the vigour of youth, inspired by the noblest of all passions, the passion for being free, and animated by piety. Here we see an old state, great indeed, but inflated and irreligious, enervated by luxury, encumbered with debts, and hanging by a thread. Can any one look without pain to the issue? May we not expect calamities that shall recover to reflection (perhaps to devotion) our libertines and atheists?

Is our cause such as gives us reason to ask God to bless it? Can we in the face of Heaven declare, "that we are not the aggressors in this war and that we mean by it, not to acquire or even preserve dominion for its own sake, not conquest, or empire, or the gratification of resentment, but solely to deliver ourselves from oppression, to gain reparation for injury, and to defend ourselves against men who would plunder or kill us?" Remember, reader whoever thou art, that there are no other just causes of war and that blood spilled with any other views must some time or other be accounted for. But not to expose myself by saying more in this way, I will now beg leave to recapitulate some of the arguments I have used and to deliver the feelings of my heart in a brief but earnest address to my countrymen.

hh. The apprehensions here expressed have been verified by the events which have happened since this was written. American privateers have spread themselves over the Atlantic. They have frightened us even on our own coasts and seized millions of British property.[73]

73. Footnote not in editions 1–13.
74. Editions 1–13 insert: "Shocking thought!"
75. Editions 1–13 insert "gambling in gaming houses."

I am hearing it continually urged, "Are they not our subjects?" The plain answer is, they are not your subjects. The people of America are no more the subjects of the people of Britain than the people of Yorkshire are the subjects of the people of Middlesex. They are your fellow-subjects.

"But we are taxed, and why should not they be taxed?" You are taxed by yourselves. They insist on the same privilege. They are taxed to support their own governments and they help also to pay your taxes by purchasing your manufactures and giving you a monopoly of their trade. Must they maintain two governments? Must they submit to be triple taxed? Has your moderation in taxing yourselves been such as encourages them to trust you with the power of taxing them?

"But they will not obey the Parliament and the laws." Say, rather, they will not obey your parliament and your laws. Their reason is, they have no voice in your parliament. They have no share in making your laws.[ii] "Neither have most of us." Then you so far want liberty, and your language is, "We are not free, why will they be free?" But many of you have a voice in parliament, none of them have. All your freehold land is represented. But not a foot of their land is represented: At worst, therefore, you are[77] only enslaved partially. [78]Were they to submit,[78] they would be enslaved totally. They are governed by parliaments chosen by themselves and by legislatures similar to yours. Why will you disturb them in the enjoyment of a blessing so valuable?[79] Is it reasonable to insist that your discretion alone shall be their law, that they shall have no constitutions of government except such as your parliament shall be pleased to leave them?

ii. "I have no other notion of slavery but being bound by a law to which I do not consent." See the case of Ireland's being bound by acts of Parliament in England, stated by William Molyneux, Esq.,[76] Dublin [William Molyneux, *The Case of Ireland's Being Bound by Acts of Parliament in England, Stated* (Dublin: Printed by and for J. R., and to be sold by R. Clavel, and A. and J. Churchill in London, 1698; with a new preface, London, Printed for J. Almon, 1770)]. In arguing against the authority of communities, and all people not incorporated, over one another I have confined my views to taxation and internal legislation. Mr. Molyneux carried his views much farther and denied the right of England to make any laws even to regulate the trade of Ireland. He was the intimate friend of Mr. Locke and writ his book in 1698, soon after the publication of Mr. Locke's *Treatise on Government.*

[In editions 1–13 the following paragraph concludes this footnote:

"What I have said in Part 1st, Sect. 3d of subjecting a number of states to a general council representing them all I suppose everyone must consider as entirely theoretical and not a proposal of anything I wish may take place under the British Empire."]

76. William Molyneux (1656–1698), philosopher and scientist; member of the Royal Society; member of the Irish parliament for Dublin University; member of Parliament for Trinity College.

77. Editions 1–13 read "can be."

78. Not in editions 1–13.

79. Editions 1–13 read "invaluable."

What is your parliament?[80] Is there not a growing intercourse between it and the court? Does it awe ministers of state as it once did? Instead of contending for a controlling power over the governments of America, should you not think more of watching and reforming your own? Suppose the worst. Suppose, in opposition to all their own declarations, that the Colonists are now aiming at independence.[jj][81] "If they can subsist without you," is it to be wondered at? Did there ever exist a community, or even an individual, that would not do the same? "If they cannot subsist without you," let them alone. They will soon come back. "If you cannot subsist without them," reclaim them by kindness, engage them by moderation and equity.[kk] It is madness to resolve to butcher them. This will make them detest and avoid you for ever. Freemen are not to be governed by force or dragooned into compliance. If capable of bearing to be so treated, it is a disgrace to be connected with them.

"If they can subsist without you and also you without them," the attempt to subjugate them by confiscating their effects, burning their towns, and ravaging their territories, is a wanton exertion of cruel ambition which, however common it has been among mankind, deserves to be called by harder names than I choose to apply to it. Suppose such an attempt was to be succeeded.[82] Would it not be a fatal preparation for subduing yourselves? Would not the disposal of American places and the distribution of an American revenue render that influence of the crown irresistible which has already stabbed your liberties?

Turn your eyes to India. There more has been done than is now attempted in America. There Englishmen, actuated by the love of plunder and the spirit of conquest, have depopulated whole kingdoms and ruined millions of innocent people by the most infamous oppression and rapacity.

jj. See on this subject the second section of the second part of the next tract, page 166.[81]

kk. Some persons, convinced of the folly as well as barbarity of attempting to keep the Colonies by slaughtering them, have very humanely proposed giving them up. But the highest authority has informed us, with great reason, "that they are too important to be given up." Dr. Tucker has insisted on the depopulation, produced by migrations from this country to the Colonies, as a reason for this measure. But unless the kingdom is made a prison to its inhabitants these migrations cannot be prevented, nor do I think that they have any great tendency to produce depopulation. When a number of people quit a country there is more employment and greater plenty of the means of subsistence left for those who remain and the vacancy is soon filled up. The grand causes of depopulation are, not migrations, or even famines and plagues, or any other temporary evils, but the permanent and slowly working evils of debauchery, luxury, high taxes, and oppression.

---

80. Editions 1–13 insert: "Powerful indeed and respectable. But. . . ."
81. Footnote not in editions 1–13.
82. Edition 13 and *Two Tracts,* edition 2, read "successful."

The justice of the nation has slept over these enormities. Will the justice of heaven sleep? Are we not now execrated on both sides of the globe?

With respect to the Colonists, it would be folly to pretend they are fault-less. They were running fast into our vices. But this quarrel gives them a salutary check. And it may be permitted on purpose to favour them, and in them the rest of mankind, by making way for establishing, in an exten-sive country possessed of every advantage, a plan of government and a growing power that will astonish the world and under which every subject of human enquiry shall be open to free discussion, and the friends of liberty, in every quarter of the globe, find a safe retreat from civil and spiritual tyranny. I hope, therefore, our brethren in America will forgive their oppressors. It is certain they know not what they are doing.

Conclusion

Having said so much of the war with America, and particularly of the danger with which it threatens us, it may be expected that I should propose some method of escaping from this danger and of restoring this once happy Empire to a state of peace and security. Various plans of pacification have been proposed and some of them by persons so distinguished by their rank and merit as to be above my applause. But till there is more of a dis-position to attend to such plans they cannot, I am afraid, be of any great service. And there is too much reason to apprehend that nothing but calamity will bring us to repentance and wisdom. In order, however, to complete my design in these observations, I will take the liberty to lay before the public the following sketch of one of the plans just referred to, as it was opened before the holidays to the House of Lords by the Earl of Shelburne[83] who, while he held the seals of the Southern Department, with the business of the Colonies annexed, possessed their confidence, without ever compromising the authority of this country, a confidence which dis-covered itself by peace among themselves, and duty and submission to the mother country. I hope I shall not take an unwarrantable liberty if, on this

---

83. William Petty, first marquis of Lansdowne, better known as Lord Shelburne (1737–1805), soldier, politician; educated at Christ Church, Oxford; member of Parliament for High Wycombe (1760–1761); member of the Irish parliament for Kerry (1761–1764); member of the House of Lords (1761–1805); member of the Irish House of Lords as Earl of Shelburne (1764–1805); secretary of state for the southern department (1766–1768); sympathizer with the American cause; opponent of American independence (1776–1781); became resigned to American independence in 1782; first lord of the treasury (1782–1783).

occasion, I use his Lordship's own words, as nearly as I have been able to collect them.[84]

"Meet the Colonies on their own ground in the last petition from the Congress to the king. The surest, as well as the most dignified mode of proceeding for this country. Suspend all hostilities. Repeal the acts which immediately distress America, namely, the last restraining act, the charter act, the act for the more impartial administration of justice, and the Quebec act. All other acts (the custom house act, the post office act, etc.) leave to a temperate revisal. There will be found much matter which both countries may wish repealed. Some which can never be given up, the principle being that regulation of trade for the common good of the Empire, which forms our palladium. Other matter which is fair subject of mutual accomodation. Prescribe the most explicit acknowledgment of your right of regulating commerce in its most extensive sense if the petition and other public acts of the Colonies have not already, by their declarations and acknowledgments, left it upon a sufficiently secure foundation. Besides the power of regulating the general commerce of the Empire, something further might be expected, provided a due and tender regard were had to the means and abilities of the several provinces, as well as to those fundamental, unalienable rights of Englishmen, which no father can surrender on the part of his son, no representative on the part of his elector, no generation on the part of the succeeding one; the right of judging not only of the mode or raising, but the quantum, and the appropriation of such aids as they shall grant. To be more explicit, the debt of England, without entering into invidious distinctions how it came to be contracted, might be acknowledged the debt of every individual part of the whole Empire, Asia, as well as America, included. Provided that full security were held forth to them, that such free aids, together with the sinking fund (Great Britain contributing her superior share) should not be left as the privy purse of the minister, but be unalienably appropriated to the original intention of that fund, the discharge of the debt, and that by an honest application of the whole fund, the taxes might in time be lessened, and the price of our manufactures consequently reduced, so that every contributory part might feel the returning benefit—always supposing the laws of trade duly observed and enforced.

"The time was, I am confident, and perhaps is, when these points might be obtained upon the easy, the constitutional and, therefore, the indispensible terms of an exemption from parliamentary taxation and an admission of the sacredness of their charters instead of sacrificing their good humour,

---

84. Shelburne's speech was made on November 10, 1775. In that speech Shelburne supported a proposal for conciliation contained in a petition from the Continental Congress which was delivered to the Earl of Dartmouth by Richard Penn on September 1, 1775. A record of that speech appears in *Parliamentary History* 18:920–927.

their affection, their effectual aids, and the act of navigation itself (which you are now in the direct road to do) for a commercial quit-rent[ll] or a barren metaphysical chimaera. How long these ends may continue attainable no man can tell. But if no words are to be relied on except such as make against the Colonies, if nothing is acceptable except what is attainable by force, it only remains to apply, what has been so often remarked of unhappy periods, *Quos deus vult*, etc."

These are sentiments and proposals of the last importance and I am very happy in being able to give them to the public from so respectable an authority as that of the distinguished peer I have mentioned to whom, I know, this kingdom, as well as America, is much indebted for his zeal to promote those grand public points on which the preservation of liberty among us depends and for the firm opposition which, jointly with many others (noblemen and commoners of the first character and abilities) he has made to the present measures.

Had such a plan as that now proposed been adopted a few months ago, I have little doubt but that a pacification would have taken place on terms highly advantageous to this kingdom. In particular, it is probable that the Colonies would have consented to grant an annual supply which, increased by a saving of the money now spent in maintaining troops among them,

ll. See the resolutions on the Nova Scotia petition reported to the House of Commons, November 29, 1775 by Lord North,[85] Lord George Germain,[86] etc. and a bill ordered to be brought in upon the said resolutions.[87] There is, indeed, as Lord Shelburne hinted, something very astonishing in these resolutions. They offer a relaxation of the authority of this country in points to which the Colonies have always consented and by which we are great gainers at the same time that, with a rigour which hazards the Empire, we are maintaining its authority in points to which they will never consent and by which nothing can be gained.

85. Frederick North, second Earl of Guilford, better known as Lord North (1732–1792), legislative architect of British policy with respect to America during the American Revolution; member of the House of Commons for Banbury (1754–1790); junior lord of the treasury (1759–1765); joint paymaster of the forces (1766–1767); chancellor of the exchequer (1767–1782); first lord of the treasury (1770–1782); joint secretary of state (1783); member of the House of Lords (1790–1792).

86. George Sackville Germain, first Viscount Sackville (1716–1785), soldier, politician; member of the House of Commons (1741–1782); secretary of war for Ireland (1751–1756); commander-in-chief of the forces on the Lower Rhine (1758–1759); lord commissioner of trade and plantations (1775–1779); secretary of state for the colonies (1779–1782).

87. On November 29, 1775, the House of Commons passed a series of resolutions on a petition from the General Assembly of Nova Scotia. That petition was presented to the Commons on October 26. The resolutions suggested that (1) a duty of 8 percent be placed on all commodities not produced in Britain and its colonies imported into Nova Scotia by an act of the General Assembly of Nova Scotia; (2) all similar taxes placed by Parliament on those commodities be removed upon the enactment of that duty by the General Assembly of Nova Scotia; (3) direct importation into Nova Scotia be allowed for certain items.

The bill to which Price refers stated that the Parliament did not stipulate, but merely suggested, the value of the duty. That bill failed. See *Parliamentary History*, 18:1021–1027.

and by contributions which might have been gained from other parts of the Empire, would have formed a fund considerable enough, if unalienably applied,[88] to redeem the public debt; in consequence of which, agreeably to Lord Shelburne's ideas, some of our worst taxes might be taken off, and the Colonies would receive our manufactures cheaper, our paper currency might be restrained, our whole force would be free to meet at any time foreign danger, the influence of the Crown would be reduced, our Parliament would become [89] less dependent,[89] and the kingdom might, perhaps, be restored to a situation of perfect safety and prosperity.

To conclude. An important revolution in the affairs of this kingdom seems to be approaching. If ruin is not to be our lot all that has been lately done must be undone and new measures adopted. At that period an opportunity (never perhaps to be recovered, if lost) will offer itself for serving essentially this country, as well as America, by putting the national debt into a fixed course of payment, by subjecting to new regulations the administration of the finances, and by establishing measures for exterminating corruption and restoring the constitution. For my own part, if this is not to be the consequence of any future changes in the ministry, and the system of corruption, lately so much improved, is to go on, I think it totally indifferent to the kingdom who are in, or who are out of power.

[90] The following fact is of so much importance that I cannot satisfy myself without laying it before the public. In a committee of the American Congress, in June 1775, a declaration was drawn up containing an offer to Great Britain, "that the Colonies would not only continue to grant extraordinary aids in time of war but also, if allowed a free commerce, pay into the sinking fund such a sum annually for one hundred years as should be more than sufficient in that time, if faithfully applied, to extinguish all the present debts of Britain. Or, provided this was not accepted, that, to remove the groundless jealousy of Britain that the Colonies aimed at independence and an abolition of the navigation act which, in truth, they had never intended and also, to avoid all future disputes about the right of making that and other acts for regulating their commerce for the general benefit, they would enter into a convenant with Britain that she should fully possess and exercise that right for one hundred years to come."[91]

---

88. Editions 1–13 have here a general reference to the Appendix.
89. Editions 1–9 read "more important."
90. Not in editions 1–13.
91. On June 25, 1775 a resolution was presented to the Continental Congress entitled, "Proposed Vindication and Offer to Parliament." The relevant passage in that resolution reads: "And we hereby declare that, on a reconciliation with Britain, we shall not only continue to grant aids in time of war, as aforesaid, but whenever she shall think fit to abolish her monopoly and give us the same privileges of trade as Scotland received at the union and allow us a free commerce with all the rest of the world, we shall willingly agree (and we doubt not it will be ratified by our constituents) to give and pay into the

At the end of the preceding tract I have had the honour of laying before the public the Earl of Shelburne's plan of pacification with the Colonies. In that plan it is particularly proposed that the Colonies should grant an annual supply to be carried to the sinking fund and unalienably appropriated to the discharge of the public debt. It must give this excellent peer great pleasure to learn, from this resolution, that even this part of his plan, as well as all the other parts, would, most probably, have been accepted by the Colonies. For though the resolution only offers the alternative of either a free trade, with extraordinary aids and an annual supply or an *exclusive* trade confirmed and extended, yet there can be little reason to doubt but that to avoid the calamities of the present contest, both would have been consented to; particularly, if, on our part, such a revisal of the laws of trade had been offered as was proposed in Lord Shelburne's plan.

The preceding resolution was, I have said, drawn up in a committee of the Congress. But it was not entered in their minutes, a severe act of Parliament[92] happening to arrive at that time which determined them not to give the sum proposed in it.[90]

---

sinking fund £100,000 sterling per annum for the term of one hundred years; which duly, faithfully and inviolably applied to that purpose, is demonstrably more than sufficient to extinguish all her present national debt, since it will in that time amount, at legal British interest, to more than £230,000,000.

"But if Britain does not think fit to accept this proportion, we, in order to remove her groundless jealousies that we aim at independence and an abolition of the Navigation Act (which hath in truth never been our intention) and to avoid all future disputes about the right of making that and other acts for regulating our commerce, do hereby declare ourselves ready and willing to enter into a convenant with Britain that she shall fully possess, enjoy, and exercise that right for a hundred years to come; the same being *bona fide* used for the common benefit." Peter Force, ed., *American Archives*, 4th series, *Containing a Documentary History of the English Colonies in North America from the King's Message to Parliament, of March 7, 1774, to the Declaration of Independence by the United States* (Washington, D.C.: Published by M. St. Clair and Peter Force, 1833), 2:1083. Hereafter cited as *Documentary History*.

92. "An act to restrain the trade and commerce of the province of Massachusetts Bay and New Hampshire, and colonies of Connecticut, and Rhode Island, and Providence Plantation, in North America, to Great Britain, Ireland, and the British islands in the West Indies; and to prohibit such provinces and colonies from carrying on any fishery on the banks of Newfoundland, or other places therein mentioned, under certain conditions and limitations," 15 George 3, ch. 10.

Additional Observations on the Nature and Value of Civil Liberty and the War with America

*Should the morals of the English be perverted by luxury;
—should they lose their colonies by restraining them &c.
—they will be enslaved; they will become insignificant
and contemptible; and* Europe *will not be able to shew
the world one nation in which she can pride herself.*

ABBÉ RAYNAL

To the Right Honourable the Lord Mayor, the Alderman, and the Commons of the City of London, this tract, containing additions to those observations of Civil Liberty, which they have honoured with their approbation, is, with the greatest respect and gratitude, inscribed, by their most obedient and humble servant, Richard Price.

Contents

Introduction

Introduction

Before the reader enters on the following tract, I shall beg leave to detain him while I give a general account of the contents of it, and make a few introductory observations.

In the first part of the *Observations on Civil Liberty*, published last winter, I gave a brief account of the nature of liberty in general, and of civil liberty in particular. That account appears to me, after carefully reconsidering it, to be just; nor do I think it in my power to improve it. In order, however, to be as explicit as possible on this subject, and to remove those misapprehensions of my sentiments into which some have fallen, I have thought proper to add the supplemental and explanatory observations, which will be found in the First Part of this pamphlet. In writing with this view, I have been led to refer often to my former pamphlet, and to repeat some of the observations in it. But as this could not have been avoided, it will, I hope, be excused.

The remarks in the Second Part, I offer to the public with all the deference due to the high station and abilities of the noble Lord, whose speech at opening the Budget in April last, has occasioned them.[1] These remarks, having been promised long ago, should have been published sooner. The reasons which have produced this delay are of little consequence to the public and, need not be mentioned.

In the first section of the second part,[2] it will, I think, appear, that I went upon as good grounds as the nature of the case admitted, when I stated the gold coin of the kingdom at about twelve millions and a half.[a] It appears now, indeed, to be some millions more. But this is a discovery made by the call of last summer which, I find, has brought in near double the sum that the best judges expected. Nothing, however, very encouraging can be inferred from hence. It only shows that a great deal of gold has been hoarded and will, probably, be again hoarded. This is the natural consequence of public diffidence and it is a circumstance which may, hereafter, greatly increase distress. Before the Revolution, according to Dr. Davenant,[3] near half the coin was hoarded and the same, undoubtedly, will be done again whenever the nation comes to be thoroughly alarmed.

In the next section of this part I have made some further observations on the contest with America. I cannot expect any other than a tragical and deplorable issue to this contest. But let events turn out as they will, I shall

---

a. See *Observations on Civil Liberty*, p. 103.

1. Lord North made the speech to which Price refers on April 24, 1776. See *Parliamentary History*, 18:1315–1322.
2. The first section of the second part is not included in this volume.
3. See footnote *t* to *Observations*.

always reflect with satisfaction that I have, though a private person of little consequence, bore my testimony from deep felt conviction against a war which must shock the feelings and the reason of every considerable person, a war in which rivers of blood must be shed, not to repel the attacks of enemies, or to maintain the authority of government *within* the realm, but to maintain sovereignty and dominion in another world.[b] I wish the advocates for the measures against America would attend to the distinction now intimated. The support of just government within the realm is always necessary, and therefore right. But to maintain, by fire and sword, dominion over the persons and the property of a people out of the realm, who have no share in its legislature, contradicts every principle of liberty and humanity. Legitimate government, let it be remembered, as opposed to oppression and tyranny, consists "only in the dominion of equal laws made with common consent, or of men over themselves; and not in the dominion of communities over communities, or of any men over other men." This is the great truth I have endeavoured to explain and defend, and happy would the world be, were a due conviction of it impressed on every human heart.

The representation I have given in this section and elsewhere, of the state of this kingdom, is, without doubt, gloomy. But it is not the effect, as some have intimated, of either a natural disposition to gloominess, or of sinister views. Few who know me will entertain such a suspicion. Valuing most what politicians and statesmen generally value least, I feel myself perfectly easy with respect to my interest as a citizen of this world; nor is there any change of situation that can make me happier except a return to privacy and obscurity. The opinion I have entertained of the present danger of the kingdom is, therefore, the effect of evidence which appears to me irresistible. This evidence I have stated to the public and every one may judge of it as he pleases. I am sensible of my own liableness to error. The measures which I condemn as the worst that ever disgraced and hazarded a great kingdom, others whose integrity I cannot question, approve; and that very situation of our affairs which I think alarming, others think prosperous. Time will determine which of these opinions is right. But supposing the latter to be so, no harm can arise from any representations which have a tendency to put us on our guard.

I have bestowed particular attention on the observations in the third section of this second part;[4] and I think the subject of this section so im-

---

b. Of all the writers against this war, the learned Dr. Tucker is the severest [see footnote g to *Observations on Civil Liberty*. Hereafter cited as *Observations*]. For if, as he maintains, contrary to repeated declarations from the throne, a separation from the Colonies would be an advantage to us, the attempt to keep them, by invasion and bloodshed, deserves a harsher censure than words can convey.

4. The third section of the second part is not included in this volume.

portant that it is probable I should not have resolved on the present publication had it not been for the opportunity it gives me to lay the observations it contains before the public. An intimation of them was given in the introduction to the third edition of the treatise on *Reversionary Payments*.[5] The nation being now once more got into a course of borrowing, and our first step having been a return to a mode of borrowing which had appeared to me absurd and detrimental, I was induced to resume the subject and to examine it with more care. And the result of an examination of only a part of the public loans will be found to be "that a capital of more than twenty millions has been a needless addition to the public debt for which no money, or any sort of equivalent has been received; and which might have been avoided, together with a great expence of interest, by only forming differently the schemes of the public loans."

The intention of the first section of the Third Part[6] is to give, in as short a compass as possible, a view of the progress of our foreign trade and its effect on the nation, from the beginning of this century and, particularly, to point out an unfavourable change which seems to have taken place since 1764.

In the second section of this part an explanation and analysis are given of all the different articles of the national debt which will probably inform every person of most that he can wish to know concerning them. I have added a general account of the debts and resources of France. This is a subject at present particularly interesting to this country and, having been informed of some important facts relating to it, I have thought proper to lay them before the public with such reflexions as have offered themselves in mentioning them.

The last section contains such of the calculations in the appendix to the *Observations on Civil Liberty* as were necessary to be reprinted in order to introduce the remarks I have added on some particulars in the state of the public income and expenditure, published not long ago by the Earl of Stair.[7] I have also meant to accommodate the purchasers of the different editions of the *Observations on Civil Liberty* who will be enabled, by this section, to possess themselves of all the material alterations and improvements which were made in that pamphlet after its first publication. The accounts, in the latter part of this tract, are so various and extensive, that it is scarcely possible there should not be some incorrectnesses in them. But the pains I have taken, and the means of information which I have

5. See footnote *i* to *Observations*.
6. The third part is not included in this volume.
7. John Dalrymple, fifth Earl of Stair (1720–1789), lawyer, soldier, politician; member of the House of Lords (1771–1789); opponent of British policy towards America. The work Price discusses is Stair's *The State of the National Debt, the National Income, and the National Expenditure. With Some Short Inferences and Reflections Applicable to the Present Dangerous Crisis* (London: Printed for J. Almon, 1776).

possessed have been such, that I cannot suspect that I have fallen into any mistakes of consequence. Should, however, any such have escaped me, it will be kind in any person to point them out with candour and to assist in making those accounts so correct and perfect as that they may serve for a basis to all future accounts of the same kind.[8] The whole concludes with an account of a resolution drawn up in a Committee of the American

---

8. In *Two Tracts-H* (See "A Note on the Editions") Price writes at this point: "The following note in Mr. Hume's *History of England* was written by him a little before his death and left with other additions to be inserted in the new edition of that history just published. It contains, therefore, a kind of dying warning from Mr. Hume to this kingdom and I have thought it proper to transcribe it and to insert it in this place, as a confirmation of similar sentiments frequently expressed in these tracts: 'The supplies granted queen Elizabeth, during a reign of forty-five years, amounted to three millions. The minister, in the war which begun in 1754, was, in some periods, allowed to lavish a sum equal to this in two months. The extreme frivolous object of the late war and the great importance of hers set this matter in still a stronger light. Money too was in most particulars of the same value in both periods. She paid eight pence a day to every foot soldier. But our late delusions have much exceeded anything known in history, not even excepting those of the Crusades. For, I suppose, there is no mathematical, still less arithmetical, demonstration that the road to the Holy Land was not the road to Paradise, as there is that the endless increase of national debt is the direct road to national ruin. But having now completely reached that goal it is needless at present to reflect on the past. It will be found in the present year (1776) that all the revenues of this island north of the Trent and west of Reading are mortgaged or anticipated forever. Could the small remainder be in a worse condition were those provinces seized by Austria and Prussia? There is only this difference, that some event might happen in Europe which would oblige those great monarchs to disgorge their acquisitions. But no imagination can figure a situation which will induce our creditors to relinquish their claims or the public to seize their revenues. So egregious indeed has been our folly that we have even lost all title to compassion under the numberless calamities that are waiting us.' Mr. Hume's History, vol. 5, page 475."

A sentence in Hume's *History* reads: "If we suppose that the supplies granted Elizabeth during a reign of forty-five years amounted to three millions, we shall not probably be much wide of the truth." In a footnote to this sentence the passage Price quotes continues as follows: "It is curious to observe that the minister in the war begun in 1754 was in some periods allowed to lavish in two months as great a sum as was granted by parliament to queen Elizabeth in forty-five years. The extreme frivolous object of the late war and the great importance of hers set this matter in still a stronger light. Money too, we may observe, was in most particulars of the same value in both periods. She paid eight pence a day to every foot soldier. But our late delusions have much exceeded anything known in history, not even excepting those of the Crusades. For I suppose there is no mathematical, still less arithmetical, demonstration that the road to the Holy Land was not the road to Paradise than there is that the endless increase of national debt is the direct road to national ruin. But having now completely reached that goal, it is needless at present to reflect on the past. It will be found in the present year, 1776, that all the revenues of this island north of Trent and west of Reading are mortgaged or anticipated for ever. Could the small remainder be in a worse condition were those provinces seized by Austria and Prussia? There is only this difference that some event might happen in Europe which would oblige those great monarchs to disgorge their claims or the public to seize their revenues. So egregious indeed has been our folly that we have even lost all title to compassion in the numberless calamities that are awaiting us." *The History of England, from the Invasion of Julius Caesar to the Revolution in MDCLXXXVIII* (Philadelphia: Printed for Robert Campbell, 1796), 4:182.

Congress in 1775, disclaiming independence, and offering an annual contribution to Britain for discharging its debts.

9 Such will be found to be the contents of the following work. Throughout the whole of it I have avoided entering into any controversy with the crowd of writers who have published remarks on my former pamphlet. I am, however, unwilling to overlook them entirely and, therefore, shall in this place, once for all, settle my accounts with them.

In the first place. Those friends (all unknown to me) who have published vindications of me, whether in separate pamphlets, or in any of the periodical publications, will, I hope, accept my gratitude and believe that, though I have been silent, I have not been inattentive to their arguments or insensible of their candour.

Secondly, those writers of opposite sentiments, who have answered me without abuse or rancour will also, I hope, accept my acknowledgments. In this number I rank the writers of the pieces enumerated below.c These

c. Experience Preferable to Theory, printed for Payne [Experience Preferable to Theory. An Answer to Dr. Price's Observations on the Nature of Civil Liberty, and the Justice and Policy of the War with America (London: Printed for T. Payne, 1776); some authorities suggest that the author was Thomas Hutchinson, governor of Massachussetts from 1771 to 1774]. Remarks on a Pamphlet Lately Published, in a Letter from a Gentleman in the Country to a Member of Parliament [Adam Ferguson,[10] Remarks on a Pamphlet Lately Published by Dr. Price, Intitled, Observations on the Nature of Civil Liberty, the Principles of Government, and the Justice and Policy of the War with America, &c., in a Letter from a Gentleman in the Country to a Member of Parliament (London, Printed for T. Cadell, 1776); see Appendix 4]. Mr. Goodricke's[11] Observations, etc. and Mr. Hey's;[12] all printed for Mr. Cadell [Henry Goodricke, Observations on Dr. Price's Theory and Principles of Civil Liberty and Government, Preceded by a Letter to

9. These eight paragraphs are omitted from the third edition of Additional Observa-

tions as published separately and from Two Tracts-T (See "A Note on the Editions"). Price says on pages xx and xxi of the third edition, at the conclusion of his introduction, "In the preceding introduction to this tract I have omitted all that I had said, in the former edition, of the writers for and against me. But it will, I hope, be taken for granted that I retain my gratitude to those friends who have vindicated me and also to those opponents who have endeavoured to set me right without rancour. As for others, their abuse gives me no pain. I have, therefore, left out all the notice I took of it, being unwilling to continue in this work anything that carries the appearance of contention and choosing to trust myself entirely to the candour of the public."

Price replies to some of his critics, however, in his General Introduction. Edmund Burke; William Markham, Archbishop of York; John Wesley; and Adam Ferguson, discussed there, are among those who contended "without abuse or rancour."

10. Adam Ferguson (1723–1816), clergyman, philosopher; educated at the University of St. Andrews and at the Divinity Hall at St. Andrews; deputy-chaplain to the 43rd regiment (1745–1754); professor of natural philosophy (1759–1764) and professor of moral philosophy (1764–1774, 1776–1785) at Edinburgh University; secretary to the British commissioners sent to America to negotiate a settlement (1778).

11. Henry Goodricke (1741–1784), member of Parliament for Lymington; opponent of the North ministry.

12. Richard Hey (1745–1835), lawyer, essayist, mathematician; educated at Magdalene College, Cambridge; fellow and tutor at Magdalene College (1782–1796).

pieces contain, I believe, all of most importance which has been against me in the way of argument and I leave every one who has read them or shall read them, to decide for himself how far they have succeeded, only desiring the justice may be done me, not to receive too easily any of the representations made in them of my sentiments. I have had, in this respect, some reason to complain of the fairest of my adversaries.

Thirdly, I must farther acknowledge myself indebted to those writers who, under the name of answers, have published virulent invectives against me. It has been some gratification to me to observe the alarm these writers have taken, and the folly they have discovered, by suffering themselves to forget that abuse and scurrility always defeat their own ends and hurt the cause they are employed to serve. I will not attempt to give any list of them. They are without number. But there is *one* who, being the ablest, it is proper I should mention. I mean the author of the three letters to Dr. Price,[15] published for Mr. Payne. This writer is likewise the author of the *Letters on the Present State of Poland;*[16] and of the *Remarks on the Acts of the Thirteenth Parliament of Great Britain;*[17] but he has been lately more known as a writer in the newspapers, under the signature of Attilius and also as the supposed author of the *Answer to the American Declaration of Independence.*[18] The following particulars will enable those, who may not yet know him sufficiently, to judge of his principles and temper.

---

a Friend, on the Pretensions of the American Colonies, in Respect of Right and Equity (York: Printed by A. Ward for J. Dodsley, T. Cadell, and R. Baldwin, London, and J. Todd in Stonegate, York, 1776); Richard Hey, *Observations on the Nature of Civil Liberty, and the Principles of Government* (London: Printed for T. Cadell and T. & J. Merrill, 1776)]. Also Mr. Wesley's[13] and Mr. Fletcher's[14] answers [John Wesley, *Some Observations on Liberty, Occasioned by a Late Tract* (London: R. Hawes, 1776); see Appendix 3. John Fletcher, *American Patriotism Farther Confronted with Reason, Scripture and the Constitution* (Shrewsbury: Printed for J. Eddowes and sold at the foundry, and by J. Buckland, London, 1776).] There may, perhaps, be some other answers of the same kind but they have not happened to fall into my hands.

---

13. John Wesley (1703–1791), clergyman, missionary, leader of methodism; missionary to Georgia (1736–1737).

14. John Fletcher (1729–1785), soldier, methodist clergyman; born in Nyon, Switzerland; minister at Madeley (1760–1785); superintendent of Lady Huntingdon's college at Trevecca in Wales (1768–1771).

15. John Lind, *Three Letters to Dr. Price, Containing Remarks on His Observations on the Nature of Civil Liberty, the Principles of Government, and the Justice and Policy of the War with America. By a Member of Lincoln's Inn, F.R.S. F.S.A.* (London: Printed for T. Payne, J. Sewell, and P. Elmsly, 1776). See Appendix 2.

16. John Lind, *Letters concerning the Present State of Poland. Together with the Manifesto of the Courts of Vienna, Petersburgh, and Berlin. And the Letters Patent of the King of Prussia* (London: Printed for T. Payne, 1773).

17. See footnote *h* to *Observations.*

18. John Lind, *An Answer to the Declaration of the American Congress . . .* (London: Printed for T. Cadell, 1776).

Civil liberty, he insists, is nothing positive. It is an *absence*. The absence of coercion, or of contraint and restraint. Not from civil governors (they are omnipotent and there can be no liberty against them[d]) but from such little despots and plunderers as common pick-pockets, thieves, house-breakers, etc.

Again, having had occasion, in my *Observations on Civil Liberty*, page [87], to take some notice of him, I studied to mention him with respect. In return for this civility he has, in his three letters just mentioned, made me the object of an abuse which would have been inexcusable had I offered him the grossest affront.

Further, such is the rage into which he has been thrown that, imagining my notions of liberty and government have been drawn from the writings of the philosophers of ancient Greece and Rome, he laments "that the Goths and Vandals, sparing their vases and urns, did destroy all their books of philosophy and politics."[e] I am much mistaken if he does not wish like-wise that all such writings were destroyed as those of Sidney,[20] Locke, Montesquieu, Blackstone,[21] etc.

I have only to add that I am truly ashamed of having, in this introduc-tion, had occasion to say so much about myself. But I hope candid allow-ances will be made for it when it is considered how much, for some time, has been said and writ about me. I now leave an open field to all who shall please to take any farther notice of me. Wishing them the same satisfaction that I have felt in *meaning* to promote peace and justice, and looking higher than this world of strife and tumult—I withdraw from politics.[9]

---

d. Their power is, however, acknowledged to be a trust, but not from the people. It must then be a trust from God, like the power of the proprietor of an estate over his tenants and cattle—charming doctrine this for Russia and Turkey! And yet such is the doctrine which this good barrister, Dr. Wesley, Dr. Cooper,[19] and others, are now propa-gating in this country [Samuel Cooper, *The Power of Christianity over the Malignant Passions, Asserted, and the True Grounds of Mutual Forbearance in Religious Opinions Explained, in a Sermon, Preached before the University of Cambridge, on Sunday, No-vember III, MDCCLXXVI* (Cambridge: J. Woodyer and T. & J. Merrill, 1776)]. See *Three Letters* [Appendix 2, pp. 243–244f.]. See likewise pages [146] and [150] of the following tract.

e. Three Letters [Appendix 2, footnote *h*].

---

19. Samuel Cooper (1739–1800), clergyman; educated at Magdalene College, Cam-bridge; curate of Great Yarmouth and rector of Morley and Yelverton, Norfolk.

20. Algernon Sidney (1622–1683), republican; soldier, member of Parliament, opponent of Cromwell, exile, executed for treason; author of *Discourses concerning Government*, 1698.

21. William Blackstone (1723–1780), legal writer and judge; professor of law at Oxford; member of Parliament for Hindon in Wiltshire (1761–1768) and for Westbury in Wilt-shire (1768–1770); justice of the Common Pleas (1770–1780).

Part I. Supplemental Observations on the Nature and Value of Civil Liberty and Free Government

Sect. I. Of the Nature of Civil Liberty and the Essentials of a Free Government.

With respect to liberty in general there are two questions to be considered:

First, what it is and, secondly, how far it is of value.

There is no difficulty in answering the first of these questions. To be free is "to be able to act or to forbear acting, as we think best;" or "to be masters of our own resolutions and conduct." It may be pretended that it is not desirable to be thus free but, without doubt, this it is to be free, and this is what all mean when they say of themselves or others that they are free.

I have observed that all the different kinds of liberty run up into the general idea of self-government.[f] The liberty of men as agents is that power of self-determination which all agents, as such, possess. Their liberty as moral agents is their power of self-government in their moral conduct. Their liberty as religious agents is their power of self-government in religion. And their liberty as members of communities associated for the purposes of civil government is their power of self-government in all their civil concerns. It is liberty in the last of these views of it that is the subject of my present enquiry and it may, in other words, be defined to be "the power of a state to govern itself by its own will." In order, therefore, to determine whether a state is free, no more is necessary than to determine whether there is any will, different from its own, to which it is subject.

When we speak of a state we mean the whole state and not any part of it; and the will of the state, therefore, is the will of the whole. There are two ways in which this will may be expressed. First, by the suffrages of all the members given in person. Or, secondly, by the suffrages of a body of representatives, in appointing whom all the members have voices. A state governed by its own will in the first of these ways enjoys the most complete and perfect liberty; but such a government being impracticable, except in very small states, it is necessary that civil communities in general should satisfy themselves with that degree of liberty which can be obtained in the last of these ways, and liberty so obtained may be sufficiently ample and at the same time is capable of being extended to the largest states.[g]

But here, before I proceed, I must desire that an observation may be

f. See *Observations on Civil Liberty*, pt. 1, sec. 1.
g. See *Observations*, pt. 1, sec. 2.

attended to which appears to me of considerable consequence. A distinction should be made between the liberty of a state and its not suffering oppression, or between a free government and a government under which freedom is enjoyed. Under the most despotic government liberty may happen to be enjoyed. But being derived from a will over which the state has no control and not from its own will, or from an accidental mildness in the administration and not from a constitution of government, it is nothing but an indulgence of a precarious nature and of little importance. Individuals in private life, while held under the power of masters, cannot be denominated free however equitably and kindly they may be treated. This is strictly true of communities as well as of individuals. Civil liberty (it should be remembered) must be enjoyed as a right derived from the Author of nature only or it cannot be the blessing which merits this name. If there is any human power which is considered as giving it, on which it depends, and which can invade or recall it at pleasure, it changes its nature and becomes a species of slavery.

But to return, the force superseding self-government in a state, or the power destroying its liberty, is of two kinds. It may be either a power without itself, or a power within itself. The former constitutes what may be properly called *external*, and the latter *internal* slavery. Were there any distant state which had acquired a sovereignty over this country, and exercised the power of making its laws and disposing its property, we should be in the first kind of slavery; and, if not totally depraved by a habit of subjection to such a power, we should think ourselves in a miserable condition; and an advocate for such a power would be considered as insulting us, who should attempt to reconcile us to it by telling us, that we were *one* community with that distant state, though destitute of a single voice in its legislature, and, on this ground, should maintain that all resistance to it was no less criminal than any resistance *within* a state to the authority of that state. In short, every state not incorporated with another by an equal representation, and yet subject to its dominion, is enslaved in this sense. Such was the slavery of the provinces subject to ancient Rome; and such is the slavery of every community, as far as any other community is master of it, or as far as, in respect of taxation and internal legislation, it is not independent of every other community. Nor does it make any difference to such a community that it enjoys within itself a free constitution of government if that constitution is itself liable to be altered, suspended, or overruled at the discretion of the state which possesses the sovereignty over it.

But the slavery most prevalent in the world has been internal slavery. In order better to explain this, it is proper to observe that all civil government being either the government of a whole by itself, or of a whole by a power extraneous to it, or of a whole by a part, the first alone is liberty and the two last are tyranny, producing the two sorts of slavery which I have mentioned. Internal slavery, therefore, takes place wherever a whole community is governed by a part and this, perhaps, is the most concise and comprehensive account that can be given of it. The part that governs may be either a single man, as in absolute monarchies, or a body of grandees, as in aristocracies. In both these cases the powers of government are commonly held for life without delegation, and descend from father to son; and the people governed are in the same situation with cattle upon an estate, which descends by inheritance from one owner to another. But farther, a community may be governed by a body of delegates and yet be enslaved. Though government by representation alone is free, unless when carried on by the personal suffrages of all the members of a state, yet *all* such government is by no means free. In order to render it so, the following requisites are necessary.

First, the representation must be complete. No state, a part of which only is represented in the legislature that governs it, is self-governed. Had Scotland no representatives in the Parliament of Britain, it would not be free; nor would it be proper to call Britain free though England, its other part, were adequately represented. The like is true, in general, of every country subject to a legislature in which some of its parts, of some classes of men in it, are represented and others not.

Secondly, the representatives of a free state must be freely chosen. If this is not the case they are not at all representatives; and government by them degenerates into government by a junto of men in the community who happen to have power or wealth enough to command or purchase their offices.

Thirdly, after being freely chosen they must be themselves free. If there is any higher will which directs their resolutions, and on which they are dependent, they become the instruments of that will; and it is that will alone that in reality governs the state.

Fourthly, they must be chosen for short terms and, in all their acts, be accountable to their constituents. Without this a people will have no control over their representatives and, in choosing them, they will give up entirely their liberty and only enjoy the poor privilege of naming, at certain intervals, a set of men whom they are to serve and who are to dispose, at their discretion, of their property and lives.

The causes of internal slavery now mentioned prevail, some of them more and others less, in different communities. With respect, in particular, to a government by representation it is evident that it deviates more or less from liberty in proportion as the representation is more or less imperfect. And, if imperfect in every one of the instances I have recited, that is, if inadequate and partial, subject to no control from the people, corruptly chosen for long terms, and, after being chosen, venal and dependent—in these circumstances a representation becomes an imposition and a nuisance and government by it is as inconsistent with true liberty as the most arbitrary and despotic government.

I have been so much misunderstood on this subject that it is necessary I should particularly observe here that my intention in this account has been merely to show what is requisite to constitute a state or a government free, and not at all to define the best form of government.[h] These are two very different points. The first is attended with few difficulties. A free state is a state self-governed in the manner I have described. But it may be free and yet not enjoy the best constitution of government. Liberty, though the most essential requisite in government, is not the only one. Wisdom, union, dispatch, secrecy, and vigour are likewise requisite; and that is the best form of government which best unites all these qualities or which, to an equal and perfect liberty, adds the greatest wisdom in deliberating and resolving, and the greatest union, force and expedition in executing.[i]

In short, my whole meaning is that the will of the community alone ought to govern, but that there are different methods of obtaining and executing this will, of which those are the best which collect into it most of the knowledge and experience of the community, and at the same time carry it into execution with most dispatch and vigour.

It has been the employment of the wisest men in all ages to contrive plans for this purpose; and the happiness of society depends so much on civil government, that it is not possible the human understanding should be better employed.

I have said in the *Observations on Civil Liberty* that "in a free state every man is his own legislator." I have been happy in since finding the same assertion in Montesquieu and also in Mr. Justice Blackstone's Commentaries.[j] It expresses the fundamental principle of our constitution; and

h. The greatest part of Mr. Goodricke's remarks are founded on this misunderstanding. He is so candid that I know he did not mean to misrepresent me and yet I cannot help thinking it hard, after repeated declarations of my preference of such a constitution as our own, to be considered as an advocate for a pure democracy. See *Observations on Dr. Price's Theory and Principles of Civil Liberty and Government*, by Mr. Goodricke.

i. One of the best plans of this kind has been, with much ability, described by Mr. de Lolme[22] in his account of the constitution of England [Jean Louis de Lolme, *The Constitution of England; Or an Account of the English Government in Which It Is Compared with the Republican Form of Government, and Occasionally with the Other Monarchies in Europe* (London: G. Kearsly, 1775)].

j. "As in a free state, every man who is supposed a free agent ought to be his own governor, so the legislative power should reside in the whole body of the people." *Spirit of Laws*, bk. 11, chap. 6.[23] See likewise Justice Blackstone's *Commentaries on the Laws of*

22. John Louis de Lolme (1740?–1807), legal advocate, writer on the English constitution, member of the Council of Two Hundred.

23. The relevant passage reads: "As in a country of liberty, every man who is supposed a free agent ought to be his own governor; the legislative power should reside in the whole body of the people." *The Spirit of the Laws*, trans. Thomas Nugent (New York: Hafner Publishing Company, 1949), 1:154. Hereafter cited as *Spirit of Laws* (1949).

the meaning of it is, plainly, that every independent agent in a free state ought to have a share in the government of it, either by himself personally, or by a body of representatives, in choosing whom he has a free vote, and therefore all the concern and weight which are possible and consistent with the equal rights of every other member of the state. But though the meaning of this assertion is so obvious, and the truth of it undeniable, it has been much exclaimed against, and occasioned no small part of the opposition which has been made to the principles advanced in the *Observations on Civil Liberty*. One even of the most candid, as well as the ablest of my opponents (whose difference of opinion from me I sincerely lament) has intimated that it implies that, in a free state, thieves and pick-pockets have a right to make laws for themselves.[k] The public will not, I hope, wonder that I choose to take little notice of such objections.

It has been said that the liberty for which I have pleaded is "a right or power in every one to act as he likes without any restraint." However unfairly this representation has been given of my account of liberty, I am ready to adopt it, provided it is understood with a few limitations. Moral liberty, in particular, cannot be better defined than by calling it "a power in every one to do as he likes." My opponents in general seem to be greatly puzzled with this; and I am afraid it will signify little to attempt explaining it to them by saying that every man's will, if perfectly free from restraint, would carry him invariably to rectitude and virtue, and that no one who acts wickedly acts as he likes, but is conscious of a tyranny within him overpowering his judgment and carrying him into a conduct for which he condemns and hates himself. "The things that he would he does not and the things that he would not, those he does."[l] He is, therefore, a slave in the properest sense.

Religious liberty, likewise, is a power of acting as we like in religion, or of professing and practising that mode of religious worship which we think most acceptable to the Deity. But here the limitation to which I have

---

England, octavo edition, vol. 1, p. 158. [William Blackstone, *Commentaries on the Laws of England* . . . (Oxford: Printed at the Clarendon Press, 1765–1769)]. Demosthenes[24] speaking in his first Phillipic, sec. 3 of certain free states, calls them *their own legislators*, αὐτονομούμενα καὶ ἐλευθερ.[25]

k. See *Remarks*, printed for Mr. Cadell, *on a Pamphlet Published by Dr. Price. In a Letter from a Gentleman in the Country to a Member of Parliament*, p. 10 [See Appendix Four, p. 256].

l. Rom. 7.

---

24. Demosthenes (384–322 B.C.), orator, leader of the Athenian opposition to Macedon.

25. The Loeb translation of the relevant passage reads: ". . . yet he [Philip] must reflect that we too, men of Athens, once held Pydna, Potidaea, and Methone and had in our own hands all the surrounding territory, and that many of the native tribes now in his service were then free and independent and were indeed more inclined to side with us than with Philip." *Demosthenes, with an English Translation*, trans. J. H. Vince (London: Heinemann, 1926–1949), p. 71.

referred must be attended to. All have the same unalienable right to this liberty and, consequently, no one has a right to such a use of it as shall take it from others. Within this limit, or as far as he does not encroach on the equal liberty of others, every one has a right to do as he pleases in religion. That the right to religious liberty goes as far as this everyone must allow who is not a friend to persecution; and that it cannot go farther is self-evident; for if it did, there would be a contradiction in the natures of things, and it would be true that everyone had a right to enjoy what everyone had a right to destroy. If, therefore, the religious faith of any person leads him to hurt another because he professes a different faith or if it carries him, in any instance, to intolerance, liberty itself requires he should be restrained and that, in such instances, he should lose his liberty.

All this is equally applicable to the liberty of man in his civil capacity and it is a maxim true universally, "that as far as any one does not molest others others ought not to molest him." All have a right to the free and undisturbed possession of their good names, properties, and lives and it is the right all have to this that gives the right to establish civil government, which is or ought to be nothing but an institution (by laws and provisions made with common consent) for guarding this right against invasion, for giving to every one, in temporals and spirituals, the power of commanding his own conduct, or of acting as he pleases and going where he will, provided he does not run foul of others. Just government, therefore, does not infringe liberty but establishes it. It does not take away the rights of mankind but protects and confirms them. I will add that it does not even create any new subordinations of particular men to one another but only gives security in those several stations, whether of authority and pre-eminence, or of subordination and dependence, which nature has established and which must have arisen among mankind whether civil government had been instituted or not. But this goes beyond my purpose in this place and more will be said of it presently.

To sum up the whole, our ideas of civil liberty will be rendered more distinct by considering it under the three following views: the liberty of the citizens, the liberty of the government, and the liberty of the community. A citizen is free when the power of commanding his own conduct and the quiet possession of his life, person, property and good name are secured to him by being his own legislator in the sense explained in page 140.[m] A government is free when constituted in such a manner as to give

m. Dr. Priestly, in his *Essay on the First Principles of Government*, makes a distinction between civil liberty and political liberty, the former of which he defines to be "the power which the members of a state ought to enjoy over their actions," and the latter, "their power of arriving at public offices or, at least, of having votes in the nomination of those who fill them."[26] This distinction forms a very proper subdivision of the liberty

26. The relevant passage reads: "Political liberty, I would say, consists in the power which the members of the state reserve to themselves of arriving at the public offices or,

this security. And the freedom of a community or nation is the same among nations that the freedom of a citizen is among his fellow-citizens. It is not, therefore, as observed in page 137, the mere possession of liberty that denominates a citizen or a community free, but that security for the possession of it which arises from such a free government as I have described, and which takes place when there exists no power that can take it away. It is in the same sense that the mere performance of virtuous actions is not what denominates an agent virtuous but the temper and habits from whence they spring, or that inward constitution and right balance of the affections which secure the practice of virtue, produce stability of conduct, and constitute a character.

I cannot imagine how it can be disputed whether this is a just account of the nature of liberty. It has been already given more briefly in the *Observations on Civil Liberty* and it is with reluctance I have repeated so much of what has been there said. But the wrong apprehensions which have been entertained of my sentiments have rendered this necessary. And, for the same reason, I am obliged to go on to the subject of the next section.

Sect. II. Of the Value of Liberty, and the Excellence of a Free Government.

Having shown in the preceding section what liberty is, the next question to be considered is how far it is valuable.

Nothing need be said to show the value of the three kinds of liberty which I have distinguished under the names of physical, moral, and religious liberty. They are, without doubt, the foundation of all the happiness and dignity of men, as reasonable and moral agents, and the subjects of the Deity. It is, in like manner, true of civil liberty that it is the foundation of the whole happiness and dignity of men as members of civil society and the subjects of civil government.

First, it is civil liberty, or such free government as I have described, that alone can give just security against oppression. One government is better than another in proportion as it gives more of this security. It is on this account that the supreme government of the Deity is perfect. There is not a possibility of being oppressed or aggrieved by it. Subjection to it is the same with complete freedom.

---

of the citizen here mentioned and it may be accommodated to all I have said on this subject by only giving some less general name to that which Dr. Priestly calls civil liberty.

---

at least, of having votes in the nomination of those who fill them and I would choose to call civil liberty that power over their own actions which the members of the state reserve to themselves and which their officers must not infringe." Joseph Priestly, *Essay on the First Principles of Government* (London: Printed for J. Dodsley, T. Cadell, and J. Johnson, 1768), pp. 12–13.

Were there any men on whose superior wisdom and goodness we might absolutely depend, they could not possess too much power and the love of liberty itself would engage us to fly to them, and to put ourselves under their direction. But such are the principles that govern human nature, such the weakness and folly of men, such their love of domination, selfishness, and depravity, that none of them can be raised to an elevation above others without the utmost danger. The constant experience of the world has verified this and proved that nothing intoxicates the human mind so much as power and that men, when they have got possession of it, have seldom failed to employ it in grinding their fellow-men and gratifying the vilest passions. In the establishment, therefore, of civil government it would be preposterous to rely on the discretion of any men. If a people would obtain security against oppression, they must seek it in themselves and never part with the powers of government out of their own hands. It is there only they can be safe. A people will never oppress themselves or invade their own rights. But if they trust the arbitrary will of any body or succession of men they trust enemies and it may be depended on that the worst evils will follow.

It follows from hence that a free government is the only government which is consistent with the ends of government. Men combine into communities and institute government to obtain the peaceable enjoyment of their rights and to defend themselves against injustice and violence. And when they endeavour to secure these ends by such a free government as I have described, improved by such arrangements as may have a tendency to preserve it from confusion, and to concentrate in it as much as possible of the wisdom and force of the community, in this case, it is a most rational and important institution. But when the contrary is done and the benefits of government are sought by establishing a government of men, and not of laws made with common consent, it becomes a most absurd institution. It is seeking a remedy for oppression in one quarter by establishing it in another and avoiding the outrages of little plunderers by constituting a set of great plunderers. It is, in short, the folly of giving up liberty in order to maintain liberty and, in the very act of endeavouring to secure the most valuable rights, to arm a body of enemies with power to destroy them.

I can easily believe that mankind, in the first and rude state of society, might act thus irrationally. Absolute governments, being the simplest forms of government, might be the first that were established. A people having experienced the happy effects of the wisdom or the valour of particular men, might be led to trust them with unlimited power as their rulers and legislators. But they would soon find reason to repent. And the time, I hope, may come when mankind in general, taught by long and dear experience, and weary of the abuses of power under slavish governments, will learn to detest them, and never to give up that self-government which, whether we consider men in their private or collective capacities, is the first of all the blessings they can possess.

Again, free governments are the only governments which give scope to the exertion of the powers of men and are favourable to their improvement. The members of free states, knowing their rights to be secure, and that they shall enjoy without molestation the fruits of every acquisition they can make, are encouraged and incited to industry. Being at liberty to push their researches as far as they can into all subjects and to guide themselves by their own judgments in all their religious and civil concerns, while they allow others to do the same, error and superstition must lose ground. Conscious of being their own governors, bound to obey no laws except such as they have given their consent to, and subject to no control from the arbitrary will of any of their fellow-citizens, they possess an elevation and force of mind which must make them great and happy. How different is the situation of the vassals of despotic power. Like cattle insured to the yoke, they are driven on in one track, afraid of speaking or even thinking on the most interesting points, looking up continually to a poor creature who is their master, their powers fettered, and some of the noblest springs of action in human nature rendered useless within them. There is nothing indeed more humiliating than that debasement of mankind which takes place in such situations.

It has been observed of free governments that they are often torn by violent contests which render them dreadful scenes of distress and anarchy. But it ought to be considered that this has not been owing to the nature of such governments but to their having been ill-modelled and wanting those arrangements and supplemental checks which are necessary to constitute a wise form of government. There is no reason to doubt but that free governments may be so contrived as to exclude the greatest part of the struggles and tumults which are arisen in free states and, as far as they cannot be excluded, they will do more good than harm. They will occasion the display of powers and produce exertions which can never be seen in the still scenes of life. They are the active efforts of health and vigour and always tend to preserve and purify. Whereas, on the contrary, the quiet which prevails under slavish governments, and which may seem to be a recommendation of them, proceeds from an ignominious tameness and stagnation of the human faculties. It is the same with the stillness of midnight or the silence and torpor of death.

Further, free governments are the only governments which are consistent with the natural equality of mankind. This is a principle which, in my opinion, has been assumed, with the greatest reason, by some of the best writers on government. But the meaning of it is not that all the subordinations in human life owe their existence to the institution of civil government. The superiorities and distinctions arising from the relation of parents to their children, from the differences in the personal qualities and abilities of men, and from servitudes founded on voluntary compacts, must have existed in a state of nature, and would now take place were all men so virtuous as to leave no occasion for civil government. The maxim, therefore, "that all men are naturally equal," refers to their state when grown up to maturity and become independent agents, capable of acquiring property, and of directing their own conduct. And the sense of it is that no one of them is constituted by the author of nature the vassal or subject of another or has any right to give law to him or, without his consent, to take away any part of his property or to abridge him of his liberty. In a state of nature one man may have received benefits from another; and this would lay the person obliged under an obligation of gratitude, but it would not make his benefactor his master or give him a right to judge for him what grateful returns he ought to make and to extort these from him. In a state of nature, also, one may possess more strength or more knowledge or more property than another, and this would give him weight and influence but it would not give him any degree of authority. There would not be one human being who would be bound to obey him. A person, likewise in a state of nature, might let out his labour or give up to another, on certain stipulated terms, the direction of his conduct, and this would so far bring him into the station of a servant; but being done by himself, and on such terms only as he chooses to consent to, it is an *instance* of his liberty; and he will always have it in his power to quit the service he has chosen or to enter into another.

This equality or independence of men is one of their essential rights.[n] It is the same with that equality or independence which now actually takes place among the different states or kingdoms of the world with respect to one another. Mankind came with this right from the hands of their Maker. But all governments which are not free are totally inconsistent with it. They imply that there are some of mankind who are born with an inherent right of dominion and that the rest are born under an obligation to subjection, and that civil government, instead of being founded on any compact, is nothing but the exercise of this right. Some such sentiments seem to be now reviving in this country and even to be growing fashionable. Most of the writers against the *Observations on Civil Liberty* argue on the supposition of a right in the few to govern the many inde-

n. See on this subject an excellent sermon entitled, *The Principles of the Revolution Vindicated*, by Dr. Watson, Regius Professor of Divinity at Cambridge[27] [Richard Watson, *The Principles of the Revolution Vindicated in a Sermon Preached before the University of Cambridge* (Cambridge: Printed by J. Archdeacon, printer to the University, 1776)].

27. Richard Watson (1737–1816), professor of chemistry at Cambridge (1764–1771), appointed Regius Professor of Divinity at Cambridge in 1771.

pendently of their own choice.ᵒ Some of these writers have gone so far as to assert, in plain language, that civil governors derive their power immediately from the Deity and are his agents or representatives, accountable to him only. And one courtly writer, in particular, has honoured them with the appellation of *our political gods*. Probably this is the idea of civil governors entertained by the author of the *Remarks on the Acts of the Thirteenth Parliament of Great Britain*, for it is not easy to imagine on what other ground he can assert that property and civil rights are derived from civil governors and their gifts to mankind.ᵖ

If these sentiments are just, civil governors are indeed an awful order of beings; and it becomes us to enquire with anxiety who they are and how we may distinguish them from the rest of mankind. Shall we take for such all, whether men or women, whom we find in actual possession of civil power, whatever may be their characters or however they may have acquired their power? This is too extravagant to be asserted. It would legalize the *American* Congress. There must then be some pretenders among civil governors and it is necessary we should know how to discover them. It is incredible that the Deity should not have made this easy to us by some particular marks and distinctions which point out to our notice his real viceregents, just as he has pointed out man, by his figures and superior powers, to be the governor of the lower creatures. In particular, these persons must be possessed of wisdom and goodness superior to those of the rest of mankind for, without this, a grant of the powers they are supposed to possess would be nothing but a grant of power to injure and oppress without remedy and without bounds. q But this is a test by which they cannot be tried. It would leave but few of them in possession of the places they hold and the rights they claim. It is not in the high ranks of life or among the great and mighty that we are to seek wisdom and goodness.

o. Some who maintain this doctrine concerning government overthrow their own system by acknowledging the right of resistance in certain cases. For, if there is such a right, the people must be judges when it ought to be exercised, a right to resist only when civil governors *think* there is reason, being a gross absurdity and nullity. The right of resistance, therefore, cannot mean less than a right in the people, whenever they think it necessary, to change their governors and to limit their power. And from the moment this is done government becomes the work of the people and governors become their trustees or agents.

p. It has been commonly reckoned that it is the end of civil government and civil laws to protect the property and rights of men but, according to this writer, civil government and civil laws create property and rights. It follows, therefore, that antecedently to civil laws men could have no property or rights and that civil governors, being the makers of civil laws, it is a contradiction to suppose that mankind can have any property or rights which are valid against the claims of their governors. See *Three Letters to Dr. Price*, [Appendix 2, p. 238 ff.] and *Remarks on the Principal Acts of the 13th Parliament of Great Britain*, p. 58, etc. and p. 191.

q. This has been done in a lower instance. Parents have been furnished with a particular affection for their children in order to prevent any abuse of their power over them.

These love the shade and fly from observation. They are to be found chiefly in the middle ranks of life and among the contemplative and philosophical who decline public employments and look down with pity on the scramble for power among mankind and the restlessness and misery of ambition. It is proper to add that it has never been hitherto understood that any superiority in intellectual and moral qualifications lays the foundation of a claim to dominion.

It is not then, by their superior endowments, that the Deity intended to point out to us the few whom he has destined to command the many. But in what other manner could they be distinguished? Must we embrace Sir Robert Filmer's[28] patriarchal scheme?[29] One would have thought that Mr. Locke has said more than enough to expose this stupid scheme.[30] One of my opponents, however, has adopted it; and the necessary inference from it is that, as there is but now one lineal descendent from Adam's eldest son, there can be but one rightful monarch of the world. But I will not abuse my reader's patience by saying more on this subject. I am sorry that in this country there should be any occasion for taking notice of principles so absurd and at the same time so pernicious.[r] I say *pernicious* for they imply

r. "In ages of darkness, and too often also in those of greater knowledge, by the perfidious arts of designing princes, and by the base servility of too many ecclesiastics who managed the superstition of the populace by the violent restraints put upon divulging any juster sentiments about the rights of mankind, the natural notions of policy were erased out of the minds of men; and they were filled with some confused imaginations of something adorable in monarchs, some representation of the Divinity, and that even in the worst of them, and of some certain divine claims in certain families. No wonder this! That millions thus look upon themselves as a piece of property to one of their fellows as silly and worthless as the meanest of them, when the like arts of superstition have made millions, nay the very artificers themselves, fall down before the block or stone they had set up, or adore monkeys, cats, and crocodiles, as the sovereign disposers of their fortunes." See Dr. Hutcheson's[31] *System of Moral Philosophy*, vol. 2, p. 280[32] [Francis Hutcheson, *A System of Moral Philosophy*, 2 vols. (London: Sold by A. Millar and T. Longman, 1755), hereafter cited as Hutcheson, *Moral Philosophy*].

28. Robert Filmer (d. 1653), political writer, strong royalist, knighted by Charles I.

29. Robert Filmer, *Patriarcha, or the Natural Power of Kings . . .* (London: Printed for R. Chiswell, 1680).

30. John Locke, *First Treatise on Civil Government, in Which the False Principles and Foundation of Sir Robert Filmer and His Followers are Detected and Overthrown* (London, 1690).

31. Francis Hutcheson (1694–1746), philosopher; founder of an academy in Dublin; professor of moral philosophy at Glasgow (1729–1746).

32. The relevant passage reads:

"In ages of darkness, and too often also in those of greater knowledge, by the perfidious arts of designing princes and by the base servility of too many ecclesiastics who managed the superstition of a populace, by the violent restraints put upon divulging any juster sentiments about the rights of mankind, the natural notions of policy were erased out of the minds of men and they were filled with some confused imaginations of something adorable in monarchs, some representation of the Divinity, and that even in the worst of them, and of some certain divine claims in certain families, abstracted from any public interests of the nations to be ruled by them, and upon these groundless attachments, the best blood of these nations hath been sacrificed by contending factions. No

that King James the Second was deposed at the Revolution unlawfully and impiously, that the present King is an usurper, and that the present government, being derived from rebellion and treason, has no right to our allegiance.

Without all doubt, it is the choice of the people that makes civil governors. The people are the spring of all civil power, and they have a right to modify it as they please.

Mankind being naturally equal according to the foregoing explanation, civil government, in its genuine intention, is an institution for maintaining that equality by defending it against the encroachments of violence and tyranny. All the subordinations and distinctions in society previous to its establishment, it leaves as it found them, only confirming and protecting them. It makes no man master of another. It elevates no person above his fellow citizens. On the contrary, it levels all by fixing all in a state of subjection to one common authority. The authority of the laws. The will of the community. Taxes are given, not imposed. Laws are regulations of common choice, not injunctions of superior power. The authority of magistrates is the authority of the state, and their salaries are wages paid by the state for executing its will and doing its business. They do not govern the state. It is the state governs them and, had they just ideas of their own stations, they would consider themselves as no less properly servants of the public than the labourers who work upon its roads or the soldiers who fight its battles. A king, in particular, is only the first executive officer, the creature of the law, and as much accountable and subject to the law as the meanest peasant.[s] And were kings properly attentive to

s. "Let not, therefore, these pretended masters of the people be allowed even to do good against the general consent. Let it be considered that the condition of rulers is exactly the same as that of the Cacique who, being asked whether he had any slaves, answered, 'Slaves? I know but one slave in all my district, and that is myself.'" See *The Philosophical and Political History of the Settlements and Trade of the Europeans in the East and West Indies*, translated from the French of the Abbé Raynal[33] by Mr. Justamond, vol. 5, p. 414[34] [Guillaume Thomas Francois Raynal, *A Philosophical and Political History of the Settlements and Trade of the Europeans in the East and West Indies*, trans. J. Justamond (London: Printed for T. Cadell, 1776). This translation is from Raynal's *Historie philosophique et politique des éstablissements & du commerce des Européens dans les Deux Indes* (Amsterdam, 1770).]

great wonder this, that millions thus look upon themselves as a piece of property to one of their fellows as silly and worthless as the meanest of them, when the like arts of superstition have made millions, nay the very artificers themselves, fall down before the block or stone they had set up, or adore monkeys, cats, and crocodiles, as the sovereign disposers of their fortunes." Hutcheson, *Moral Philosophy*, 2:280–281.

33. Guillaume Thomas Francois Raynal (1713–1796), French political writer and propagandist; writer of histories on the Netherlands, the English Parliament, and the colonies in India and America; refused to serve in the States General because he opposed violence.

34. The relevant passage reads:
"Let not therefore these pretended masters of the people be allowed even to do good

their duty, and as anxious as they should be about performing it, they could not easily avoid sinking under the weight of their charge.

The account now given is, I am fully persuaded, in every particular, a true account of what civil government *ought* to be and it teaches us plainly the great importance and excellence of *free* government. It is this only that answers the description I have given of government, that secures against oppression, that gives room for that elevation of spirit and that exertion of the human powers which is necessary to human improvement, or that is consistent with the ends of government, with the rights of mankind, and their natural equality and independence. Free government, therefore, only, is just and legitimate government.

It follows farther from the preceding account that no people can lawfully surrender or cede their liberty. This must appear to any one who will consider that when a people make such a cession, and the extensive powers of government are trusted to the discretion of any man or body of men, they part with the powers of life and death and give themselves up a prey to oppression, that they make themselves the instruments of any injustice in which their rulers may choose to employ them, by arming them against neighbouring states and, also, that they do this not only for themselves but for their posterity. I will add, that if such a cession has been made or if through any causes a people have lost their liberty, they must have a right to emancipate themselves as soon as they can.[t] In attempting this, indeed, they ought to consider the sufferings which may attend the struggle and the evils which may arise from a defeat. But at the same time it will be proper to consider that the sufferings attending such a struggle must be temporary, whereas the evils to be avoided are permanent and that liberty is a blessing so inestimable, "that whenever there appears any probability of recovering it, a people should be willing to run many hazards

t. See *Observations*, p. [78–79]. "The rights of mankind are so sacred that no prescription of tyranny or arbitrary power can have authority enough to abolish them." Mr. Hume's *Essays*, vol. 3, "Essay on the Coalition of Parties."[35]

---

against the general consent. Let it be considered that the condition of those rulers is exactly the same as that of the cacique who, being asked whether he had any slaves, answered, 'Slaves! I know but one slave in all my district and that is myself.' " Guillaume Thomas Francois Raynal, *A Philosophical and Political History of the Settlements and Trade of the Europeans in the East and West Indies*, trans. J. O. Justamond (London: Printed for W. Strahan and T. Cadell, 1783), 8:32.

35. The relevant passage reads: "Though obliged to acknowledge, that precedents in favour of prerogative had uniformly taken place during many reigns before Charles the First, they [the Whigs] thought that there was no reason for submitting any longer to so dangerous an authority. Such might have been their reasoning: as the rights of mankind are for ever to be deemed sacred, no prescription of tyranny or arbitrary power can have authority sufficient to abolish them." David Hume, "Of the Coalition of Parties," in *Essays Moral, Political and Literary* (Oxford: Oxford University Press, 1963), p. 469. Hereafter cited as Hume, *Essays* (1963).

and even not to repine at the greatest expence of blood or treasure."[u]

I am very sensible that civil government, as it actually exists in the world, by no means answers to the account I have given of it. Instead of being an institution for guarding the weak against the strong we find it an institution which mades the strong yet stronger and gives them a systematical power of oppressing. Instead of promoting virtue and restraining vice, encouraging free enquiry, establishing liberty, and protecting alike all peaceable persons in the enjoyment of their civil and religious rights, we see a savage despotism, under its name, laying waste the earth, unreasonably elevating some and depressing others, discouraging improvement, and trampling upon every human right. That force of states which ought to be applied only to their own defence we see continually applied to the purpose of attack and used to extend dominion by conquering neighbouring communities. Civil governors consider not themselves as servants but as masters. Their stations they think they hold in their own right. The people reckon their property, and their possessions, a common stock from which they have a right to take what they will and of which no more belongs to any individual than they are pleased to leave him.[v]

What a miserable perversion is this of a most important institution? What a grievance is government so degenerated? But this perversion furnishes no just argument against the truth of the account I have given. Similar degeneracies have prevailed in other instances of no less importance.

Reason in man, like the will of the community in the political world, was intended to give law to his whole conduct and to be the supreme controlling power within him. The passions are subordinate powers, or an executive force under the direction of reason kindly given to be, as it were, wind and tide to the vessel of life in its course through this world to future

u. "Mankind have been generally a great deal too tractable and hence so many wretched forms of power have always enslaved nine tenths of the nations of the world, where they have the fullest right to make all efforts for a change." Dr. Hutcheson's *Moral Philosophy,* vol. 2, p. 280.[36]

v. See *Remarks on the Acts of the Thirteenth Parliament of Great Britain,* p. 34, etc. "Is not the same reasoning applicable to taxes paid for the support of civil government? Are not these too the property of the civil magistrate?" *ibid.,* p. 56.[37] If I understand this writer, his meaning is not only that the taxes which the civil magistrate has imposed are his property but also any which he shall please to impose.

---

36. Price quotes Hutcheson verbatim.

37. The relevant passage reads:

"Tythes, for instance, is a tax, and a very heavy and perhaps impolitic one too. Yet it appears at first sight that in the payment of this tax we do not give up any part of our property. The meanest farmer will understand you when you tell him, that nine sheaves belong to (are the property of) himself and the tenth belongs to (is the property of) the parson. . . .

"Is not the same reasoning applicable to taxes paid for the support of civil governors? Are not these too the property of the civil magistrate?" John Lind, *Remarks on the Principal Acts of the Thirteenth Parliament of Great Britain* (London: Printed for T. Payne, 1775), pp. 57–58.

honour and felicity. How different from this is the actual state of man? Those powers which were destined to govern are made to serve and those powers which were destined to serve are allowed to govern. Passion guides human life and most men make no other use of their reason than to justify whatever their interest or their inclinations determine them to do.

Religion likewise (the perfection of reason) is, in its true nature, the inspirer of humanity and joy and the spring of all that can be great and worthy in a character; and were we to see its genuine effects among mankind, we should see nothing but peace and hope and justice and kindness, founded on that regard to God and to his will which is the noblest principle of action. But how different an aspect does religion actually wear? What is it, too generally, in the practice of mankind, but a gloomy and cruel superstition, rendering them severe and sour, teaching them to compound for wickedness by punctuality in religious forms and prompting them to harrass, persecute and exterminate one another?

The same perversion has taken place still more remarkably in Christianity, the perfection of religion. Jesus Christ has established among Christians an absolute equality. He has declared that they have but *one* master, even himself and that they are all brethren and, therefore, has commanded them not to be called masters and, instead of assuming authority over one another, to be ready to wash one another's feet.[w] The princes of the gentiles, he says, exercise lordship over them and are flattered with high titles[x] but he has ordained that it shall not be so amongst his followers and that if any one of them would be chief he must be the servant of all. The clergy in his church are, by his appointment, no more than a body of men chosen by the different societies of Christians to conduct their worship and to promote their spiritual improvement without any other powers than those of persuasion and instruction. It is expressly directed that they shall not make themselves lords of God's heritage or exercise dominion over the faith of Christians, but be helpers of their joy.[y] Who can, without astonishment, compare these appointments of Christianity with the events which have happened in the Christian church? That religion which thus inculcates humility and forbids all domination and the end of which was to produce peace on earth and good will among men has been turned into an occasion of animosities the most dreadful and of ambition the most destructive. Notwithstanding its mildness and benignity and the tendency it has to extinguish in the human breast pride and malevolence, it has been the means of arming the spirits of men with unrelenting fury against one another. Instead of peace, it has brought a sword, and its professors, instead of washing one another's feet, have endeavoured to tread on one

w. Matt. 23:8–12; John 13:14.
x. Luke 22:25, etc.
y. 1 Pet. 5:3; 2 Cor. 1:24.

another's necks. The ministers, in particular, of Christianity, became, soon after its establishment, an independent body of spiritual rulers, nominating one another in perpetual succession, claiming, by divine right, the highest powers and forming a hierarchy which by degrees produced a despotism more extravagant than any that ever before existed on this earth.

A considerate person must find difficulties in enquiring into the causes and reasons of that depravity of human nature which has produced these evils and rendered the best institutions liable to be so corrupted. This enquiry is much the same with the enquiry into the origin of moral evil which has in all ages puzzled human wisdom. I have at present nothing to do with it. It is enough for my purpose in these observations that the facts I have mentioned prove undeniably that the state of civil government in the world affords no reason for concluding that I have not given a just account of its true nature and origin.

I have shown at the beginning of this section that it is free government alone that can preserve from oppression, give security to the rights of a people, and answer the ends of government. It is necessary I should here observe that I would not be understood to mean that there can be no kind or degree of security for the rights of a people under any government which cannot be denominated free. Even under an absolute monarchy or an aristocracy there may be laws and customs which, having gained sacredness by time, may restrain oppression and afford some important securities. Under governments by representation there must be still greater checks on oppression provided the representation, though partial, is uncorrupt and also frequently changed. In these circumstances there may be so much of a common interest between the body of representatives and the people, and they may stand so much on one ground, that there will be no temptations to oppression. The taxes which the representative body impose they will be obliged themselves to pay, and the laws they make, they will make with the prospect of soon returning to the situation of those for whom they make them and of being themselves governed by them.

It seems particularly worth notice here that as far as there are any such checks under any government they are the consequence of its partaking so far of liberty and that the security attending them is more or less in proportion as a government partakes more or less of liberty. If, under an absolute government, fundamental laws and long established institutions give security in any instances, it is because they are held so sacred that a despot is afraid to violate them or, in other words, because a people, not being completely subdued, have still some control over the government. The like is more evidently true under mixed governments of which a house of representatives, fairly chosen and freely deliberating and resolving, forms a part; and it is one of the highest recommendations of such governments that, even when the representation is most imperfect, they have a tendency to give more security than any other governments. Under other governments it is the fear of exciting insurrections by contradicting established maxims that restrains oppression. But as, in general, a people will bear much, and are seldom driven to resistance till grievances become intolerable, their rulers can venture far without danger and, therefore, under such governments are very imperfectly restained. On the contrary, if there is an honest representation, vested with powers like to those of our House of Commons, the redress of grievances, as soon as they appear, will be always easily attainable and the rulers of a state will be under a necessity of regarding the first beginnings of discontent. Such, and greater than can be easily described, are the advantages of even an imperfect representation in a government. How great then must be the blessing of a complete representation?[z] It is this only gives full security and that can properly denominate a people free.

It deserves to be added here, that as there can be no private character so abandoned as to want all virtue, so there can be no government so slavish as to exclude every restraint upon oppression. The most slavish and, therefore, the worst governments are those under which there is nothing to set bounds to oppression besides the discretion and humanity of those who govern. Of this kind are the following governments.

First, all governments purely despotic. These may be either monarchical, or aristocratical. The latter are the worst, agreeably to a common observation, that it is better to have one master than many. The appetites of a single despot may be easily satiated but this may be impossible where there is a multitude.

Secondly, all provincial governments. The history of mankind proves these to be the worst of all governments and that no oppression is equal to that which one people are capable of practising towards another. I have mentioned some of the reasons of this in the *Observations on Civil Liberty*, Part I. sect. 3. Bodies of men do not feel for one another as individuals do. The odium of a cruel action, when shared among many, is not regarded. The master of slaves working on a plantation, though he may keep them down to prevent their becoming strong enough to emancipate themselves,

z. He who wants to be convinced of the practicability, even in this country, of a complete representation, should read a pamphlet lately published, the title of which is *Take Your Choice* [John Cartwright,[38] *The Legislative Rights of the Commonalty Vindicated; or, Take Your Choice! Representation and Respect: Imposition and Contempt. Annual Parliaments and Liberty: Long Parliaments and Slavery* (London: Printed for J. Almon, 1777)].

38. John Cartwright (1740–1824), political reformer; served in the navy; appointed major to the Nottingham militia, but was not active after 1775 because of his sympathies with the American cause; in 1776 he began activities that gained him the title of "Father of Reform."

yet is led by interest, as well as humanity, to govern them with such moderation as to preserve their use. But these causes will produce more of this good effect, when the slaves are under the eye of their proprietor and form a part of his family than when they are settled on a distant plantation where he can know little of them and is obliged to trust them to the management of rapacious servants.

It is particularly observable here that free governments, though happier in themselves, are more oppressive to their provinces than despotic governments. Or, in other words, that the subjects of free states are worse slaves than the subjects of states not free.*aa* This is one of the observations which Mr. Hume represents as an universal axiom in politics.*bb* "Though," says he, "free governments have been commonly the most happy for those who partake of their freedom, yet are they the most oppressive and ruinous to their provinces and this observation may be fixed as an universal axiom in politics. What cruel tyrants were the Romans over the world during the time of their commonwealth? After the dissolution of the commonwealth the Roman yoke became easier upon the provinces, as Tacitus informs us, and it may be observed, that many of the worst emperors (Domitian, for instance) were very careful to prevent all oppression of the provinces. The oppression and tyranny of the Carthaginians over their subject states in Africa went so far, as we learn from Polybius (Lib. I. cap. 72) that not content with exacting the half of all the produce of the ground, which of itself was a very high rent, they also loaded them with many other taxes. If we pass from ancient to modern times we shall always find the observation to hold. The provinces of absolute monarchies are always better treated than those of free states."[39]

---

aa. "A free subject of a free state" is a contradiction in terms. See the *Proclamation for a Fast* [*Proclamation for a Fast. In Congress, Saturday, March 16, 1776* (Philadelphia: Printed by John Dunlap, 1776) (Broadside)].

bb. Mr. Hume's *Essays*, vol. 1, essay 4, p. 31.

---

39. The relevant passage reads:

"It may easily be observed, that though free governments have been commonly the most happy for those who partake of their freedom; yet are they the most ruinous and oppressive of their provinces: and this observation may, I believe, be fixed as a maxim of the kind we are here speaking of. When a monarch extends his dominions by conquest, he soon learns to consider his old and his new subjects as on the same footing; because, in reality, all his subjects are to him the same, except the few friends and favourites with whom he is personally acquainted. . . . But a free state necessarily makes a great distinction, and must always do so, till men learn to love their neighbours as well as themselves. The conquerors, in such a government, are all legislators, and will be sure to contrive matters, by restrictions on trade, and by taxes, so as to draw some private, as well as public advantage from their conquests. . . . What cruel tyrants were the Romans over the world during the time of their commonwealth! It is true, they had laws to prevent oppression in their provincial magistrates; but Cicero informs us, that the Romans could not better consult the interests of the provinces than by repealing these very laws. For, in that case, says he, our magistrates, having entire impunity, would plunder no more than would satisfy their own rapaciousness; whereas, at present, they must also satisfy

Thirdly, among the worst sorts of governments I reckon all governments by a corrupt representation. There is no instance in which the trite observation is more true than in this, "that the best things when corrupted become the worst." A corrupt representation is so far from being any defence against oppression that it is a support to it. Long established customs, in this case, afford no security because, under the sanction of such a representation, they may be easily undermined or counteracted; nor is there any injury to a people which, with the help of such an instrument, may not be committed with safety. It is not, however, every degree of corruption, that will destroy the use of a representation and turn it into an evil so dreadful. In order to this, corruption must pass a certain limit. But every degree of it tends to this, saps the foundation of liberty, and poisons the fountain of legislation. And when it gets to its last stage and has proceeded its utmost length, when, in particular, the means by which candidates get themselves chosen are such as admit the worst but exclude the best men, a House of Representatives becomes little better than a sink into which is collected all that is most worthless and vile in a kingdom. There cannot be a greater calamity than such a government. It is impossible there should be a condition more wretched than that of a nation, once free, so degenerated.

Conclusion.

It is time to dismiss this subject. But I cannot take a final leave of it (and probably of all subjects of this kind) without adding the following reflections on our own state in this kingdom.

It is well known that Montesquieu has paid the highest compliment to this country by describing its constitution of government in giving an account of a perfect government, and by drawing the character of its inhabitants in giving an account of the manners and characters of a free people. "All (he says) having, in free states, a share in government, and the laws not being made for some more than others, they consider themselves as monarchs and are more properly confederates than fellow-subjects. No one

that of their judges, and of all the great men in Rome, of whose protection they stand in need. . . . After the dissolution of the commonwealth, the Roman yoke became easier upon the provinces, as Tacitus informs us; and it may be observed, that many of the worst emperors, Domitian, for instance, were careful to prevent all oppression on the provinces. . . . The oppression and tyranny of the Carthaginians over their subject states in Africa went so far, as we learn from Polybius, that, not content with exacting the half of all the produce of the land, which of itself was a very high rent, they also loaded them with many other taxes. If we pass from ancient to modern times, we shall still find the observation to hold. The provinces of absolute monarchies are always better treated than those of free states." Hume, "That Politics May be Reduced to a Science," *Essays* (1963), pp. 17–19.

citizen being subject to another, each sets a greater value on his liberty
than on the glory of any of his fellow citizens. Being independent, they are
proud, for the pride of kings is founded on their independence. They are
in a constant ferment and believe themselves in danger even in those
moments when they are most safe. They reason but it is indifferent whether
they reason well or ill. It is sufficient that they do reason. Hence springs
that liberty which is their security. This state, however, will lose its liberty.
It will perish when the legislative power shall become more corrupt than
the executive." *cc*

Such is the account which this great writer gave, many years ago, of the
British constitution and people. We may learn from it that we have nothing to fear from that disposition to examine every public measure, to
censure ministers of state, and to be restless and clamorous, which has
hitherto characterized us. On the contrary, we shall have everything to fear
when this disposition is lost. As soon as a people grow secure and cease to
be quick in taking alarms they are undone. A free constitution of government cannot be preserved without an earnest and unremitting jealousy.
Our constitution, in particular, is so excellent that it is the properest object of such a jealousy. For my own part, I admire so much the general
frame and principles of it that I could be almost satisfied with that representation of the kingdom which forms the most important part of it, had
I no other objection to this representation than its inadequateness. Did it
consist of a body of men, fairly elected for a short term, by a number of
independent persons, of all orders in every part of the kingdom, equal to
the number of the present voters and were it, after being elected, under no
undue influence, it would be a security of such importance that I should be
less disposed to complain of the injustice done, by its inadequateness, to

---

cc. *Spirit of Laws*, bk. 19, chap. 27.[40]

40. The relevant passage reads:
"In a country where every man has, in some sort, a share in the administration of
the government, the women ought scarcely to live with the men. They are therefore
modest, that is, timid; and this timidity constitutes their virtue: whilst the men without
a taste for gallantry plunge themselves into a debauchery, which leaves them at leisure,
and in the enjoyment of their full liberty.
"Their laws not being made for one individual more than another, each considers
himself a monarch; and, indeed, the men of this nation are rather confederates than
fellow-subjects. . . .
"In a free nation it is very often a matter of indifference whether individuals reason
well or ill; it is sufficient that they do reason: hence springs that liberty which is a
security from the effects of these reasonings.
"But in a despotic government, it is equally pernicious whether they reason well or
ill; their reasoning is alone sufficient to shock the principle of that government. . . .
"As no subject fears another, the whole nation is proud: for the pride of kings is
founded only on their independence.
"Free nations are haughty; others may more properly be called vain." *Spirit of Laws*
(1949), pp. 314–315.

the greatest part of the kingdom by depriving them of one of their natural and unalienable rights. To such a body of representatives we might commit, with confidence, the guardianship of our rights knowing that, having one interest with the rest of the state, they could not violate them or that if they ever did, a little time would bring the power of gaining redress without tumult or violence. Happy the people so blessed. If wise, they will endeavour, by every possible method, to preserve the purity of their representation and, should it have degenerated, they will lose no time in effecting a reformation of it. But if, unhappily, infection should have pervaded the whole mass of the state, and there should be no room to hope for any reformation, it will be still some consolation to reflect that slavery, in all its rigour, will not immediately follow. Between the time in which the securities of liberty are undermined and its final subversion there is commonly a flattering interval during which the enjoyment of liberty may be continued in consequence of fundamental laws and rooted habits which cannot be at once exterminated. And this interval is longer or shorter according as the progress of corruption is more or less rapid and men in power more or less attentive to improve favourable opportunities. The government of this country, in particular, is so well balanced, and the institutions of our common law are so admirable, and have taken such deep root, that we can bear much decay before our liberties fall. Fall, however, they must, if our public affairs do not soon take a new turn. That very evil which, according to the great writer I have quoted, is to produce our ruin, we see working everywhere and increasing every day. The following facts, among many others, show too plainly whither we are tending and how far we are advanced.

First, it seems to me, that a general indifference is gaining ground fast among us. This is the necessary effect of increasing luxury and dissipation but there is another cause of it which I think of with particular regret. In consequence of having been often duped by false patriots and found that the leaders of opposition, when they get into places, forget all their former declarations, the nation has been led to a conviction that all patriotism is imposture and all opposition to the measures of government nothing but a struggle for power and its emoluments. The honest and independent part of the nation entertain at present most of this conviction and, therefore, having few public men to whom they can look with confidence, they give up all zeal, and sink into inactivity and despondence.

Secondly, at the Revolution the House of Commons acquired its just weight in the constitution and, for some years afterwards it was often giving much trouble to men in power. Of late, it is well known, that means have been tried and a system adopted for quieting it. I will not say with what success. But I must say, that the men whose policy this has been have struck at the very heart of public liberty and are the worst traitors this kingdom ever saw. "If ever, (says Judge Blackstone) it should happen, that the independency of any one of the three branches of our legislature should be lost, or that it should become subservient to the views of either of the other two, there would soon be an end of our constitution. The legislature would be changed from that which was originally set up by the general consent and fundamental act of the society; and such a change, however effected, is according to Mr. Locke (who perhaps carries his theory too far) at once an entire dissolution of the bands of government, and the people are thereby reduced to a state of anarchy, with liberty to constitute to themselves a new legislative power." *dd*

Thirdly, soon after the Revolution bills for triennial parliaments passed both Houses in opposition to the court.*ee* At the accession septennial parliaments were established. Since this last period many attempts have been made, by the friends of the constitution, to restore triennial parliaments and, formerly, it was not without difficulty that the ministry were able to defeat these attempts. The division in the House of Commons in 1735, on a bill for this purpose, was 247 to 184.[43] I need not say that now all such attempts drop of themselves. So much are the sentiments of our representatives changed in this instance that the motion for such a bill, annually made by a worthy member of the House of Commons,[44] can scarcely produce a serious debate or gain the least attention. For several years, at the beginning of the last reign, the House of Commons constantly passed pension and place bills which were as constantly rejected by the House of Lords. At present, no one is so romantic as ever to think of introducing any such bills into the House of Commons.

Fourthly, standing armies have in all ages been destructive to the liberties of the states into which they have been admitted. Montesquieu ob-

---

dd. Introduction to the *Commentaries on the Laws of England*, p. 48.[41] See also bk. 1, chap. 8.

ee. In 1692 King William rejected a bill for triennial parliaments after it had passed both Houses. But in a following year he thought proper to give his assent to it.[42]

---

41. The relevant passage reads: "For if ever it should happen that the independence of any one of the three [branches of government] should be lost, or that it should become subservient to the views of either of the other two, there would soon be an end of our constitution. The legislature would be changed from that, which was originally set up by the general consent and fundamental act of the society; and such a change, however effected, is according to Mr. Locke (who perhaps carries his theory too far) at once an entire dissolution of the bands of government; and the people would be reduced to a state of anarchy, with liberty to constitute to themselves a new legislative power." William Blackstone, *Commentaries on the Laws of England*, bk. 1 (Oxford: Printed at the Clarendon Press, 1765; reprint of 1st ed., London: Dawsons of Pall Mall, 1966), pp. 51–52.

42. "An act for the frequent meeting and calling of Parliaments," 6 William 3, ch. 2.

43. On March 13, 1733, a motion was made to repeal the Septennial Act. That motion was defeated by a vote of 247 to 184. See *Journals of Commons*, 22:279.

44. These motions were made by John Sawbridge. See, for example, *Parliamentary History*, 17:322–327; 690–696; 1050–1051.

serves that the preservation of liberty in England requires that it should have no land forces.*ff* Dr. Ferguson calls the establishment of standing armies "a fatal refinement in the present state of civil government."*gg* Mr. Hume pronounces "our standing army a mortal distemper in the British constitution of which it must inevitably perish."*hh* Formerly the nation was apprehensive of this danger and the standing army was a constant subject of warm debate in both Houses of Parliament. The principal reason then assigned for continuing it was the security of the House of Hanover against the friends of the Pretender. This is a reason which now exists no more, the House of Hanover being so well established as not to want any such security. The standing army also is now more numerous and formidable than ever and yet all opposition to it is lost and it is become in a manner a part of the constitution.

Fifthly, for many years after the accession the national debt was thought an evil so alarming that the reduction of it was recommended every year from the throne to the attention of Parliament as an object of the last importance. The fund appropriated to this purpose was called the only hope of the kingdom and when the practice of alienating it began, it was reckoned a kind of sacrilege and zealously opposed in the House of Commons and protested against in the House of Lords. But now, though the debt is almost tripled, we sit under it with perfect indifference and the sacred fund, which repeated laws had ordered to be applied to no other purpose than the redemption of it, is always alienated of course and become a

---

ff. Spirit of Laws, bk. 19, chap. 27.

gg. History of Civil Society, pt. 6, sec. 5.[45] [Adam Ferguson, *An Essay on the History of Civil Society* (Edinburgh: Printed for A. Millar and T. Cadell, London, and for A. Kincaid and J. Bell, Edinburgh, 1767)].

hh. Political Discourses, essay 12, p. 301[46] [David Hume, *Political Discourses* (Edinburgh: Printed by R. Fleming for A. Kincaid and A. Donaldson, 1752)].

---

45. The relevant passage reads: ". . . by forming a distinction between civil and military professions, by committing the keeping and the enjoyment of liberty to different hands, has prepared the way for the dangerous alliance of faction with military power, in opposition to mere political forms and the rights of mankind.

"A people who are disarmed in compliance with this fatal refinement, have rested their safety on the pleadings of reason and of justice at the tribunal of ambition and of force." Adam Ferguson, *An Essay on the History of Civil Society*, 6th ed. (London: Printed for T. Cadell, in the Strand, and for W. Creech, and Bell and Bradfute, at Edinburgh 1793), pt. 6, sec. 5, pp. 452–453. Hereafter cited as Ferguson, *Civil Society*, 6th ed.

46. The relevant passage reads:

"The plan of limited monarchy, however corrected, seems still liable to three great inconveniences. First, it removes not entirely, though it may soften the parties of court and country. Secondly, the king's personal character must still have great influence on the government. Thirdly, the sword is in the hands of a single person, who will always neglect to discipline the militia, in order to have a pretence for keeping up a standing army." In a footnote to the last sentence quoted Hume says, "It is evident that this is a mortal distemper in the British government of which it must at last inevitably perish." Hume, "Idea of a Perfect Commonwealth," *Essays* (1963), p. 513.

constant part of the current supplies and much more an encouragement to dissipation than a preservative from bankruptcy.

Sixthly, nothing is more the duty of the representatives of a nation than to keep a strict eye over the expenditure of the money granted for public services. In the reign of King William, the House of Commons passed almost every year bills for appointing commissioners for taking, stating and examining the public accounts and, particularly, the army and navy debts and contracts. In the reign of Queen Ann such bills became less frequent. But since the accession only two motions have been made for such bills, one in 1715,[47] and the other in 1741;[48] and both were rejected.

Seventhly, I hope I may add, that there was a time when the kingdom could not have been brought to acquiesce in what was done in the case of the Middlesex election.[49] This is a precedent which, by giving the House of Commons the power of excluding its members at discretion, and of introducing others in their room on a minority of votes, has a tendency to make it a self-created House and to destroy entirely the right of representation. And a few more such precedents would completely overthrow the constitution.

Lastly, I cannot help mentioning here the addition which has been lately made to the power of the Crown by throwing into its hands the East-India Company. Nothing more unfavourable to the security of public liberty has been done since the Revolution. And should our statesmen, thus strengthened by the patronage of the East, be farther strengthened by the conquest and patronage of the West, they will indeed have no small reason for triumph and there will be little left to protect us against the encroachments and usurpations of power. Rome sank into slavery in consequence of enlarging its territories and becoming the center of the wealth of conquered provinces and the seat of universal empire. It seems the appointment of Providence that free states, when not contented with self-government and prompted by the love of domination they make themselves masters of other states, shall lose liberty at the same time that they take it away and, by subduing, be themselves subdued. Distant and dependent provinces can be governed only by a military force. And a military force which governs abroad will soon govern at home. The Romans were so sensible of this that they made it treason for any of their generals to march their armies over the Rubicon into Italy. Caesar, therefore, when he came to this river, hesitated; but he passed it, and enslaved his country.

---

47. The bill Price mentions was presented to the House of Commons on May 25, 1715. See *Journals of Commons*, 18:138–139.

48. See footnote 30 to the *General Introduction*, p. 56.

49. Price refers here to the expulsion of John Wilkes from the House of Commons. Wilkes was elected to Parliament for Middlesex on March 28, 1768, and was expelled from Parliament on February 4, 1769. For a concise account of this episode, see *Dictionary of National Biography*, s.v. "Wilkes, John."

"Among the circumstances (says Dr. Ferguson) which in the event of national prosperity and in the result of commercial arts, lead to the establishment of despotism, there is none perhaps that arrives at this termination with so sure an aim as the perpetual enlargement of territory. In every state the freedom of its members depends on the balance and adjustment of its interior parts; and the existence of any such freedom among mankind depends on the balance of nations. In the progress of conquest those who are subdued are said to have left their liberties. But, from the history of mankind, to conquer or to be conquered has appeared in effect the same."[ii]

Many more facts of this kind might easily be enumerated but these are sufficient. They show with sad evidence how fast we have, for some time, been advancing towards the greatest of all public calamities.

We may also infer from the preceding observations that there is only one way in which our deliverance is possible, and that is by restoring our grand national security. This is the object which our great men in opposition ought to hold forth to the kingdom and to bind themselves by some decisive tests to do all they can to obtain. That patriotism must be spurious which does not carry its views principally to this. Without it, nothing is of great importance to the kingdom and even an accommodation with America would only preserve a limb, and save from present danger, while a gangrene was left to consume the vitals.

But probably we are gone too far and corruption has struck its roots too deep to leave us much room for hope. Mr. Hume has observed that as the affairs of this country are not likely to take a turn favourable to the establishment of a perfect plan of liberty, "an absolute monarchy is the easiest death, the true euthanasia of the British constitution."[jj] If this observation is just, our constitution (should no great calamity intervene) is likely, in some future period, to receive a very quiet dissolution. At present, however, it must be acknowledged that we enjoy a degree of liberty, civil and religious, which has seldom been paralleled among mankind. We ought to

ii. *History of Civil Society*, pt. 4, sec. 5.[50]
jj. See Mr. Hume's *Essays*, vol. 1, p. 91.[51]

---

50. Price quotes Ferguson verbatim except that where Price has "(says Mr. Ferguson)" Ferguson has "therefore." Price wrongly cites this passage to be in part 4, section 5. Part 4 of Ferguson's work contains no section 5. See Ferguson, *Civil Society*, 6th ed., pp. 454–455.

51. The relevant passage reads:
"It is well known, that every government must come to a period, and that death is unavoidable to the political, as well as to the animal body. But, as one kind of death may be preferable to another, it may be inquired, whether it be more desirable for the British constitution to terminate in a popular government, or in an absolute monarchy? Here I would frankly declare, that though liberty be preferable to slavery, in almost every case; yet I should rather wish to see an absolute monarch than a republic in this island. . . . Absolute monarchy, therefore, is the easiest death, the true euthanasia of the British constitution." Hume, "Whether the British Government Inclines More to Absolute Monarchy or to a Republic," *Essays* (1963), pp. 52–53.

rejoice in this happiness and to be grateful to that benevolent disposer of all events who blesses us with it. But, at the same time, our hearts must bleed when we reflect that, the supports of it having given way, it is little more than a sufferance which we owe to the temper of the times, the lenity of our governors, and some awe, in which the friends of despotism are still held, by the voice and spirit of the uncorrupted part of the kingdom. May these causes, if no better securities can be hoped for, long delay our fate.

It must not be forgotten that all I have now said is meant on the supposition that our affairs will proceed smoothly till, by a common and natural progress, we have gone the round of other nations once free and are brought to their end. But it is possible this may not happen. Our circumstances are singular and give us reason to fear that we have before us a death which will not be easy or common.

Part II

. . . .

Sect. II. Of the State of the Nation and the War with America.

At the beginning of the preceding section I have taken notice of the flattering account which was given, at opening the budget in April last, of the state of the kingdom with respect to its commerce, revenue, and opulence. On that account I shall beg leave to offer the following reflections.

First, the observations in the last section prove, I think, that it is not so well supported by facts as there is reason to wish. I am sensible, indeed, that we never made a more gay and splendid appearance. But no considerate person will draw much encouragement from hence. The pride and security, that luxury, venality and dissipation which give us this appearance, are melancholy symptoms and have hitherto been the forerunners of distress and calamity.

Secondly, when this account was given there was a particular end to be answered by it. Additional taxes were to be imposed and it was necessary to reconcile the public to the prospect of a great increase of its burdens in order to carry on the war with America. On other occasions different accounts had been given. In order to prove the justice of taxing the Americans the weight of our own taxes had been often insisted upon and the difficulty of raising a sufficient force among ourselves to reduce them had been urged as a reason for seeking and employing, at a great expence, the assistance of foreign powers. On such occasions I have heard our unhappy and embarrassed situation mentioned and, at the end of the last session of Parliament, one of our greatest men, whose opinion in favour of coercion had contributed to bring us into our present situation, acknowledged the distress attending it and represented the vessel of the state as having never before rode in so dangerous a storm. This is, without doubt, the truth. But, if the account on which I am remarking was just, we were then safe and happy nor was the vessel of the state ever wafted by more gentle and prosperous gales.

But the reflection which, on this occasion, has given me most pain is the following.

If, without America, we can be in a state so flourishing, a war to reduce America must be totally inexcuseable. I wish I could engage attention to this. War is a dreadful evil and those who involve a people in it needlessly will find they have much to answer for. Nothing can ever justify it but the necessity of it to secure some essential interest against unjust attacks. But, it seems there is no interest to be secured by the present war. The revenue has never flourished so much as since America has been rendered hostile to us and it is now reckoned by many a decided point that little depends on the American trade. It follows, then, that if the end of the present war is to "obtain a revenue," it is a revenue we do not want; if "to maintain authority," it is an authority of no use to us. Must not humanity shudder at such a war? Why not let America alone if we can subsist without it? Why carry fire and sword into a happy country to do ourselves no good?

Some of the very persons who depreciate the value of the colonies, as a support to our revenue and finances, yet say that we are now under a necessity of reducing them or perishing. I wish such persons would give an account of the causes which, according to their ideas, create this dreadful necessity. Is it the same that led Haman of old to reckon all his honours and treasures nothing to him while Mordecai the Jew would not bow to him? Or, are we become so luxurious that luxury even in the revenue is become necessary to us and so depraved that, like many individuals in private life, having lost self-dominion, we cannot subsist without dominion over others?

It must not be forgotten that I speak here on the supposition that it is possible for this country to be as safe and prosperous without America as some have asserted, and as was implied in what was said at opening the last budget. This is far from being my own opinion. Some time or other we shall, in all probability, feel severely, in our commerce and finances, the loss of the colonies. As a source of revenue they are, I think, of great importance to us but they are still more important as supports to our navy and an aid to us in our wars. It appears now that there is a force among them so formidable and so growing that, with its assistance, any of the great European powers may soon make themselves masters of all the West Indies and North America; and nothing ought to be more alarming to us than that our natural enemies see this and are influenced by it. With the colonies united to us we might be the greatest and happiest nation that ever existed. But with the colonies separated from us, and in alliance with France and Spain, we are no more a people. They appear, therefore, to be indeed worth any price. Our existence depends on keeping them. But how are they to be kept? Most certainly not by forcing them to unconditional submission at the expence of many millions of money and rivers of blood. The resolution to attempt this is a melancholy instance of that infatuation which sometimes influences the councils of kingdoms. It is attempting to keep them by a method which, if it succeeds, will destroy their use and make them not worth the having and which, if it does not succeed, will throw them into the scale of rival powers, kindle a general war, and undo the empire.

The extension of our territories in America, during the last war, increased the expence of our peace-establishment from 2.400,000£ *per ann.* to four millions *per ann.* Almost all the provinces in America, which used to be ours, are now to be conquered. Let the expence of this be stated at 25 or 30 millions or, at a capital bearing a million *per annum* interest. America recovered by the sword must be kept by the sword and forts and garrisons must be maintained in every province to awe the wretched inhabitants and to hold them in subjection. This will create another addition of expence and both together cannot, I suppose, be stated at less than two millions *per annum.* But how is such an increase of revenue to be procured? The colonies, desolated and impoverished, will yield no revenue. The surplusses of the sinking fund have, for many years, formed a necessary part of the current and ordinary supplies. It must, therefore, be drawn from new taxes. But can the kingdom bear such an increase of taxes? Or, if it can, where shall we find a surplus for discharging an enormous debt of above 160 millions? And what will be our condition when the next foreign war shall add two millions *per annum* more to our expences? Indeed, this is a frightful prospect. But it will be rendered infinitely more frightful by carrying our views to that increase of the power of the Crown which will arise from the increase of the army, from the disposal of new places without number, and the patronage of the whole continent of North America.

These consequences have been stated moderately on the supposition that we shall succeed in subduing America and that, while we are doing it, our natural enemies will neglect the opportunity offered them and continue to satisfy themselves with assisting America indirectly. But should the contrary happen, I need not say what will follow.

Some time ago this horrid danger might have been avoided and the colonies kept by the easiest means. By a prudent lenity and moderation. By receiving their petitions. By giving up the right we claim to dispose of their property and to alter their governments. By guaranteeing to them, in these respects, a legislative independence[kk] and establishing them in the possession of equal liberty with ourselves. This a great and magnanimous nation should have done. This, since the commencement of hostilities, would have brought them back to their former habits of respect and subordination and might have bound them to us for ever.

Montesquieu has observed that England, in planting colonies, should have commerce, not dominion, in view, the increase of dominion being incompatible with the security of public liberty. Every advantage that could arise from commerce they have offered us without reserve and their language to us has been, "Restrict us as much as you please in acquiring property by regulating our trade for your advantage but claim not the disposal of that property after it has been acquired. Be satisfied with the authority you exercised over us before the present reign. Place us where we were in 1763." On these terms they have repeatedly sued for a reconciliation. In return, we have denounced them rebels and with our fleets in their ports and our bayonets at their breasts have left them no other alternative than to acknowledge our supremacy and give up rights they think most sacred or stand on the defensive and appeal to heaven. They have chosen the latter.

In this situation, if our feelings for others do not make us tremble, our feelings for ourselves soon may. Should we suffer the consequences I have intimated our pride will be humbled. We shall admire the plans of mod-

kk. "There is something," says a great writer, "so unnatural in supposing a large society, sufficient for all the good purposes of an independent political union, remaining subject to the direction and government of a distant body of men who know not sufficiently the circumstances and exigencies of this society, or in supposing this society obliged to be governed solely for the benefit of a distant country, that it is not easy to imagine there can be any foundation for it in justice or equity. The insisting on old claims and tacit conventions to extend civil power over distant nations and form grand unwieldy empires, without regard to the obvious maxims of humanity, has been one great source of human misery," System of Moral Philosophy, by Dr. Hutcheson, vol. 2, p. 309.[52] In the section from whence this quotation is taken, Dr. Hutcheson discusses the question, "When [do] colonies have a right to be released from the dominion of the parent state?" And his general sentiment seems to be that they acquire such a right, "Whenever they are so increased in numbers and strength as to be sufficient by themselves for all the good ends of a political union."[53] Such a decision given by a wise man, long before we had any disputes with the colonies, deserves, I think, particular notice.

52. Price quotes Hutcheson verbatim. See Hutcheson, Moral Philosophy, 2:309.
53. The relevant passage reads:
"Nay as the end of all political unions is the general good of those thus united, and this good must be subordinated to the more extensive interests of mankind. If the plan of the mother country is changed by force, or degenerates by degrees from a safe, mild, and gentle limited power, to a severe and absolute one; or if under the same plan of polity, oppressive laws are made with respect to the colonies or provinces; and any colony is so increased in numbers and strength that they are sufficient by themselves for all the good ends of political union; they are not bound to continue in their subjection, when it is grown so much more burdensome than was expected." Hutcheson, Moral Philosophy, 2:308.

eration and equity which, without bloodshed or danger, would have kept America. We shall wish for the happiness of former times and remember, with anguish, the measures which many of us lately offered their lives and fortunes to support.

I must not conclude these observations without taking particular notice of a charge against the colonies which has been much insisted on. "They have," it is said, "always had independency in view; and it is this, chiefly, that has produced their present resistance." It is scarcely possible there should be a more unreasonable charge. Without all doubt, our connexion with them might have been preserved for ages to come (perhaps for ever) by wise and liberal treatment. Let any one read a pamphlet, published in 1761 by Dr. Franklin, and entitled, *The interest of Great Britain with respect to her Colonies*,[54] and let him deny this if he can. Before the present quarrel there prevailed among them the purest affection for this country and the warmest attachment to the House of Hanover. And since the present quarrel began, and not longer ago than the beginning of last winter, independency was generally dreaded among them. There is the fullest evidence for this and all who are best acquainted with America must know it to be true. As a specimen of this evidence, and of the temper of America till the period I have mentioned, I will just recite the following facts.

In the resolutions of the assembly which met at Philadelphia, July 15, 1774, after making the strongest professions of affection to Britain and duty to their sovereign, they declare their abhorrence of every idea of an unconstitutional independence on the parent state.[55] An assembly of delegates from all the towns of the county of Suffolk (of which Boston is the capital) delivered in September, 1774, to General Gage, a remonstrance against fortifying Boston-neck.[56] In this remonstrance they totally disclaim

54. Benjamin Franklin, *The Interest of Great Britain Considered, with Regard to Her Colonies, and the Acquisition of Canada and Guadaloupe. To Which are Added, Observations Concerning the Increase of Mankind, Peopling of Countries, &c.* (London: Printed for T. Becket, 1760).

55. Two resolutions passed by the Pennsylvania Council on July 15, 1774, read as follows: "[Resolved] Unanimously, 1. That we acknowledge ourselves, and the inhabitants of this Province, liege subjects of his Majesty King George the Third, to whom they and we owe and will bear true and faithful allegiance.

"Unanimously, 2. That as the idea of an unconstitutional independence on the parent state is utterly abhorrent to our principles, we owe the unhappy differences between Great Britain and the Colonies with the deepest distress and anxiety of mind, as fruitless to her, grievous to us, and destructive of the best interests of both." *Documentary History*, 1:555–556.

56. On September 9, 1774, an unofficial gathering of delegates from the towns and districts of Suffolk County, Massachusetts, approved a remonstrance to be delivered to General Gage. In that remonstrance the delegates ask Gage not to fortify the south entrance to Boston for the purpose of intercepting all trade between Boston and the country. They continue by saying: "We have been informed, that your excellency, in consequence of the application of the select men of Boston, has, indeed, disavowed any

every wish of independence. The same is done in the instructions given by several colonies to the first deputies chosen for a general Congress.57 In the petition of the first Congress to the King they declare they shall always, carefully and zealously, endeavour to support and maintain their connexion with Great Britain.58 In the memorial of the same Congress to the people of this country they repeat this assurance.59 In the order of the Congress which met in May, 1775, for a general fast, they call upon all America to unite in beseeching the Almighty to avert the judgments with which they were threatened and to bless their rightful Sovereign that so a

---

intention to injure the town in your present manoeuvres, and expressed your purpose to be for the security of the troops and his majesty's subjects in the town, we are therefore at a loss to guess, may it please your excellency, from whence your want of confidence in the loyal and orderly people of this vicinity could originate; a measure, so formidable, carried into execution from a pre-conceived though causeless jealousy of the insecurity of his majesty's troops and subjects in the town, deeply wounds the loyalty, and is an additional injury to the faithful subjects of this county, and affords them a strong motive for this application: We therefore intreat your excellency to desist from your design, assuring your excellency, that the people of this county, are by no means disposed to injure his majesty's troops. . . ." *Journals of Congress Containing Their Proceedings from September 5, 1774, to January 1, 1776,* (Philadelphia: Folwell's Press, 1800), 1:18–19. Hereafter cited as *Journals of Congress.*

57. In the "Instructions for the Deputies Appointed to Meet in General Congress on the Part of This Colony [Virginia]" it is stated: "And that they [the deputies for Virginia] may be better informed of our sentiments touching the conduct we wish them to observe on this important occasion, we desire that they will express, in the first place, our faith and true allegiance to his Majesty King George the Third, our lawful and rightful Sovereign; and that we are determined, with our lives and fortunes, to support him in the legal exercise of all his just rights and prerogatives; and, however misrepresented, we sincerely approve of a constitutional connection with Great Britain, and wish most ardently a return of that intercourse of affection and commercial connection that formerly united both countries, which can only be effected by a removal of those causes of discontent which have of late unhappily divided us." *Documentary History,* 1:689. See also Pennsylvania's "Instructions from the Committee to the Representatives in Assembly Met," *Documentary History,* 1:558–593; and "New Jersey Resolutions," *Documentary History,* 1:624–625.

58. On October 26, 1774, the Continental Congress approved a petition to be sent to the King. A passage from that petition reads:

"We ask but for peace, liberty, and safety. We wish not a diminution of the prerogative, nor do we solicit the grant of any new right in our favour. Your royal authority over us, and our connexion with Great-Britain, we shall always carefully and zealously endeavour to support and maintain." *Journals of Congress,* 1:66.

59. On October 21, 1774, the Continental Congress approved an address to the people of Great Britain. In that address, one passage reads:

"It is with the utmost regret, however, that we find ourselves compelled, by the over-ruling principles of self-preservation, to adopt measures detrimental, in their consequences, to numbers of our fellow-subjects in Great-Britain and Ireland. But, we hope, that the magnanimity and justice of the British nation will furnish a parliament of such wisdom, independence, and public spirit, as may save the violated rights of the whole empire, from the devices of wicked ministers and evil counsellors, whether in or out of office; and thereby restore that harmony, friendship, and fraternal affection, between all the inhabitants of his majesty's kingdoms and territories, so ardently wished for, by every true and honest American." *Journals of Congress,* 1:43.

reconciliation might be brought about with the parent state.[60] And in their declaration setting forth the causes of their taking arms they warn us, "that, should they find it necessary, foreign assistance was undoubtedly attainable," but at the same time declare "that they did not mean to dissolve the union which had so long and so happily subsisted between them and this country, that necessity had not yet driven them to that desperate measure or induced them to excite any other nation to war against us, and that they had not raised armies with ambitious designs of forming independent states, but solely for the protection of their property against violence and the defence of that freedom which was their birth-right." [61] In the instructions delivered Nov. 9, 1775, by a committee of the representatives of the province of Pennsylvania to their delegates in the third general congress they enjoin them, in behalf of the province, "utterly to reject any propositions, should such be made, that might lead to a separation from the mother country." [62]

---

60. On June 12, 1775, the Continental Congress passed a resolution calling for a general fast. A passage in that resolution reads:

"This Congress, therefore, considering the present critical, alarming and calamitous state of these colonies, do earnestly recommend that Thursday, the 20th day of July next, be observed, by the inhabitants of all the English colonies on this continent, as a day of public humiliation, fasting and prayer; that we may, with united hearts and voices, unfeignedly confess and deplore our many sins; and offer up our joint supplications to the all-wise, omnipotent, and merciful Disposer of all events; humbly beseeching him to forgive our iniquities, to remove our present calamities, to avert those desolating judgments, with which we are threatened, and to bless our rightful sovereign, king George the third, and to inspire him with wisdom to discern and pursue the true interest of his subjects, that a speedy end may be put to the civil discord between Great-Britain and the American colonies, without farther effusion of blood. . . ." *Journals of Congress,* 1:109–110.

61. The declaration to which Price refers was approved by the Continental Congress on July 6, 1775. The relevant passage from that declaration reads:

"Our cause is just. Our union is perfect. Our internal resources are great, and, if necessary, foreign assistance is undoubtedly attainable. . . .

"Lest this declaration should disquiet the minds of our friends and fellow-subjects in any part of the empire, we assure them that we mean not to dissolve that union which has so long and so happily subsisted between us, and which we sincerely wish to see restored. Necessity has not yet driven us into that desperate measure, or induced us to excite any other nation to war against them. We have not raised armies with ambitious designs of separating from Great-Britain, and establishing independent states. We fight not for glory or conquest. We exhibit to mankind the remarkable spectacle of a people attacked by unprovoked enemies, without any imputation or even suspicion of offence. They boast of their privileges and civilization, and yet proffer no milder conditions than servitude or death.

"In our own native land, in defence of the freedom that is our birth-right, and which we every enjoyed till the late violation of it—for the protection of our property, acquired solely by the honest industry of our fore-fathers and ourselves, against violence actually offered, we have taken up arms." *Journals of Congress,* 1:138–139.

62. On November 9, 1775, John Morton, Speaker of the Pennsylvania Council signed, by that council's order, a set of further instructions to the delegates to the Continental Congress. A passage from those instructions reads: "Though the oppressive measures of the British Parliament and Administration have compelled us to resist their violence by

What reason can there be for thinking the colonies not sincere in all these declarations? In truth, it was not possible they should be otherwise than sincere for so little did they think of war, at the time when most of these declarations were made, that they were totally unprepared for it. And, even when hostilities were begun at Lexington in April, 1775, they were so destitute of every instrument of defence, particularly ammunition, that half the force which is now invading them would have been sufficient to conquer them at once.

I will beg leave to add on this occasion the following extracts from letters, written by some leading persons at New York, the genuineness of which may be depended on.

New York, August 3, 1775. "I am sensible of the many artifices and falsehoods which have been used to bias the minds of your countrymen who believe evil reports of us and, particularly, that we are aiming at independence. Of this be assured, that even Hancock and Adams are averse to independence. There was a lie current last week that the congress had finally agreed upon independence to take place the 10th of March next, should not our grievances be redressed before that time. I wrote to one of our delegates to enquire whether this report was true. In his answer he declares, upon his honour, that he believed there was not one man in the Congress who would dare to make a motion tending to independence or, that if any one did, two could not be found to support the motion. None but those who are on the spot can conceive what a spirit is gone forth among all ranks and degrees of men. We deserve to be free. It is a heavy sacrifice we are making. Trade is at an end. We expect our city to be knocked about our ears. But I declare solemnly, I will submit to all, and die in a loghouse in the wilds of America, and be free, rather than flourish in servitude." In a subsequent letter, dated New York, Jan. 3, 1776, the same person writes as follows: "It is in the power of the ministry to annihilate all our disputes by restoring us to the situation we were in at the conclusion of the last war. If this is done we shall immediately return to our allegiance. But if not, be assured that an awful scene will be opened in the spring. Let me repeat a caution to you; believe not the insinuations of our enemies, who would make you all believe that independence is what America aims at. It is an insidious falsehood. Madmen will be found in all large societies. It would be singular were there none such to be found in a body of three millions of people and upwards. But they are like a grain of sand on the sea shore."

Another person writes thus: New York, Nov. 2, 1775. "We love and

---

force of arms, yet we strictly enjoin you, that you, in behalf of this Colony, dissent from, and utterly reject, any propositions, should such be made, that may cause or lead to a separation from our Mother Country, or a change of the form of this Government." *Documentary History*, 3:1408.

honour our King. He has no subjects in all his dominions more attached to his person, family and government, notwithstanding the epithet of rebels bestowed upon us. No charge is more unjust than the charge that we desire an independence on Great Britain. Ninety-nine in a hundred of the inhabitants of this country deprecate this as the heaviest of evils. But if administration will persist in their present measures, this will and must inevitably be the event; for submit to the present claims of the British parliament, while unrepresented in it, you may be assured they never will. And what deserves notice is that all the violence of Britain only unites the Americans still more firmly together and renders them more determined to be free or die. This spirit is unconquerable by violence but they may be easily won by kindness. Serious people of all denominations among us, episcopal and non-episcopal, are much employed in prayer to God for the success of the present struggles of America. They consider their cause as the cause of God and, as such, they humbly commit it to him, confident of success in the end, whatever blood or treasure it may cost them." [63]

Since these letters were written, the sentiments of America, with respect to independence, have been much altered. But it should be remembered that this alteration has been owing entirely to ourselves; I mean, to the measures of the last winter and summer, and particularly the following.

First, the rejection of the petition from the Congress brought over by Governor Penn. In this petition they professed, in strong language, that they still retained their loyalty to the King and attachment to this country and only prayed, "that they might be directed to some mode by which the united applications of the colonies might be improved into a happy reconciliation and that, in the meantime, some measures might be taken for preventing their farther destruction and for repealing such statutes as more immediately distressed them." [64] The colonies had often petitioned before

---

63. All available evidence indicates that these three letters have not survived. They are not among some three hundred I have seen. Price was cautious in his correspondence with his American friends through this period, and among some of them even had a code number, 176. I am fairly confident that he or his wife destroyed many such letters.

64. On July 8, 1775, the Continental Congress approved a petition to the King to be carried by Richard Penn, Lieutenant Governor of Pennsylvania. The relevant passage from that petition reads:

"We, therefore, beseech your majesty, that your royal authority and influence may be graciously interposed to procure us relief from our afflicting fears and jealousies, occasioned by the system before mentioned, and to settle peace through every part of your dominions, with all humility submitting to your majesty's wise consideration whether it may not be expedient for facilitating those important purposes that your majesty be pleased to direct some mode, by which the united applications of your faithful colonists to the throne, in pursuance of their common councils, may be improved into a happy and permanent reconciliation; and that, in the mean time, measures may be taken for preventing the further destruction of the lives of your majesty's subjects; and that such statutes as more immediately distress any of your majesty's colonies may be repealed." *Journals of Congress,* 1:142.

without being heard. They had, therefore, little hope from this application and meant that, if rejected, it should be their last.

Secondly, the last prohibitory bill, by which our protection of them was withdrawn, their ships and effects confiscated, and open war declared against them.

Thirdly, employing foreign troops to subdue them. This produced a greater effect in America than is commonly imagined. And it is remarkable that even the writers in America who answered the pamphlet entitled *Common Sense* acknowledge that should the British ministry have recourse to foreign aid it might become proper to follow their example and to embrace the necessity of resolving upon independence.[ll]

I have, further, reason to believe that the answer to the last petition of the City of London, presented in March, 1776, had no small share in producing the same effect.[mm,67]

ll. See *Common Sense*, and *Plain Truth*, p. 44. Published for Mr. Almon [Thomas Paine,[65] *Common Sense; Addressed to the Inhabitants of America . . . To Which Is Added an Appendix; Together with an Address to the People Called Quakers . . .* (Philadelphia: Printed and sold by W. and T. Bradford, 1776; reprinted, London, for J. Almon, 1776). James Chalmers,[66] Candidus, *Plain Truth; Addressed to the Inhabitants of America, Containing Remarks on a Late Pamphlet, Entitled Common Sense . . .* (Philadelphia: Printed and sold by R. Bell, 1776; reprinted, London, for J. Almon, 1776). For details on the authorship and publication of *Plain Truth*, see Thomas R. Adams, "The Authorship and Printing of *Plain Truth* by Candidus," *The Papers of the Bibliographical Society of America* 49 (1955):230–248. Hereafter cited as Adams, "Authorship of *Plain Truth*."]

mm. The colonies, I am assured, were not perfectly unanimous till they saw this answer.

65. Thomas Paine (1757–1809), revolutionary political pamphleteer, emigrated from England to America in 1775; secretary to the committee on foreign affairs of the Continental Congress (1777–1779); clerk of the Pennsylvania Assembly (1779); emigrated from New Jersey to Europe in 1787; wrote the first part of *The Rights of Man* in 1791; outlawed from England in 1792; made a French citizen by the National Assembly in 1792; elected to the Convention for Pas de Calais; deprived of his French citizenship in 1793 and imprisoned as an Englishman; released in 1794 and returned to the convention; returned to live in America in 1802.

66. James Chalmers (d. 1806), born in Scotland; lived in the West Indies when young; moved to Philadelphia in 1760 and later to Kent County, Maryland; raised and commanded the Maryland Loyalist Regiment as Lieutenant Colonel; fought at the battle of Germantown; lived in Canada and London after the Revolution. See Adams, "Authorship of *Plain Truth*."

67. The petition to which Price refers was dated March 22, 1776, and was addressed to the king and Parliament. A passage from that petition reads: "We humbly and earnestly beseech your majesty that the most solemn, clear, distinct and unambiguous specification of those just and honourable terms which your majesty, with both houses of Parliament, mean to grant to the Colonies, may precede the dreadful operations of your armament. Every colour and suspicion of injustice and oppression will then be removed from the proceedings of the mother-country; and if those just and honourable terms are not submitted to, your majesty will undoubtedly be enabled to meet what will then be rebellion with the zealous hearts and hands of a determined, loyal, and united people."
The King's reply to that petition reads as follows:
"I deplore, with the deepest concern, the miseries which a great part of my subjects

By these measures, and others of the same kind, those colonists who had all along most dreaded and abhorred independence were at last reconciled to it. I can, however, say from particular information, that even so lately as the month of June last an accommodation might have been obtained with the colonies on a reasonable and moderate plan without giving up any one of the rights claimed by this country except that of altering their characters and disposing of their property. And, as it would have restored peace and prevented the desolating calamities into which America and Britain are now plunged, no friend to humanity can avoid regretting that such a plan, when offered, was not adopted. But our rulers preferred coercion and conquest. And the consequence has been that the colonies, after being goaded and irritated to the utmost, resolved to disengage themselves and directed the Congress to declare them independent states, which was accordingly done, as is well known, on the 4th of July last. Since that time they have probably been making applications to foreign powers and it is to be feared that now we may in vain offer them the very terms for which they once sued. All this is the necessary consequence of the principles by which human nature is governed. There was a time when, perhaps, we should ourselves have acted with more violence and, instead of remonstrating and praying, as America has done, have refused the most advantageous terms when offered with defiance and under an awe from a military force. Had King William, instead of coming over by invitation to deliver us, invaded us and, at the head of an army, offered us the Bill of Rights, we should, perhaps, have spurned at it and considered liberty itself as no better than slavery when enjoyed as a boon from an insolent conqueror. But we have all along acted as if we thought the people of America did not possess the feelings and passions of men, much less of Englishmen. It is indeed strange our ministers did not long ago see that they had mistaken the proper method of treating the colonies and that, though they might be gradually influenced to any thing, they could be dragooned to nothing. Had King James the Second avoided violence and been a little more patient and secret in pursuing his views he might have gained all he wished for. But an eager haste and an open avowal of the odious claims of prerogative ruined him. This has been since considered and a plan both here and in Ireland less expeditious indeed, but more sure, has been pursued.[nn] And had the same plan been pursued in America

nn. I am sorry to differ from those respectable persons who have proposed placing America on the same ground with Ireland. If the same ground of law is meant, it is

in North America have brought upon themselves by an unjustifiable resistance to the constitutional authority of this kingdom; and I shall be ready and happy to alleviate those miseries by acts of mercy and clemency, whenever that authority is established, and the now existing rebellion is at an end. To obtain these salutary purposes, I will invariably pursue the most proper and effectual means." *Documentary History*, 5:462–463.

the whole empire might in time have been brought, without a struggle, to rest itself quietly in the lap of corruption and slavery. It may, therefore, in the issue prove happy to the colonies that they have not been thought worthy of any such cautious treatment. Our coercive measures have done all for them that their warmest patriots could have desired. They have united them among themselves and bound them together under one government. They have checked them in the career of vicious luxury, guarded them against any farther infection from hence, taught them to seek all their resources within themselves, instructed them in the use of arms, and led them to form a naval and military power which may, perhaps, in time, become superior to any force that can attack them, and prove the means of preserving from invasion and violence, a government of justice and virtue, to which the oppressed in every quarter of the globe may fly and find peace, protection, and liberty. In short, these measures have, in all probability, hastened that disruption of the new from the old world which will begin a new era in the annals of mankind and produce a revolution more important, perhaps, than any that has happened in human affairs.[oo] As a friend, therefore, to the general interest of mankind I ought, probably, to rejoice in these measures and to bless that all-governing Providence which, often, out of the evil intended by wretched mortals, brings the greatest

---

already done, for our laws give us the same power over Ireland that we claim over America. If the same ground of practice is meant, it has been most unfortunate for Ireland and would be equally so for America.

oo. See the Abbé Raynal's reflections on this subject at the end of the 18th book of his *History of the European Settlements in the East and West Indies.* "Is it not likely," says this writer, "that the distrust and hatred which have of late taken place of that regard and attachment which the English colonies felt for the parent country may hasten their separation from one another? Every thing conspires to produce this great disruption, the era of which it is impossible to know. Every thing tends to this point: The progress of good in the new hemisphere and the progress of evil in the old. In proportion as our people are weakened, and resign themselves to each other's dominion, population and agriculture will flourish in America and the arts make a rapid progress. And that country rising out of nothing will be fired with the ambition of appearing with glory in its turn on the face of the globe. O posterity! ye, peradventure, will be more happy than your unfortunate and contemptible ancestors." Mr. Justamond's translation.[68]

---

68. The relevant passage reads: "Is it not likely that the distrust and hatred which have of late taken place of that regard and attachment which the provinces formerly felt for the parent country may bring on a separation? Thus everything conspires to produce this great disruption, the era of which it is impossible to know. Every thing tends to show this point; the progress of good in the new hemisphere and the progress of evil in the old. . . . In proportion as our people are weakened and resign themselves to each other's dominion, population and agriculture will flourish in America. The arts, transplanted by our means, will make a rapid progress; and that country, rising out of nothing, will be fired with the ambition of appearing with glory in its turn on the face of the globe and in the history of the world. O posterity! Ye, peradventure, will be more happy than your unfortunate and contemptible ancestors." Guillaume Thomas Francois Raynal, *The Philosophical and Political History of the Settlements and Trade of the Europeans in the East and West Indies* (London: Printed for T. Cadell, 1776), 4:390–391.

good. But when I consider the present sufferings which these measures must occasion, and the castastrophe with which they threaten Great Britain, I am shocked and feel myself incapable of looking forward, without distress, to the fate of an empire, once united and happy, but now torn to pieces and falling a sacrifice to despotic violence and blindness. Under the impression of these sentiments, and dreading the awful crisis before us, I cannot help, however important my voice, crying out to this country. "Make no longer war against *yourselves*. Withdraw your armies from your colonies. Offer your power to them as a protecting, not a destroying power. Grant the security they desire to their property and charters and renounce those notions of dignity which lead you to prefer the exactions of force to the offerings of gratitude and to hazard everything to gain nothing. By such wisdom and equity America may, perhaps, be still preserved and that dreadful breach healed which your enemies are viewing with triumph and all Europe with astonishment."

But what am I doing? At the moment I am writing this the possibility of a reconciliation may be lost. America may have formed an alliance with France. And the die may be cast.

Part III

. . . .

[*Resolution of a Committee of the American Congress in June 1775*]

[69]The paper from which I have taken the following account came into my hands after almost the whole of this work had been printed off. It contains a fact of so much importance that I cannot satisfy myself without laying it before the public. In a committee of Congress in June, 1775, a declaration was drawn up containing an offer to Great Britain, "that the Colonies would not only continue to grant extraordinary aids in time of war, but also, if allowed a free commerce, pay into the sinking fund such a sum annually for one hundred years as should be more than sufficient in that time, if faithfully applied, to extinguish all the present debts of Britain. Or, provided this was not accepted, that, to remove the groundless jealousy of Britain that the Colonies aimed at independence and an abolition of the Navigation Act, which, in turn, they had never intended; and also, to avoid all future disputes about the right of making that and other Acts for regulating their commerce for the general benefit, they would en-

---

69. Price clearly considered this section to be highly important since he includes it both here and at the conclusion of *Observations*. See pp. 122–123.

ter into a covenant with Britain, that she should fully possess and exercise this right for one hundred years to come."

At the end of the *Observations on Civil Liberty* I had the honour of laying before the public the Earl of Shelburne's plan of pacification with the Colonies. In that plan it is particularly proposed that the Colonies should grant an annual supply to be carried to the sinking fund and unalienably appropriated to the discharge of the public debt. It must give this excellent Peer great pleasure to learn, from this resolution, that even this part of his plan, as well as all the other parts, would, most probably, have been accepted by the Colonies. For though the resolution only offers the alternative of either a free trade, with extraordinary aids and an annual supply, or an exclusive trade confirmed and extended, yet there can be little reason to doubt but that to avoid the calamities of the present contest, both would have been consented to; particularly, if, on our part, such a revisal of the laws of trade had been offered as was proposed in Lord Shelburne's plan.

The preceding resolution was, I have said, drawn up in a committee of the Congress. But it was not entered in their minutes, a severe Act of Parliament happening to arrive at that time, which determined them not to give the sum proposed in it.[69]

Observations on the Importance of the American Revolution, and the Means of Making it a Benefit to the World. To which is Added, a letter from M. Turgot, Late Comptroller-General of the Finances of France

To the Free and United States of America, the following Observations are humbly offered, as a last testimony of the good-will of the Author.

Contents

---

1. Appendix and tables not in edition 1 and not included in this volume.

Advertisement[2]

Having reason to hope I should be attended to in the American States and thinking I saw an opening there favourable to the improvement and best interests of mankind I have been induced to convey thither the sentiments and advice contained in the following *Observations*. They were, therefore, originally intended only for America. The danger of a spurious edition has now obliged me to publish them in my own country.

I should be inexcusable did I not take this opportunity to express my gratitude to a distinguished writer (the Count de Mirabeau)[3] for his translation of these *Observations* into French, and for the support and kind civility with which it has been accompanied.

Mr. Turgot's[4] letter formed a part of this tract when it was conveyed to America. I have now given a translation of it.

I think it necessary to add that I have expressed myself in some respects too strongly in the conclusion of the following *Observations*. By accounts from persons the best informed, I have lately been assured that no such dissensions exist among the American States as have been given out in this country, that the new governments are in general well settled and the people happy under them and that, in particular, a conviction is becoming universal of the necessity of giving more strength to that power which forms and which is to conduct and maintain their union.

March, 1785.

Of the Importance of the Revolution which has Established the Independency of the United States.

Having, from pure conviction, taken a warm part in favour of the British colonies (now the United States of America) during the late war, and been exposed, in consequence of this, to much abuse and some danger, it must be supposed that I have been waiting for the issue with anxiety. I am

---

2. Advertisement not in edition 1.

3. Comte Honoré Gabriel Riqueti de Mirabeau (1749–1791), French statesman and author; author of *La traduction d'un pamphlet du docteur Price, intitulé: Observations on the Importance of the American Revolution and the means of making it a benefit to the world; accompagnée de reflexions et de notes traducteur* (London: J. Johnson, 1784).

4. Anne Robert Jacques Turgot (1727–1781), French economist and author; minister of finance (1774–1776).

thankful that my anxiety is removed and that I have been spared to be a witness to that very issue of the war which has been all along the object of my wishes. With heart-felt satisfaction, I see the revolution in favour of universal liberty which has taken place in America, a revolution which opens a new prospect in human affairs, and begins a new era in the history of mankind, a revolution by which Britons themselves will be the greatest gainers, if wise enough to improve properly the check that has been given to the despotism of their ministers and to catch the flame of virtuous liberty which has saved their American brethren.

The late war, in its commencement and progress, did great good by disseminating just sentiments of the rights of mankind and the nature of legitimate government by exciting a spirit of resistance to tyranny which has emancipated one European country and is likely to emancipate others, and by occasioning the establishment in America of forms of government more equitable and more liberal than any that the world has yet known. But in its termination the war has done still greater good by preserving the new governments from that destruction in which they must have been involved, had Britain conquered by providing, in a sequestered continent possessed of many singular advantages, a place of refuge for oppressed men in every region of the world, and by laying the foundation there of an empire which may be the seat of liberty, science and virtue, and from whence there is reason to hope those sacred blessings will spread till they become universal and the time arrives when kings and priests shall have no more power to oppress, and that ignominious slavery which has hitherto debased the world is exterminated. I therefore think I see the hand of Providence in the late war working for the general good.[5]

Reason, as well as tradition and revelation, lead us to expect that a more improved and happy state of human affairs will take place before the consummation of all things. The world has hitherto been gradually improving. Light and knowledge have been gaining ground and human life at present compared with what it once was, is much the same that a youth approaching to manhood is compared with an infant.

Such are the natures of things that this progress must continue. During particular intervals it may be interrupted but it cannot be destroyed. Every present advance prepares the way for farther advances and a single experiment or discovery may sometimes give rise to so many more as suddenly to raise the species higher and to resemble the effects of opening a new sense or of the fall of a spark on a train that springs a mine. For this reason mankind may at last arrive at degrees of improvement which we cannot now even suspect to be possible. A dark age may follow an enlightened age but, in this case, the light, after being smothered for a time, will break

---

5. Edition 1 adds "and can scarcely avoid crying out, It was the Lord's doing."

out again with a brighter lustre. The present age of increased light, considered as succeeding the ages of Greece and Rome and an intermediate period of thick darkness, furnishes a proof of the truth of this observation. There are certain kinds of improvement which, when once made, cannot be entirely lost. During the dark ages the improvements made in the ages that preceded them remained so far as to be recovered immediately at the resurrection of letters and to produce afterwards that more rapid progress in improvement which has distinguished modern times.

There can scarcely be a more pleasing and encouraging object of reflection than this. An accidental observation of the effects of gravity in a garden has been the means of discovering the laws that govern the solar system[a] and of enabling us to look down with pity on the ignorance of the most enlightened times among the ancients. What new dignity has been given to man, and what additions have been made to his powers, by the invention of optical glasses, printing, gun-powder, etc. and by the late discoveries in navigation, mathematics, natural philosophy, etc.?[b][7]

But among the events in modern times tending to the elevation of mankind there are none probably of so much consequence as the recent one which occasions these observations. Perhaps I do not go too far when I say that, next to the introduction of Christianity among mankind, the American revolution may prove the most important step in the progressive course of human development. It is an event which may produce a general diffusion of the principles of humanity and become the means of setting free mankind from the shackles of superstition and tyranny by leading them to see and know "that nothing is fundamental but impartial enquiry, an honest mind, and virtuous practice, that state policy ought not to be applied to the support of speculative opinions and formularies of faith, that the members of a civil community are confederates, not subjects; and

a. This refers to an account given of Sir Isaac Newton in the Preface to Dr. Pemberton's[6] view of his philosophy [Henry Pemberton, *A View of Sir Isaac Newton's Philosophy* (London: Printed by S. Palmer, 1728)].

b. Who could have thought, in the first ages of the world, that mankind would acquire the power of determining the distances and magnitudes of the sun and planets? Who, even at the beginning of this century, would have thought that in a few years mankind would acquire the power of subjecting to their wills the dreadful force of lightning, and of flying in aerostatic machines? The last of these powers, though so long undiscovered, is only an easy application of a power always known. Many similar discoveries may remain to be made which will give new directions of the greatest consequence to human affairs, and it may not be too extravagant to expect that (should civil governments throw no obstacles in the way) the progress of improvement will not cease till it has excluded from the earth most of its worst evils and restored that paradisaical state which, according to the Mosaic history, preceded the present state.[7]

6. Henry Pemberton (1694–1771), physician and writer; member of the Royal Society; close friend of Newton; editor of third edition of Newton's *Principia*; became professor of physics at Gresham College in 1728.

7. Footnote added in edition 2.

their rulers, servants, not masters. And that all legitimate government consists in the dominion of equal laws made with common consent, that is, in the dominion of men over themselves and not in the dominion of communities over communities, or of any men over other men."[c8]

Happy will the world be when these truths shall be everywhere acknowledged and practised upon. Religious bigotry, that cruel demon, will be then laid asleep. Slavish governments and slavish hierarchies will then sink and the old prophecies be verified, "that the last universal empire upon earth shall be the empire of reason and virtue, under which the gospel of peace (better understood) *shall have free course and be glorified, many will run to and fro and knowledge be increased, the wolf dwell with the lamb and the leopard with the kid, and nation no more lift up a sword against nation."*[9]

It is a conviction I cannot resist that the independence of the English colonies in America is one of the steps ordained by Providence to introduce these times and I can scarcely be deceived in this conviction if the United States should escape some dangers which threaten them and will take proper care to throw themselves open to future improvements and to make the most of the advantages of their present situation. Should this happen, it will be true of them as it was of the people of the Jews, that *in them all the families of the earth shall be blessed.*[10] It is scarcely possible they should think too highly of their own consequence. Perhaps, there never existed a people on whose wisdom and virtue more depended or to whom a station of more importance in the plan of Providence has been assigned. They have begun nobly. They have fought with success for themselves and for the world and, in the midst of invasion and carnage, established forms of government favourable in the highest degree to the rights of mankind. But they have much more to do, more indeed than it is possible properly to represent. In this address my design is only to take notice of a few great points which seem particularly to require their attention in order to render them permanently happy in themselves and useful to mankind. On these points I shall deliver my sentiments with freedom, conscious I mean well, but, at the same time, with real diffidence, conscious of my own liableness to error.

c. These are the words of Montesquieu.[8]

---

8. This is the syntax of Price. The words (and phrases) are drawn from Montesquieu's discussion of the republican form of government and the laws in relation to a democratic or free society. The general ideas expressed by Price range throughout *The Spirit of the Laws.* The passages and particular ideas are primarily from Book 11, chapter 6, and from Book 19, chapter 27, but also from Books 1 through 5, particularly bk. 3, chap. 3 and bk. 5, chap. 3. Others are drawn from bk. 12, chaps. 2 and 4; bk. 8, chap. 3; bk. 24, chap. 1; and bks. 25 and 26. Price's footnote added in edition 2.

9. Isaiah 11:6 and 2:4.

10. Genesis 28:14.

Of the Means of Promoting Human Improvement and Happiness in the United States. And first, of Public Debts.

It seems evident that what first requires the attention of the United States is the redemption of their debts and making compensation to that army which has carried them through the war. They have an infant credit to cherish and rear which, if this is not done, must perish and with it their character and honour for ever. Nor is it conceivable they should meet with any great difficulties in doing this. They have a vast resource peculiar to themselves in a continent of unlocated lands possessing every advantage of soil and climate. The settlement of these lands will be repaid,[11] the consequence of which must be a rapid increase of their value. By disposing of them to the army and to emigrants the greatest part of the debts of the United States may probably be sunk immediately. But had they no such resource, they are very capable of bearing taxes sufficient for the purpose of a gradual redemption. Supposing their debts to amount to nine millions sterling, carrying interest at $5\frac{1}{2}$ *per cent.* taxes producing a revenue of a million *per ann.* would pay the interest, and at the same time leave a surplus of half a million *per ann.* for a *sinking fund*, which would discharge the principal in thirteen years. A surplus of a quarter of a million would do the same in $20\frac{1}{2}$ years. After discharging the principal, the appropriated revenue being no longer wanted, might be abolished, and the states eased of the burden of it. But it would be imprudent to abolish it entirely. £100,000 *per ann.* reserved, and faithfully laid out in clearing unlocated lands and other improvements, would in a short time increase to a treasure (or continental patrimony) which would defray the whole expenditure of the union and keep the States free from debts and taxes for ever.[d] Such a reserve would (supposing it improved so as to produce a profit of 5 *per cent*). increase to a capital of three millions in 19 years, 30 million in 57 years, 100 millions in 81 years, and 261 millions in 100 years. But supposing it capable of being improved so as to produce a profit of 10 *per cent.* It would increase to five millions in 19 years, 100 millions in 49 years, and 10,000 millions in 97 years.

It is wonderful that no state has yet thought of taking this method to

---

d. The lands, forests, imposts, etc., etc., which once formed the patrimony of the crown in England, bore most of the expences of government. It is well for this kingdom that the extravagance of the crown has been the means of alienating this patrimony, for the consequence has been making the crown dependent on the people. But in America such a patrimony would be continental property, capable of being applied only to public purposes, in the way which the public (or its delegates) would approve.

11. Edition 1 reads "rapid."

make itself great and rich. The smallest appropriation in a sinking fund, never diverted, operates in cancelling debts, just as money increases at compound interest and is, therefore, omnipotent.[e] But, if diverted, it loses all its power. Britain affords a striking proof of this. Its sinking fund (once the hope of the kingdom) has, by the practice of alienating it, been rendered impotent and useless. Had it been inviolably applied to the purposes for which it was intended, there would, in the year 1775, have been a surplus in the revenue of more than five millions *per ann*. But instead of this we were then encumbered with a debt of 137 millions, carrying an interest of near 4½ millions and leaving no surplus of any consequence. This debt has been since increased to 280 millions, carrying an interest (including expences of management) of nine millions and a half.[f][12] A monstrous bubble—and [13]if no very strong measures are soon taken to reduce[13] it within the limits of safety it must[14] produce a dreadful convulsion. Let the United States take warning. Their debts at present are moderate. A sinking fund, guarded against misapplication,[g] may soon extinguish them and prove a resource in all events of the greatest importance.[15]

I must not, however, forget that there is *one* of their debts on which no sinking fund can have any effect and which it is impossible for them to discharge. A debt, greater, perhaps, than has been ever due from any country and which will be deeply felt by their latest posterity. But it is a debt of *gratitude* only, of gratitude to that General who has been raised up by Providence to make them free and independent and whose name must shine among the first in the future annals of the benefactors of mankind.

The measure now proposed may preserve America forever from too great an accumulation of debts and, consequently, of taxes—an evil which is likely to be the ruin not only of Britain but of other European states. But there are measures of yet greater consequence which I wish ardently to recommend and inculcate.

e. One penny put out at our Saviour's birth to 5 per cent. compound interest would, before this time, have increased to a greater sum than would be contained in two hundred millions of earth's all solid gold. But if put out to simple interest it would have amounted to no more than seven shillings and six-pence. All governments which alienate funds destined for reimbursements choose to improve money in the last rather than the first of these ways.

f. See the Postscript to a pamphlet entitled, *The State of the Finances of the Kingdom, at Signing the Preliminary Articles of Peace in January 1783*, printed for Mr. Cadell. [By Richard Price.][12]

g. When not thus guarded public funds become the worst evils by giving to the rulers of states a command of revenue for the purposes of corruption.

12. Footnote not in edition 1.

13. Edition 1 reads "as no effectual measures are likely to be taken (or perhaps can now be taken) for reducing."

14. Edition 1 inserts "some time or other."

15. Edition 1 adds: "Let such a fund be established. Could a sacredness be given it like that of the ark of God among the Jews, it would do the same service."

For the sake of mankind, I wish to see every measure adopted that can have a tendency to preserve peace in America and to make it an open and fair stage for discussion and the seat of perfect liberty.

Of Peace,
And the Means of Perpetuating it.

Civil government is an expedient for collecting the wisdom and force of a community or confederacy in order to preserve its peace and liberty against every hostile invasion, whether from within or from without. In the latter of these respects, the United States are happily secured but they are far from being equally happy in the former respect. Having now, in consequence of their successful resistance of the invasion of Britain, united to their remoteness from Europe, no external enemy to fear, they are in danger of fighting with one another. This is their greatest danger and providing securities against it is their hardest work. Should they fail in this America may some time or other be turned into a scene of blood and instead of being the hope and refuge of the world may become a terror to it.

When a dispute arises among individuals in a state an appeal is made to a court of law, that is, to the wisdom and justice of the state. The court decides. The losing party acquiesces or, if he does not, the power of the state forces him to submission and thus the effects of contention are suppressed and peace is maintained. In a way similar to this peace may be maintained between any number of confederated states and I can almost imagine that it is not impossible but that by such means universal peace may be produced and all war excluded from the world. Why may we not hope to see this begun in America? The Articles of Confederation make considerable advances towards it. When a dispute arises between any of the states they order an appeal to Congress, an enquiry by Congress, a hearing, and a decision.[16] But here they stop. What is most of all necessary is omitted. No provision is made for enforcing the decisions of Congress and this renders them inefficient and futile. I am by no means qualified to point out the best method of removing this defect. Much must be given up for this purpose, nor is it easy to give up too much. Without all doubt the powers of Congress must be enlarged. In particular, a power must be given it to collect, on certain emergencies, the force of the confederacy, and to employ it in carrying its decisions into execution. A state against which a

16. The Articles of Confederation and Perpetual Union, art. 9. See *Federal and State Constitutions*, pt. 1, pp. 9–11.

decision is made will yield of course when it knows that such a force exists and that it allows no hope from resistance.

By this force I do not mean a standing army. God forbid that standing armies should ever find an establishment in America. They are everywhere the grand supports of arbitrary power and the chief causes of the depression of mankind. No wise people will trust their defence out of their own hands or consent to hold their rights at the mercy of armed slaves. Free states ought to be bodies of armed citizens, well regulated and well disciplined, and always ready to turn out, when properly called upon, to execute the laws, to quell riots, and to keep the peace. Such, if I am rightly informed, are the citizens of America. Why then may not Congress be furnished with a power of calling out from the confederated states quotas of militia sufficient to force at once the compliance of any state which may show an inclination to break the union by resisting its decisions?

I am very sensible that it will be difficult to guard such a power against abuse and, perhaps, better means of answering this end are discoverable. In human affairs, however, the choice generally offered us is "of two evils to take the least." We choose the restraint of civil government because a less evil than anarchy and, in like manner, in the present instance, the danger of the abuse of power and of its being employed sometimes to enforce wrong decisions, must be submitted to, because a less evil than the misery of intestine wars. Much, however, may be done to lessen this danger. Such regulations as those in the ninth of the Articles of Confederation will, in a great measure, prevent hasty and partial decisions. The rotation established by the fifth article will prevent that corruption of character which seldom fails to be produced by the long possession of power, and the right reserved to every state of recalling its delegates when dissatisfied with them, will keep them constantly responsible and cautious.

The observations now made must be extended to money transactions. Congress must be trusted with a power of procuring supplies for defraying the expenses of the confederation, of contracting debts, and providing funds for discharging them; and this power must not be capable of being defeated by the opposition of any minority in the states.

In short, the credit of the United States, their strength, their respectableness abroad, their liberty at home, and even their existence, depend on the preservation of a firm political union; and such an union cannot be preserved without giving all possible weight and energy to the authority of that delegation which constitutes the union.

Would it not be proper to take periodical surveys of the different states, their numbers of both sexes in every stage of life, their condition, occupations, property, etc.? Would not such surveys, in conjunction with accurate registers of births, marriages and deaths at all ages, afford much important instruction by showing that laws govern human mortality, and what situations, employments, and civil institutions are most favourable to the health and happiness of mankind? Would they not keep constantly in view the progress of population in the states and the increase or decline of their resources? But, more especially, are they not the only means of procuring the necessary information for determining accurately and equitably the proportions of men and money to be contributed by each state for supporting and strengthening the confederation?

Of Liberty.

The next point I would insist on, as an object of supreme importance, is the establishment of such a system of perfect liberty, religious as well as civil, in America as shall render it a country where truth and reason shall have fair play and the human powers find full scope for exerting themselves and for showing how far they can carry human improvement.

The faculties of man have hitherto, in all countries, been more or less cramped by the interference of civil authority in matters of speculation, by tyrannical laws against heresy and schism, and by slavish hierarchies and religious establishments. It is above all things desirable that no such fetters on reason should be admitted into America. I observe, with inexpressible satisfaction, that at present they have no existence there. In this respect the governments of the United States are liberal to a degree that is unparalleled. They have the distinguished honour of being the first states under heaven in which forms of government have been established favourable to universal liberty. They have been thus distinguished in their infancy. What then will they be in a more advanced state, when time and experience, and the concurring assistance of the wise and virtuous in every part of the earth shall have introduced into the new governments corrections and amendments which will render them still more friendly to liberty and more the means of promoting human happiness and dignity? May we not see the dawning of brighter days on earth and a new creation rising. But I must check myself. I am in danger of being carried too far by the ardor of my hopes.

The liberty I mean includes in it liberty of conduct in all civil matters, liberty of discussion in all speculative matters, and liberty of conscience in all religious matters. And it is then perfect when under no restraint except when used to injure any one in his person, property, or good name, that is, except when used to destroy itself.

In liberty of discussion, I include the liberty of examining all public measures and the conduct of all public men and of writing and publishing on all speculative and doctrinal points.

Of Liberty of Discussion.

It is a common opinion that there are some doctrines so sacred, and others of so bad a tendency, that no public discussion of them ought to be allowed. Were this a right opinion all the persecution that has been ever practised would be justified. For, if it is a part of the duty of civil magistrates to prevent the discussion of such doctrines, they must, in doing this, act on their own judgments of the nature and tendency of doctrines and, consequently, they must have a right to prevent the discussion of all doctrines which they think to be too sacred for discussion or too dangerous in their tendency and this right they must exercise in the only way in which civil power is capable of exercising it, "by inflicting penalties on all who oppose sacred doctrines, or who maintain pernicious opinions." In Mohammedan countries, therefore, civil magistrates have a right to silence and punish all who oppose the divine mission of Mohammed, a doctrine there reckoned of the most sacred nature. The like is true of the doctrines of transubstantiation, worship of the Virgin Mary, etc. in Popish countries, and of the doctrines of the Trinity, satisfaction, etc. in Protestant countries. In England itself, this principle has been acted upon and produced the laws which subject to severe penalties all who write or speak against the supreme divinity of Christ, the Book of Common Prayer, and the Church Articles of Faith. All such laws are right, if the opinion I have mentioned is right. But in reality civil power has nothing to do with any such matters and civil governors go miserably out of their proper province whenever they take upon them the care of truth, or the support of any doctrinal points. They are not judges of truth and if they pretend to decide about it they will decide wrong. This all the countries under heaven think of the application of civil power to doctrinal points in every country but their own. It is, indeed, superstition, idolatry, and nonsense, that civil power at present supports almost everywhere under the idea of supporting sacred truth and opposing dangerous error. Would not, therefore, its perfect neutrality be the greatest blessing? Would not the interest of truth gain unspeakably were all the rulers of states to aim at nothing but keeping the peace, or did they consider themselves as bound to take care, not of the future, but the present interest of men, not of their souls and their faith but of their persons and property, not of any ecclesiastical, but secular matters only?

All the experience of past time proves that the consequence of allowing civil power to judge of the nature and tendency of doctrines must be making it a hindrance to the progress of truth and an enemy to the improvement of the world.

Anaxagoras was tried and condemned in Greece for teaching that the sun and stars were not deities but masses of corruptible matter. Accusations of a like kind contributed to the death of Socrates. The threats of bigots and the fear of persecution prevented Copernicus from publishing, during his whole lifetime, his discovery of the true system of the world. Galileo was obliged to renounce the doctrine of the motion of the earth and suffered a year's imprisonment for having asserted it. And so lately as the year 1742, the best commentary on the first production of human genius (Newton's *Principia*) was not allowed to be printed at Rome because it asserted this doctrine and the learned commentators were obliged to prefix to their work a declaration that on this point they submitted to the decisions of the supreme pontiffs. Such have been and such (while men continue blind and ignorant) will always be the consequence of the interposition of civil governments in matters of speculation.

When men associate for the purpose of civil government they do it not to defend truth or to support formularies of faith and speculative opinions but to defend their civil rights and to protect one another in the free exercise of their mental and corporeal powers. The interference, therefore, of civil authority in such cases is directly contrary to the end of its institution. The way in which it can best promote the interest and dignity of mankind (as far as they can be promoted by the discovery of truth) is by encouraging them to search for truth wherever they can find it and by protecting them in doing this against the attacks of malevolence and bigotry. Should any attempt be made by contending sects to injure one another, its power will come in properly to crush the attempt and to maintain for all sects equal liberty by punishing every encroachment upon it. The conduct of a civil magistrate, on such an occasion, should be that of Gallio the wise Roman proconsul who, on receiving an accusation of the apostle Paul, would not listen to it, but drove from his presence the accusers who had laid violent hands upon him, after giving them the following admonition: "If it were a matter of wrong or wicked lewdness, reason would require that I should bear with you. But if it be a question of words and names and the law, look you to it. For I will be no judge of such matters." (Acts xviii.12, etc.) How much happier would the world have been had all magistrates acted in this manner? Let America learn this important lesson and profit by the experience of past times. A dissent from established opinions and doctrines has indeed often miserably disturbed society and produced mischief and bloodshed. But it should be remembered that this has been owing to the establishment of the points dissented from and the use of civil power to enforce the reception of them. Had civil government done its duty, left all free, and employed itself in procuring instead of restraining fair discussion, all mischief would have been avoided and mankind would have been raised higher than they are in knowledge and improvement.

When Christianity, that first and best of all the means of human improvement, was first preached it was charged with turning the world upside down. The leaders of Jewish and pagan establishments were alarmed and by opposing the propagation of it converted a religion of peace and love into an occasion of violence and slaughter and thus verified our Lord's prophecy, that he was come *not to send peace, but a sword on earth.*[17] All this was the effect of the misapplication of the powers of government. Instead of creating, they should have been employed in preventing such mischief and been active only in causing the Christian cause to receive a fair hearing and guarding the propagators of it against insult. The like observation may be made concerning the first reformers. What we all see would have been right in pagan and Popish governments with respect to Christianity and the Reformation would it not be now right in Christian or Protestant governments, were any attempts made to propagate a new religion or any doctrines advanced opposite to those now held sacred? Such attempts, if unsupported by reason and evidence, would soon come to nothing. An imposture[18] cannot stand the test of fair and open examination. On the contrary, the cause of truth will certainly be served by it. Mohammedanism would have sunk as soon as it rose, had no other force than that of evidence been employed to propagate it; and it is an unspeakable recommendation of Christianity that it made its way till it became the religion of the world in one of its most enlightened periods, by evidence only, in opposition to the strongest exertions of civil power. There cannot be a more striking proof that nothing but fair discussion is necessary to suppress error and to propagate truth. I am grieved, indeed, whenever I find any Christians showing a disposition to call in the aid of civil power to defend their religion. Nothing can be more disgraceful to it. If it wants such aid it cannot be of God. Its corruption and debasement took place from the moment that civil power took it under its patronage and this corruption and debasement increased till at last it was converted into a system of absurdity and superstition more gross and more barbarous than paganism itself. The religion of Christ disclaims all connexion with the civil establishments of the world. It has suffered infinitely by their friend-

17. Matthew 10:34.
18. Edition 1 reads "imposter."

ship. Instead of silencing its opponents let them be encouraged to produce their strongest arguments against it. The experience of Britain has lately shown that this will only cause it to be better understood and more firmly believed.

I would extend these observations to all points of faith, however sacred they may be deemed. Nothing reasonable can suffer by discussion. All doctrines really sacred must be clear and incapable of being opposed with success. If civil authority interposes it will be to support some misconception or abuse of them.

That immoral tendency of doctrines which has been urged as a reason against allowing the public discussion of them must be either avowed and direct or only a consequence with which they are charged. If it is avowed and direct such doctrines certainly will not spread. The principles rooted in human nature will resist them and the advocates of them will be soon disgraced. If, on the contrary, it is only a consequence with which a doctrine is charged, it should be considered how apt all parties are to charge the doctrines they oppose with bad tendencies. It is well known, that Calvinists and Arminians, Trinitarians and Socinians, Fatalists and Freewillers, are continually exclaiming against one another's opinions as dangerous and licentious. Even Christianity itself could not, at its first introduction, escape this accusation. The professors of it were considered as atheists because they opposed pagan idolatry and their religion was on this account reckoned a destructive and pernicious enthusiasm. If, therefore, the rulers of a state are to prohibit the propagation of all doctrines in which they apprehend immoral tendencies an opening will be made, as I have before observed, for every species of persecution. There will be no doctrine, however true or important, the avowal of which will not in some country or other be subjected to civil penalties. Undoubtedly, there are doctrines which have such tendencies. But the tendencies of speculative opinions have often very little effect on practice. The Author of nature has planted in the human mind principles and feelings which will operate in opposition to any theories that may seem to contradict them. Every sect, whatever may be its tenets, has some salvo for the necessity of virtue. The philosophers who hold that matter and motion have no existence except in our own ideas are capable of believing this only in their closets. The same is true of the philosophers who hold that nothing exists but matter and motion and at the same time teach that man has no self-determining power, that an unalterable fate governs all things, and that no one is any thing that he can avoid being or does any thing that he can avoid doing. These philosophers when they come out into the world act as other men do. Common sense never fails to get the better of their theories and I know that many of them are some of the best [19]as well as the ablest[19] men in the

---

19. Not in edition 1.

world and the warmest friends to the true interests of society. Though their doctrine may seem to furnish an apology for vice their practice is an exhibition of virtue and a government which would silence them would greatly injure itself. Only overt acts of injustice, violence or defamation, come properly under the cognizance of civil power. Were a person now to go about London teaching that "property is founded in grace," I should, were I a magistrate, let him alone while he did nothing but teach, without being under any other apprehension than that he would soon find a lodging in Bedlam. But were he to attempt to carry his doctrine into its consequences by actually stealing, under the pretence of his right as a saint to the property of his neighbours, I should think it my duty to lay hold of him as a felon without regarding the opinion from which he acted.

I am persuaded that few or no inconveniences would arise from such a liberty. If magistrates will do their duty as soon as violence begins or any overt acts which break the peace are committed no great harm will arise from their keeping themselves neutral till then. Let, however, the contrary be supposed. Let it be granted that civil authority will in this case often be too late in its exertions; the just inference will be, not that the liberty I plead for ought not be allowed but that there will be two evils between which an option must be made and the least of which must be preferred. One is the evil just mentioned. The other includes in it every evil which can arise from making the rulers of states judges of the tendency of doctrines, subjecting freedom of enquiry to the control of their ignorance, and perpetuating darkness, intolerance and slavery. I need not say which of these evils is the least.

Of Liberty of Conscience and Civil Establishments of Religion.

In liberty of conscience I include much more than toleration. Jesus Christ has established a perfect equality among his followers. His command is that they shall assume no jurisdiction over one another and acknowledge no master besides himself. It is, therefore, presumption in any of them to claim a right to any superiority or pre-eminence over their brethren. Such a claim is implied whenever any of them pretend to tolerate the rest. Not only all Christians but all men of all religions ought to be considered by a state as equally entitled to its protection as far as they demean themselves honestly and peaceably. Toleration can take place only where there is a civil establishment of a particular mode of religion, that is, where a predominant sect enjoys exclusive advantages and makes the encouragement of its own mode of faith and worship a part of the constitution of the state but at the same time thinks fit to suffer the exercise of other modes of faith and worship. Thanks be to God, the new American States are at present strangers to such establishments. In this respect, as well as many others, they have shown, in framing their constitutions, a degree of wisdom and liberality which is above all praise.

Civil establishments of formularies of faith and worship are inconsistent with the rights of private judgment. They engender strife. They turn religion into a trade. They shore up error. They produce hypocrisy and prevarication. They lay an undue bias on the human mind in its enquiries and obstruct the progress of truth. Genuine religion is a concern that lies entirely between God and our own souls. It is incapable of receiving any aid from human laws. It is contaminated as soon as worldly motives and sanctions mix their influence with it. Statesmen should countenance it only by exhibiting in their own example a conscientious regard to it in those forms which are most agreeable to their own judgments and by encouraging their fellow citizens in doing the same. They cannot as public men give it any other assistance. All besides that has been called a public leading in religion, has done it an essential injury, and produced some of the worst consequences.

The Church Establishment in England is one of the mildest [20]and best[20] sort. But even here what a snare has it been to integrity? And what a check to free enquiry? What dispositions favourable to despotism has it fostered? What a turn to pride and narrowness and domination has it given the clerical character? What struggles has it produced in its members to accommodate their opinions to the subscriptions and tests which it imposes? What a perversion of learning has it occasioned to defend obsolete creeds and absurdities? What a burden is it on the consciences of some of its best clergy who, in consequence of being bound down to a system they do not approve, and having no support except that which they derive from conforming to it, find themselves under the hard necessity of either prevaricating or starving? No one doubts but that the English clergy in general could with more truth declare that they do not, than that they do, give their unfeigned assent to all and every thing contained in the thirty-nine articles and the Book of Common Prayer and yet, with a solemn declaration to this purpose, are they obliged to enter upon an office which above all offices requires those who exercise it to be examples of simplicity and sincerity. Who can help execrating the cause of such an evil?

But what I wish most to urge is the tendency of religious establishments to impede the improvement of the world. They are boundaries prescribed by human folly to human investigation and enclosures which intercept the light and confine the exertions of reason. Let any one imagine to himself

20. Added in edition 2.

what effects similar establishments would have in philosophy, navigation, metaphysics, medicine, or mathematics. Something like this took place in logic and philosophy while the *ipse dixit* of Aristotle and the nonsense of the schools maintained an authority like that of the creeds of churchmen. And the effect was a longer continuance of the world in the ignorance and barbarity of the dark ages. But civil establishments of religion are more pernicious. So apt are mankind to misrepresent the character of the Deity and to connect his favour with particular modes of faith that it must be expected that a religion so settled will be what it has hitherto been—a gloomy and cruel superstition bearing the name of religion.

It has been long a subject of dispute, which is worst in its effects on society, such a religion or speculative atheism. For my own part, I could almost give the preference to the latter. Atheism is so repugnant to every principle of common sense that it is not possible it should ever gain much ground or become very prevalent. On the contrary, there is a particular proneness in the human mind to superstition and nothing is more likely to become prevalent. Atheism leaves us to the full influence of most of our natural feelings and social principles and these are so strong in their operation that in general they are a sufficient guard to the order of society. But superstition counteracts these principles by holding forth men to one another as objects of divine hatred and by putting them on harassing, silencing, imprisoning and burning one another in order to do God service. Atheism is a sanctuary for vice by taking away the motives to virtue arising from the will of God and the fear of a future judgment. But superstition is more a sanctuary for vice by teaching men ways of pleasing God without moral virtue and by leading them even to compound for wickedness by ritual services, by bodily penances and mortifications, by adorning shrines, going [on] pilgrimages, saying many prayers, receiving absolutions from the priest, exterminating heretics, etc. Atheism destroys the sacredness and obligation of an oath. But [21] has there not been also a religion (so called) which has done this by leading its professors to a persuasion that there exists a power on earth[21] which can dispense with the obligations of oaths, that pious frauds are right, and that faith is not to be kept with heretics?

It is indeed only a rational and liberal religion, a religion founded on just notions of the Deity as a being who regards equally every sincere worshipper and by whom all are alike favoured as far as they act up to the light they enjoy, a religion which consists in the imitation of the moral perfections of an almighty but benevolent governor of nature who directs for the best all events, in confidence in the care of his providence, in resignation to his will, and in the faithful discharge of every duty of piety and morality from a regard to his authority and the apprehensions of a

---

21. Edition 1 reads ". . . is there not also a religion (so called) which does this by teaching that there is a power . . . ."

future righteous retribution. It is only *this* religion (the inspiring principle of every thing fair and worthy and joyful and which in truth is nothing but the love of God and man and virtue warming the heart and directing the conduct)—it is only *this* kind of religion that can bless the world or be an advantage to society. This is the religion that every enlightened friend to mankind will be zealous to promote. But it is a religion that the powers of the world know little of and which will always be best promoted by being left free and open.

I cannot help adding here that such in particular is the *Christian* religion. Christianity teaches us that there is none good but one, that is, God, that he willeth all men to be saved and will punish nothing but wickedness, that he desires mercy and not sacrifice (benevolence rather than rituals), that loving him with all our hearts, and loving our neighbour as ourselves, is the whole of our duty, and that in every nation he that feareth him and worketh righteousness is accepted of him. It rests its authority on the power of God, not of man, refers itself entirely to the understandings of men, makes us the subjects of a kingdom that is not of this world, and requires us to elevate our minds above temporal emoluments and to look forwards to a state beyond the grave where a government of perfect virtue will be erected under that Messiah who has *tasted death for every man*.[22] What have the powers of the world to do with such a religion? It disclaims all connection with them, it made its way at first in opposition to them and, as far as it is now upheld by them, it is dishonoured and vilified.

The injury which civil establishments do to Christianity may be learnt from the following considerations.

First, the spirit of religious establishments is opposite to the spirit of Christianity. It is a spirit of pride and tyranny in opposition to the Christian lowly spirit, a contracted and selfish spirit, in opposition to the Christian enlarged and benevolent spirit, the spirit of the world in opposition to the Christian heavenly spirit.

Secondly, religious establishments are founded on a claim of authority in the Christian church which overthrows Christ's authority. He has in the scriptures given his followers a code of laws to which he requires them to adhere as their only guide. But the language of the framers of church establishments is, "We have authority in controversies of faith and power to decree rites and ceremonies. We are the deputies of Christ upon earth who have been commissioned by him to interpret his laws and to rule his church. You must therefore follow us. The scriptures are insufficient. Our interpretations you must receive as Christ's laws, our creeds as his doctrine, our inventions as his institutions."

It is evident, as the excellent Hoadly has shown, that these claims turn Christ out of the government of his own kingdom and place usurpers on

---

22. Hebrews 2:9.

his throne. They are therefore derogatory to his honour and a submission to them is a breach of the allegiance due to him. They have been almost fatal to true Christianity and attempts to enforce them by civil penalties have watered the Christian world with the blood of saints and martyrs.

Thirdly, the difficulty of introducing alterations into church establishments after they have been once formed is another objection to them. Hence it happens that they remain always the same amidst all changes of public manners and opinions[h] and that a kingdom even of Christians may go on for ages in idolatrous worship after a general conviction may have taken place that there is but one [23]being who is the proper object of religious adoration and that this one being is that one only living and true God who sent Christ into the world and who is his, no less than he is our, God and father.[23] What a sad scene of religious hypocrisy must such a discordance between public conviction and the public forms produce?

At this day in some European countries the absurdity and slavishness of their hierarchies are seen and acknowledged but, being incorporated with the state, it is scarcely possible to get rid of them.

What can be more striking than the state of England in this respect? The system of faith and worship established in it was formed above two hundred years ago when Europe was just emerging from darkness and barbarity. The times have since been growing more enlightened but without any effect on the establishment. Not a ray of the increasing light has penetrated it. Not one imperfection, however gross, has been removed. The same articles of faith are subscribed. The same ritual of devotion is practised. There is reason to fear that the absolution of the sick, which forms a part of this ritual, is often resorted to as a passport to heaven after a wicked life and yet it is continued. Perhaps nothing more shocking to reason and humanity ever made a part of a religious system than the damning clauses in the Athanasian creed and yet the obligation of the clergy to declare assent to this creed, and to read it as a part of the public devotion, remains.

The necessary consequence of such a state of things is that, fourthly, Christianity itself is disgraced and that all religion comes to be considered as a state trick and a barbarous mummery. It is well known that in some Popish countries there are few Christians among the higher ranks of men, the religion of the state being in those countries mistaken for the religion of the Gospel. This indeed shows a criminal inattention in those who fall

---

h. This is an inconvenience attending civil as well as ecclesiastical establishments which has been with great wisdom guarded against in the new American constitutions by appointing that there shall be a revisal of them at the end of certain terms. This will leave them always open to improvement without any danger of those convulsions which have usually attended the correction of abuses when they have [ac]quired a sacredness by time.

---

23. Edition 1 reads "object of religious worship, namely, the God and Father of our Lord Jesus Christ."

into such a mistake, for they ought to consider that Christianity has been grievously corrupted and that their ideas of it should be taken from the New Testament only. It is, however, so natural to reckon Christianity to be that which it is held out to be in all the establishments of it, that it cannot but happen that such an error will take place and produce some of the worst consequences. There is probably a greater number of rational Christians (that is, of Christians upon enquiry) in England than in all Popish countries. The reason is that the religious establishment here is Popery reformed and that a considerable body dissent from it and are often inculcating the necessity of distinguishing between the Christianity established by law and that which is taught in the Bible. Certain it is that, till this distinction is made, Christianity can never recover its just credit and usefulness.

Such then are the effects of civil establishments of religion. May heaven soon put an end to them. The world will never be generally wise or virtuous or happy till these enemies to its peace and improvement are demolished. Thanks be to God, they are giving way before increasing light. Let them never show themselves in America. Let no such monster be known there as human authority in matters of religion. Let every honest and peaceable man, whatever is his faith, be protected there and find an effectual defence against the attacks of bigotry and intolerance. In the United States may religion flourish. They cannot be very great and happy if it does not. But let it be a better religion than most of those which have been hitherto professed in the world. Let it be a religion which enforces moral obligations, not a religion which relaxes and evades them, a tolerant and catholic religion, not a rage for proselytism, a religion of peace and charity, not a religion that persecutes, curses and damns. In a word, let it be the genuine Gospel of peace lifting above the world, warming the heart with the love of God and his creatures, and sustaining the fortitude of good men by the assured hope of a future deliverance from death and an infinite reward in the everlasting kingdom of our Lord and Saviour.

From the preceding observations it may be concluded that it is impossible I should not admire the following article in the declaration of rights which forms the foundation of the Massachusetts constitution. "In this state every denomination of Christians demeaning themselves peaceable and as good subjects of the commonwealth shall be equally under the protection of the law and no subordination of any one sect or denomination to another shall ever be established by law."[i,24]

i. The North Carolina constitution also orders that there shall be no establishment of any one religious church or denomination in that state in preference to any other.[25]

---

24. Mass. Const. pt. 1, art. 3 (1780). The relevant passage reads: "And every denomination of Christians, demeaning themselves peaceably and as good subjects of the commonwealth, shall be equally under the protection of the law; and no subordination of any

This is liberal beyond all example. I should, however, have admired it more had it been more liberal and the words, *all men of all religions* been substituted for the words, *every denomination of Christians.*

It appears farther from the preceding observations that I cannot but dislike the religious tests which make a part of several of the American constitutions. In the Massachusetts constitution it is ordered that all who take seats in the House of Representatives or Senate shall declare "their firm persuasion of the truth of the Christian religion."[26] The same is required by the Maryland constitution as a condition of being admitted into any places of profit or trust.[27] In Pennsylvania every member of the House of Representatives is required to declare that he "acknowledges the Scriptures of the Old and New Testament to be given by divine inspiration."[28] In the state of Delaware, that "he believes in God the Father, and in Jesus Christ his only Son, and in the Holy Ghost, one God blessed for evermore."[29] All this is more than is required even in England where, though every person however debauched or atheistical is required to receive the sacrament as a qualification for inferior places, no other religious test is imposed on members of parliament than a declaration against popery. It is an observation no less just than common that such tests exclude only honest men. The dishonest never scruple them.

Montesquieu probably was not a Christian. Newton and Locke were not Trinitarians and therefore not Christians according to the commonly received ideas of Christianity. Would the United States, for this reason, deny such men, were they living, all places of trust and power among them?

---

one sect or denomination to another shall ever be established by law." *Federal and State Constitutions*, pt. 1, pp. 957–958.

25. N.C. Const. art. 34 (1776). See *Federal and State Constitutions*, pt. 2, pp. 1413–1414.

26. Mass Const. ch. 6, art. 1 (1780). The relevant passage reads:

"Any person chosen governor, lieutenant-governor, councillor, senator, or representative, and accepting the trust, shall, before he proceed to execute the duties of his place or office, make and subscribe the following declaration, viz:

" 'I, A. B., do declare that I believe the Christian religion, and have a firm persuasion of its truth. . . .' " *Federal and State Constitutions*, pt. 1, p. 970.

27. Md. Const. art. 55 (1776). See *Federal and State Constitutions*, pt. 1, p. 828.

28. See footnote 24 to the *General Introduction*, pp. 54–55.

29. Del. Const. art. 22 (1776). The relevant passage reads:

"Every person who shall be chosen a member of either house, or appointed to any office or place of trust, before taking his seat, or entering upon the execution of his office, . . .

". . . [shall] make and subscribe the following declaration, to wit:

" 'I, A B, do profess faith in God the Father, and in Jesus Christ His only Son, and in the Holy Ghost, one God, blessed for evermore; and I do acknowledge the holy scriptures of the Old and New Testament to be given by divine inspiration." *Federal and State Constitutions*, pt. 1, p. 276.

Of Education.

Such is the state of things which I wish to take place in the united American states. In order to introduce and perpetuate it, and at the same time to give it the greatest effect on the improvement of the world, nothing is more necessary than the establishment of a wise and liberal plan of education. It is impossible properly to represent the importance of this. So much is left by the author of nature to depend on the turn given to the mind in early life, and the impressions then made, that I have often thought there may be a secret remaining to be discovered in education which will cause future generations to grow up virtuous and happy and accelerate human improvement to a greater degree than can at present be imagined.

The end of education is to direct the powers of the mind in unfolding themselves and to assist them in gaining their just bent and force. And, in order to do this, its business should be to teach how to think, rather than what to think; or to lead into the best way of searching for truth, rather than to instruct in truth itself. As for the latter, who is qualified for it? There are many indeed who are eager to undertake this office. All parties and sects think they have discovered truth and are confident that they alone are its advocates and friends. But the very different and inconsistent accounts they give of it demonstrate they are utter strangers to it and that it is better to teach nothing than to teach what they hold out for truth. The greater their confidence, the greater is the reason for distrusting them. We generally see the warmest zeal where the object of it is the greatest nonsense.

Such observations have a particular tendency to show that education ought to be an initiation into candour rather than into any systems of faith, and that it should form a habit of cool and patient investigation rather than an attachment to any opinions.

But hitherto education has been conducted on a contrary plan. It has been a contraction, not an enlargement of the intellectual faculties, an injection of false principles hardening them in error, not a discipline enlightening and improving them. Instead of opening and strengthening them, and teaching to think freely, it hath cramped and enslaved them and qualified for thinking only in one track. Instead of instilling humility, charity, and liberality, and thus preparing for an easier discovery and a readier admission of truth, it has inflated with conceit and stuffed the human mind with wretched prejudices.[j]

j. [At the end of the English translation of Turgot's letter in edition 2, Price indicates that the following footnote should be inserted here: "The imperfection of real knowledge may often produce unreasonable incredulity. Had the best philosophers been told a few years ago 'that there existed fishes which had the command of lightning and which

The more has been learnt from such education, the more it becomes necessary to unlearn. The more has been taught in this way, of so much the more must the mind be emptied before true wisdom can enter. Such was education in the time of the first teachers of Christianity. By furnishing with skill in the arts of disputation and sophistry, and producing an attachment to establish systems, it turned the minds of men from truth and rendered them more determined to resist evidence and more capable of evading it. Hence it happened that this heavenly instruction, when first communicated, was to the Jews a stumbling block, and to the Greeks foolishness and that, in spite of miracles themselves, the persons who rejected with most disdain, and who opposed it with most violence, were those who had been educated in colleges and were best versed in the false learning of the times. And had it taught the true philosophy instead of the true religion, the effect would have been the same. The doctrine "that the sun stood still, and that the earth moved around it," would have been reckoned no less absurd and incredible, than the doctrine of a crucified Messiah. And the men who would have treated such an instruction with most contempt would have been the wise and the prudent, that is, the proud sophists and learned doctors of the times, who had studied the Ptolemaic system of the world and learnt, by cycles and epicycles, to account for all the motions of the heavenly bodies.

In like manner, when the improvement of Logic in Mr. Locke's *Essay on the Human Understanding* was first published in Britain, the persons readiest to attend to it and to receive it were those who had never been trained in colleges and whose minds, therefore, had never been perverted by an instruction in the jargon of the schools. To the deep professors of the time it appeared (like the doctrine taught in his book on the reasonableness of Christianity) to be a dangerous novelty and heresy and the University of Oxford, in particular, condemned and reprobated the author. The like happened when Sir Isaac Newton's discoveries were first published. A romance (that is, the philosophy of Descartes) was then in possession of the philosophical world. Education had rivetted it in the minds of the learned and it was twenty-seven years before Newton's *Principia* could gain sufficient credit to bring it to a second edition. Such are the prejudices which have generally prevailed against new lights. Such the impediments which have been thrown in the way of improvement by a narrow plan of education. Even now the principal object of education (especially in divinity) is to teach established systems as certain truths and to qualify for successfully defending them against opponents and thus to arm the mind against conviction and render it impenetrable to farther

------

used it to kill their prey' they would have scouted the information as absurd and ridiculous.''])

light. Indeed, were it offered to my option which I would have, the plain sense of a common and untutored man, or the deep erudition of the proud scholars and professors in most universities, I should eagerly prefer the former, from a persuasion that it would leave me at a less distance from real wisdom. An unoccupied and simple mind is infinitely preferable to a mind warped by systems and the entire want of learning better than a learning such as most of that is which hitherto has been sought and admired, a learning which puffs up, while in reality it is nothing but profounder ignorance and more inveterate prejudice.

It may be worth adding here that a narrow education (should it ever happen not to produce the evils now mentioned) will probably produce equal evils of a contrary nature. I mean that there will be danger when persons so educated come to see the absurdity of some of the opinions in which they have been educated that they will become prejudiced against them all and, consequently, throw them all away and run wild into scepticism and infidelity. At present, in this part of the world, this is a very common event.

I am by no means qualified to give a just acount of the particular method in which education ought to be conducted so as to avoid these evils, that is, so as to render the mind free and unfettered, quick in discerning evidence, and prepared to follow it from whatever quarter and in whatever manner it may offer itself. But certain it is that the best mode of education is that which does this most effectually, which guards best against silly prejudices, which enflames most with the love of truth, which disposes most to ingenuity and fairness, and leaves the mind most sensible of its own need of farther information. Had this been always the aim of education mankind would now have been farther advanced. It supposes, however, an improved state of mankind and when once it has taken place it will quicken the progress of improvement.

I have in these observations expressed a dislike of systems but I have meant only to condemn that attachment to them as standards of truth which has been too prevalent. It may be necessary in education to make use of them or of books explaining them. But they should be used only as guides and helps to enquiry. Instruction in them should be attended with a fair exhibition of the evidence on both sides of every question and care should be taken to induce, as far as possible, a habit of believing only on an overbalance of evidence, and of proportioning assent in every case to the degree of that overbalance, without regarding authority, antiquity, singularity, novelty, or any of the prejudices which too commonly influence assent. Nothing is so well fitted to produce this habit as the study of mathematics. In these sciences no one ever thinks of giving his assent to a proposition till he can clearly understand it and see it proved by a fair deduction from propositions previously understood and proved. In these sciences the mind is insured to close and patient attention, shown the nature of just reasonings, and taught to form distinct ideas and to expect clear evidence in all cases before belief. They furnish, therefore, the best exercise for the intellectual powers, and the best defence against that credulity and precipitation and confusion of ideas which are the common sources of error.

There is, however, a danger even here to be avoided. Mathematical studies may absorb the attention too much, and when they do they contract the mind by rendering it incapable of thinking at large by disqualifying it for judging of any evidence except mathematical and, consequently, disposing it to an unreasonable scepticism on all subjects which admit not of such evidence. There have been many instances of this narrowness in mathematics.

But to return from this digression, I cannot help observing on this occasion, with respect to Christianity in particular, that education ought to lead to a habit of judging of it as it is in the code itself of Christianity, that the doctrines it reveals should be learned only from a critical and fair enquiry into the sense of this code, and that all instruction in it should be a preparation for making this enquiry and a communication of assistance in examining into the proofs of its divine original and in determining to what degree of evidence these proofs amount, after allowing every difficulty its just weight. This has never yet been the practice among Christians. The New Testament has been reckoned hitherto an insufficient standard of Christian Divinity and, therefore, formularies of human invention pretending to explain and define it (but in reality misrepresenting and dishonouring it) have been substituted in its room, and teaching these has been called teaching Christianity. And it is very remarkable that in the English universities 30 lectures on the New Testament are seldom or ever read 30 and that, through all Christendom, it is much less an object of attention than the systems and creeds which have been fathered upon it.

I will only add on this subject that it is above all things necessary, while instruction is conveyed, to convey with it a sense of the imbecility of the human mind and of its great proneness to error, and also a disposition even on points which seem the most clear, to listen to objections and to consider nothing as involving in it our final interest but an honest heart.

Nature has so made us that an attachment must take place within us to opinions once formed, and it was proper that we should be so made, in order to prevent that levity and desultoriness of mind which must have been the consequence had we been ready to give up our opinions too easily and hastily. But this natural tendency, however wisely given us, is apt to exceed its proper limits and to render us unreasonably tenacious. It ought,

---

30. Edition 1 reads "no lectures on the New Testament are ever read or even suffered to be read."

therefore, like all our other natural propensities, to be carefully watched and guarded, and education should put us upon doing this. An observation before made should, in particular, be inculcated, "that all mankind have hitherto been most tenacious when most in the wrong and reckoned themselves most enlightened when most in the dark." This is, indeed, a very mortifying fact but attention to it is necessary to cure that miserable pride and dogmaticalness which are some of the worst enemies to improvement. Who is there that does not remember the time when he was entirely satisfied about points which deeper reflection has shown to be above his comprehension? Who, for instance, does not remember a time when he would have wondered at the question, "Why does water run down hill?" What ignorant man is there who is not persuaded that he understands this perfectly? But every improved man knows it to be a question he cannot answer, and what distinguishes him in this instance from the less improved part of mankind is his knowing this. The like is true in numberless other instances. One of the best proofs of wisdom is a sense of our want of wisdom; and he who knows most possesses most of this sense.

In thinking of myself I derive some encouragement from this reflection. I now see that I do not understand many points which once appeared to me very clear. The more I have inquired, the more sensible I have been growing of my own darkness and a part of the history of my life is that which follows.

In early life I was struck with Bishop Butler's[31] *Analogy of Religion Natural and Revealed to the Constitution and Course of Nature.*[32] I reckon it happy for me that this book was one of the first that fell into my hands. It taught me the proper mode of reasoning on moral and religious subjects and particularly the importance of paying a due regard to the imperfection of human knowledge. His sermons also, I then thought, and do still think, excellent. Next to his works I have always been an admirer of the writings of Dr. Clarke.[33] And I cannot help adding, however strange it may seem, that I owe much to the philosophical writings of Mr. Hume which I likewise studied early in life. Though an enemy to his scepticism, I have profited by it. By attacking, with great ability, every principle of truth and reason, he put me upon examining the ground upon which I stood and taught me not hastily to take any thing for granted. The first fruits of my

---

31. Joseph Butler (1692–1752), clergyman and moral philosopher; bishop of Bristol (1738–1750); dean of St. Paul's, London (1740–1752); bishop of Durham (1750–1752).

32. Joseph Butler, *The Analogy of Religion, Natural and Revealed, to the Constitution and Course of Nature,* 3d ed. (London: John and Paul Knapton, 1740).

33. Samuel Clarke (1675–1729), philosopher, author, theologian, correspondent with Leibniz; successively, rector at Drayton and St. Bennet's, and chaplain in ordinary to Queen Anne, who later made him rector of St. James, Westminster; delivered the Boyle lectures at St. Paul's in 1704 and 1705.

reading and studies were laid before the public in a treatise entitled *A Review of the Principal Questions and Difficulties in Morals.*[34] This publication has been followed by many others on various subjects. And now, in the evening of a life devoted to enquiry and spent in endeavours (weak indeed and feeble) to serve the best interests, present and future, of mankind, I am waiting for the Great Teacher, convinced that the order of nature is perfect, that infinite wisdom and goodness govern all things, and that Christianity comes from God, but at the same time puzzled by many difficulties, anxious for more light, and resting with full and constant assurance only on this one truth—that the practice of virtue is the duty and dignity of man and, in all events, his wisest and safest course.

Of the Dangers to Which the American States are Exposed.

In the preceding observations, I have aimed at pointing out the means of promoting the progress of improvement in the United States of America. I have insisted, particularly, on the importance of a just settlement of the Federal Union and the establishment of a well-guarded and perfect liberty in speculation, in government, in education, and in religion. The United States are now setting out and all depends on the care and foresight with which a plan is begun which hereafter will require only to be strengthened and ripened. This is, therefore, the time for giving them advice and mean advice (like the present) may suggest some useful hints. In this country when any improvements are proposed or any corrections are attempted of abuses so gross as to make our boasts of liberty ridiculous,[k] a clamour im-

k. The majority of the British House of Commons is chosen by a few thousands of the dregs of the people who are constantly paid for their votes. Is it not ridiculous to call a country so governed free? See a striking account of the state of the British parliamentary representation in Mr. Burgh's *Political Disquisitions*, 1:39, etc.[35] [36] It was proposed to the convention for settling the Massachusetts constitution that one of the two houses which constitute the general court of that state should be a representation of persons and the other a representation of property and that the body of the people should appoint only the electors of their representatives. By such regulations corruption in the choice of representatives would be rendered less practicable and it seems the best method of concentrating in the legislature as much as possible of the virtue and ability of the state and of making its voice always an expression of the will and best sense of the people. On this plan also the number of members constituting a legislature might be

34. (London: Printed for T. Cadell, 1758; 2d ed., 1769; 3d ed., 1787). The second and third editions omit 'and Difficulties' from the title. The Clarendon Press of Oxford published the *Review* in 1948, edited by D. D. Raphael.

35. See footnote *b* to *Observations*, p. 71.

36. Added in edition 2.

mediately arises against innovation, and an alarm spreads lest the attempt to repair should destroy. In America no such prejudices can operate. There abuses have not yet gained sacredness by time. There the way is open to social dignity and happiness and reason may utter her voice with confidence and success.

Of Debts and Internal Wars.

I have observed in the introduction to this address that the American States have many dangers to shun. In what follows I shall give a brief recital of some of the chief of these dangers.

The danger from an endless increase of public debts has been already sufficiently noticed.

Particular notice has been likewise taken of the danger from internal wars. Again and again, I would urge the necessity of pursuing every measure and using every precaution which can guard against this danger. It will be shocking to see in the new world a repetition of all the evils which have hitherto laid waste the old world, war raging where peace and liberty were thought to have taken their abodes, the points of bayonets and the mouths of cannon settling disputes, instead of the collected wisdom of the confederation—and perhaps one restless and ambitious state rising by bloody conquest above the rest and becoming a sovereign state, claiming impiously (as Britain once did) "full authority to make laws that shall bind its sister states in all cases whatever," and drawing to itself all advantages at their expence. I deprecate this calamity. I shudder when I consider how possible it is and hope those persons are mistaken who think that such are the jealousies which govern human nature, and such the imperfections of the best human arrangements, that it is not within the reach of any wisdom to discover any effectual means of preventing it without encroaching too much on the liberty and independence of the states. I have mentioned an enlargement of the powers of Congress. Others have proposed a consolidation of the powers of government in one parliament representing all the states and superseding the particular parliaments by which they are now separately governed. But it is obvious that this will be attended with greater inconveniences and encroach more on the liberty of the states than the enlargement I have proposed of the powers of Congress. If such a parliament is not to supersede any of the other parliaments it will be the same with Congress as at present constituted.

---

much lessened. This is a circumstance of particular consequence to which the United States in some future period of their increase will find it necessary to attend. It has been often justly observed that a legislative body very numerous is little better than a mob.[26]

Of an Unequal Distribution of Property.

It is a trite observation that "dominion is founded on property." Most free states have manifested their sense of the truth of this observation by studying to find out means of preventing too great an inequality in the distribution of property. What tumults were occasioned at Rome, in its best times, by attempts to carry into execution the agrarian laws? Among the people of Israel, by the direction of heaven, all estates which had been alienated during the course of fifty years returned to their original owners at the end of that term. One of the circumstances that has been most favourable to the American states in forming their new constitutions of government has been the equality which subsists among them.

The happiest state of man is the middle state between the savage and the refined or between the wild and the luxurious state. Such is the state of society in Connecticut and some others of the American provinces where the inhabitants consist, if I am rightly informed, of an independent and hardy yeomanry, all nearly on a level, trained to arms, instructed in their rights, clothed in home-spun, of simple manners, strangers to luxury, drawing plenty from the ground, and that plenty gathered easily by the hand of industry and giving rise to early marriages, a numerous progeny, length of days, and a rapid increase; the rich and the poor, the haughty grandee and the creeping sycophant, equally unknown, protected by laws which (being of their own will) cannot oppress, and by an equal government which, wanting lucrative places, cannot create corrupt canvassings and ambitious intrigue.[1] O distinguished people! May you continue long thus happy and may the happiness you enjoy spread over the face of the whole earth! But I am forgetting myself. There is danger that a state of society so happy will not be of long duration, that simplicity and virtue will give way to depravity, that equality will in time be lost, the cursed lust of domineering show itself, liberty languish, and civil government gradually degenerate into an instrument in the hands of the few to oppress and plunder the many. Such has hitherto been the progress of evil in human affairs. In order to give them a better turn some great men (Plato, Sir Thomas Moore,[37] Mr. Wallace,[38] etc.) have proposed plans which, by establishing

---

1. In this state, and also the state of Massachusetts, New Jersey, etc., any attempt to canvas, or even the expression of a wish to be chosen, will exclude a candidate from a seat in the House of Representatives. The same is true of any stain on his moral character.

---

37. Thomas More (1478–1535), English saint, humanist, martyr; Lord Chancellor (1529–1532); author of *Utopia*.

38. Robert Wallace (1697–1771), clergyman; successively, minister of New Greyfriars, Edinburgh, New North Church, and royal chaplain for Scotland and a dean of the Chapel Royal; author of *Dissertation on the Numbers of Mankind in Ancient and Modern Times* (1653).

a community of goods and annihilating property, would make it impossible for any one member of a state to think of enslaving the rest or to consider himself as having interest distinct from that of his fellow citizens. Such theories are in speculation pleasing, nor perhaps are they wholly impracticable. Some approaches to them may hereafter be made and schemes of government may take place which shall leave so little besides personal merit to be a means of distinction as to exclude from society most of the causes of evil. But be this as it will, it is out of doubt that there is an equality in society which is essential to liberty and which every state that would continue virtuous and happy ought as far as possible to maintain. It is not in my power to describe the best method of doing this. I will only observe that there are three enemies to equality against which America ought to guard.

First, granting hereditary honours and titles of nobility. Persons thus distinguished, though perhaps meaner than the meanest of their dependants, are apt to consider themselves as belonging to a higher order of beings and made for power and government. Their birth and rank necessarily dispose them to be hostile to general liberty, and when they are not so, and discover a just zeal for the rights of mankind, it is always a triumph of good sense and virtue over the temptations of their situation. It is, therefore, with peculiar satisfaction that I have found in the Articles of Confederation an order that no titles of nobility shall be ever granted by the United States. Let there be honours to encourage merit, but let them die with the men who have earned them. Let them not descend to posterity to foster a spirit of domination and to produce a proud and tyrannical aristocracy. In a word, let the United States continue for ever what it is now their glory to be—a confederation of states prosperous and happy, without lords, without bishops,^m and without kings.

Secondly, the right of primogeniture. The tendency of this to produce an improper inequality is very obvious. The disposition to raise a name by accumulating property in one branch of a family is a vanity no less unjust and cruel than dangerous to the interest of liberty, and no wise state will encourage or tolerate it.

Thirdly, foreign trade is another of the enemies against which I wish to caution the United States. But this operates unfavourably to a state in so many more ways than by destroying that equality which is the basis of liberty that it will be proper to take more particular notice of it.

m. I do not mean by bishops any officers among Christians merely spiritual; but lords spiritual, as distinguished from lords temporal, or clergymen raised to preeminence and invested with civil honours and authority by a state establishment.

I must add that by what is here said I do not mean to express a general preference of a republican constitution of government. There is a degree of political degeneracy which unfits for such a constitution. Britain, in particular, consists too much of the high and the low (of scum and dregs) to admit of it. Nor will it suit America should it ever become equally corrupt.

Of Trade, Banks, and Paper Credit.

Foreign trade has, in some respects, the most useful tendency. By creating an intercourse between distant kingdoms it extends benevolence, removes local prejudices, leads every man to consider himself more as a citizen of the world than of any particular state and, consequently, checks the excesses of that love of our country[n] which has been applauded as one of the noblest, but which really is one of the most destructive, principles in human nature. Trade also, by enabling every country to draw from other countries conveniences and advantages which it cannot find within itself, produces among nations a sense of mutual dependence and promotes the general improvement. But there is no part of mankind to which these uses of trade are of less consequence than the American states. They are spread over a great continent and make a world within themselves. The country they inhabit includes soils and climates of all sorts, producing not only every necessary, but every convenience of life. And the vast rivers and widespread lakes which intersect it create such an inland communication between its different parts as is unknown in any other region of the earth. They possess then within themselves the best means of the most profitable traffic and the amplest scope of it. Why should they look much farther? What occasion have they for being anxious about pushing foreign trade or even about raising a great naval force? Britain, indeed, consisting as it does of unarmed inhabitants, and threatened as it is by ambitious and powerful neighbours, cannot hope to maintain its existence long after becoming open to invasion by losing its naval superiority. But this is not the case with the American states. They have no powerful neighbours to dread. The vast Atlantic must be crossed before they can be attacked. They are all a well trained militia and the successful resistance which, in their infancy and without a naval force, they have made to the invasion of the first European power will probably discourage and prevent all future in-

n. The love of our country is then only a noble passion when it engages us to promote the internal happiness of our country and to defend its right and liberties against domestic and foreign invasion, maintaining at the same time an equal regard to the rights and liberties of other countries. But this has not been its most common effects. On the contrary, it has in general been nothing but a spirit of rivalship between different communities, producing contention and a thirst for conquest and dominion. What is his country to a Russian, a Turk, a Spaniard, etc. but a spot where he enjoys no right and is disposed of by owners as if he was a beast? And what is his love to his country but an attachment to degradation and slavery? What was the love of their country among the Jews but a wretched partiality for themselves and a proud contempt for other nations? Among the Romans also what was it, however great in many of its exertions, but a principle holding together a band of robbers in their attempts to crush all liberty but their own? Christianity has wisely omitted to recommend this principle. Had it done this, it would have countenanced a vice among mankind. It has done what is infinitely better. It has recommended universal benevolence.

vasions. Thus singularly happy, why should they seek connections with Europe and expose themselves to the danger of being involved in its quarrels? What have they [to] do with its politics? Is there any thing very important to them which they can draw from thence—except infection? Indeed, I tremble when I think of that rage for trade which is likely to prevail among them. It may do them infinite mischief. All nations are spreading snares for them and courting them to a dangerous intercourse. Their best interest requires them to guard themselves by all proper means and, particularly, by laying heavy duties on importations. But in no case will any means succeed unless aided by manners. In this instance, particularly, there is reason to fear that an increasing passion for foreign frippery will render all the best regulations ineffectual. And should this happen, that simplicity of character, that manliness of spirit, that disdain of tinsel in which true dignity consists, will disappear. Effeminacy, servility, and venality will enter and liberty and virtue be swallowed up in the gulf of corruption. Such may be the course of events in the American states. Better infinitely will it be for them to consist of bodies of plain and honest farmers, 39than of39 opulent and splendid merchants. Where in these states do the purest manners prevail? Where do the inhabitants live most on an equality and most at their ease? Is it not in those inland parts where agriculture gives health and plenty and trade is scarcely known? Where, on the contrary, are the inhabitants more selfish, luxurious, loose, and vicious and at the same time most unhappy? Is it not along the sea coasts and in the great towns where trade flourishes and merchants abound? So striking is the effect of these different situations on the vigour and happiness of human life that in the one, population would languish did it receive no aid from emigrations while in the other, it increases to a degree scarcely ever before known.

But to proceed to some observations of a different nature, the United States have, I think, particular reason to dread the following effects of foreign trade. By increasing importation to feed luxury and gratify prodigality it will carry out their coin and occasion the substitution of a delusive paper currency, the consequence of which will be that ideal wealth will take place of real, and their security come to depend on the strength and duration of a bubble. I am very sensible that paper credit is one of the greatest of all conveniences but this makes it likewise one of the greatest of all temptations. A public bank (while it can circulate its bills) facilitates commerce and assists the exertions of a state in proportion to its credit. But when it is not carefully restricted and watched, when its emissions exceed the coin it can command and are carried near the utmost length that the confidence of the public will allow and when in consequence of this, its permanence comes to depend on the permanence of public credulity, in

---

39. Edition 1 reads "rather than."

these circumstances, a bank, though it may for a time (that is, while a balance of trade too unfavourable does not occasion a run and no events arise which produce alarm) answer all the ends of a mine from which millions may be drawn in a minute and, by filling a kingdom with cash, render it capable of sustaining any debts, and give it a kind of omnipotence. In such circumstances, I say, notwithstanding these temporary advantages, a public bank must at last prove a great calamity and a kingdom so supported, at the very time of its greatest exertions, will be only striving more violently to increase the horror of an approaching convulsion.

The United States have already verified some of these observations and felt in some degree the consequences to which I have alluded. They have been carried through the war by an emission of paper which had no solid support and which now has lost all value. It is indeed surprising that, being secured on no fund and incapable of being exchanged for coin, it should ever have obtained a currency or answered any important purpose.

Unhappily for Britain, it has used the means of giving more stability to its paper credit and been enabled by it to support expences greater than any that have been yet known, and to contract a debt which now astonishes, and may hereafter produce a catastrophe that will terrify the world. A longer duration of the late war would have brought on this catastrophe immediately. The peace has put it off for the present. God grant, if still possible, that measures may be adopted which shall put it off for ever.

Of Oaths.

Oaths are expedients to which all states have had recourse in order to obtain true information and ascertain facts by securing the veracity of witnesses. But I know not how to relish that imprecation which always makes a part of an oath. Perhaps there is no such necessity for it as is commonly imagined. An affirmation solemnly made, with laws inflicting severe penalties on falsehood when detected, would probably answer all the ends of oaths. I am, therefore, disposed to wish that in the United States imprecatory oaths may be abolished and the same indulgence in this respect granted to all which is now granted to the Quakers. But I am afraid they will think this too dangerous an experiment and what is of most consequence is to avoid, first, such a multiplicity of oaths as will render them too familiar and, secondly, a slight manner of administering them. England, in this respect, seems to be sunk to the lowest possible degree of degeneracy. Oaths among us are required on so many occasions, and so carelessly administered as to have lost almost all their use and efficacy. It has been asserted that, including oaths of office, oaths at elections, custom-house oaths, etc., etc. there are about a million of perjuries committed in this kingdom annually. This is one of the most atrocious of our national iniquities and it is a wonder if we are not to be visited for it with some of the severest of God's judgments.

Of the Negro Trade and Slavery.

The negro trade cannot be censured in language too severe. It is a traffic which, as it has been hitherto carried on, is shocking to humanity, cruel, wicked, and diabolical. I am happy to find that the United States are entering into measures for discountenancing it and for abolishing the odious slavery which it has introduced. Till they have done this, it will not appear they deserve the liberty for which they have been contending. For it is self-evident that if there are any men whom they have a right to hold in slavery, there may be *others* who have had a right to hold *them* in slavery.° I am sensible, however, that this is a work which they cannot accomplish at once. The emancipation of the negroes must, I suppose, be left in some measure to be the effect of time and of manners. But nothing can excuse the United States if it is not done with as much speed, and at the same time with as much effect, as their particular circumstances and situation will allow. I rejoice that on this occasion I can recommend to them the example of my own country. In Britain, a negro becomes a freeman the moment he sets his foot on British ground.

Conclusion.

Such is the advice which I would humbly (but earnestly) offer to the United States of America. Such are the means by which they may become the seats of liberty, science, peace, and virtue, happy within themselves and a refuge to the world.

o. See a remonstrance, full of energy, directed to the United States on this subject, by a very warm and able friend to the rights of mankind, in a tract, entitled *Fragment of an Original Letter on the Slavery of the Negroes, Written in the Year 1776*, but published in 1784, by Thomas Day, Esq.[40] [Thomas Day, *Fragment of an Original Letter on the Slavery of the Negroes; Written in the Year 1776* (London: Printed for John Stockdale, 1784)].

40. Thomas Day (1748–1789), humanist, philosopher, critic, poet, philanthropist.

Often, while employed in writing these papers, have I wished for a warning voice of more power. The present moment, however auspicious to the United States if wisely improved, is critical and, though apparently the end of all their dangers, may prove the time of their greatest danger. I have, indeed, since finishing this address, been mortified more than I can express by accounts which have led me to fear that I have carried my ideas of them too high and deceived myself with visionary expectations. And should this be true, should the return of peace and the pride of independence lead them to security and dissipation, should they lose those virtuous and simple manners by which alone republics can long subsist, should false refinement, luxury, and irreligion[41] spread among them, excessive jealousy distract their governments, and clashing interests, subject to no strong control, break the federal union, the consequence will be that the fairest experiment ever tried in human affairs will miscarry and that a revolution which had revived the hopes of good men and promised an opening to better times will become a discouragement to all future efforts in favour of liberty and prove only an opening to a new scene of human degeneracy and misery.

41. Edition 1 reads "impiety."

Letter from M. Turgot

Advertisement.[1]

The following letter was written by the late M. Turgot, Comptroller General (in the years 1774, 1775, and 1776) of the finances of France. It contains observations in which the United States are deeply concerned and, for this reason, I now convey it to them, not doubting but that the eminence of M. Turgot's name and character will recommend it to their attention, and that it will do honour to his memory among all the friends of public liberty.

Translation.[2]
To Dr. Price, London.

Paris, March 22, 1778

Sir,

Mr. Franklin by your desire has put into my hands the last edition of your *Observations on Civil Liberty*, etc. for which I think myself doubly

---

1. Price's comment in the first advertisement that he has now given a translation of Turgot's letter suggests that there might be an edition of *Observations on the Importance of the American Revolution, and the Means of Making It a Benefit to the World* (hereafter cited as *Benefit*) without Turgot's letter or with it only in French. Evidence is quite strong that no such edition exists. From the standpoint of internal argument, there is an interpretation of Price's comment that does not require it: He may have thought of *Benefit* as a unit and of Turgot's letter as an addition to it. He credits a friend with the English translation of it in the 1785 edition but gives no credit to anyone for the more awkward translation of the 1784 edition, which suggests that the translation might have been his own. This could be a sufficient reason for mentioning the translation of Turgot's letter "now." From the standpoint of external evidence, an extensive search in England and the United States has not located such a copy. The edition of 1784, which I have been calling the first, contains an English translation although not the French text as in the 1785 edition. Finally, there is the correspondence with Franklin and Jefferson. See Appendix 8, Price to Franklin, July 12, 1784; Jefferson to Price, February 1, 1785; Price to Jefferson, March 21, 1785; and Jefferson to Price, August 7, 1785. In particular, combining the letter to Franklin with Price's advertisement, it would seem that the texts of *Benefit* and of the letter might have been printed separately but never published separately.
    Lastly, it should be noted that the English translation differs somewhat from the original, and not only in terms of the two different translations in the two editions. As M. Laboucheix puts it, the text given in Price's *Benefit* "est légèrement différent." He refers to the letter in *Oeuvres de Turgot*, ed. Gustave Schelle (Paris, 8e, 1913–1923), 5:532–540. *Richard Price, Théoricien de la Révolution Américaine*, pp. 274–275.
    2. The first edition of *Benefit* contains a translation of Turgot's letter which differs from the translation in the second edition. The first edition translation is generally

indebted to you. In the first place, for the work itself, of which I have long known the value and read with great avidity, notwithstanding the multiplicity of my engagements, when it was first published. And in the next place, for the politeness you have shown in leaving out the imputation of want of address,[a] which you intermixed with the handsome things you said of me in your additional observations. I might have merited this im-

a. What is here said refers to the following account of M. Turgot's administration in the second tract on *Civil Liberty and the War with America*, p. 150, etc. "A new reign produced a new minister of finance in France, whose name will be respected by posterity for a set of measures as new to the political world as any late discoveries in the system of nature have been to the philosophical world. Doubtful in their operation, as all untried measures must be, but distinguished by their tendency to lay a solid foundation for endless peace, industry, and a general enjoyment of the gifts of nature, arts and commerce, the edicts issued during his administration exhibit indeed a phenomenon of the most extraordinary kind. An absolute King rendering a voluntary account to his subjects and inciting his people to think, a right which it has been the business of all absolute princes and their ministers to extinguish. In these edicts the King declared in the most distinct terms against a bankruptcy, etc., while the minister applied himself to increase every public resource by principles more liberal than France or any part of Europe ever had in serious contemplation. [3]It is much to be regretted that the opposition he met with and the intrigues of a court should have deprived the world of those lights which must have resulted from the example of such an administration."[3] In this passage I had, in the first edition, mentioned improperly Mr. Turgot's want of address among the other causes of his dismission from power. This occasioned a letter from him to inform me of the true reasons of his dismission and begun that correspondence, of which this letter is a part, and which continued till his death. It may not be improper to add here that his successor was Mr. Necker,[4] author of the interesting *Treatise on the Administration of the Finances of France*, just published, and that in the passage just quoted, the following notice is taken of this appointment [Jacques Necker, *De l'administration des finances de la France* (Paris?, 1784)]. "After a short interval a nomination, in some respects still more extraordinary, took place in the court of France. A court, which a few years since was distinguished by its bigotry and intolerance, has raised a Protestant, the subject of a small but virtuous republic, to a decisive lead in the regulation of its finances. It is to be presumed that so singular a preference will produce an equally singular exertion of integrity and talents."

[In edition 1 this footnote reads: "What is here said refers to an account of M. Turgot's administration in the second tract on *Civil Liberty and the War with America*, p. 150, etc. In the first edition of this tract I had mentioned improperly his "want of address" among the other causes of his dismission from power. This occasioned a letter from him to inform me of the true reasons of his dismission and begun that correspondence of which this letter is a part and which continued till his death."]

more cumbersome than that in the second edition. Price may have done it himself. He adds a note in the second edition at the end of the French text:
"It is not easy to do justice in English to many parts of the preceding letter. The following translation of it will, however, I hope, be found to be nearly correct; and I think myself greatly obliged to the gentleman who has been so good as to favour me with it."

3. In three editions of *Additional Observations* published separately and in the first edition of *Two Tracts* this passage reads: "It is much to be regretted that the intrigues of a court, want of address, or perhaps want of due regard to that degree of public conviction which must influence more or less in a despotic as well as free state should have deprived the world of those lights which must have resulted from the example of such an administration."

4. Jacques Necker (1732–1804), economist, popular figure; director general of the treasury of France (1776–1777); director general of finance (1777–1781; 1788–1790).

putation if you had in view no other "want of address" than incapacity to
unravel the springs of those intrigues that were employed against me by
some people who are much more expert in these matters than I am, or ever
shall be, or indeed ever desire to be. But I imagined you imputed to me a
want of address which made my opinions grossly clash with the general
opinions of my countrymen, and in that respect I thought you neither did
justice to me nor to my country, where there is a degree of understanding
much superior to what you generally suppose in England, and where it is
more easy, perhaps, than even with you, to bring back the public to hearken
to reason.

I have been led to judge thus by the infatuation of your people in the
absurd project of subduing America, till the affair of Burgoyne[5] began to
open their eyes, and by the system of monopoly and exclusion which has
been recommended by all your writers on commerce (except Mr. Adam
Smith[6] and Dean Tucker), a system which has been the true source of your
separation from your colonies. I have also been led to this opinion by all
your controversial writings upon the questions which have occupied your
attention these twenty years and in which, till your observations appeared,
I scarce recollect to have read one that took up these questions on their
proper ground. I cannot conceive how a nation which has cultivated every
branch of natural knowledge with such success should have made so little
progress in the most interesting of sciences, that of the public good, a science
in which the liberty of the press, which she alone enjoys, ought to have
given her a prodigious advantage over every other nation in Europe. Was
it national pride which prevented you from profiting by this advantage?
Or was it because you were not altogether in so bad a condition as other
nations, that you have imposed upon yourselves in your speculations so
far as to be persuaded that your arrangements were complete? Is it party
spirit and a desire of being supported by popular opinion which has re-
tarded your progress, by inducing your political writers to treat as vain
metaphysics[b] all those speculations which aim at establishing the rights and
true interests of nations and individuals upon fixed principles. How comes
it that you are almost the first of the writers of your country who has given
a just idea of liberty and shown the falsity of the notion so frequently
repeated by almost all republican writers, "that liberty consists in being

b. See Mr. Burke's *Letter to the Sheriffs of Bristol*.

---

5. John Burgoyne (1722–1792), British general, playwright; member of Parliament;
after the American Revolution, commander-in-chief in Ireland; one of the managers in
the impeachment trial of Warren Hastings. On October 17, 1777, Burgoyne surrendered
a force of 9,000 troops to American General Horatio Gates at Saratoga. News of Burgoyne's surrender prompted Louis XVI of France to sign a treaty with the Americans.
6. Adam Smith (1723–1790), Scottish economic philosopher; advocate of the freedom
of economic enterprise; author of *Enquiry into the Nature and Causes of the Wealth of
Nations*, 1776.

subject only to the laws," as if a man could be free while oppressed by an unjust law. This would not be true even if we could suppose that all the laws were the work of an assembly of the whole nation, for certainly every individual has his rights, of which the nation cannot deprive him, except by violence and an unlawful use of the general power. Though you have attended to this truth and have explained yourself upon this head, perhaps it would have merited a more minute explanation, considering how little attention is paid to it even by the most zealous friends of liberty.

It is likewise extraordinary that it was not thought a trivial matter in England to assert "that one nation never can have a right to govern another nation"—"that a government where such a principle is admitted can have no foundation but that of force, which is equally the foundation of robbery and tyranny"—"and that the tyranny of a people is the most cruel and intolerable, because it leaves the fewest resources to the oppressed." A despot is restrained by a sense of his own interest. He is checked by a remorse or by the public opinion. But the multitude never calculate. The multitude are never checked by remorse and will even ascribe to themselves the highest honour when they deserve only disgrace.

What a dreadful commentary on your book are the events which have lately befallen the English nation? For some months they have been running headlong to ruin. The fate of America is already decided. Behold her independent beyond recovery. But will she be free and happy? Can this new people, so advantageously placed for giving an example to the world of a constitution under which man may enjoy his rights, freely exercise all his faculties, and be governed only by nature, reason and justice—can they form such a constitution? Can they establish it upon a neverfailing foundation and guard against every source of division and corruption which may gradually undermine and destroy it?

I confess that I am not satisfied with the constitutions which have hitherto been formed by the different states of America. It is with reason that you reproach the state of Pennsylvania with exacting a religious test from those who become members of the body of representatives. There are much worse tests in the other states, and there is one (I believe the Jerseys) which requires[c] a declaration of faith in the *divinity* of Jesus Christ. I observe that by most of them the customs of England are imitated, without any particular motive. Instead of collecting all authority into one center, that of the nation, they have established different bodies, a body of representatives, a council, and a governor, because there is in England a House of

c. It is the constitution of Delaware that imposes the test here meant. [See footnote 29 to *Benefit*.] That of the Jerseys, with a noble liberality, orders that there shall never in that province be any establishment of any one religious sect in preference to another and that all Protestants of all persuasions shall enjoy equal rights and privileges.[7]

7. N.J. Const. art. 18 (1776). See *Federal and State Constitutions*, pt. 2, p. 1313.

Commons, a House of Lords, and a King. They endeavour to balance these different powers, as if this equilibrium, which in England may be a necessary check to the enormous influence of royalty, could be of any use in republics founded upon the equality of all the citizens, and as if establishing different orders of men was not a source of divisions and disputes. In attempting to prevent imaginary dangers they create real ones and in their desire to have nothing to fear from the clergy they unite them more closely by one common proscription. By excluding them from the right of being elected into public offices they become a body distinct from the state. Wherefore should a citizen, who has the same interest with others in the common defense of liberty and property, be excluded from contributing to it his virtue and knowledge? Is it because he is of a profession which requires knowledge and virtue? The clergy are only dangerous when they exist as a distinct body in the state and think themselves possessed of separate rights and interests and a religion established by law, as if some men had a right to regulate the consciences of other men, or could have an interest in doing this, as if an individual could sacrifice to civil society opinions on which he thinks his eternal salvation depends, as if, in short, mankind were to be saved or damned in communities. Where true toleration (that is, where the absolute incompetency of civil government in matters of conscience) is established, there the clergyman, when admitted into the national assembly, becomes a simple citizen; but when excluded, he becomes an ecclesiastic.

I do not think they are sufficiently careful to reduce the kind of business with which the government of each state is charged within the narrowest limits possible, nor to separate the objects of legislation from those of a local and particular administration, nor to institute local permanent assemblies, which by discharging almost all the functions in the detail of government, make it unnecessary for the general assemblies to attend to these things, and thereby deprive the members of the general assemblies of every means, and perhaps of every desire, of abusing a power which can only be applied to general objects, and which, consequently, must be free from the influence of the little passions by which men usually are agitated.

I do not find that they attend to the great distinction (the only one which is founded in nature between two classes of men) between landholders and those who are not landholders, to their interests, and of course to their different rights respecting legislation, the administration of justice and police, their contributions to the public expence, and employment.

No fixed principle of taxation is established. They suppose that each state may tax itself according to its own fancy by establishing either personal taxes or taxes on consumption and importation, that is, that each state may assume to itself an interest contrary to the interest of the other states.

They also everywhere suppose that they have a right to regulate commerce. They even delegate authority to executive bodies, and to governors, to prohibit the exportation of certain commodities on certain occasions. So far are they from being sensible that the right to an entire liberty in commerce is the consequence of the right of property. So much are they still involved in the mist of European illusions.

In the general union of the States I do not observe a coalition, a fusion of all the parts to form one homogeneous body. It is only a jumble of communities too discordant, and which retain a constant tendency to separation, owing to the diversity in their laws, customs and opinions, to the inequality in their present strength; but still more, to the inequality in their advances to greater strength. It is only a copy of the Dutch republic, with this difference, that the Dutch republic had nothing to fear, as the American republic has, from the future possible increase of any one of the provinces. All this edifice has been hitherto supported upon the erroneous foundation of the most ancient and vulgar policy, upon the prejudice that nations and states, as such, may have an interest distinct from the interest which individuals have to be free, and to defend their property against the attacks of robbers and conquerors, an interest in carrying on a more extensive commerce than other states, in not purchasing foreign merchandise, and compelling foreigners to consume their produce and manufactures, an interest in possessing more extensive territories and acquiring such and such a province, island or village, an interest in inspiring other nations with awe and gaining a superiority over them in the glory of arts, sciences, and arms.

Some of these prejudices are fomented in Europe from the ancient rivalship of nations and the ambition of princes which compel every state to keep us an armed force to defend itself against the attack of neighbours in arms and to look upon a military force as the principal object of government. America is likely in no long time to enjoy the happiness of having no external enemy to dread, provided she is not divided within herself. She ought, therefore, to estimate properly those pretended interests and causes of discord which alone are likely to be formidable to her liberty. On that sacred principle, "liberty of commerce considered as a natural right flowing from the possession of property," all the pretended interests of commerce must vanish. The supposed interest in possessing more or less territory disappears on this principle, "that a territory does not belong to nations, but to the individuals who are proprietors of the lands." The question whether such a canton or such a village belongs to such a province or such a state ought not to be determined by the interest in it pretended by that province or that state, but by the interest the inhabitants of the canton or village have in assembling for transacting their affairs in the place most convenient for them. This interest, measured by the greater or less distance that a man can go from his home to attend to important affairs without injuring his private concerns, forms a natural boundary to the jurisdiction of states, and establishes an equipoise[d] of extent and strength between them which must remove every danger of inequality and every pretence to superiority.

There can be no interest in being feared when nothing can be demanded and when men are in a situation not to be attacked by a considerable force with any hope of success.

The glory of arms is nothing to those who enjoy the happiness of living in peace.

The glory of arts and sciences belongs to every man who can acquire it. There is here ample scope. The field of discovery is boundless and all profit by the discoveries of all.

I imagine that the Americans are not as sensible of these truths as they ought to be in order to secure the happiness of their posterity. I do not blame their leaders. It was necessary to provide for the necessities of the moment by such a union as they could form against a present and most formidable enemy. They have not leisure to consider how the errors of the different constitutions and states may be corrected, but they ought to be afraid of perpetuating these errors and to endeavour by all means to reconcile the opinions and interests of the different provinces and to unite them by bringing them to one uniform set of principles.

To accomplish this they have great obstacles to surmount:

In Canada, an order of Roman Catholic clergy, and a body of nobles.

In New England, a rigid puritanical spirit which has been always somewhat intolerant.[e]

In Pennsylvania, a very great number of inhabitants laying it down as a religious principle that the profession of arms is unlawful, and refusing to join in the arrangements necessary to establish the military force of the state by uniting the character of the citizen with that of the soldier and militiaman, in consequence of which the business of war is made to be the business of mercenaries.

In the southern colonies, an inequality of fortune too great and, what is worse, a great number of blacks, whose slavery is incompatible with a good political constitution and who, if emancipated, would occasion great embarrassment by forming two distinct people in one state.

In all of them, various prejudices, an attachment to established forms, a habit of paying certain taxes, and a dread of those which must be sub-

d. This seems to be a particular of much consequence. The great inequality now existing, and which is likely to increase, between the different states, is a very unfavourable circumstance, and the embarrassment and danger to which it exposes the union ought to be guarded against as far as possible in laying out future states.

e. This has been *once* true of the inhabitants of New England, but it is not so now. See p. 199.

stituted for them, a vanity in those colonies which think themselves most powerful and a wretched beginning of national pride. I imagine that the Americans must aggrandize themselves not by war, but by agriculture. If they neglect the immense deserts which are at their backs, and which extend all the way to the western sea, their exiles and fugitives from the severity of the laws will unite with the savages and settle that part of the country, the consequence of which will be that bodies of banditti will ravage America, as the barbarians of the North ravaged the Roman Empire, and subject the states to the necessity of keeping the frontiers always guarded and remaining in a state of continual war.

The colonies next to the frontier will of course be better disciplined than the rest and this inequality of military force will prove a dreadful incentive to ambition. The remedy for this inequality would be to keep a standing army, to which every state should contribute in proportion to its population, but the Americans, who have the fears that the English ought to have, dread nothing so much as a standing army. In this they are wrong. There is nothing more easy than to combine a standing army with a militia, so as to improve the militia, and gain additional security for liberty. But it is no easy matter to calm their apprehensions on that head.

Here are a number of difficulties; and perhaps the private interests of powerful individuals will unite with the prejudices of the multitude to check the efforts of true philosophers and good citizens.

It is impossible not to wish ardently that this people may attain to all the prosperity of which they are capable. They are the hope of the world. They may become a model to it. They may prove by fact that men can be free and yet tranquil and that it is in their power to rescue themselves from the chains in which tyrants and knaves of all descriptions have presumed to bind them under the pretence of the public good. They may exhibit an example of political liberty, of religious liberty, of commercial liberty, and of industry. The asylum they open to the oppressed of all nations should console the earth. The ease with which the injured may escape from oppressive governments will compel princes to become just and cautious and the rest of the world will gradually open their eyes upon the empty illusions with which they have been hitherto cheated by politicians. But for this purpose America must preserve herself from these illusions and take care to avoid being what your ministerial writers are frequently saying she will be—an image of our Europe, a mass of divided powers contending for territory and commerce and continually cementing the slavery of the people with their own blood.

All enlightened men, all the friends of humanity, ought at this time to unite their lights to those of the American sages and to assist them in the great work of legislation. This, sir, would be a work worthy of you. I wish it was in my power to animate your zeal in this instance. If I have in this letter indulged too free an effusion of my sentiments, this has been my only motive and it will, I hope, induce you to pardon me for tiring you. I wish indeed that the blood which has been spilt, and which will continue for some time to be spilt in this contest, may not be without its use to the human race.

Our two nations are about doing much harm to each other and probably without the prospect to either of any real advantage. An increase of debts and public burdens (perhaps a national bankruptcy) and the ruin of a great number of individuals will prove the result. England seems to me to be more likely to suffer by these evils, and much nearer to them, than France. If instead of going to war you had at the commencement of your disputes endeavoured to retreat with a good grace, if your statesmen had then consented to make those concessions which they will infallibly be obliged to make at last, if the national opinion would have permitted your government to anticipate events which might have been foreseen, if, in short, you had immediately yielded to the independence of America without entering into any hostilities I am firmly persuaded your nation would have lost nothing. But you will now lose what you have already expended and what you are still to expend, you will experience a great diminution of your commerce for some time and great interior commotions if driven to a bankruptcy and, at any rate, a great diminution of weight in foreign politics. But this last circumstance I think of little consequence to the real happiness of a people, for I cannot agree with the Abbé Raynal in your motto.*f*

I do not believe all this will make you a contemptible nation or throw you into slavery. On the contrary, your misfortunes may have the effect of a necessary amputation. They are perhaps the only means of saving you from the gangrene of luxury and corruption. And if they should terminate in the amendment of your constitution, by restoring annual elections, and distributing the right of suffrages for representation so as to render it more equal and better proportioned to the interests of the represented, you will perhaps gain as much as America by this revolution, for you will preserve your liberty, and with your liberty, and by means of it, all your other losses will be speedily repaired.

By the freedom with which I have opened myself to you, sir, upon these delicate points, you will judge to the esteem with which you have inspired

f. This refers to the following words (taken from Mr. Justamond's translation of the Abbé Raynal's *History of the European Settlements*) in the title page of the *Second Tract on Civil Liberty*: "Should the morals of the English be perverted by luxury, should they lose their colonies by restraining them, etc. they will be enslaved. They will become insignificant and contemptible and Europe will not be able to show the world one nation in which she can pride herself."

me and the satisfaction I feel in thinking there is some resemblance between our sentiments and views. I depend on your[g] confining this confidence to yourself. I even beg that you will not be particular in answering me by the post, for your letter will certainly be opened at our post-offices, and I shall be found much too great a friend to liberty for a minister, even though a discarded minister.

I have the honour to be with all possible respect, sir,

Your most humble,

and most obedient servant,

TURGOT.

g. In compliance with Mr. Turgot's desire, this letter was kept private during his life. Since his death I have thought the publication of it a duty which I owe to his memory, as well as to the United States and the world. I can add, with much satisfaction, that my venerable friend and the excellent philosopher and statesman whose name introduces this letter and also that some intimate friends of Mr. Turgot's, who have been consulted on this subject, concur with me in this sentiment.

Appendices

The following selections show some of the context in which Price wrote. They include some fairly extensive passages from a representative sample of the critics whom Price mentions explicitly in his *General Introduction*, the Introduction to *Additional Observations*, or elsewhere, as well as extensive selections from his sermon of February 10, 1779, his most explicitly political sermon during the period of the American Revolution, and correspondence with several American Revolutionary leaders.

The selections from Edmund Burke indicate an initial agreement with Price, but on grounds of practicality and *noblesse oblige*, quite different from Price's ethical and theoretical foundations. This difference appears more explicitly in Burke's "Letter to the Sheriffs of Bristol" when he criticizes Price for his "metaphysics." (His vitriolic attack on Price in the opening passages of *Reflections on the Revolution in France* refers to Price's later political sermon of November 4, 1789, published as "A Discourse on the Love of our Country.") The selection from John Lind is representative of a number of negative attacks based on personal abuse more than argumentation. The selections from John Wesley, Adam Ferguson and William Markham, by contrast, offer argued criticisms, decreasing in personal abuse from Markham to Wesley to Ferguson. They also exemplify a continued appeal to historical and constitutional grounds, in contrast to Price's ethical and theoretical grounds, again decreasing in this respect in the same order, reaching considerable philosophical power in Ferguson. In addition to its intrinsic interest the correspondence illustrates Price's detailed knowledge of the situation in America and the high regard in which he was held by American leaders.

Appendix One. On Conciliation with the Colonies (March 22, 1775) *Edmund Burke*

. . . .

The proposition is peace. Not peace through the medium of war; not peace to be hunted through the labyrinth of intricate and endless negotiations; not peace to arise out of universal discord fomented from principle, in all parts of the empire; not peace to depend on the juridical determination of perplexing questions or the precise marking the shadowy boundaries of a complex government. It is simple peace, sought in its natural course, and in its ordinary haunts—it is peace sought in the spirit of peace, and laid in principles purely pacific. I propose, by removing the ground of the difference, and by restoring the *former unsuspecting confidence of the colonies in the mother country,* to give permanent satisfaction to your people; and (far from a scheme of ruling by discord) to reconcile them to each other in the same act, and by the bond of the very same interest which reconciles them to British government.

My idea is nothing more. Refined policy ever has been the parent of confusion, and ever will be so as long as the world endures. Plain good intention, which is as easily discovered at the first view as fraud is surely detected at last, is, let me say, of no mean force in the government of mankind. Genuine simplicity of heart is an healing and cementing principle. My plan, therefore, being formed upon the most simple grounds imaginable, may disappoint some people when they hear it. It has nothing to recommend to it the pruriency of curious ears. There is nothing at all new and captivating in it. . . .

. . . .

I mean to give peace. Peace implies reconciliation, and, where there has been material dispute, reconciliation does in a manner always imply concession on the one part or on the other. In this state of things I make no difficulty in affirming that the proposal ought to originate from us. Great and acknowledged force is not impaired, either in effect or in opinion, by an unwillingness to exert itself. The superior power may offer peace with honour and with safety. Such an offer from such a power will be attributed to magnanimity. But the concessions of the weak are the concessions of fear. When such a one is disarmed he is wholly at the mercy of his superior, and he loses for ever that time and those chances which, as they happen to all men, are the strength and resources of all inferior power.

The capital leading questions on which you must this day decide are these two: First, whether you ought to concede; and secondly, what your concession ought to be. On the first of these questions we have gained (as I have just taken the liberty of observing to you) some ground. But I am sensible that a good deal more is still to be done. Indeed, sir, to enable us to determine both on the one and the other of these great questions with a firm and precise judgment, I think it may be necessary to consider distinctly the true nature and the peculiar circumstances of the object which we have before us. Because after all our struggle, whether we will or not, we must govern America according to that nature and to those circumstances, and not according to our own imaginations, nor according to abstract ideas of right—by no means according to mere general theories of government, the resort to which appears to me, in our present situation, no better than arrant trifling. I shall therefore endeavour, with your leave, to lay before you some of the most material of these circumstances in as full and as clear a manner as I am able to state them.

The first thing that we have to consider with regard to the nature of the object is—the number of people in the colonies. I have taken for some years a good deal of pains on that point. I can by no calculation justify myself in placing the number below two millions of inhabitants of our own European blood and colour, besides at least 500,000 others, who form no inconsiderable part of the strength and opulence of the whole. This, sir, is, I believe, about the true number. . . .

.   .   .   .

The trade with America alone is now within less than £500,000 of being equal to what this great commercial nation, England, carried on the beginning of this century with the whole world! If I had taken the largest year of those on your table it would rather have exceeded. But it will be said, is not this American trade an unnatural protuberance that has drawn the juices from the rest of the body? The reverse. It is the very food that has nourished every other part into its present magnitude. Our general trade has been greatly augmented, and augmented more or less in almost every part to which it ever extended; but with this material difference, that of the six millions which in the beginning of the century constituted the whole mass of our export commerce, the colony trade was but one-twelfth part; it is now (as a part of sixteen millions) considerably more than a third of the whole. This is the relative proportion of the importance of the colonies at these two periods; and all reasoning concerning our mode of treating them must have this proportion as its basis, or it is a reasoning weak, rotten, and sophistical.

.   .   .   .

I pass therefore to the colonies in another point of view, their agriculture. This they have prosecuted with such a spirit that, besides feeding plentifully their own growing multitude, their annual export of grain, comprehending rice, has some years ago exceeded a million in value. Of their last harvest, I am persuaded they will export much more. At the beginning of the century some of these colonies imported corn from the mother country. For some time past, the Old World has been fed from the New. The scarcity which you have felt would have been a desolating famine if this child of your old age, with a true filial piety, with a Roman charity, had not put the full breast of its youthful exuberance to the mouth of its exhausted parent.

As to the wealth which the colonies have drawn from the sea by their fisheries, you had all that matter fully opened at your bar. . . . When I contemplate these things, when I know that the colonies in general owe little or nothing to any care of ours, and that they are not squeezed into this happy form by the constraints of watchful and suspicious government, but that, through a wise and salutary neglect, a generous nature has been suffered to take her own way to perfection; when I reflect upon these effects, when I see how profitable they have been to us, I feel all the pride of power sink, and all presumption in the wisdom of human contrivances melt and die away within me. My rigour relents. I pardon something to the spirit of liberty.

I am sensible, sir, that all which I have asserted in my detail, is admitted in the gross, but that quite a different conclusion is drawn from it. America, gentlemen say, is a noble object. It is an object well worth fighting for. Certainly it is, if fighting a people be the best way of gaining them. Gentlemen in this respect will be led to their choice of means by their complexions and their habits. Those who understand the military art will of course have some predilection for it. Those who wield the thunder of the state may have more confidence in the efficacy of arms. But I confess, possibly for want of this knowledge, my opinion is much more in favour of prudent management than of force, considering force not as an odious, but a feeble instrument for preserving a people so numerous, so active, so growing, so spirited as this in a profitable and subordinate connection with us.

First, sir, permit me to observe that the use of force alone is but *temporary*. It may subdue for a moment, but it does not remove the necessity of subduing again; and a nation is not governed which is perpetually to be conquered.

My next objection is its *uncertainty*. Terror is not always the effect of force, and an armament is not a victory. If you do not succeed, you are without resource; for, conciliation failing, force remains, but force failing, no further hope of reconciliation is left. Power and authority are sometimes bought by kindness, but they can never be begged as alms by an impoverished and defeated violence.

A further objection to force is, that you *impair the object* by your very endeavours to preserve it. The thing you fought for is not the thing which you recover, but depreciated, sunk, wasted, and consumed in the contest. Nothing less will content me than *whole America*. I do not choose to consume its strength along with our own, because in all parts it is the British strength that I consume. I do not choose to be caught by a foreign enemy at the end of this exhausting conflict; and still less in the midst of it. I may escape, but I can make no assurance against such an event. Let me add, that I do not choose wholly to break the American spirit, because it is the spirit that has made the country.

Lastly, we have no sort of *experience* in favour of force as an instrument in the rule of our colonies. Their growth and their utility has been owing to methods altogether different. Our ancient indulgence has been said to be pursued to a fault. It may be so. But we know, if feeling is evidence, that our fault was more tolerable than our attempt to mend it, and our sin far more salutary than our penitence.

These, sir, are my reasons for not entertaining that high opinion of untried force by which many gentlemen, for whose sentiments in other particulars I have great respect, seem to be so greatly captivated. But there is still behind a third consideration concerning this object, which serves to determine my opinion on the sort of policy which ought to be pursued in the management of America, even more than its population and its commerce—I mean its *temper and character*.

In this character of the Americans, a love of freedom is the predominating feature which marks and distinguishes the whole; and as an ardent is always a jealous affection, your colonies become suspicious, restive, and untractable whenever they see the least attempt to wrest from them by force or shuffle from them by chicane what they think the only advantage worth living for. This fierce spirit of liberty is stronger in the English colonies probably than in any other people of the earth; and this from a great variety of powerful causes, which, to understand the true temper of their minds and the direction which this spirit takes, it will not be amiss to lay open somewhat more largely.

.   .   .   .

Then, sir, from these six capital sources: of descent, of form of government, of religion in the northern provinces, of manners in the southern, of education, of the remoteness of situation from the first mover of government—from all these causes a fierce spirit of liberty has grown up. It has grown with the growth of the people in your colonies, and increased with the increase of their wealth; a spirit that unhappily meeting with an exercise of power in England which, however lawful, is not reconcilable to any ideas of liberty, much less with theirs, has kindled this flame that is ready to consume us.

I do not mean to commend either the spirit in this excess or the moral causes which produce it. Perhaps a more smooth and accommodating spirit of freedom in them would be more acceptable to us. Perhaps ideas of liberty might be desired more reconcilable with an arbitrary and boundless authority. Perhaps we might wish the colonists to be persuaded that their liberty is more secure when held in trust for them by us (as their guardians during a perpetual minority) than with any part of it in their own hands. The question is, not whether their spirit deserves praise or blame, but what, in the name of God, shall we do with it? . . .

. . . .

My idea, therefore, without considering whether we yield as matter of right, or grant as matter of favour, is *to admit the people of our colonies into an interest in the constitution*; and, by recording that admission in the journals of Parliament, to give them as strong an assurance as the nature of the thing will admit that we mean for ever to adhere to that solemn declaration of systematic indulgence.

. . . .

All this, I know well enough, will sound wild and chimerical to the profane herd of those vulgar and mechanical politicians, who have no place among us; a sort of people who think that nothing exists but what is gross and material; and who, therefore, far from being qualified to be directors of the great movement of empire, are not fit to turn a wheel in the machine. But to men truly initiated and rightly taught, these ruling and master principles which, in the opinion of such men as I have mentioned, have no substantial existence, are in truth everything and all in all. Magnanimity in politics is not seldom the truest wisdom; and a great empire and little minds go ill together. If we are conscious of our situation, and glow with zeal to fill our place as becomes our station and ourselves, we ought to auspicate all our public proceedings on America with the old warning of the church, *Sursum corda!* We ought to elevate our minds to the greatness of that trust to which the order of Providence has called us. By adverting to the dignity of this high calling, our ancestors have turned a savage wilderness into a glorious empire, and have made the most extensive, and the only honourable conquests, not by destroying, but by promoting the wealth, the number, the happiness of the human race. Let us get an American revenue as we have got an American empire. English privileges have made it all that it is; English privileges alone will make it all it can be.

In full confidence of this unalterable truth, I now (*quod felix faustumque sit*) lay the first stone of the temple of peace; and I move you—

"That the colonies and plantations of Great Britain in North America, consisting of fourteen separate governments, and containing two millions and upwards of free inhabitants, have not had the liberty and privilege of electing and sending any knights and burgesses, or others, to represent them in the High Court of Parliament."

Appendix Two. Three Letters to Dr. Price *John Lind*

Preface.

It was not, I confess, from any high opinion I had entertained of Dr. Price's political or philosophical abilities, that I sat down to read his *Observations*. Not the writer, but the subject, engaged me. At first I gave them only a cursory perusal; on that perusal they seemed to present to me what I had expected, abuse of terms, confusion of ideas, intemperate ebullitions of misguided zeal, gloomy pictures of a disturbed imagination; all the effect I apprehended from the book arose from the opinion which I was told the public had of the author. I could not bring myself to conceive that by anything in these *Observations* a single person would be convinced who was not convinced before but I could easily conceive that many people might embrace that side of the question, on hearing that Dr. Price had written in favour of it.

Considering the Doctor as a man of integrity, as expressing what he really felt, I honoured the motive which led him to the work, and only smiled at the execution of it. For probity I gave him credit; I lamented only that he had no clearer views; in a word, my respect for the man converted into pity what I might otherwise have felt for the author.

Soon however it appeared that no common pains were taken to circulate, or (in the bookseller's phrase) to *puff* the work. I did not hastily give up my opinion of the Doctor's integrity. To his friends then, and not to him, was I candid enough to attribute these indecent manoeuvres.

He has acted, thought I, with no unbecoming dignity. He contents himself with telling us that "the *Observations* are important as well as just," that "he could not make himself easy without offering them to the public." And why should he not put himself at ease? It is not his fault that the zeal of his friends is too fierce to be restrained, too headstrong to be guided.

The quick circulation of the work they seem indeed to have considered as essential to the very being of this sinking country, as the only means of snatching "the kingdom from an edge so perilous." Circulate therefore it must, at whatever rate. Large extracts from it they got inserted in the public papers, they held it out to the world as unanswerable. They went a step farther—for the gentlemen are inventive—they declared the ministry had used undue means to suppress the sale of it; and at last—for the gentlemen are modest—they proposed that a subscription should be set on foot to enable the sons of freedom to distribute gratis this manual of liberty, physical and moral, religious and civil.[a]

a. The Doctor has completely justified the application of this term *manual*. A cheap edition of this pamphlet has been advertised for a guinea a hundred, in the same manner

The zeal of his friends stopped not here: these were only marks of private approbation; they determined that the stamp of public applause should be set on these important observations. How to obtain it? That was the question.

A certain court there is, "distinguished" we are told "for giving an example of zeal in the cause of liberty;"[b] not quite so distinguished for discernment perhaps but at least as ductile as that of the Areopagus of old. Here then they determined to apply. They aimed at no common things: a vote of thanks, the freedom of the city, a gold box. They aimed, and they succeeded. The great council of the city bestowed on the writer of a six-penny pamphlet what was thought an adequate reward for the services of a Pitt.

If before the Doctor's friends had given proofs of invention and modesty, here they gave proofs of political skill and management. Their party had been prepared by circular letters; all was still, till the avowed business of day was over, and many of those not in the secret were retired; then, in defiance of a standing order and an established custom,[c] such was the eloquence of one man,

"Whose voice sonorous charms the listening cit"—

---

as *manuals* of devotion, *quack* medicines, etc. This and the other proposals alluded to, appeared at the time in several of the public papers.

b. See Dr. Price's letter to the town clerk. Not always was the city of London so distinguished for giving an example of zeal in the cause of liberty. So at least we learn from unexceptionable authority, from the learned sister of the present patriotic lord mayor. On the servility of the city she is frequently and pointedly severe. She represents it, in her *History of the Commonwealth and Usurpation,* as alternately licking the hand that flattered, and crouching beneath the whip that threatened [probably Catharine (Sawbridge) Macaulay, *The History of England, from the Accession of James I to the Elevation of the House of Hanover,* vol. 5: *From the Death of Charles I to the Restoration of Charles II* (London: Printed for Edward and Charles Dilly, 1771)]. Did the parliament gain power? With the good citizens the parliament was all in all. Did Cromwell drive out the parliament? Cromwell was their lord. Cromwell dies, the parliament resumes the reins; the memory of Cromwell becomes odious, again the parliament is all in all. Lambert heads the army, and establishes a military council; the parliament is nothing, Lambert and his council are the deliverers of the nation. Monk disperses Lambert; Monk is their hero. Monk proposes to restore the second Charles without a single stipulation in favour of the people; it was the city of London that "was the centre of all the wicked cabals which produced the return of national slavery;" it was the city of London which was "among the most forward in offering service incense to the new established idol." As our days have produced neither Lamberts, nor Cromwells, nor Monks, the good city is content to be driven by *meaner* men.

c. If I am rightly informed, and I have my information from a deputy of one of the wards, there is a standing order, "That when any question is moved, which affects the city case, that question shall stand over to another court." This order was dispensed with in the present case. It is likewise customary, "That when a motion is made to confer the freedom of the city on a stranger, that motion shall stand over to another court." This custom was broke through. From the same authority I learn that of some few more than a hundred members who are said to have been present at the passing of this vote, eighty had been previously prepared by private circular letters to vote in favour of the motion.

The Doctor's arguments were first resolved, by these competent judges, to be unanswerable; then public thanks, the freedom of the city in a gold box were voted, as but adequate rewards for writing *Observations*, which many of the voters frankly owned they had never read.

In courtiers to be sure such a conduct would have been intolerable. To have waited till the house was thin, the members in opposition retired, and then to have given the public money to one of his own dependents would, and deservedly, have damned a minister. But when patriots are to be served, oh! the case is altered. To recompence a patriot author, a grant of public honours and of public money may be smuggled, to serve a patriot candidate, the mansion of the chief magistrate may be turned into a cake-house. "*To the pure, all things are pure.*"

It was scarcely possible that such repeated efforts should be altogether without effect, curiosity at least would be excited, men would be tempted to give a second and more attentive perusal to a book, on which so wise a body as the city of London had bestowed so uncommon a reward. On this second perusal my opinion of the writer remained the same, of the man my opinion wavered.

It wavered—but not long. When I saw him lend his hand to these manoeuvres, publish his *cheap* edition,[d] charged with gross miscalculations, yet refusing either to disprove the charge or retract his errors because forsooth his accusers are nameless; charged with false reasoning, and defending himself by the most servile of all pleas—that some body else had argued so before him; scattering firebrands around him; and when he thought all was in flame, retiring snugly to his own cell, and calling out, "I love quiet too well," to explain the reasons or vindicate the propriety of my conduct; then indeed my opinion of the man no longer wavered: from that moment his integrity as a man, and his abilities as a writer, stood with me in equal estimation.

He who runs a-tilt at a whole nation is surely a fair object of attack; in this case particularly no apology could be necessary; every critique upon such a work must be considered as a favour done to the author and his friends. He who criticizes, contributes to circulate a work and such, in the opinion both of the author and his friends, is the merit of this work, that to extend its circulation is to extend his fame, and to accomplish their wishes. . . .

d. The reader may be informed here as well as anywhere that the edition referred to in the following letters is this cheap edition, called I think the ninth.

Letter I. Of the Nature of Liberty in General.

. . . .

Right, Sir, is a mere legal term; "where no law is, there is no transgres-sion;" *e* so says an apostle. With equal truth he might have said, "where no law is, there is no right." *f*

How is it that a man acquires a right to a thing? By the declaration of the legislator that he may use and enjoy that thing; joined to a promise of the legislator, expressed or implied, that he will restrain every other person from depriving him of that thing or from troubling him in the use or enjoyment of it. How is it that a man acquires a right to do or to forbear any act? By the declaration of the legislator that he may do or forbear it joined to a promise of the legislator, expressed or implied, that he will re-strain every other person from constraining him to forbear the one or to do the other.

As to things, antecedently to law, a man may have the use and enjoyment of them, but he cannot have the right to them. That is, he may have pos-session, but he cannot have property. As to acts, he may be in the habit of doing, or forbearing, but he cannot have the right of exercising that habit. For till there be some law, tacit or expressed, he cannot be sure that others will be restrained from troubling him in the exercise of it. He may be free, but, without law, he cannot have the right to freedom.

When therefore you talk of a natural right, you must presuppose a Law of Nature which has established that right. But where is this Law of Nature to be found? Who has produced it? *g*

Not to enter into discussions which would lead us too far, it may be sufficient to observe that when men talk of a law of nature, they mean only certain imaginary regulations which appear to them to be fit and expedient. It is in this sense, sir, that I conceive the phrase to have been used by you. When therefore you say that a man has a natural right to the use and en-joyment of any thing or to do or forbear any act, I conceive you to mean no more than that it appears to you to be fit and expedient that such a right should be established.

And can you seriously imagine, sir, that a full and perfect liberty that

e. Romans 4:15.

f. See a book lately published called *A Fragment on Government,* pp. 179, 180 [Jeremy Bentham, *A Fragment on Government; Being an Examination of what is Delivered, on the Subject in General, in the Introduction to Sir William Blackstone's Commentaries . . .* (London: T. Payne, 1776)].

g. "Law," as is justly observed by Mr. De Lolme, "is the expression of will." The law of nature then must be the expression of will—but of whose will? Of nature's? But what is nature? Or is it the expression of the will of God who is sometimes called the Author of Nature? But if this be the case, where is the difference between this and what is called the Law of Revelation?

is a total absence of coercion, of constraint and restraint, is among the things to which every member of society should have an established un-alienable right? You cannot think so; for, though you will not allow that "it belongs to the nature of government to entrench upon private liberty," yet in the same breath you allow that government may restrain liberty because liberty may "be used to destroy liberty."

Supposing the law of nature to have been produced, supposing it to have established the right of liberty, still that right cannot be unalienable. It must, to a degree at least, be alienated in a state of society, if by society you mean, as it appears you do mean, a state of government. Such a state implies laws. All laws are coercive; the effect of them is either to restrain or to constrain. They either compel us to do or to forbear certain acts. The law which secures my property is a restraint upon you; the law which secures your property is a restraint upon me. By what magic then is it that you contrive to bestow on every member of society an unalienable right to be free from that restraint which is one of the two cements by which, and by which alone, society is held together? . . .

Letter II. Of Civil Liberty, and the Principles of Government.

. . . .

Wild indeed then must be the notions which one would naturally expect from you when you come to treat of the complicated concerns of a large state. The truth is, however, that in neither case do we meet with a single opinion of your own; nothing but the crude ideas of unthinking writers, adopted hastily and (it may sound harsh, but truth requires me to add) very awkwardly expressed.

You had read (and who has not read?) that "the political writers of antiquity would not allow more than three regular forms of government."[h] To one of these three it seems they gave the name of a *democracy* and in this form, some men have told us, "the sovereign power was lodged in the hands of an aggregate assembly consisting of all the members of the community."[i]

You had read too (and who has not read?) that democracies, that is, governments of all, have existed? You never stopped to enquire whether, or in what sense, the fact was true—whether by the term *all* were really meant all the inhabitants of a country or only all those of a certain class and

h. Blackstone's *Commentaries*, 1:49. I know it is a dangerous heresy, but I will avow it. Oft have I wished that the rage of the Goths and Vandals had spared all the buildings and vases of the ancients; most freely in return would I have pardoned the destruction of all their books of philosophy and politics.
i. Blackstone's *Commentaries*, 1:49.

denomination.*ʲ All* was the word and at once you determined that in your little state all the inhabitants, in general, should at one and the same moment be governors and governed.

You had read (and without reading one might have guessed) that "when a state becomes numerous or when the different parts of it are removed to distances from one another," this meeting of all would be impracticable. And "hence," you tell us, "a diminution of liberty necessarily arises."

I was quite frightened at this intelligence and actually on the point of setting out for Lucca or Ragusa. But the next paragraph quieted my alarms. "In these circumstances," (these dreadful circumstances of living in a large and opulent country) all is not lost; though we cannot catch liberty by the foretop, yet, "such near approaches may be made to it as shall answer all the purposes of government and, at the same time, secure every right of human nature." Thank God! A man may live in England without being quite a brute.

What then is the way of approaching to this unknown divinity without advancing a single step towards it? *"Quis facis per alterum facis per te."* You cannot get thither yourself, but then you may send another person in your stead and that you know brings you there too. You cannot participate in the powers of legislation individually and personally, but a number of you may club together, appoint one or more substitutes to participate for you, and then (can anything be plainer?) you are participating yourselves. I am not turning your positions into ridicule. I am stating them precisely as you yourself have stated them. Let the reader judge between us.

"Though the members of a state should not be capable of giving their suffrages on public measures individually and personally, they may do this by the appointment of substitutes." Do *this*? Do what? Give their suffrages on public measures, individually and personally. This is the only thing that has been mentioned. Again, "All the individuals that compose a great state cannot be admitted to an immediate participation in the powers of legislation and government, yet they may participate in these powers by a delegation of them to a body of representatives." That is, by putting the power in the hands of another, we may, we do, actually retain in it our own.

But to go on, these substitutes must have a name. Two occurred to you— *representatives* and *delegates*; the one familiar to an English ear, the other sweet-sounding to the ear of an American. Of these we may take our choice.

The next thing to be considered is the manner of appointing them. And

j. The truth is, as we have observed before, speaking of the state of Athens, that by the term *citizens* was meant a certain class of inhabitants who, in consequence of certain qualifications, had a right of voting in the public councils and it is all of this class only who participated in the legislation. When this class happened to be numerous, the government was called a democracy.

here you seemed to be on the point of becoming more reasonable than in the formation of your little state. In a little state the personal consent of every individual was necessary to every act of legislation; in a large state the suffrages of the majority are sufficient to appoint substitutes.[k] Not that all difficulties are removed by this concession: you had already supposed that the members of a large state were so numerous and the different parts of it removed to such distances from one another that all the members of it could not meet together to give their suffrages individually and personally. Yet meet they must and give their suffrages, too, individually and personally, for the election of substitutes. All and each of these substitutes are to be chosen "by the unbiassed voices of a majority of the state." Now, hitherto at least, the word 'state' has been used by you to denote the aggregate body of all the inhabitants of a country. It should seem, then, that every individual making part of this body is to give his suffrage in the choice of every representative. It should seem that no representative is to act without a decided majority of all these individuals in his favour. This I think we may fairly conclude to be your meaning. Were it not, some qualification, some restriction, would have been thrown in. But nothing of that sort do we meet with.

The representatives being thus chosen and chosen only for a short term, they are, I suppose, to be invested with certain powers.[l] What are these powers? Small enough God knows—dealt out with a very sparing hand. Your representatives are to be very good and do what they are bid and no more. For first they are to be subject to "the instructions of the unbiassed voices of a majority of the state." At the outset indeed you had agreed that all the members of your large state were not capable of giving their suffrages on public measures, individually and personally. But this was a hasty concession; why should you not revoke it? Why not convene all the members of the community for the very purpose of giving their suffrages

k. In the same page the Doctor again changes his mind. A majority, after all, is but a part, though a large part, of the whole. And if substitutes be "chosen by a part only of the state," down we go to the very abyss of slavery. These inaccuracies we see are not uncommon with our correct author.

l. What the Doctor means by a *short* term, he has not expressly declared. I suppose he means a year. To this interpretation I am led by a passage in his letter to the Town Clerk. It is this: "The testimony of approbation which they," meaning his *Observations*, "have received from a body so respectable, *annually* elected by the first city in the world, will, it may be hoped, lead the public to fix their views more on such measures as shall save a sinking constitution and preserve us from impending ruin." The reader will observe the stress intended to be laid on the phrase *annually* elected. Were it allowable to suppose so *good* a man subject to vanity, one would be tempted to imagine that the Doctor was drawing a secret comparison between the value of this approbation conferred on his *Observations* by these *annual unbiassed* officers and the approbation conferred by a *venal septennial* parliament on a Hawke or a Saunders. Who can doubt whether of the two speaks the voice of the people? Who can doubt to which of the heroes the title of *Saviour*, of *Preserver*, of his country most properly belongs? *Credant arma togae.*

on public measures? For I suppose you will allow that to give instructions to the representatives—instructions which must be obeyed—is, in the strictest sense of the word, to give their suffrages on public measures.[m]

But this is not all. The representatives are not only to be chosen for a short term and instructed by the unbiassed voices of a majority of the state, but being only trustees, they are to be subject to the control of some other body. As an individual, I can appoint a trustee, I can prescribe to him the extent of the trust and the uses he shall make of it. If he exceeds the bounds of that trust, if he perverts it to other uses, I know where to apply for a control. The judicial power affords it—the judicial power to which I and my trustee must alike submit. But when the majority of the people have appointed this public trustee, where shall they apply for a controlling power? To themselves you tell us; there can be no power to which they ought to submit, "for theirs is the only real omnipotence." And therefore the representatives are to be subject, not only to the instruction, but to "the control of the constituents," that is, of an unbiassed majority of the state. For of no other constituents have you spoken.

Indeed, my good Doctor, if your state is to meet together so often for the frequent (I suppose annual) election of its representatives for the purpose of instructing them, that is, of prescribing to them what they are to do, for the purpose of controlling them, that is, judicially punishing them when they shall have done more or less or otherwise than they ought to have done, you might as well let the state do its own business. It is mere children's play to choose representatives.

Having rendered your representatives so dependent on the instructions and control of their constituents, you have, no doubt, attained the object you had in view—the constitution of a free state. We have your own word for it: "To be free is to be guided by one's own will and to be guided by the will of another is the characteristic of servitude. This is particularly applicable to political liberty. That state is free which is guided by its own will or (which comes to the same) by the will of an assembly appointed by itself and accountable to itself."

Here then our business is done. According to your own assertion that

m. There are two countries in Europe where the electors retain this power of instructing their representatives, Poland and the Seven Provinces. What good effects have arisen from it in Poland is obvious to all Europe. The Seven Provinces are seven distinct sovereignties confederated together in one republic. Each province considered separately is an aristocracy. The government of each is in the hand of a senate or *vrootschap* in the election of which the people have no more share than they have in the election of a Pope. It cannot but be seen that there is a wide difference between substitutes chosen by a senate and deputed to a general council by separate states, each having its own local, separate and, in many occurrencies, opposite interests, and representatives chosen by the middling and inferior classes of a large community to provide for the common interests of one, single, undivided state. It is easy to be conceived that the right of instructing their substitutes may be practicable and salutary in the former case and dangerous, if not impracticable, in the other.

constitution is most "perfect and complete" which is most free. According to your own account that constitution is most free where the government is lodged either in the hands of the people themselves or in those of representatives, chosen by the people, accountable to the people.

What whim possessed you, sir, what qualm had seized you, to throw down in a moment the edifice you had been labouring so long to erect? In the same page we learn that this is no longer the most perfect constitution of government. For in the same page it is you tell us that "in order to form the most perfect constitution of government there may be the best reasons for joining to such a body of representatives an hereditary council consisting of men of the first rank in the state with a supreme executive magistrate at the head of all."[n] And what, I pray you, are the best reasons for such a junction? One, and that the first recited, is given us in these words: "This will form useful checks in a legislature." Checks upon whom? Upon that very body of men by whose will alone we were told but a few lines before a free people can be governed. So then to be free is, at one and the same time, to be guided solely by our own will, or the will of substitutes appointed by ourselves and accountable to ourselves, and to be guided by the will of these substitutes conjointly with the concurrent will of a second body of men and the will of yet a single person at the head of all, neither of which latter are to be substitutes, neither of which latter are to be appointed by ourselves or accountable to ourselves.

. . . .

How is it that liberty is established by law? To whom and against whom is it given? Whether the circumstance which distinguishes that which is generally called a free from that which is called a despotic state be this, namely, that the persons in whose hands the supreme power is lodged in a free state have indeed less power than those in whose hands it is lodged in a despotic state? Whether you are justified by experience in supposing that to constitute a free state it is necessary to vest the supreme power in the hands of the people at large?

Liberty we have said is the absence of coercion. Perfect Liberty would be a total absence of coercion. Civil liberty means not this. It means only a partial absence of coercion; and that enjoyed by one or more of that class of persons in a state of civil or political society who are called subjects and with respect only to others of that same class? How is this liberty created by law? To whom and against whom is it given? It is given to that subject or class of subjects upon whom the law does not operate and against all other subjects upon whom the law does operate.

n. The reader will observe the inaccuracy of which our correct author is guilty in speaking of this hereditary council. It is to consist of "men of the first rank in the state." Rank is not one of the requisites which the candidate is to possess. It is an acquisition which he makes in consequence of becoming one of the hereditary council.

Suppose, for instance, there were but one religion established or even tolerated in a country and that the ministers of that religion were the only persons permitted to speak in public on the subject of religion. To this class of citizens, called ministers, the liberty of speaking in public on the subject of religion would be then reserved. But how? Not by any operation of the law on them, but by its operation on every other subject whom it would restrain from troubling them in the free performance of this act. But the restraint upon other subjects in this case would be twofold. They would be restrained from troubling this particular class in the free performance of this particular act and they would be again restrained from performing that act themselves. Supposing this last restraint never to have been imposed and all the subjects would in this instance have been free; supposing the restraint to be taken off and they would again become free. In either case how is this liberty bestowed on all? Precisely in the same manner as in the former supposition it would be bestowed on a particular class of subjects—by the operation of the law, not on the individual who means to do the act in question, but on every other person who may attempt to restrain him from doing it.

We may perhaps be told that this idea of civil liberty is imperfect, that civil liberty includes an absence of coercion with respect to that person or assemblage of persons who are called governors. I profess I do not see how this can be established by law. Law we have said is the expression of will. That person or assemblage of persons, the expression of whose will constitutes law, are governors. Is it then likely, is it indeed possible that they should give liberty against themselves? The very attempt to do it, I mean directly and openly, would be destructive of civil liberty, properly so called, of that liberty, I mean, which we have just described and which only should be called by this name. For the truth of this I may appeal to the history of Rome in ancient days, to that of Poland in our own. In both these states, in proportion as the power of the governors has been openly and directly checked, the civil liberty of the subject has been checked with it. The governors, as such, could not indeed infringe the liberty of the subject, but then neither could they protect the accused against the abuse of power on the part of the magistrate nor the feeble against the oppression of the more powerful individual. And too, that when this impotence of the governors has produced, as it naturally must produce, a state of anarchy and confusion, they have been compelled to have recourse to the most violent methods to protect the state against either the attacks of foreign foes or the cabals of factious and over-powerful citizens. Such was at Rome the appointment of a dictator or of a consul armed with the dictatorial power conveyed by that arbitrary and unlimited commission of *"videat consul ne quid respublica detrimenti capiat;"* such is in Poland the yet more dreadful tyranny of a confederation. . . .

Appendix Three. Some Observations on Liberty Occasioned by a Late Tract *John Wesley*

1. It was with great expectation that I read Dr. Price's *Observations on the Nature of Civil Liberty, the Principles of Government, and the Justice and Policy of the War with America*; and I was not disappointed. As the author is a person of uncommon abilities, so he has exerted them to the uttermost in the tract before us, which is certainly a masterpiece of its kind. He has said all that can be said upon the subject, and has digested it in the most accurate manner; and candour requires us to believe that he has wrote with an upright intention, with a real design to subserve the interest of mankind in general, as well as the subjects of the British empire. But as the Doctor is a friend to liberty, so he can "think and let think." He does not desire that we should implicitly submit to the judgment, either of him or any other fallible man; and will not therefore be displeased at a few further observations on the same subject. This subject is,

2. The liberty which is now claimed by the confederate colonies in America. In order to understand this much-controverted question, I would set aside everything not essential to it. I do not therefore now inquire, whether this or that measure be consistent with good policy; or, whether it is likely to be attended with good or ill success. I only want to know, is their claim right or wrong? Is it just or unjust?

3. What is it they claim? You answer, "Liberty." Nay, is it not independency? You reply, "That is all one, they do claim it, and they have a right to it."

To independency? That is the very question. To liberty they have an undoubted right, and they enjoy that right. (I mean, they did, till the late unhappy commotions.) They enjoyed their liberty in all full a manner as I do, or any reasonable man can desire.

"What kind of liberty do they enjoy?" Here you puzzle the cause, by talking of physical and moral liberty. What you speak of both is exactly true, and beautifully expressed. But both physical and moral liberty are beside the present question and the introducing them can answer no other end than to bewilder and confuse the reader. Therefore, to beg the reader "to keep these in his view," is only begging him to look off the point in hand. You desire him, in order to understand this, to attend to something else! "Nay, I beg him to look straight forward, to mind this one thing, to fix his eye on that liberty, and that only, which is concerned in the present question. And all the liberty to which this question relates is either religious or civil liberty."

4. "Religious liberty is a liberty to choose our own religion, to worship

246   Appendix Three. Observations

God according to our own conscience. Every man living, as a man, has a right to this, as he is a rational creature. The Creator gave him this right when he endowed him with understanding, and every man must judge for himself, because every man must give an account of himself to God. Consequently, this is an unalienable right, it is inseparable from humanity, and God did never give authority to any man, or number of men, to deprive any child of man thereof, under any colour or pretence whatever."[a]

Now, who can deny that the colonies enjoy this liberty to the fulness of their wishes?

5. Civil liberty is a liberty to dispose of our lives, persons, and fortunes, according to our own choice and the laws of our country.

I add, *according to the laws of our country*. For, although, if we violate these, we are liable to fines, imprisonment, or death, yet if, in other cases, we enjoy our life, liberty, and goods, undisturbed, we are free, to all reasonable intents and purposes.

Now, all this liberty the confederate colonies did enjoy, till part of them enslaved the rest of their countrymen; and all the loyal colonies do enjoy it at the present hour. None takes away their lives, or freedom, or goods; they enjoy them all quiet and undisturbed.

"But the King and Parliament can take them all away." But they do not; and, till it is done, they are freemen. The supreme power of my country can take away either my religious or civil liberty but, till they do, I am free in both respects. I am free now, whatever I may be by and by. Will any man face me down, I have no money now, because it may be taken from me tomorrow?

6. But the truth is, what they claim is not liberty, it is independency. They claim to be independent of England, no longer to own the English supremacy.

A while ago, they vehemently denied this, for matters were not then ripe. And I was severely censured for supposing they intended any such thing. But now the mask is thrown off. They frankly avow it, and Englishmen applaud them for so doing!

Nay, you will prove that not only the colonies, but all mankind, have a right to it; yea, that independency is of the very essence of liberty and that all who are not independent are slaves.

Nay, if all who are not independent are slaves, then there is no free nation in Europe, then all in every nation are slaves except the supreme powers. All in France, for instance, except the King; all in Holland, except the Senate; yea, and these too, King and Senate both are slaves, if (as you say) they are dependent upon the people. So, if the people depend on their governors, and their governors on them, they are all slaves together.

a. See my tract, entitled, *Thoughts upon Liberty* [John Wesley, *Thoughts upon Liberty. By an Englishman*, 1772].

Mere play with words. This is not what all the world means by liberty and slavery; therefore, to say, "If the Parliament taxes you without your consent, you are a slave," is mere quibbling. Whoever talks thus should say honestly, "Reader, I give you warning, I affix a new sense, not the common one, to these words, *liberty* and *slavery*." Take the words in this sense, and you may prove there are slaves enough in England, as well as America; but if we take them in the old, common sense, both the Americans and we are free men.

. . . .

14. "Nay, not only the Americans, but all men, have a right to be self-governed and independent." You mean, they had a right thereto, before any civil societies were formed. But when was that time when no civil societies were formed? I doubt hardly since the flood and, wherever such societies exist, no man is independent. Whoever is born in any civilized country is, so long as he continues therein, whether he chooses it or no, subject to the laws and to the supreme governors of that country. Whoever is born in England, France, or Holland, is subject to their respective governors and "must needs be subject to the power, as to the ordinance of God, not only for wrath, but for conscience' sake." He has no right at all to be independent or governed only by himself but is in duty bound to be governed by the powers that be, according to the laws of the country. And he that is thus governed, not by himself, but the laws, is, in the general sense of mankind, a free man, not that there ever existed any original compact between them and those governors. But the want of this does not make him a slave nor is any impeachment to his liberty and yet this free man is, by virtue of those laws, liable to be deprived, in some cases, of his goods, in others, of his personal freedom, or even of his life. And all this time he enjoys such a measure of liberty as the condition of civilized nations allows, but no independency. That chimera is not found, no, not in the wilds of Africa or America.

Although, therefore, these subtle metaphysical pleas for universal independency appear beautiful in speculation, yet it never was, neither can be, reduced to practice. It is in vain to attempt it.

. . . .

22. To set this whole matter in another light, I beg leave to repeat the sum of a small tract lately published.[b] Have not the people, in every age and nation, the right to dispose of the supreme power, of investing therewith whom they please, and upon what conditions they see good? Consequently, if those conditions are not observed, they have a right to take it

b. *Thoughts on the Origin of Power* [John Wesley, *Thoughts concerning the Origin of Power* (Bristol: Printed by W. Pine, 1772)].

away. To prove this it is argued, "All men living are naturally equal, none is above another, and all are naturally free masters of their own actions; therefore, no man can have any power over another, but by his own consent: therefore, the power which any governors enjoy must be originally derived from the people, and presupposes an original compact between them and their first governors."

23. But, who are the people? Are they every man, woman, and child? Why not? Is it not one fundamental principle, that "all persons living are naturally equal, that all human creatures are naturally free, masters of their own actions, that none can have any power over them, but by their own consent?" Why, then, should not every man, woman, and child, have a voice in placing their governors, in fixing the measure of their power, and the conditions on which it is intrusted? And why should not every one have a voice in displacing them too? Surely they that gave the power have a right to take it away. By what argument do you prove that women are not naturally as free as men? And if they are, why have they not as good a right to choose their governors? Who can have any power over free, rational creatures, but by their own consent? And are they not free by nature as well as we? Are they not rational creatures?

24. But suppose we exclude women from using their natural right, by might overcoming right, what pretence have we for excluding men like ourselves barely because they have not lived one-and-twenty years? "Why, they have not wisdom or experience to judge of the qualifications necessary for governors." I answer, (1) Who has? how many of the voters in Great Britain? one in twenty? one in an hundred? If you exclude all who have not this wisdom, you will leave few behind. But, (2) Wisdom and experience are nothing to the purpose. You have put the matter upon another issue. Are they men? That is enough. Are they human creatures? Then they have a right to choose their own governors, and indefeasible right, a right inherent, inseparable from human nature. "But in England they are excluded by law." Did they consent to the making of that law? If not, by your original supposition, it can have no power over them. I therefore utterly deny that we can, consistently with that supposition, exclude either women or minors from choosing their own governors.

25. But suppose we exclude these by main force, are all that remain, all men of full age, the people? Are the males, then, that have lived one-and-twenty years allowed to choose their own governors? Not in England, unless they are freeholders, and have forty shillings a year. Worse and worse! After depriving half the human species of their natural right for want of beard, after having deprived myriads more for want of a stiff beard, for not having lived one-and-twenty years, you rob others, many hundred thousands, of their birthright for want of money! Yet not altogether on this account neither; if so, it might be more tolerable. But here is an Eng-

lishman who has money enough to buy the estates of fifty freeholders and yet he must not be numbered among the people because he has not two or three acres of land! How is this? By what right do you exclude a man from being one of the people because he has not forty shillings a year; yea, or not a groat? Is he not a man whether he be rich or poor? Has he not a soul and a body? Has he not the nature of a man, consequently, all the rights of a man, all that flow from human nature and, among the rest, that of not being controlled by any but by his own consent?

"But he that has not a freehold is excluded by law." By a law of his own making? Did he consent to the making of it? If he did not, what is that law to him? No man, you aver, has any power over another but by his own consent. Of consequence, a law made without his consent is, with regard to him, null and void. You cannot say otherwise without destroying the supposition that "none can be governed but by his own consent."

26. See now to what your argument comes. You affirm, all power is derived from the people and presently exclude one half of the people from having any part or lot in the matter. At another stroke, suppose England to contain eight millions of people, you exclude one or two millions more. At a third, suppose two millions left, you exclude three-fourths or these; and the poor pittance that remains, by I know not what figure of speech, you call the people of England!

27. Hitherto we have endeavoured to view this point in the mere light of reason and, even by this, it appears, that this supposition, which has been palmed upon us as undeniable, is not only false, not only contrary to reason, but contradictory to itself; the very men who are most positive that the people are the source of power, being brought into an inextricable difficulty, by that single question, "Who are the people?" reduced to a necessity of either giving up the point, or owning that by *the people*, they mean scarce a tenth part of them.

28. But we need not rest the matter entirely on reasoning. Let us appeal to matter of fact; and, because we cannot have so clear a prospect of what is at a distance, let us only take a view of what has been in our own country. I ask, then, when did the people of England (suppose you mean by that word only half a million of them) choose their own governors? Did they choose (to go no further) William the Conqueror? Did they choose King Stephen or King John? As to those who regularly succeeded their fathers, the people are out of the question. Did they choose Henry the Fourth, Edward the Fourth, or Henry the Seventh? Who will be so hardy as to affirm it? Did the people of England, or but fifty thousand of them, choose Queen Mary, or Queen Elizabeth, or King James the First? Perhaps you will say, "If the people did not give King Charles the supreme power, at least they took it away." No; the people of England no more took away his power, than they cut off his head. "Yes; the Parliament did, and they are

the people." No; the Parliament did not. The House of Commons is not the Parliament any more than it is the nation. Neither were those who then sat the House of Commons, no, nor one quarter of them. But, suppose they had been the whole House of Commons, yea, or the whole Parliament, by what rule of logic will you prove that seven or eight hundred persons are the people of England? "Why, they are the delegates of the people; they are chosen by them." No, not by one half, not by a quarter, not by a tenth part of them. So that the people, in the only proper sense of the word, were innocent of the whole affair.

29. "But, you will allow, the people gave the supreme power to King Charles the Second at the Restoration." I will allow no such thing unless, by the people, you mean General Monk and ten thousand soldiers. "However, you will not deny that the people gave the power to King William at the Revolution." I will; the Convention were not the people, neither elected by them. So that still we have not a single instance, in above seven hundred years, of the people of England's conveying the supreme power either to one or more persons.

30. So much both for reason and matter of fact. But one single consideration will bring the question to a short issue. It is allowed no man can dispose of another's life but by his own consent. I add, No, nor with his consent; for no man has a right to dispose of his own life. The Creator of man has the sole right to take the life which he gave. Now, it is an indisputable truth, *Nihil dat quod non habet.*—"None gives what he has not." It follows that no man can give to another a right which he never had himself, a right which only the Governor of the world has, even the wiser heathens being judges, but which no man upon the face of the earth either has or can have. No man, therefore, can give the power of the sword, any such power as gives a right to take away life. Wherever it is, it must descend from God alone, the sole disposer of life and death.

31. The supposition, then, that the people are the origin of power, or that "all government is the creature of the people," though Mr. Locke himself should attempt to defend it, is utterly indefensible. It is absolutely overturned by the very principle on which it is supposed to stand, namely, that "a right of choosing his governors belongs to every partaker of human nature." If this be so, then it belongs to every individual of the human species; consequently, not to freeholders alone, but to all men; not to men only, but to women also; not only to adult men and women, to those who have lived one-and-twenty years, but to those that have lived eighteen or twenty, as well as those who have lived threescore. But none did ever maintain this, nor probably ever will; therefore, this boasted principle falls to the ground and the whole superstructure with it. So common sense brings us back to the grand truth, "There is no power but of God."

32. I may now venture to "pronounce, that the principles on which you have argued are incompatible with practice," even the universal practice of mankind, as well as with sound reason and it is no wonder "that they are not approved by our governors," considering their natural tendency, which is to unhinge all government, and to plunge every nation into total anarchy.

This, in truth, is the tendency of the whole book, a few passages of which I shall now recite, begging leave to make a few remarks upon them. But I must ask the reader's pardon if I frequently say the same thing more than once for, otherwise, I could not follow the author.

33. "All the members of a state," (which necessarily include all the men, women, and children) "may intrust the powers of legislation with any number of delegates, subject to such restrictions as they think necessary." This is "incompatible with practice." It never was done from the beginning of the world, it never can, it is flatly impossible in the nature of the thing. "And thus, all the individuals that compose a great state partake of the power of legislation and government." *All the individuals*! Mere quixotism! Where does that state exist? Not under the canopy of heaven. "In this case, a state is still free," (but this case has no being) "if the representatives are chosen by the unbiassed voices of the majority." Hold! This is quite another case, you now shuffle in a new term. The *majority* we were not talking of, but *all the members* of a state. The majority are not *all the individuals* that compose it and pray, how came the minority to be deprived of those rights which you say are "unalienable from human nature?" "But we disguise slavery, keeping up the form of liberty, when the reality is lost." It is not lost; I now enjoy all the real liberty I can desire, civil as well as religious. The liberty you talk of was never found; it never existed yet. But what does all this lead to, but to stir up all the inhabitants of Great Britain against the government?

34. To inflame them still more, you go on: "Liberty is more or less complete, according as the people have more or less share in the government." This is altogether contrary to matter of fact. The greater share the people have in the government, the less liberty, either civil or religious, does the nation in general enjoy. Accordingly, there is most liberty of all, civil and religious, under a limited monarchy; there is usually less under an aristocracy, and least of all under a democracy. What sentences then are these: "To be guided by one's own will, is freedom; to be guided by the will of another, is slavery"? This is the very quintessence of republicanism but it is a little too barefaced for, if this is true, how free are all the devils in hell, seeing they are all guided by their own will! And what slaves are all the angels in heaven since they are all guided by the will of another! See another stroke: "The people have power to model government as they

please." What an admirable lesson to confirm the people in their loyalty to the government! Yet again: "Government is a trust, and all its powers a delegation." It is a trust, but not from the people. "There is no power but of God." It is a delegation, namely, from God, for "rulers are God's ministers," or delegates.

.   .   .   .

Appendix Four. Remarks on a Pamphlet Lately Published by Dr. Price *Adam Ferguson*

In a Letter to a Member of Parliament.

. . . .

Sir,

I send you some remarks on Dr. Price's pamphlet concerning which you do me the honour to desire my opinion. A gentleman who gives his name to the public is entitled to have the fairest construction put upon his words, and I shall be extremely sorry if, in differing from Dr. Price, any expression escape from me that is too abrupt for the respect that is due to him. As I am a mere commentator, I am likely to be as dull as the rest of my fraternity but shall, nevertheless, abide by the order, and confine myself to the matter, that is suggested by my author.

You will please to observe that the Doctor rests his argument on a definition of civil liberty which is, therefore, a principal subject of these remarks. He considers liberty under four general divisions, *physical liberty, moral liberty, religous liberty,* and *civil liberty.*[a] The first is the *principle of spontaneity.* The second is the *power of following our own sense of right and wrong.* The third, the *power of exercising the religion we like best.* And the fourth, of civil liberty, is the *power of a civil society or state to govern itself by its own discretion.*

The Doctor, in the following inference from all these definitions collated together, puts liberty in contradistinction to restraint, and makes restraint, in every case, the essence of slavery. In all these cases, he says, *there is a force which stands opposed to the agent's own will and which, as far as it operates, produces servitude.* And he concludes the whole deduction with observing that, *as far as in any instance the operation of any cause comes in to restrain the power of self-government, so far slavery is introduced. Nor do I think,* he adds, *that a preciser idea than this of liberty and slavery can be formed.*

I am under the necessity, however of owning that this idea is somewhat perplexing to me. It does not appear that upon this idea of liberty any civil community can be formed without introducing slavery. For even where the collective body are sovereigns they are seldom unanimous and the minority must ever submit to a power that stands opposed to their own will.

In this, however, the loss of liberty may be supposed unavoidable, for it is common to say that men, by entering into society, give up a part of their natural liberty.

a. See Sec. 1, [pp. 67–68].

But there is yet another difficulty. If liberty be opposed to restraint, I am afraid it is inconsistent with the great end of civil government itself, which is to give people security from the effect of crimes and disorders, and to preserve the peace of mankind.

The liberty of any single man, in this sense of a freedom from restraint, would be the servitude of all. In Turkey, perhaps in Brandenburgh, there are persons who pretend to this liberty but I believe that no one can devise a more plentiful source of slavery than this. The liberty of every separate district or corporation in a state would be national independence and, as far as the humour for it should spread, would threaten every community with the loss of every incorporated member that has a pretence for separation or a fancy to set up for itself.

I confess I am somewhat surprised that Dr. Price, who quotes Montesquieu with so much regard on other occasions, should have overlooked what he has said on this. Among the other mistaken notions of liberty, this celebrated writer observes, *that some have confounded the power of the people with the liberty of the people.*[b] *That in democracies the people seem to do what they please, but that liberty does not consist in doing what we please. It consists in being free to do what we ought to incline, and in not being obliged to do what we ought not to incline.*[c] *We ought to remember,* he continues, *that independence is one thing and liberty another. That if any citizen were free to do what he pleased, this would be an extinction of liberty, for every one else would have the same freedom.*[d]

If the Doctor persist in his definition of civil liberty it will be difficult to support the high encomium which he bestows upon it. For it would be a real curse to numbers of mankind to be left to do what they please. Certain instances we have had of this liberty in the case of despotic princes who were taught to think that they had a right to do what they pleased; but they were, in consequence of this liberty, the completest wretches that have appeared in the history of mankind.

Whether we say or no with Montesquieu that the power of the people is not the liberty of the people, it may be said with confidence that the power of the people is not the happiness of the people. Corrupt and vicious men assembled in great bodies cannot have a greater curse bestowed upon them, than the power of governing themselves.

It is possible that the Doctor may have meant to qualify his definition and the encomium of civil liberty by supposing that it was preceded by moral liberty, and if he did this would be rather an awkward way of informing us that liberty consists in the freedom to do what is just and innocent. In the meantime, and till moral liberty is fully established in the

b. *L'Esprit des Loix*, livre 2, chap. 2.
c. *Ibid.*, chap. 3.
d. *Ibid.*

world, we shall do well to prepare some restraint for the inclinations of men and be contented with a liberty which secures to us the possession of our rights while it restrains us from invading the rights of others.

Here, however, I am obliged to look forward some pages, and must confess that the Doctor himself has qualified his description of liberty in some such manner as this; *A free state,* he says, *at the same time that it is free itself, makes all its members free by excluding licentiousness and guarding their persons and property and good name against insult.*[e] That is to say, when we bring together the two parts of the Doctor's description, that a free state produces servitude, to produce liberty. Or, as he concludes the paragraph himself, that *government restrains liberty when used to destroy liberty.*

This collision of words, I confess, renders the precision of the Doctor's former idea somewhat suspicious, but we must be contented with the good meaning and only regret that the qualification of the general definition had not come sooner and that it is not more uniformly kept in view through the piece. If a writer should insist that the inhabitants of St. Giles have a right to seize the houses in Grosvenor Square and afterwards, upon a difficulty stated, should qualify his doctrine by saying that he affirmed the right only on a supposition that they had bought the subjects in question, and had paid for them, his doctrine might be true on the whole but his manner of stating it, by leaving out so important a condition till it was required to solve an objection, especially if he dropped it afterwards through the whole of his argument, might appear somewhat exceptionable. It is probable that some of the parties concerned would be in such haste to avail themselves of the right, that they would not stay to think of the condition. And I apprehend with some regret that the Doctor may have readers who will reason on his definition of liberty and think themselves entitled to do what they please without attending to the qualification that is afterwards brought to explain it.

My impatience to have a satisfactory account of this important subject, by collating together the descriptions and limitations of my author, has carried me a few pages too fast; I think myself now, however, authorised to conclude with the consent of the Doctor, that civil liberty is not precisely a power to do what we please, but the security of our rights; and that a person may be free, although contrary to his own will he is obliged to pay his debts, and even to contribute to the revenue of the state. And if the Doctor insists that liberty still implies a freedom from restraint, he will please to observe that nothing can give a more complete freedom from unjust restraint than the perfect security that we cannot be wronged. This is the freedom which Montesquieu holds forth to our esteem, and I presume it is that liberty on which Dr. Price bestows his encomium, notwith-

e. Pp. [72] and [73].

standing his apparent partiality to the freedom of doing what we please. I now return to the place at which I met my author.[f]

The doctor, in every step of his argument, is somewhat hurried by his own definition. *In every free state*, he says, *every man is his own legislator, all taxes are free gifts for public services.* It may be fair to ask in what part of the world such a state does, or ever did exist? Or what sort of laws thieves and pickpockets are likely to make against theft? Or how much of his property the miser is likely to bring to the coffers of the public?

In most free states the populace has as much need to be guarded against the effect of their own folly and errors as against the usurpation of any other person whatever. And the essence of political liberty is such an establishment as gives power to the wise and safety to all. The exercise of power in popular assemblies has a mixture of effects, good and bad. It teaches a people, as it did the Athenians, to become wits, critics, and orators. It gives to every man one chance against being oppressed, in allowing him to appear for himself. But it places him, when accused, before rash, precipitate, prejudiced, and inequitable judges; he is no more his own legislator than he is the master of the people. And he is in fact subject to a power which is of all others the most unstable, capricious, and arbitrary, bound by no law and subject to no appeal. For this reason, Mr. Montesquieu has very wisely said that democracy and aristocracy are not by their nature free governments.[g] They are inferior in this respect to certain species of monarchy where law is more fixed and the abuses of power are better restrained.

The Doctor farther observes, or concludes, from his definition, *that civil liberty in the most perfect degree can be enjoyed only in small states, where every member is capable of giving his suffrage in person, and of being chosen into public offices.*[h] It is true that democracy is tolerable only in small states and the Doctor certainly means to speak of democracy when he makes this inference on the subject of liberty. But even in the smallest states the preservation of public consistency and justice, the security of private rights, must ever recommend some mixture of aristocratical power that may prove a check on the caprice of the people, and such a mixture took place in all the happiest institutions of antiquity.

The Doctor owns that although liberty be most perfect in small states, it is not altogether banished from great ones! For, *where all the members of a state are not capable of giving their suffrages on public measures individually and personally they may do this by the appointment of substitutes or representatives.*[i]

In this concession the Doctor begins to elude the force of his own defini-

f. P. [69].
g. *L'Esprit des Loix*, livre 9, chap. 5.
h. P. [70].
i. *Ibid.*

tion and when we consider how little in some cases the constituent may know of what his representative does, it appears that, by this device, men may be their own legislators without so much as knowing that laws are enacted or proposed. And even America, at the distance of three thousand miles of sea, may enjoy its freedom by sending substitutes or representatives to the Parliament of Great Britain.

This indeed is one of the happiest institutions of mankind and might be of use in small as well as in great states by giving every order of the people that share in the legislature of their country which is necessary to guard their own rights without enabling them to usurp on the rights of others. But I must still contend that the liberty of every class and order is not proportioned to the power they enjoy but to the security they have for the preservation of their rights.

. . . .

Dr. Price infers from his argument that no one community can have *any power over the property or legislation of another that is not incorporated with it by a just and adequate representation.*[j]

In this passage, by the word power, he certainly means the right to have such a power, for it is an undoubted fact that many states have had the power. Even the admired and happy republics of Switzerland and Holland have their subject towns and provinces, and this nascent republic of New England too, if it acquire the independence which, under the denomination of liberty is projected for it, may come to have its subject towns and provinces and, among the foremost, some of those who are now so ready to become partners of its revolt against the state.

I do not contend for the right to any such power in any actual case but I contend not only for the reality of the power but for the right likewise in some supposable cases. No writer on the law of nature, that I know of, has denied that states or bodies politic may perform every act that any private party can perform, and, if this be admitted, it follows that they may, either by contract or forfeiture, become tributary or subject to another state or body politic, as much as a single man may become the servant or debtor of another single man by stipulation or forfeiture.

This maxim of the law of nature, I confess, does not bind the Americans to contribute to the supply of the British Empire unless it can be shown that they have received all the benefit of subjects and therefore have stipulated to perform all the duties of subjects by the same tacit convention that binds every inhabitant of Great Britain.

I agree with the Doctor that the subjection of one state to another is inexpedient and often calamitous for both but this will not preclude one member of the same state, who has always made common cause with an-

j. P. [75].

other, from having a very just claim to expect a joint contribution to the common support.

After what has passed between Great Britain and her colonies, whoever pretends that Great Britain should drop every claim of a return and the colonies refuse to make any return, under every possible security to their property, must have very high notions of the generosity incumbent on the one party and as low notions of what is incumbent on the other. Nay, but they have traded with us, and this is enough; and have not we traded with them? Have they given us their goods for nothing? Or have they been careful to receive value? Or have they taken less value than other nations would have taken? These questions should be answered before we are told that their trade has repaid us for all the blood and treasure we have expended in the common cause and before it can be admitted that in the heights of prosperity, at which they may arrive, they are not bound under any form, or with any precautions, for the remainder of their property, to contribute any part of it whatever to the common supplies of the Empire.

.   .   .   .

Dr. Price, being to consider the justice of the war, recites all the pleas that may be offered by the state in support of coercive measures. These pleas he supposes to be, *the necessity of war to preserve the unity of the empire, our superiority, our pretensions as the parent state, the return due for our benefits, our sovereignty in the territory of America.* The Doctor will own that union is at least a desirable object and will pardon our endeavours to preserve it by the same means that states, the most moderate, have employed for this purpose: the policy of a common interest, a common sense of duty, and the authority of a common government. If any one contend that we ought to rely on either of the former principles to the exclusion of the latter, and that we ought to resign either the authority or the force which government on occasion must exert, I should suspect that he does not wish to have us united, nor even to leave us possessed of the common resources for the preservation of peace and good order that all nations have employed within their dependencies.

I mean not to argue from the second topic. Nations do not found obligations of allegiance and duty on difference of wealth, numbers of people, or the supposed precedency of scholars and learned men. I hope the remaining title, however, will not be so slightly treated. The name of parent state is not an empty sound. It carries the authority by which civil rights are established and modified. If America derive nothing from this authority why did its settlers take any charters from the crown of Great Britain? Or if they were emancipated by these charters why is not their emancipation expressed in some such terms as the following? *Whereas certain persons mean to depart this our kingdom and form states apart, we hereby emancipate such persons, discharge their allegiance to us, and discontinue our protection.* If, on the contrary, they took possession of their settlements by grants of the Crown, if they have been uniformly considered as British subjects, amenable to the law and under the protection of the state, what title have they now to withdraw their allegiance because their settlements were made in America, any more than if they had been on Hounslow Heath or on Finchley Common? The charters, the precedents, the statutes on which this right of the state is founded, can no more be disputed than the charters, precedents, and statutes on which the constitution of the state, respecting any other part of its power, is established. The utmost any party can plead is that circumstances are changed and require a new system of policy, or at least some additional precautions, to give to the British subjects of America the same security, or a security as nearly as possible the same, with that which is enjoyed by their fellow subjects at home.

Exaction of gratitude is but an ungracious plea; the fact is that the state protected and encouraged that part of her subjects on the same mixed motives of political interest and affection that she protects and encourages every other member of the community, and there is no other member that has not an equal title to reject the claim of gratitude. It may again be repeated that considering what has passed between Great Britain and her colonies, the Americans will be found to act an odious part in this contest; they are not satisfied with the enjoyment of their municipal governments and such a mode of contributing to the supplies of the empire as may be consistent with the safety of their persons and their properties.

The sovereignty of a territory and the property of its land, everywhere admits of a distinction. The state is undoubtedly sovereign of all the territory on which any of her subjects, under her protection, and by her charters and grants, have made any settlements; and the territory of North America was, and is, subject to all the claims of sovereignty under the limitation of statutes and charters. I write from memory, but appeal to the original deeds, whether some of them did not give an exemption from taxation during a limited time, with an evident implication that at the expiration of that term they should be subject to taxation like other British subjects. And whether others did not limit taxation to specific duties, mentioned with a like implication, that the right of taxation was entire while the exercise of that right was restricted.

. . . .

Dr. Price, in the second section of the second part of his pamphlet, in which he inquires, *whether the war with America is justified by the principles of the constitution,* affects to consider the Americans as a separate people; and inquires, *whether the war be made to establish our constitu-*

tion among them. If this question has any meaning at all, I apprehend it should stand, whether, by the present constitution of the state, the legislature of Great Britain is in possession of a right to impose taxes and to enact laws binding in America? If they be in possession of such a right, have they been known to abuse it? They have been in possession of the right and scarcely at all exerted it. But the Americans are now alarmed and think that this right may be abused; let them come forward, therefore, and urge the precautions necessary to be taken against this abuse. If they will accept of no security below that of independency and total separation of commonwealth this, I apprehend, they must acquire at the point of the sword. But other and better remedies for the evil may yet be expected from the councils of a state that has been as remarkable for moderation as for resolution in the conduct of great affairs.

Advocates in this cause perpetually quote the spirit and principles of the British constitution against the letter and the fact. Do they mean its primeval state, the intention of its founder, or something else that they fancy concerning it? Its primeval state is very little known and if it were could not be admitted as the rule of proceeding in opposition to subsequent establishments and compacts. In that state which is called the feudal constitution the King had his domain or royal estate, and had no other claim on his subjects but their personal services in his wars. When he wanted some extraordinary supply he summoned his vassals together and made his proposition to them for that purpose; they deliberated and refused or granted, sometimes in commutation for military services and sometimes as a voluntary gift. The constitution was gradually raised upon these foundations. The Parliament became what it is, and the state in possession of a maxim that the King can raise no supplies without consent of Parliament. This is the origin and this is the fact in our constitution and, right or wrong, till within these few years, or few months, within the British territory of Europe, Asia, Africa, and America, Parliament was supposed omnipotent and irresistible. What change may now be made to accommodate forms to new situations I hope may still be determined by a better decision than that of the sword. But, till that is determined, I hope that every good subject will pay a proper respect to the fact and the letter of the constitution whatever fancy he may have about the spirit of it. We may wish for improvements in the laws of the state but, till these are made, we must abide by the law as it stands.

· · · · · · · · · · · · · · · · · · · ·

Appendix Five. A Sermon Preached Before the Incorporated Society for the Propagation of the Bible in Foreign Parts   *William Markham, Lord Archbishop of York*

Daniel vii. ver. 14

And there was given him dominion, and glory, and a kingdom, that
all people, nations and languages should serve him: His dominion is an
everlasting dominion, which shall not pass away, and his kingdom
that which shall not be destroyed.

. . . .

Avoiding therefore both passionate excesses and unprofitable sorrows
let us look rather towards a correction of the evil, and in our way to that
let us consider by what probable causes our religious and civil interests
in America are reduced to this calamitous situation.

Of these causes, I am afraid that too many may be charged to mistakes
or inattentions in government, perhaps in every government that has
subsisted since the colonies were first established. Whatever there is of
that sort is a fitter subject for each man's particular reflexion than for a
public discussion in this place. It will be more suitable as well as more
profitable to us at this time, to consider whether the evil may in any part
be ascribed to the present state of our morals and opinions.

A fair estimate of the first might probably enable us to account for the
latter. But however applicable to the occasion such a disquisition may be,
it is more than I can now attempt.

I shall content myself therefore with making a short observation upon
some loose opinions which have been lately current on two very important
subjects, religious and civil liberty.

It has been the practice of sectaries to claim much more than they are
disposed to give and some, who when possessed of power, used it sufficiently, have afterwards made pretensions to an unrestrained right of
preaching and propagating their opinions. How these pretensions are
founded it may be difficult to say, except it be on some mistaken texts of
scripture which apply to the observance of the Jewish ritual but are now
made to carry a releasement from the law of the state under a notion of
Christian liberty. It is true that the secret intercourse between a man's
spirit and his creator excludes all foreign cognizance. But it is not so
when sects are formed, assemblies convened, a distinct system of doctrine
framed, and men appointed to propagate them.

In this state of things every legal government, by its inherent right of providing for its own safety, is justified in enquiring what those doctrines are. They may be immoral, they may be seditious, they may be subversive of society itself. It was a favourite doctrine in the last century that dominion is founded in grace. Those therefore who were pleased to call themselves the saints of the earth thought they had a good right to all the power and all the property in the universe.

The history of fanaticism will furnish many such examples.

The truth is that in our frail and fallible condition even religion can with difficulty keep itself undefiled from the world. It gathers some impurities in its passage. When a sect therefore is established it usually becomes a party in the state, it has its interests, it has its animosities, together with a system of civil opinions by which it is distinguished at least as much as by its religion. Upon these opinions, when contrary to the well-being of the community, the authority of the state is properly exercised.

[1] The laws enacted against Papists have been extremely severe, but they were not founded on any difference in religious sentiments. The reasons upon which they were founded are purely political.

The Papists acknowledged a sovereignty different from that of the state and some of the opinions which they maintained made it impossible to give any security for their obedience. We are usually governed by traditional notions and are apt to receive the partialities and aversions of our fathers, but new dangers may arise; and if at any time another denomination of men should be equally dangerous to our civil interests, it would be justifiable to lay them under similar restraints.[1]

Upon these subjects Christianity has made no alteration, it has left the systems of civil polity, and the duties annexed to them, exactly as they were before. Our Saviour's discourses all related to the actions of private men and the gospel was equally given to the Jew and to the Gentile, to the bond and to the free.

Let Christianity therefore be spared, it lends no aid to these extravagances, any more than to those on the general subject of civil liberty.

It is the usual artifice of faction to look for something colourable, by which the ignorant and unwary may be deceived, and this is commonly effected by the adoption of a false, or the misapplication of a true, principle.

What is assumed upon the present occasion is the glorious nature of liberty. Of this there can be no question, and I hope that no times will be so wretchedly debased, as to make it a question in this free country. It is certainly the first and most valuable of all human possessions. It realizes and secures all the rest and by those who are in the enjoyment of it ought to be maintained at all hazards. But it remains to be settled, wherein does it consist? I have sometimes thought it a misfortune that a thing so valuable

---

1. Price quotes from this passage in footnote *e* to the *General Introduction*.

and important, should have no word in our language to express it except one which goes to everything that is wild and lawless.

If therefore we would avoid abusing our understanding with the ideas of savage liberty, which have no place in regulated society, we should use it with an addition, such as legal, or civil liberty. ²It seems to consist in a freedom from all restraints except such as established law imposes, for the good of the community, to which the partial good of each individual is obliged to give place.²

As there are in the nature of things, but two sorts of government, that of law, and that of force, it wants no argument to prove that under the last freedom cannot subsist. If it subsists, therefore, it must be under law and of necessity that law must be supreme, for if it is not supreme its power must be abridged by its enemy, force. The foundation therefore of legal freedom is the supremacy of law. It has been acknowledged as such by all commonwealths from the beginning of the world as the only power which can protect our rights from their natural adversaries, despotism and anarchy. These indeed have usually gone together, for no anarchy ever prevailed, which did not end in despotism.

The passions of men are restless and enterprizing, the occasions which time may present to them are innumerable, and the possible situations of things much more various than any wisdom can foresee. But the supremacy of law is a steady and uniform rule to which those, who mean well, may in all circumstances safely adhere.

To those, indeed, who mean delinquency it is not very favourable. This they were aware of and have therefore substituted another rule, by which every man's honour or interest is to be made the measure of his obedience.

By this system of political rights, ambition, revenge, envy, and avarice, with the other bad passions, the controlling of which is the very intent and meaning of law, are all let loose, and those dear interests, for the protection of which we trust in law, are at once abandoned to outrage.

It is wonderful that so weak a system should find stability, even in popular madness. It is wonderful that extreme folly should not be more innocent. But it is most wonderful that those who have anything to lose should adopt such a system.

Do they hold their distinctions and fortunes by any other tenure than that of law? And will they put them to the hazard for the chance of gaining something better in the uproar?

This would be a more desperate species of gaming than any other which is known, even in these times. But nothing is too mean for the uses of parties especially as they are now constituted. Parties once had a principle belonging to them, absurd perhaps, and indefensible, but still carrying a notion of duty, by which honest minds might easily be caught.

2. Price quotes from this sentence in footnote *d* to the *General Introduction.*

But they are now combinations of individuals who, instead of being the sons and servants of the community, make a league for advancing their private interests. It is their business to hold high the notion of political honour. 3I believe and trust it is not injurious to say that such a bond is no better than that by which the lowest and wickedest combinations are held together and that it denotes the last stage of political depravity.3

There is another point, in the clearing of which the common cause of legal freedom is intimately concerned. Those who maintain these doctrines justify themselves by the Glorious Revolution. Are the cases in any view similar? Or did the leaders in that great business act upon principles such as theirs? Many went into that enterprize who were of different complexions and characters and with very different designs and motives. Some who but little before, when they thought it their interest, were ready enough to have betrayed the constitution. But the best and honestest among them stood forth avowedly as supporting the supremacy of law. Have these men done the same? Or have they not, in every step of the American contest, assailed and insulted it? They have maintained that a charter which issues from the King's sole pleasure is valid against an act of Parliament. They have maintained that a king of England has the power to discharge any number of his subjects that he pleases from the allegiance that is due to the state.

They used their best endeavours to throw the whole weight and power of the colonies into the scale of the crown, but we thank God's good providence that we had a prince upon the throne whose magnanimity and justice were superior to such temptations. Of those men therefore they have taken the name, but not the principles and have so far aspersed their memory.

My subject, I hope, will excuse me for the notice I have taken of these mischievous opinions. I consider them as relating, not indeed to the rebellion itself, for that rests upon wickedness only, but to the specious fallacies by which it is so shamelessly defended.

This discourse has, I am afraid, been already lengthened beyond the usual limits. I shall therefore add but very little more. I wish it could be in comfortable words that those who have been patient in tribulation might likewise rejoice in hope. 4Our prospects indeed have long been dark. We may now perhaps discover a ray of brightness,4 but for the continuance and encrease of it we must rely on the wisdom of our governors in confidence that necessity will at last provide those remedies which foresight did not, that the dependence of the colonies may be no longer nominal; and for our spiritual interests, we hope the reasoning which was so just in the case of Canada, that if you allowed their religion you must allow a mainte-

---

3. Price quotes from this sentence in footnote e to the General Introduction.
4. Price gives a modified quotation of this passage on page 52 of the General Introduction.

nance for their clergy, will be thought at least equally strong, when it pleads for our own church: that those who are disposed to worship God in peace and charity may be thought entitled to a regular and decent support for their ministers, that they may not continue to want the important office of confirmation, without the benefit of which even a toleration is not complete, and that those who have a call to the ministry may not be obliged to seek ordination at an expence which is very grievous and with the hazards of a long voyage which has been already fatal to many of them. We have surely a right to expect that the only established church should not, against all example, remain in a state of oppression and that whatever encouragements may be afforded, they should rather be for the professing it than against it.

As to what relates to the delinquents we, for our parts, should wish to say, Go and sin no more. But the interests of great states require securities that are not precarious.

Our chief reliance however must always be on the mercies of God, who has already so often interposed with mighty deliverances in behalf of this church and nation, that He, of whose providence it is the distinctive character to produce harmony and order out of apparent confusion, to whose eternal mind futurity is always present, and who, from the beginning of time, has so directed the blind operations of sinful men that they should all contribute to the shining forth of that light which was to lighten the Gentiles, may now also, by the excellency of his power, make the sweet water to flow from bitter fountains and, even in our present distresses lay the foundation of our future tranquility.

To him we offer up our humble and fervent prayers that he may once more comfort his people, that the hearts of the froward may be turned, and the disobedient brought to the wisdom of the just. *Amen.*

Appendix Six. A Letter to John Farr and John Harris, Esqrs, (Sheriffs of the City of Bristol) *Edmund Burke*

Liberty, if I understand it at all, is a *general* principle, and the clear right of all the subjects within the realm or of none. Partial freedom seems to me a most invidious mode of slavery. But, unfortunately, it is the kind of slavery the most easily admitted in times of civil discord; for parties are but too apt to forget their own future safety in their desire of sacrificing their enemies. People without much difficulty admit the entrance of that injustice of which they are not to be the immediate victims. In times of high proceeding it is never the faction of the predominant power that is in danger; for no tyranny chastises its own instruments. It is the obnoxious and the suspected who want the protection of law; and there is nothing to bridle the partial violence of state factions but this: "that whenever an act is made for a cessation of law and justice, the whole people should be universally subjected to the same suspension of their franchises." The alarm of such a proceeding would then be universal. It would operate as a sort of *call of the nation*. It would become every man's immediate and instant concern to be made very sensible of the *absolute necessity* of this total eclipse of liberty. They would more carefully advert to every renewal, and more powerfully resist it. These great determined measures are not commonly so dangerous to freedom. They are marked with too strong lines to slide into use. No plea, nor pretence, of *inconvenience or evil example* (which must in their nature be daily and ordinary incidents) can be admitted as a reason for such mighty operations. But the true danger is, when liberty is nibbled away, for expedients, and by parts. . . .

. . . .

Not only our policy is deranged, and our empire distracted, but our laws and our legislative spirit appear to have been totally perverted by it. We have made war on our Colonies, not by arms only, but by laws. As hostility and law are not very concordant ideas, every step we have taken in this business has been made by trampling on some maxim of justice, or some capital principle of wise government. What precedents were established, and what principles overturned (I will not say of English privilege, but of general justice) in the Boston Port, the Massachusetts Charter, the Military Bill, and all that long array of hostile acts of Parliament by which the war with America has been begun and supported! Had the principles of any of these acts been first exerted on English ground they would probably have expired as soon as they touched it. But by being removed from our persons they have rooted in our laws, and the latest posterity will taste the fruits of them.

Nor is it the worst effect of this unnatural contention that our *laws* are corrupted. Whilst *manners* remain entire, they will correct the vices of law, and soften it at length to their own temper. But we have to lament that in most of the late proceedings we see very few traces of that generosity, humanity, and dignity of mind which formerly characterized this nation. War suspends the rules of moral obligation, and what is long suspended is in danger of being totally abrogated. Civil wars strike deepest of all into the manners of the people. They vitiate their politics, they corrupt their morals, they pervert even the natural taste and relish of equity and justice. By teaching us to consider our fellow citizens in a hostile light, the whole body of our nation becomes gradually less dear to us. The very names of affection and kindred, which were the bond of charity whilst we agreed, become new invectives to hatred and rage, when the communion of our country is dissolved. We may flatter ourselves that we shall not fall into this misfortune. But we have no charter of exemption that I know of from the ordinary frailties of our nature.

What but that blindness of heart which arises from the frenzy of civil contention could have made any persons conceive the present situation of the British affairs as an object of triumph to themselves, or of congratulations to their sovereign? Nothing surely could be more lamentable to those who remember the flourishing days of this kingdom than to see the insane joy of several unhappy people, amidst the sad spectacle which our affairs and conduct exhibit to the scorn of Europe. We behold (and it seems some people rejoice in beholding) our native land, which used to sit the envied arbiter of all her neighbours, reduced to a servile dependence on their mercy, acquiescing in assurances of friendship which she does not trust, complaining of hostilities which she dares not resent, deficient to her allies, lofty to her subjects, and submissive to her enemies; whilst the liberal government of this free nation is supported by the hireling sword of German boors and vassals; and three millions of the subjects of Great Britain are seeking for protection to English privileges in the arms of France!

. . . .

Indeed our affairs are in a bad condition. I do assure those gentlemen who have prayed for war, and have obtained the blessing they have sought, that they are at this instant in very great straits. The abused wealth of this country continues a little longer to feel its distemper. As yet they, and their German allies of twenty hireling states, have contended only with the unprepared strength of our own infant Colonies. But America is not subdued. Not one unattacked village which was originally adverse throughout that vast continent has yet submitted from love or terror. You have the ground you encamp on, and you have no more. The cantonments of your troops and your dominions are exactly of the same extent. You spread devastation, but you do not enlarge the sphere of authority.

The events of this war are of so much greater magnitude than those who either wished or feared it ever looked for, that this alone ought to fill every considerate mind with anxiety and diffidence. Wise men often tremble at the very things which fill the thoughtless with security. For many reasons I do not choose to expose to public view all the particulars of the state in which you stood with regard to foreign powers during the whole course of the last year. Whether you are yet wholly out of danger from them is more than I know or than your rulers can divine. But even if I were certain of my safety, I could not easily forgive those who had brought me into the most dreadful perils, because by accidents, unforeseen by them or me, I have escaped.

Believe me, gentlemen, the way still before you is intricate, dark, and full of perplexed and treacherous mazes. Those who think they have the clue may lead us out of this labyrinth. We may trust them as amply as we think proper; but as they have most certainly a call for all the reason which their stock can furnish, why should we think it proper to disturb its operation by inflaming their passions? . . .

. . . .

I think I know America. If I do not my ignorance is incurable, for I have spared no pains to understand it; and I do most solemnly assure those of my constituents who put any sort of confidence in my industry and integrity, that everything that has been done there has arisen from a total misconception of the object; that our means of originally holding America, that our means of reconciling with it after quarrel, of recovering it after separation, of keeping it after victory, did depend and must depend in their several stages and periods, upon a total renunciation of that unconditional submission, which has taken such possession of the minds of violent men. The whole of those maxims upon which we have made and continued this war must be abandoned. Nothing indeed (for I would not deceive you) can place us in our former situation. That hope must be laid aside. But there is a difference between bad and the worst of all. Terms relative to the cause of the war ought to be offered by the authority of Parliament. An arrangement at home promising some security for them ought to be made. By doing this, without the least impairing of our strength, we add to the credit of our moderation, which in itself is always strength more or less.

I know many have been taught to think that moderation in a case like this is a sort of treason, and that all arguments for it are sufficiently answered by railing at rebels and rebellion and by charging all the present or future miseries which we may suffer on the resistance of our brethren. But I would wish them in this grave matter, and if peace is not wholly removed from their hearts, to consider seriously, first, that to criminate and recriminate never yet was the road to reconciliation in any difference amongst men. In the next place, it would be right to reflect that the American English (whom they may abuse if they think it honourable to revile the absent) can, as things now stand, neither be provoked at our railing nor bettered by our instruction. All communication is cut off between us, but this we know with certainty that, though we cannot reclaim them, we may reform ourselves. If measures of peace are necessary, they must begin somewhere, and a conciliatory temper must precede and prepare every plan of reconciliation. Nor do I conceive that we suffer anything by thus regulating our own minds. We are not disarmed by being disencumbered of our passions. Declaiming on rebellion never added a bayonet or a charge of powder to your military force, but I am afraid that it has been the means of taking up many muskets against you.

. . . .

When I was amongst my constituents at the last summer assizes, I remember that men of all descriptions did then express a very strong desire for peace, and no slight hopes of attaining it from the commission sent out by my Lord Howe. And it is not a little remarkable, that, in proportion as every person showed a zeal for the court measures, he was then earnest in circulating an opinion of the extent of the supposed powers of that commission. When I told them that Lord Howe had no powers to treat, or to promise satisfaction on any point whatsoever of the controversy, I was hardly credited—so strong and general was the desire of terminating this war by the method of accommodation. As far as I could discover, this was the temper then prevalent through the kingdom. The king's forces, it must be observed, had at that time been obliged to evacuate Boston. The superiority of the former campaign rested wholly with the colonists. If such powers of treaty were to be wished whilst success was very doubtful, how came they to be less so since his Majesty's arms have been crowned with many considerable advantages? Have these successes induced us to alter our mind, as thinking the season of victory not the time for treating with honour or advantage? Whatever changes have happened in the national character, it can scarcely be our wish that terms of accommodation never should be proposed to our enemy, except when they must be attributed solely to our fears. It has happened, let me say unfortunately, that we read of his Majesty's commission for making peace, and his troops evacuating his last town in the Thirteen Colonies, at the same hour and in the same gazette. It was still more unfortunate that no commission went to America to settle the troubles there, until several months after an act had been passed to put the Colonies out of the protection of this government, and to divide their trading property, without a possibility of restitution, as spoil among the seamen of the navy. The most abject submission on the part of the Colonies could not redeem them. There was no man on that whole continent, or within three thousand miles of it, qualified by law to follow allegiance with protection or submission with pardon. A proceeding of this kind has no example in history. Independency, and independency with an enmity (which, putting ourselves out of the question, would be called natural and much provoked) was the inevitable consequence. How this came to pass the nation may be one day in an humour to inquire.

All the attempts made this session to give fuller powers of peace to the commanders in America were stifled by the fatal confidence of victory and the wild hopes of unconditional submission. There was a moment favourable to the king's arms, when, if any powers of concession had existed on the other side of the Atlantic, even after all our errors, peace in all probability might have been restored. But calamity is unhappily the usual season of reflection; and the pride of men will not often suffer reason to have any scope, until it can be no longer of service.

I have always wished that as the dispute had its apparent origin from things done in Parliament and as the acts passed there had provoked the war that the foundations of peace should be laid in Parliament also. I have been astonished to find that those whose zeal for the dignity of our body was so hot as to light up the flames of civil war should even publicly declare that these delicate points ought to be wholly left to the crown. Poorly as I may be thought affected to the authority of Parliament, I shall never admit that our constitutional rights can ever become a matter of ministerial negotiation.

I am charged with being an American. If warm affection towards those over whom I claim any share of authority be a crime, I am guilty of this charge. But I do assure you (and they who know me publicly and privately will bear witness to me) that [1]if ever one man lived more zealous than another for the supremacy of Parliament and the rights of this imperial crown, it was myself. Many others, indeed, might be more knowing in the extent of the foundation of these rights.[1] [2]I do not pretend to be an antiquary, a lawyer, or qualified for the chair of professor in metaphysics. I have never ventured to put your solid interests upon speculative grounds. My having constantly declined to do so have been attributed to my incapacity for such disquisitions; and I am inclined to believe it is partly the cause.[2] I never shall be ashamed to confess that where I am ignorant I am diffident. I am indeed not very solicitous to clear myself of this imputed incapacity, because men, even less conversant than I am in this kind of

1. Price quotes this passage in footnote c to the General Introduction.
2. Price inaccurately quotes this passage in footnote c to the General Introduction.

subtleties, and placed in stations to which I ought not to aspire, have, by the mere force of civil discretion, often conducted the affairs of great nations with distinguished felicity and glory.

When I first came into a public trust I found your Parliament in possession of an unlimited legislative power over the colonies. I could not open the statute book without seeing the actual exercise of it, more or less, in all cases whatsoever. This possession passed with me for a title. It does so in all human affairs. No man examines into the defects of his title to his paternal estate or to his established government. Indeed, common sense taught me that a legislative authority not actually limited by the express terms of its foundation, or by its own subsequent acts, cannot have its powers parcelled out by argumentative distinctions, so as to enable us to say that here they can and there they cannot bind. Nobody was so obliging as to produce to me any record of such distinctions, by compact or otherwise, either at the successive formation of the several colonies or during the existence of any of them. If any gentlemen were able to see how one power could be given up (merely on abstract reasoning) without giving up the rest, I can only say that they saw further than I could. Nor did I ever presume to condemn any one for being clear-sighted when I was blind. I praise their penetration and learning, and hope that their practice has been correspondent to their theory.

I had, indeed, very earnest wishes to keep the whole body of this authority perfect and entire as I found it—and to keep it so, not for our advantage solely, but principally for the sake of those on whose account all just authority exists: I mean the people to be governed. For I thought I saw that many cases might well happen in which the exercise of every power comprehended in the broadest of legislature might become, in its time and circumstances, not a little expedient for the peace and union of the Colonies against themselves, as well as for their perfect harmony with Great Britain. Thinking so (perhaps erroneously, but being honestly of that opinion), I was at the same time very sure that the authority of which I was so jealous could not, under the actual circumstances of our plantations, be at all preserved in any of its members, but by the greatest reserve in its application, particularly in those delicate points in which the feelings of mankind are the most irritable. They who thought otherwise have found a few more difficulties in their work than (I hope) they were thoroughly aware of, when they undertook the present business. I must beg leave to observe that it is not only the invidious branch of taxation that will be resisted but that no other given part of legislative rights can be exercised without regard to the general opinion of those who are to be governed. That general opinion is the vehicle and organ of legislative omnipotence. Without this, it may be a theory to entertain the mind but it is nothing in the direction of affairs. The completeness of the legislative authority of Parliament *over this kingdom* is not questioned; and yet many things indubitably included in the abstract idea of that power and which carry no absolute injustice in themselves, yet being contrary to the opinions and feelings of the people, can as little be exercised as if Parliament in that case had been possessed of no right at all. I see no abstract reason, which can be given, why the same power which made and repealed the High Commission Court and the Star Chamber might not revive them again; and these courts, warned by their former fate, might possibly exercise their powers with some degree of justice. But the madness would be unquestionable as the competence of that parliament which should attempt such things. If anything can be supposed out of the power of human legislature, it is religion. I admit, however, that the established religion of this country has been three or four times altered by act of Parliament and, therefore, that a statute binds even in that case. But we may very safely affirm that, notwithstanding this apparent omnipotence, it would be now found as impossible for King and Parliament to alter the established religion of this country as it was to King James alone when he attempted to make such an alteration without a parliament. 3 In effect, to follow, not to force the public inclination, to give a direction, a form, a technical dress, and a specific sanction, to the general sense of the community is the true end of legislature.3

. . . .

If there be one fact in the world perfectly clear it is this: "That the disposition of the people of America is wholly averse to any other than a free government;" and this is indication enough to any honest statesman how he ought to adapt whatever power he finds in his hands to their case. If any ask me what a free government is, I answer that, for any practical purpose, it is what the people think so; and that they, and not I, are the natural, lawful, and competent judges of this matter. If they practically allow me a greater degree of authority over them than is consistent with any correct ideas of perfect freedom, I ought to thank them for so great a trust and not to endeavour to prove from thence that they have reasoned amiss, and that, having gone so far, by analogy, they must hereafter have no enjoyment but by my pleasure.

If we had seen this done by any others, we should have concluded them far gone in madness. It is melancholy as well as ridiculous to observe the kind of reasoning with which the public has been amused, in order to divert our minds from the common sense of our American policy. There are people who have split and anatomised the doctrine of free government as if it were an abstract question concerning metaphysical liberty and necessity, and not a matter of moral prudence and natural feeling. They have disputed whether liberty be a positive or a negative idea; whether it does

---

3. Price quotes this passage in footnote *b* to the *General Introduction*.

not consist in being governed by laws without considering what are the laws or who are the makers; whether man has any rights by nature; and whether all the property he enjoys be not the alms of his government, and his life itself their favour and indulgence. Others, corrupting religion as these have perverted philosophy, contend that Christians are redeemed into captivity, and the blood of the Saviour of mankind has been shed to make them the slaves of a few proud and insolent sinners. These shocking extremes provoking to extremes of another kind, 4speculations are let loose as destructive to all authority4 as the former are to all freedom; and every government is called tyranny and usurpation which is not formed on their fancies. In this manner the stirrers-up of this contention, not satisfied with distracting our dependencies and filling them with blood and slaughter, are corrupting our understandings; they are endeavouring to tear up, along with practical liberty, all the foundations of human society, all equity and justice, religion, and order.

Civil freedom, gentlemen, is not, as many have endeavoured to persuade you, a thing that lies hid in the depth of abstruse science. It is a blessing and a benefit, not an abstract speculation; and all the just reasoning that can be upon it is of so coarse a texture as perfectly to suit the ordinary capacities of those who are to enjoy, and of those who are to defend it. Far from any resemblance to those propositions in geometry and metaphysics, which admit no medium, but must be true or false in all their latitude, social and civil freedom, like all other things in common life, are variously mixed and modified, enjoyed in very different degrees, and shaped into an infinite diversity of forms, according to the temper and circumstances of every community. The *extreme* of liberty (which is its abstract perfection, but its real fault) obtains nowhere, nor ought to obtain anywhere. Because extremes, as we all know, in every point which relates either to our duties or satisfactions in life, are destructive both to virtue and enjoyment. Liberty too must be limited in order to be possessed. The degree of restraint it is impossible in any case to settle precisely. But it ought to be the constant aim of every wise public council to find out, by cautious experiments and rational, cool endeavours, with how little, not how much, of this restraint the community can subsist. For liberty is a good to be improved, and not an evil to be lessened. 5It is not only a private blessing of the first order, but the vital spring and energy of the state itself, which has just so much life and vigour as there is liberty in it.5 But whether liberty be advantageous or not (for I know it is a fashion to decry the very principle) none will dispute that peace is a blessing; and peace must in the course of human affairs be frequently bought by some indulgence and toleration at

---

4. Price gives a modified quotation of this passage on page 50 of the *General Introduction*.

5. Price quotes this passage in footnote *c* to the *General Introduction*.

least to liberty. For as the Sabbath (though of divine institution) was made for man, not man for the Sabbath, government, which can claim no higher origin or authority, in its exercise at least, ought to conform to the exigencies of the time and the temper and character of the people with whom it is concerned, and not always to attempt violently to bend the people to their theories of subjection. The bulk of mankind on their part are not excessively curious concerning any theories, whilst they are really happy; and one sure symptom of an ill-conducted state is the propensity of the people to resort to them.

But when subjects, by a long course of such ill conduct, are once thoroughly inflamed, and the state itself violently distempered, the people must have some satisfaction to their feelings more solid than a sophistical speculation on law and government. Such was our situation, and such a satisfaction was necessary to prevent recourse to arms; it was necessary towards laying them down: it will be necessary to prevent the taking them up again and again. Of what nature this satisfaction ought to be I wish it had been the disposition of Parliament seriously to consider. It was certainly a deliberation that called for the exertion of all their wisdom.

I am, and ever have been, deeply sensible of the difficulty of reconciling the strong presiding power, that is so useful towards the conservation of a vast, disconnected, infinitely diversified empire, with that liberty and safety of the provinces, which they must enjoy (in opinion and practice at least) or they will not be provinces at all. I know, and have long felt, the difficulty of reconciling the unwieldy haughtiness of a great ruling nation, habituated to command, pampered by enormous wealth, and confident from a long course of prosperity and victory, to the high spirit of free dependencies, animated with the first glow and activity of juvenile heat, and assuming to themselves as their birthright some part of that very pride which oppresses them. They who perceive no difficulty in reconciling these tempers (which however to make peace must some way or other be reconciled), are much above my capacity or much below the magnitude of the business. Of one thing I am perfectly clear, that it is not by deciding the suit, but by compromising the difference that peace can be restored or kept. They who would put an end to such quarrels, by declaring roundly in favour of the whole demands of either party, have mistaken, in my humble opinion, the office of a mediator.

. . . .

I have the honour to be, gentlemen, your most obedient and faithful humble servant,

Edmund Burke.

Beaconsfield, April 3, 1777.

P.S. You may communicate this letter in any manner you think proper to my constituents.

Appendix Seven. A Sermon Delivered to a Congregation of Protestant Dissenters at Hackney   *Richard Price*

Advertisement.

The following discourse was composed in some haste, and without any particular attention to the style; and it is now published, with the addition of a few Notes, partly in compliance with the request of some who heard it; and, partly, because it has been misrepresented. The notice which the author has taken of public measures, is such as came necessarily in his way in discussing the subject he had chosen, and in considering the present state of the kingdom. This, however, is the first time in which he has entered into politics in the pulpit, and, perhaps, it may be the last.

GEN. XVIII. 32. And he said, O let not the Lord be angry, and I will speak but this once. Peradventure ten shall be found there. And he said, I will not destroy it for ten's sake.

You must all of you recollect that these words are represented as addressed to the Deity by the Patriarch Abraham, when he was interceding with him for the city of Sodom. There can scarcely be a more affecting representation; and it is not possible that on the present occasion, I should speak to you on a properer subject. The calamity by which Sodom and the whole country round it was destroyed, is one of the most ancient as well as the most tremendous events, of which we have any account in history. We have a particular relation of it in the xixth chapter of this book of Genesis; and, throughout all the subsequent parts of scripture, it is referred to, and held forth as an example and a warning to other countries. Thus in Jude we read, that *Sodom and Gommorah, and the cities about them, had been set forth for an example, suffering the vengeance of eternal fire;* that is, a fire which totally consumed them, and which appeared to be even still burning, and would probably burn till the end of the world. So likewise in the prophecy of Jeremiah, the Lth chapter and 40th verse, it is said that *Babylon should no more be inhabited for ever; and that as God had overthrown Sodom and Gommorah, and the neighbouring cities, so should Babylon be overthrown.* And in Deuteronomy the xxixth and 23d, the prophetical denunciation against the children of Israel is, that if *they forsook the Lord, and served other gods, their land should be turned into brimstone and salt and burning, like the overthrown of Sodom and Gommorah.* And in Luke xvii. and 28th and following verses, our Lord, in admonishing his disciples to vigilance directs them to think of the security and carelessness of the inhabitants of Sodom, before God *rained fire and brimstone from Heaven, and destroyed them all*. It is in allusion also to this event that in the Revelation (ch. xix. 20, and xxi. 8.) the future extirpation of anti-Christian delusion, and of the workers of iniquity, is expressed by their being cast into a lake burning with fire and brimstone.

. . . .

The warning and admonitions which such accounts give should engage us to love and to seek righteousness above all things. When we consider what it is we cannot wonder that it stands so high in the estimation of the Deity. It is his image in our souls. It is the foundation of all honour and dignity. It is the order by which the universe subsists. God, therefore, must delight in those who practice it and we may with reason expect that his favour will extend itself to their connections and that, in their account, their families, their friends, and their country will be best. I have been showing you that the Sacred History strongly inculcates this upon us. God will pardon a guilty nation for the sake of the righteous in it, if they are not too few. So we read in Jer. v. 1. *Run ye through the streets of Jerusalem, and see in the broad places thereof, if you can find any one who executeth judgment, and seeketh the truth, and I will pardon Jerusalem*. I can scarcely set before you a properer motive to the practice of virtue. If you are virtuous you may save your country by engaging God's favour to it. Do you then love your country? Have you any desire to be the means of preserving and blessing it? If you have, do all you can to increase the number of the virtuous in it or, should you despair of success in this, resolve at least that you will unite yourselves to that number. Thus will you be your country's best friends, make yourselves powerful intercessors with the Deity for it, and stand in the gap between it and calamity. But should wickedness become so prevalent as to render calamity necessary though, in this case, your country must suffer, yet care will be taken of you. Perhaps you may be directed to some means of escaping from the common ruin and a Zoar, or an Ark, may be provided for you from whence you may view the storm, and find yourselves safe. Methinks the friends of truth and virtue may now look across the Atlantic and entertain some such hope. But should there be no resource of this kind left the righteous will at least find resources of infinite value in their own minds, in the testimony of a good conscience, in the consolations of divine grace, and the prospect of that country where they shall possess an undefiled and incorruptible inheritance.

My inclinations would lead me to address you some time longer in this way. But I must hasten to some observations of a different kind. My principal design on this occasion was to set before you the chief particulars in the characters of those righteous men who are a blessing to their country and to point out to you the necessary dependence of the salvation of a country on such characters. I shall now desire your attention to what I shall say on these heads.

With respect to the character of those righteous men who are likely to save a country I would observe, first, that they love their country and are zealous for its rights. They obey the laws of the legislature that protects them, contribute cheerfully to its support, and are solicitous, while they give to God the things that are God's, to give also to Caesar the things that are Caesar's. They are, therefore, loyal subjects. That is, they do all they can to promote the good order of the state by complying with its laws and bearing a constant and inviolable allegiance to it. This alone is genuine loyalty, and not any attachment to the persons of princes arising from a notion of their sacredness. There cannot be any notion more stupid or debasing. The people are the fountain of all civil jurisdiction and *theirs* is the true majesty in a state. There is no individual who, as a member of any community, is more sacred than another except as far as he is invested with the authority of the community and employed in executing its will. Civil governors are, in the intention of nature and reason, the servants[a] of the public and whenever, forgetting this, they imagine they possess inherent rights of dominion and attempt to establish their own authority and to govern by their own will, they become dangerous enemies; and all that is valuable to a state requires they should be opposed. The righteous citizen, therefore, whose character I am describing, at the same time that he is loyal, can have no notion of passive obedience and non-resistance. His duty obliges him to enquire into his rights and to be jealous of them, to attend to the manner in which the trust of government is discharged and to do his part towards keeping the springs of legislation pure and checking the progress of oppression. Thus only can he prove himself a worthy and useful citizen.[b] It is a sad mistake to think that private men have nothing to do

a. King James the First, in his first speech to his parliament, declared, that "he should never be ashamed to confess it his principal honour to be the great servant of the commonwealth." But in the very same speech he calls his people his natural vassals. It is, therefore, plain, he made this declaration from the same affected humility, or rather insolence, which has led the Pope to give himself the title of *Servant of Servants.*

b. It is common to assert that resistance can be justified only in cases of extreme oppression. Mankind, in consequence of indolence and want of union, have generally acted agreeably to this principle but it has lost the world its liberty. It implies that resistance ought to be avoided while oppression is growing and till it becomes too late to resist successfully without setting every thing afloat and producing dreadful convulsions. The truth is that oppression cannot be resisted too soon and that all the tendencies to it ought to be watched. Had this been always done tyranny would have been crushed in its birth and mankind would have been always happy. If an equal and virtuous representation of the people of a state makes an essential part of its legislature this may be done easily and every grievance may be redressed as soon as it appears without disturbance or tumult; and this forms one of the distinguishing excellencies of such a constitution of government as ours. But if through a general degeneracy the representation becomes partial and corrupt, a despotism may arise from such a form of government, which will

with the administration of public affairs, that there are *mysteries* in civil government of which they are not judges and that, instead of complaining, it is their duty always to yield and follow. This is the same with saying that in every community the body of the people are only a herd of cattle, made to be led and disposed of as their owners please. Had such a vile principle been always acted upon there would now have been no such thing as a free government upon earth and every human right would have been overwhelmed under an universal and savage despotism. It is thus that in religion a set of holy usurpers have pretended that there are mysteries in religion of which the people are not judges and into which they should not enquire and that, for this reason, they ought to resign to *them* the direction of their faith and consciences. It would be a disgrace to virtue to suppose that it requires an acquiescence in such insolent claims or that it is a part of the character of a righteous man that he is always ready to crouch to every tyrant and never exercises his own judgment or shows any sense of his own dignity as a rational creature and a freeman. Away with all such degrading and miserable sentiments. Let us remember that we are men and not cattle, that the sovereignty in every country belongs to the people and that a righteous man is the best member of every community and the best friend to his species by being the most irreconcileable to slavery, the most sensible to every encroachment on the rights of mankind, the most zealous for equal and universal liberty, and the most active in endeavouring to propagate just sentiments of religion and government. In short, a virtuous man must be a firm and determined patriot. Power cannot awe him. Money cannot bribe him. He scruples no labour or expence in supporting any necessary measures of government; but at the same time he will resist any oppressive measures. If he is an elector he is sure to give an uninfluenced and honest vote. If he is a magistrate he is strictly just and impartial, a terror to evil doers, and a praise to all who do well. If he is a senator he is uncorrupt and faithful. In every station he studies to promote the peace and prosperity of his country. He possesses integrity to assist in directing its councils and courage to defend its honour and to fight its battles against all enemies.

Such is a righteous man in his public capacity or as a member of a state.

---

be the very worst possible and under which no hope may be left from a calamity that shall destroy the means of corruption and awaken repentance.

Mr. Linguet, in a letter to Voltaire, says of the people that they are condemned to have only hands and that mischief arises and all is lost the moment they are put upon thinking. Voltaire observes in reply that, on the contrary, all is lost when they are treated like a herd of bulls for, in this case, they will use their horns, and sooner or later gore their owners to death. See letters 8th and 9th in the collection of M. de Voltaire's original letters. Certain it is, indeed, that much greater evils are to be dreaded from the fury of a people ignorant and blind than from the resistance and jealousy of a people inquisitive and enlightened.

I must go on to observe that in his private capacity he practises every private and social virtue. He is industrious in his calling, upright in his dealings, and true to his engagements. He is a good husband, a good parent, a good neighbour, and a good friend, as well as a good citizen. Within the circle of his family and acquaintance he maintains the same regard to equity and liberty that he does in the more extended circle of his fellow subjects and fellow men. He renders to all their dues, honour to whom honour, custom to whom custom, and always acts to others as he desires that others would act to him. He is charitable and generous, as far as his abilities reach, but he avoids all parade and ostentation and fixes his expences below his income, that he may enjoy that happy independence which will place him above temptation. In every transaction of commerce his fairness may be depended on. In the execution of every trust he is exact and faithful. He shuns all the excesses of pleasure and voluptuousness, never suffers his passions to carry him beyond the bounds of chastity and temperance, and within the inclosure of his own breast, where only one eye observes him, he is as just and fair and candid as he appears to be on the open stage of the world.

Once more, he is conscientious and diligent in the discharge of all the duties of religion. This is the crowning part of his character. It is religion gives dignity and efficacy to all our moral and public principles; nor is it possible there should be a consistent character of virtue without it. A virtuous man, therefore, must be a religious man. He worships God in private, in his family, and in public. He is governed in his whole conduct by a regard to the Deity, looks to him in all that happens, and joins constantly with his fellow creatures in those social exercises of piety which are the proper expressions of the homage and fealty which he owes to him as the Supreme Governor and Judge.

I will on this subject only add that the three particulars I have named are inseparable in a righteous character. Public virtue cannot subsist without private, nor can public and private virtue subsist without religion. As a truly virtuous and religious man must be a patriot, so a true patriot must be a virtuous and religious man. The obligations of righteousness are the same in all their branches, and a righteous man cannot violate them habitually in any instance. Is it likely that a man who is false to private engagements will not be also false to public ones, or that a man who, in his family is a tyrant, will not be likewise a tyrant as a magistrate? Is it likely that a man who has given up to his passions his internal liberty should be a true friend to liberty, or that a man who will cheat his tradesmen or betray his friends will not give a wicked vote, and betray his country? Can you imagine that a spendthrift in his own concerns will make an economist in managing the concerns of others, that a wild gamester will take due care of the stake of a kingdom, or that an unprincipled debauchee will make an upright judge or a sound statesman? Can a man who shows no regard to God his Maker, or to Christ his Saviour, who is such an enemy to society as to neglect countenancing, by his example, those forms of worship on which the order of society depends, and so void of the fundamental principles of goodness as to be capable of being habitually atheistical in his conduct; can, I say, such a person possess any great regard for the interests of society? Let us reject all such absurd imaginations. Treachery, venality and villainy must be the effects of dissipation, voluptuousness and impiety. These vices sap the foundations of virtue.[c] They render men necessitous and supple and ready at any time to sacrifice their consciences or to fly to a court in order to repair a shattered fortune and procure supplies for prodigality. Let us remember these truths in judging of men. Let us consider that true goodness is uniform and consistent and learn never to place any great confidence in those pretenders to public spirit who are not men of virtuous characters. They may boast of their attachment to a public cause but they want the living root of persevering virtue and should not be depended on.

Having given you this account of righteous men, I am next to take notice of the causes which produce that dependence, intimated in my text, of the fate of a country on such men. This dependence is derived, first, from the natures of things. Such men are the health and vigour of a state. They are the order that preserve it from anarchy, and the vital springs which give it life and motion. When they are withdrawn a nation as necessarily falls into ruin as a building falls when its pillars are destroyed, or as an animal body putrifies when the fluids stagnate and the animal functions cease to be performed. There is a distant country, once united to us, where every inhabitant has in his house (as a part of his furniture) a book on law and government, to enable him to understand his civil rights, a musket to enable him to defend these rights, and a Bible to enable him to understand and practice his religion. What can hurt such a country? We have invaded, and for some time have been endeavouring to subdue this country. Is it any wonder that we have not succeeded? How secure must it be while it preserves its virtue, against all attacks?

But, secondly, the dependence of states on the virtuous men in it is not only thus derived from the necessary course and operations of causes and effects but from the positive will of the Deity. There is an invisible and almighty power which overrules the operations of natural causes and presides over all events. This power is a righteous power, and it must be friendly to the righteous and, therefore, will direct events for the advantage

c. Some of the expressions in this passage, and a few others in the latter part of this discourse, may perhaps be too strong. But I am not at liberty to suppress them. Every candid person must see that my views are *general* and, should any one imagine the contrary, he will greatly injure me.

of the country where they reside. In consequence of the particular favour of God to them, and his delight in them, they stay his hand when lifted up to scourge a nation; and we may consider him as saying, in the words already quoted, Gen. xix. 22. *I cannot do any thing till you are gone.*

I am in danger of being too tedious on this subject. Nothing now remains but that I conclude with briefly applying the whole to the present state of this country.

On this occasion I feel myself much at a loss how to address you, not knowing whether I should do it in the way of encouragement or despair. When I think of this congregation, when I recollect the many worthy persons among my acquaintance and friends and consider what multitudes more there must be that I can never know, and in situations where perhaps I should not expect to find them—when I make only such reflections, I feel comfort, and am disposed to conclude that all may be well and that the number of the virtuous among us is still considerable enough to save us.

But when I extend my views and look abroad into the world, when I consider the accounts I am often hearing of the court, the camp, and the senate, and the profligacy that prevails almost every where, I fall back into diffidence, and am ready to believe there is no room for hope. There are, it is true, among all our parties, political and religious, many excellent characters still left but the comfort they give me is damped by the following considerations.

First, they are a smaller number than they were. Public and private virtue has been for some time declining. Never, perhaps, was there a time when men showed so little regard to decency in their vices or were so shameless in their venality and debaucheries. When men are wanted for the business of any department of the state, do you ever find that only honest men are sought for or that it is, on such an occasion, any objection to a man that he scoffs at religion or that he is known to be a drunkard, a gamester, an adulterer, or an atheist? What vacancies would be made in public offices were all but men of pure manners and independent integrity taken from them?

As to religion, nothing is plainer than that it was never at so low an ebb. Even among Protestant non-conformists, the places of worship are almost deserted. In this great metropolis several of our best congregations have sunk to nothing. Many are sinking and few flourish. Our religious zeal is dying and the most valuable part of the dissenting interest is likely soon to be ground to death between enthusiasm on the one hand and luxury and fashion on the other.

But, secondly, another discouraging circumstance in our present state is that a considerable part of the righteous themselves, or of that description of men to whom we must look for the salvation of the kingdom, are only nominally righteous. They are a smaller number than they were and of this number many are false and hollow. Nothing, indeed, is more discouraging than to find that a man has been secretly wicked who, for many years, has carried with him every appearance of the strictest probity and piety. We are all of us often making discoveries of this kind and they have a tendency to destroy in us all confidence in our fellow creatures. Take away from the honest men all that are dishonest, and from the religious men all the hypocrites, and what a melancholy reduction will be made of a party which, without such a reduction, would be too small? Among the persons to whom it is natural for us to look for the defence of our country are those in high life, and among our senators, who have taken up the cry of public liberty and virtue and oppose the oppressions of power. They seem, indeed, a glorious band and it is impossible not to admire their zeal. But alas! How often have we been duped by their professions? How often has their zeal proved to be nothing but a cover for ambition and a struggle for places? How many instances have there been of their forgetting all their declarations as soon as they have got into power? How often do you hear of their extravagance and immoralities? I have more than once, in the preceding discourse, spoken of patriotism. I have mentioned it as one of the first and best qualities of a righteous man. But I have done this with pain on account of the disgrace into which what is so called has fallen. Patriotism, like religion, is an excellent thing. But true patriotism, like true religion, is a scarce thing. In the state, as well as in the church, there are abominable impostors who have blasted the credit of these divine excellencies to such a degree that they cannot be mentioned as parts of a good character without an apology. Is it possible there should be a worse symptom in the state of a kingdom? How mortifying is it to find the nation's best friends falling so short as they do of our wishes? What measures for restoring a dying constitution? What reformation of abuses, what public points do they hold forth to us, and pledge themselves to accomplish? How little does it signify who are in, and who are out of power, if the constitution continues to bleed and that system of corruption is not destroyed which has been for some time destroying the kingdom? In short, where will you find the disinterested patriots who are ready, in this time of distress, to serve their country for nothing?[d] Where will you find the honest statesmen who are above making use of undue influence and will trust for support to the rectitude of their measures, the virtuous electors or representatives who fear an oath and have no price, or the professors of religion who cannot be induced to do any thing mean or base? I wish not to be mistaken. I am far from meaning that none such can be found. I have acknowledged (and it is all my encouragement) that such may be found among all our

d. One such the nation has lately heard of with admiration. I believe I am happy enough to know some more; and though their services may not be called for, God will recompense them.

parties.*e* I only mean to intimate a doubt whether they are not blended with so many hypocrites, and decreased so much in number, as now no longer to make a body of men very discernible, and of sufficient consequence to save us. Would to God there was no reason for entertaining this doubt.

Perhaps we are, in general, too much disposed always to think the present times the worst. I am, probably, myself under the influence of this disposition but, after studying to be upon my guard against it, I find myself incapable of believing that miserable declensions have not taken place among us.

As an evidence of this, and a farther alarming circumstance in the state of the nation, I would mention to you that levity and dissipation and rage for pernicious diversions which prevail among us. Not long ago play-houses were confined to London. But now there is scarcely a considerable town in the kingdom without them. In manufacturing towns they produce very bad effects and yet there are not many of these towns where they are not established. Think here, particularly, of those scenes of lewdness and intemperance, our masquerades. These are late improvements in our public pleasures but I question whether in Sodom itself any thing much worse could have been found. We answer, indeed, too nearly to the account given by our Saviour of this city before its destruction. *They eat and drank. They married and were given in marriage. They bought and sold, and planted and builded.* That is, they enjoyed themselves in ease and mirth. They gave themselves up to sensuality and criminal indulgencies without thinking of any danger. *But the same day that Lot went out, it rained fire and brimstone from Heaven and destroyed them all.* Luke xvii. 28. With similar gaiety and security do we now give ourselves up to intrigue and dissipation in the midst of danger. Heaven is angry with us and our existence is threatened but it seems to give us no concern. In the course of a few years we have been reduced from the highest principle of glory to the brink of ruin. A third of the empire is lost; and at the same time we see powerful enemies combining against us, our commerce languishing, and our debts and taxes, already insupportable, increasing fast and likely soon to crush us. Not long ago this would have produced an alarm which nothing could have quieted. In the last war, particularly, I remember that only the loss of Minorca threw

e. In this I differ extremely from the learned and worthy and very liberal Bishop of Exeter who (in a sermon preached on the 30th of January last, before the Lords spiritual and temporal) calls the great men who for some time have been opposing measures which have brought the kingdom near its last struggles, "a desperate and daring faction." It is probable, therefore, that he thinks no good men can be found among them. This, at least, must be the opinion of the Archbishop of York who, in a noted sermon, has called them a body of men who are held together by the same bond that keeps together the "lowest and wickedest combinations," that is, "rogues and thieves," as this censure was expressed in the pulpit. I have in this discourse been a little free in delivering censures but had I delivered any such censures as these, I should have thought myself inexcusable.

the kingdom into a commotion which cost an admiral his life and produced a change of measures. But now, though in a condition unspeakably worse, the kingdom is insensible. We fly to feasts and amusements and dance the round of pleasure. The same measures go on. The same ministers direct these measures, and sometimes we hear of new emoluments conferred upon them, just as if, instead of having brought us into imminent danger, they had saved us. One would have thought it impossible that the stupefaction of luxury and vice could have proceeded so far in so short a period. But such torpors, like mortifications before death, have been the common forerunners of calamity. Seldom has it happened, when debauchery and extravagance and a pompous manner of living have come to their height, that they have not been followed by a sudden transition to slavery and misery.

I shall mention to you but one circumstance more that checks my hopes. I mean the fact just alluded to, or the uniform effect of all our public measures for the last four or five years. This is so remarkable, as naturally to dispose us to conclude that we are indeed forsaken by Heaven. Nothing has prospered. Several opportunities for getting back to security and peace have been neglected. Offers of reconciliation, which once would have been joyfully accepted, have been made too late. Every step has plunged us deeper into difficulties so that now we see a quarrel about tea, which lenity and wisdom might have accommodated immediately, increased into a war more destructive than any in which this country has been ever engaged. Must we not in this see the hand of Providence? Does it not give us reason to fear that God, having no intentions of mercy towards us, has infatuated our councils? Will you give me leave to mention one particular proof of this observation?

At the time the alliance with France was notified it seems to me that an opening was left by which we might have got back to safety and peace. The alliance was commercial, and not exclusive.*f* We might have consented to it and determined to withdraw our forces from the colonies. Our situation was such as rendered this necessary and, in consequence of its, we might in time have recovered their confidence and secured, by a family compact, every advantage that could be derived from a connection with them. But we had not fortitude enough to consider properly our situation nor wisdom and magnanimity enough to conform to it. National safety was forced to give way to national dignity. Hostilities against France were begun immediately. And now, with our strength spent, and public credit tottering, we seem to be just entering into a war with the combined powers of France, Spain, and America.

This is, indeed, a prospect so frightful, that I must turn my attention

f. It was to become what it now is (offensive and defensive) only in the event of its being resisted by this country.

from it. Never did so dark a cloud hang over this nation. May Heaven avert the storm or, if it must break, may its fury be mitigated and the issue directed to the general advantage of the interest of truth, liberty and virtue. But, whatever happens, may you and I be found of the number of those righteous persons who have acted the part of faithful citizens and with whom all shall go well for ever.

FINIS.

Appendix Eight. Selected Correspondence

Charles Chauncy[1] to Price[2]

Boston
May 30, 1774

Reverend and dear Sir,

Yours of last November I have received, for which I thank you. The enclosed pamphlet you might with good reason hope would have produced some good effect.[3] So far as I am capable of judging (and my poor judgment perfectly agrees with the judgment of the most sensible men we have among us, to whom I have given opportunity of reading your book), you have clearly and demonstrably pointed out the way in which the nation may be saved from sinking under the heavy debt that lies upon them. I can attribute it to nothing but a spirit of infatuation in those who are entrusted with the management of your public affairs, that you are so evidently hastening to a state of ruin. And this, as I imagine, will be the case with respect to the American Colonies, should they tamely submit to the tyranny of those British ministers who are endeavouring to enslave us. But, I trust in God, we have more virtue and resolution than to sit still and suffer chains to be fastened on us. The late act of Parliament, shutting up the port of Boston, and putting it out of the power of thousands of poor innocents to preserve themselves from starving, is so palpably cruel, barbarous, and inhumane, that even those who are called the friends of government complain bitterly of it; nor do I know of any whose eyes are not opened to see plainly that despotism, which must end in slavery, is the plan to be carried into execution. This British edict which, without all doubt, was an intended blow at the liberties of all the American Colonies will, I believe, under the blessing of Providence, be the very thing which will bring salvation to us. The town of Boston, the Massachusetts Province, and the other colonies, far from being intimidated by the horrid severity and injustice of this Port Act, are rather filled with indignation, and more strongly spirited than ever to unite in concerting measures to render void

---

1. Charles Chauncy (1705–1787), graduated from Harvard College in 1721; ordained in 1727; minister of the First Church, Boston.

2. *Proceedings of the Massachusetts Historical Society*, 2nd. series (Boston: The Society, 1903), 17:266–268. Hereafter cited as MHSP (1903).

3. "Probably the new edition of Price's pamphlet entitled 'Appeal to the Public on the Subject of the National Debt' [London, Printed for T. Cadell, 1772; 4th ed., 1774]— Eds." MHSP (1903).

its designed operation. We have found by experience that no dependence can be had upon merchants, either at home, or in America, so many of them are so mercenary as to find within themselves a readiness to become slaves themselves, as well as to be accessory to the slavery of others, if they imagine they may, by this means, serve their own private separate interest. Our dependence, under God, is upon the landed interest, upon our freeholders and yeomanry. By not buying of the merchants what they may as well do without, they may keep in their own pockets two or three millions sterling a year which would otherwise be exported to Great Britain. I have reason to think the effect of this barbarous Port Act will be an agreement among the freeholders and yeomanry of all the colonies, not to purchase of the merchants any goods from England, unless some few excepted ones, till we are put into the enjoyment of our constitutional rights and privileges. The plain truth is, we can in America live within ourselves, and it would be much for our interest not to import a great deal from England; and as things are now carrying on with such a high hand, I believe the Americans will see where their interest lies. We need only to pursue what is certainly our interest, and the nation at home will suffer a thousand times more than we shall in this part of the world; and I am ready to think they will find this to be a truth from their own perceptions in a little time. But I cannot enlarge, as I am at present much indisposed. I should not indeed on this account have written now, but that I knew not how long it would be before I could have another opportunity of writing.

I send you herewith *Observations on the Boston Port Bill* by a young lawyer, of a sprightly genius and strong powers.[4] They were penned in haste, but you will readily perceive that they are highly pertinent and spirited.

I am, wishing you all happiness, with great respect

Your friend and humble servant,
Charles Chauncy.

---

4. Josiah Quincy, *Observations on the Act of Parliament Commonly Called the Boston Port Bill; with Thoughts on Civil Society and Standing Armies* (Boston: Printed for and sold by Edes and Gill, 1774).

Josiah Quincy, Jr. (1744–1775), graduated from Harvard College in 1763; defended the British soldiers involved in the Boston Massacre (with John Adams); wrote many political essays on the American cause; died at thirty-one of tuberculosis.

John Winthrop[1] to Price[2]

Cambridge, New England
September 20, 1774

Reverend Sir,[3]

I am very sensible I ought to make an apology for addressing a gentleman of your distinction in the learned world. Indeed, the great satisfaction
and instruction I have derived from your excellent writings, and your
goodness to me in communicating your curious papers on the aberration,
through the hands of our common friend Dr. Franklin, merit my most
grateful acknowledgments, yet I should scarcely have adventured to trouble
you with a letter, on account of anything that related merely to myself. It is
a much more important cause, sir, that urges me on to the freedom I now
take. It is the cause of distressed America, groaning under the hand of an
oppressive power which threatens its ruin. The fate of millions is now at
stake. The measures pursued by administration for ten years past, evidently
designed to abridge the colonists of their liberties, one after another, were
truly alarming and of the most dangerous tendency. But they appear to
be trifles when compared with the acts passed in the last session of Parliament which, I believe, are not to be paralleled in the British annals. The
Act for Shutting Up the Port of Boston struck everybody with astonishment; that cruel act which, by putting a stop to the trade on which the
town wholly depended, must immediately have starved or driven away almost all the inhabitants, had they not been supported by the very generous
contributions of our sister colonies, even in the farthest part of the continent. But this act, shocking as it was, seemed to be swallowed up in another
which quickly followed it, of more extensive and more fatal operation, the
Act for Better Regulating the Government of the Province of the Massachusetts Bay which has, in fact, dissolved the government. It has mutilated
the Charter, so as to leave only an empty phantom remaining and, by
depriving the people of every privilege, has erected an absolute despotism
in the province. The councillors who, by charter, were to be elected annually by the General Court (subject, however, to the Governor's negative)
are to be appointed by mandamus from the King; the judges, who before
were paid by the General Court, are now made totally dependent on the
Crown for their salaries as well as their commissions; all other civil officers,
as justices of the peace, sheriffs, etc., are removable by the Governor at his

---

1. John Winthrop (1714–1779), astronomer, physicist, mathematician; graduated from
Harvard College in 1732; became the second Hollis Professor of Mathematics and Natural
Philosophy at Harvard in 1738.
2. MHSP (1903), pp. 271–273.
3. "A strip of paper has been pasted over the address.—Eds." MHSP (1903).

sole pleasure, even without the advice or consent of this mandamus council; the juries for trials, whose names were before drawn out of a box at a town meeting, in the manner of a lottery, which effectually precluded all design or collusion, are now to be returned by the sheriff. By this arrangement, it is evident, the Governor has it in his power to command what verdict he pleases in any case. To crown all, the third act was passed, entitled for the more impartial administration of justice. By this act, any of the soldiers who should kill the inhabitants may, at the Governor's pleasure, be sent to any other colony or to Great Britain for trial. The manifest design of which is, to empower the military to kill the inhabitants without danger or fear of punishment.

The Governor insists on acting according to this new plan. The people are determined to adhere to the old one; so that we have neither legislative nor executive powers in the province. Things are running fast into confusion; and it seems as if it were designed to irritate the people into something which might be called rebellion. At all events, the people will never submit to the new system. Their minds are universally agitated, to a degree not to be conceived by any person at a distance; and they are determined to abide all extremities, even the horrors of a civil war, rather than crouch to so wretched a state of vassallage. And these are the sentiments, not of a contemptible faction, as has been represented, nor of this province only, but of every colony on the continent. They all consider Boston as suffering in a common cause, and themselves as deeply interested in the event. For though the vengeance is immediately directed against Boston and this province, they all expect the same treatment in their turn, unless they tamely submit to the exorbitant power lately claimed by Parliament over them; which they will never be brought to do. To submit to such a power would be to hold their lives, liberties and properties by the precarious tenure of the will of a British minister. The sanction of Parliament, in their apprehension, makes no difference in the case; they know full well in what manner parliamentary affairs are managed. Besides, they do not acknowledge the Commons of Great Britain as their representatives. If the Ministry are resolved to push their schemes, nothing but desolation and misery is to be expected.

I have given but a slight sketch of the present situation of affairs here, omitting many matters of great moment. Mr. Quincy, who will have the honor to wait upon you with this letter, can give you a much more distinct account than I can pretend to do by writing. He is a gentleman of the law, and eminent in his profession, and is making a voyage to England, with hopes of doing some service to his native country; and I humbly hope you will be pleased to favor him with your countenance.

I cannot but persuade myself, that a gentleman of so enlarged an understanding and so benevolent an heart as the author of the *Dissertation on*

Providence, etc.,[4] will excuse the freedom of this application which, I am sure, proceeds from an unexceptionable motive, the love of my country, and that he will be ready to use the influence which his high reputation justly gives him, as far as he can with propriety, in favor of the oppressed.

With sentiments of the highest esteem and respect, I am, reverend sir,

Your most humble servant,[5]

Chauncy to Price[1]

Boston
January 10, 1775

Reverend and dear Sir,

Yours of October 8th, with the enclosed pamphlets, I have received, for which I heartily thank you. It is strange nothing which has happened among us from September 2nd to the day of the date of your letter, should have been known in England. It is easy to conceive that the news conveyed to the ministry by the *Scarborough* should be secreted, but not so easy to be accounted for that the private letters which went by her should be profoundly silent also.

What came into event here before the 26th of September, when Mr. Quincy embarked for London, I shall say nothing about, as you have doubtless had opportunity of hearing from him an exact and true account of facts till that time. Since then the fortifications at the only entrance into Boston by land have, at no small expence, been completed; the troops which were at New York, New Jersey, Philadelphia, and Canada sent for and brought to town, in addition to those that were here before, making in all eleven regiments, besides several companies of the artillery. You can't easily imagine the greatness of our embarrassment, especially if it be remembered that the town, while filled with troops, is at the same time encompassed with ships of war, and the harbour so blocked up as that an entire stop is put to trade, only as it is carried on at the amazing charge of transporting everything from Salem, not less than 28 miles by land. Can it in reason be thought that Americans, who were freeborn, will submit to such cruel tyranny? They will sooner lose their heart's blood. Not fears, but the livery

---

4. *Four Dissertations: I. On Providence. II. On Prayer. III. On the Reasons for Expecting that Virtuous Men Shall Meet after Death in a State of Happiness. IV. On the Importance of Christianity, the Nature of Historical Evidence and Miracles* (London: Printed for T. Cadell, 1767).

5. "A strip of paper has been pasted over the signature, but the letter is docketed in Dr. Price's hand 'Professor Winthrop'.—Eds." MHSP (1903).

1. MHSP (1903), pp. 275–278.

of the troops among us, pointing them out as subjects of the same sovereign with ourselves, is the true and only reason they were either suffered to come, or to continue here, without molestation. Had they been French or Spanish troops they would have been cut off long before now, as they easily might have been. It is given out by the tools of government that more ships of war and more regiments will soon be sent to humble or destroy us. The colonists are not intimidated by such threatenings, neither would they be should they be carried into execution. They are sensible that contending with Great Britain would be like a mouse's contending with a lion, could her ships of war sail upon the land as they do upon the water. But in a contest with America her ships can annoy none of our inland towns, and but a few only of our towns upon the seacoast for want of depth of water. And should they even destroy these, England would suffer more than America, as a greater debt than the worth of all these places would, by that means, be at once cancelled.

The people in England have been taught to believe that five or six thousand regular troops would be sufficient to humble us into the lowest submission to any parliamentary acts however tyrannical. But we are not so ignorant in military affairs and unskilled in the use of arms as they take us to be. A spirit for martial skill has strongly catched from one to another throughout at least the New England Colonies. A number of companies in many of our towns are already able to go through the military exercise in all its forms with more dexterity and a better grace than some of the regiments which have been sent to us; and even all our men from 20 to 60 years of age are either formed or forming into companies and regiments under officers of their own choosing, to be steadily tutored in the military art. It is not doubted but next spring we shall have at least one hundred thousand men well qualified to come forth for the defence of our liberties and rights, should there be a call for it. We have besides in the New England Colonies only a much greater number of men who, the last war, were made regulars by their services than your troops now in Boston. I can't help observing to you here that we have in this town a company of boys, from about 10 to 14 years of age, consisting of 40 to 50, who, in the opinion of the best judges, can go through the whole military exercise much more dexterously than a very great part of the regulars have been able to do since they have been here.

I would not suggest by anything I have said, that we have the least disposition to contend with the parent states. It is our earnest universal desire to be at peace and to live in love and harmony with all our fellow subjects. We shall not betake ourselves to the sword unless necessarily obliged to it in self-defence, but in that case, so far as I can judge, it is the determination of all North America to exert themselves to the utmost, be the consequence what it may. They choose death rather [than] to live in slavery, as they must do, if they submit to that despotic government which has been contrived for them.

The accounts I have seen in some of the London newspapers, affirming that Governor Gage and Lord Piercy have been killed, and that a number of houses have been pulled down, are without the least foundation in truth, and must be numbered among the many abominable falsehoods which are continually transmitted home by those detestable inhabitants here, to whose lies it is owing that we have been brought into our present distressing circumstances.

The result of the Continental Congress I should have sent you but that it has probably reached home by this time, or doubtless will long before a copy of it would, was it to go by this opportunity. I cannot but look upon it an occurrence in our favor truly extraordinary, that so many colonies, so distant from one another, and having each their separate interest, should unite in sending delegates to meet in one general body upon the present occasion, and that those delegates (52, I think) should, upon a free and full debate among themselves, be so united in what they have done. I have been assured by our Massachusetts delegates, since their return from Philadelphia, that there was in no article more than one or two dissentients and in almost every one perfect unanimity. And it is as extraordinary that the doings of the Congress should be so universally adopted as a rule of conduct strictly to be adhered to. Effectual care has been taken in all the colonies, counties, and towns that the non-consumption agreement, in special, be punctually complied with, and committees of inspection are constituted to see that this is done; and their care upon this head has been the more earnest as they are universally sensible that no non-importation agreement among merchants will signify anything unless they are obliged to keep to it by not being able to sell their goods, should they send for them. You may receive it as a certain fact that, in conformity to one of the articles agreed to by the Continental Congress, all the merchandise that has arrived from Great Britain since the first of December has been sold, or is now selling, at vendue, and whatever it fetches beyond the prime cost and charges, is to relieve the Boston sufferers under their present distresses; and it may be depended on, that whatever goods come after the first of February will be sent back without being opened. You can't easily conceive the universality and zeal of all sorts of persons in all the colonies to carry fully into effect whatever the Congress have recommended in order to put an entire stop to our commerce with England, till the acts we complain of are repealed.

Those who call themselves the friends of government, but are its greatest enemies, are continually endeavouring, in all the ways they can devise, to foment divisions among the people, and to lead them, in particular, into an ill opinion of some here that there are among us those who are employed upon the hire of unrighteousness to do all that lies in their power to effect a submission to the late acts which would enslave us; but whether this be so or not, you may rely on it as the truth of fact that, notwithstanding all their efforts, the inhabitants of these colonies, one it may be in an hundred excepted, are firmly united in their resolution to defend themselves against any force which may be used with them to deprive them of the rights they have a just claim to, not only as men made of one blood with the rest of the human species, but as Englishmen, and Englishmen born heirs to a royal grant of charter rights and privileges.

We are told (perhaps to affrighten us) by those who join with the ministry in carrying their plan of despotism into effect, that every port on the continent will be blocked up next spring by English ships of war. But this we know cannot be done, as the seacoast on this continent is of such large extent, and we have so great a number of harbours, rivers, and inlets, inacessable by any ships of war so as to do us harm. Besides, administration, by such a conduct as this, would in the most effectual manner co-operate with the American congress in putting a stop to all commerce with Great Britain, which would, perhaps, be more hurtful to you than to us; for we should, notwithstanding, have all the necessaries and most of the comforts of life, and be far more happy than we could be were we to be enslaved.

I can't help assuring you as an evidence that the Colonies continue united in supporting the common cause, that they are almost daily sending to this town for its relief, flour, indian corn, beef, pork, mutton, butter, cheese, and in a word every thing necessary for the comfort as well as support of life; and we have all the encouragement we can desire to depend upon their going on to do thus while our circumstances are such as to require their help.

I fear I have tried your patience but I must, notwithstanding, add this further that a most malignant fever rages among the troops. Three, four, and five have sometimes been buried in a day. Many of them are now sick. There is no abatement of the disease. Blessed be God, few or none of the town-people have taken the infection. The troops, by desertion and death, are amazingly lessened, which we certainly know, notwithstanding the care of the officers to hide it from us.

I am, dear sir, with all due respect,

Your friend [and] humble servant,
Charles Chauncy

Price to Chauncy[1]

Newington
February 25, 1775

Dear Sir,

I cannot avoid embracing the opportunity offered me by Mr. Quincy's return of writing to you. I am very sorry for the bad state of health into which Mr. Quincy has fallen. This has rendered him incapable of carrying into execution some of the views with which he came here. But he is now better and I hope will be restored in health to his family. He is indeed an able, faithful, and zealous friend to his country and I have been happy in my acquaintance with him. He can inform you of what is passing here and of my sentiments with respect to the public affairs which now engage so much attention. But neither my sentiments, nor those of persons of more weight, can be of much importance to you. It is from themselves that our brethren in America must look for deliverance. They have, in my opinion, infinitely the advantage in this dispute. If they continue firm and unanimous it must have a happy issue, nothing being more certain than that the consequences of the present coercive measures must in a year or two be so felt in this kingdom as to rout the present despotic ministry and to bring in new men who will establish the rights and liberties of the Colonies on a plan of equity, dignity and permanence. In such circumstances, if the Americans relax, or suffer themselves to be intimidated or divided, they will indeed deserve to be slaves. For my own part, were I in America I would go barefoot, I would cover myself with skins and endure any inconveniences sooner than give up the vast stake now depending, and I should be encouraged in this by knowing that my difficulties would be temporary, and that I was engaged in a last struggle for liberty, which perseverance would certainly crown with success. I speak with earnestness because thoroughly convinced that the authority claimed by this country over the Colonies is a despotism which would leave them none of the rights of freemen, and because also I consider America as a future asylum for the friends of liberty here, which it would be a dreadful calamity to lose.

By the government which our ministers endeavour to establish in New England, and that which they have established in Canada, we see what sort of government they wish for in this country; and as far as they can succeed in America, their way will be paved for success here. Indeed the influence of the crown has already in effect subverted liberty here; and should this influence be able to establish itself in America, and gain an accession of strength from thence, our fate would be sealed, and all security for the sacred blessing of liberty would be destroyed in every part of the British

---

1. MHS*P* (1903), pp. 278–281.

dominions. These are sentiments that dwell much upon my heart, and I am often repeating them.

You must have been informed before this time that Lord Chatham introduced into the House of Lords about three weeks ago a bill containing a plan of pacification, which was rejected at the first reading in a manner the most unprecedented and contemptuous. In a few days after this, both Houses in an address to his Majesty declared the Province of Massachusetts Bay in rebellion, petitioned for an enforcement of the late acts, and offered to stand by his Majesty with their lives and fortunes. But at the beginning of last week, to the amazement of everybody, the ministry took a new turn and, though they had repeatedly declared that their object was not to draw money from the Colonies, yet on the 20th of last month, a motion was made in the House by Lord North to the following purport: "That it was the opinion of that House, that when any of his Majesty's colonies shall make provision, according to their several circumstances, for contributing their proportion towards the common defence and the support of their respective governments (such proportion to be raised by their own assemblies and disposable by Parliament) it will be proper, if such proposal should be approved by Parliament, and for so long as it shall be so approved, to forbear in respect of such colonies imposing upon them or levying any taxes." By this resolution Lord North said he hoped the horrors of a civil war might be avoided, and yet more gained from the Colonies than could be gained by any coercion of them. After a debate of near seven hours (during which some of the members chose to amuse themselves with cards in one of the rooms adjoining to the House) the motion was agreed to by a majority of 274 to 88; and it was reported and confirmed last Monday, but is not to be formed into a bill. At the same time, the hostile plan before adopted is to go on. No firelock, as the Solicitor-General said in the House, is to be taken from a gun or rudder from a ship; the bill now in Parliament for destroying the New England fishery is to pass; none of the acts of last spring are to be repealed; and General Gage's reinforcement, consisting of eight regiments, besides dragoons, marines and ships of war, is to embark. I am told also that two bills more against New England are intended, one for destroying the Connecticut, Rhode Island, and New Hampshire charters, and another for attaining some of the leading men in your province.

These are measures that want no comment. Lord North's motion, though called a concession, is certainly, considered in all its circumstances, more properly an insult. An armed robber who demands my money might as well pretend he makes a concession by suffering me to take it out of my own pocket rather than search there for it himself. I cannot imagine, therefore, that this motion will have any other effect on the Colonies than to render them more united and determined.

With respect to the people in Massachusetts Bay, were they inclined to trust this opinion of the House of Commons by consenting to pay such contributions as the House shall require, they could not be benefited by it without giving up their old charter and together with it their whole right of legislation; for it is only from an assembly under the new charter that any proposals can be received.

Were there not so many melancholy instances of the pliableness of the House of Commons, it would be wonderful that the same House that had one day declared war against the Colonies should, almost the next day, on a sudden fright in the Cabinet, agree to a proposal supposed conciliatory. You may learn from hence our condition and what that power is which claims a right to make laws for America that shall bind it in all cases whatever. The design of the ministry by this step is to produce differences among the colonies or, as Lord North said in the House of Commons, to break at least one link in the chain, in consequence of which he thinks the whole may fall to pieces. New York, in particular, the ministry have in view, and they imagine that they have reason to depend on succeeding there. But frantic must that colony be that will suffer itself to be ensnared. Indeed our ministers have all along acted from the persuasion that you are all fools and cowards. I have said that the design of Lord North's motion is to disunite. I must add that it is intended also to create delays and gain time; for as with you all depends on losing no time, so with us all depends on gaining time (to corrupt and divide).

But I must conclude. Forgive your oppressors. I believe they know not what they do; but at the same time make them know that you will be free. My heart bleeds for the sufferings of your province; but, if it be not your own fault, all will end well. God is on the side of liberty and justice.

With the best wishes and the greatest regard, I am, dear sir,

Your sincere friend and very humble servant.

I have been long waiting with impatience for a letter from you. I writ in December last to Mr. Winthrop in answer to a letter with which he favoured me by Mr. Quincy. Be so good as to deliver my best respects to him. Dr. Franklin tells me that he shall write by this conveyance. America cannot have an abler or better friend.

Winthrop to Price[1]

Reverend and dear Sir,

Your favor of December 19th last, which came to hand but last week, gave me the highest satisfaction. I most heartily thank you for the expressions of your kindness towards me, for the honor you have done my letter, and for the farther honor of admitting me to your future correspondence, an indulgence I highly prize and shall not fail to make use of.

All America is greatly indebted to you for the sympathetic concern you express for their distresses, and for your exertions in their behalf; and I have no doubt would be happy, if it were in your power to make them so. But it is one of the principal sources of human misery, and one of the greatest mysteries of Providence, that the powers of this world are almost always in very different hands, are lodged with persons who have very different modes of thinking and very different objects of pursuit. Were the case otherwise, were no persons advanced to power but such as had ability to comprehend and a disposition to pursue the proper means for promoting the great end of government, the good of the people, there would be no grievances to complain of, and this world would soon become a kind of paradise. But this is too much to be expected till the millennial state or till, by the universal prevalence of Christ's heavenly doctrine, the virtue, and by consequence the liberty, peace and happiness of mankind are established upon a solid foundation.

The kind reception you gave my friend Mr. Quincy emboldens me to recommend to your notice another friend and near neighbor of mine, Francis Dana, Esq. He is a sensible, ingenious, modest gentleman who was in the practice of the law but can now have no employment in that way, and has always appeared a true friend to liberty. He will be able to give you full satisfaction as to the situation of affairs here, and inform you of many particulars which I cannot so well do in writing. But to show my readiness to obey your commands, I shall give the best account I can.

The people of Boston passed tolerably well through the winter by the help of the generous donations of this and the other colonies. I am well informed that not less than 7000 persons depend on these donations for their daily bread, and there is a multitude of others who, having something beforehand, and yet being cut off from their business, are now spending their all and must quickly be reduced to poverty. The people through the province, ever since so many of the mandamus councillors resigned their

---

1. MHSP (1903), pp. 283–286.

places, have had as little disturbance among them as in any of the colonies although there has been a total suspension of government. Our executive courts are shut up and we have no legislature. What supplies the place of this, in some measure, is a Provincial Congress, composed of delegates chosen by the several towns, in the manner of a house of representatives. Though they assume no authority, their recommendations have the same regard paid to them by the body of the people as used to be paid to laws enacted in form. All this while we were willing to flatter ourselves that the papers sent home by the Continental Congress would make some impression and incline the ministry to accommodate this unhappy controversy upon equitable terms. I have the satisfaction to find that their address to the people of England meets with your approbation and, I hope, that to the King does so likewise. But the last address to the two Houses has extinguished every spark of hope. The ministry have stopped their ears to the voice of reason and justice, and steeled their hearts against the feelings of humanity. Having been fairly foiled in the field of argument and tried, as it is said, the force of bribery and corruption in America, which has been so sucessfully practised at home, they have now recourse to the *ratio ultima*, and we have nothing in prospect but the horrors of war. The people of Boston, notwithstanding repeated insults from the soldiery, were willing to suppose that the works which the general threw up last fall at the only entrance into the town were designed merely for his own defence. But he has been making preparations since, which indicate *offensive* war. He has provided a great number of wagons and other military implements which can be of no use but for a march into the country. But what his particular operations will be, can be known only by the execution of them. The people of Boston are quitting the town in great numbers, so that the first city in America is likely soon to be in a great measure deserted, or inhabited chiefly by regiments and those who arrogate to themselves the title *friends of government*; and one of the finest harbors in the world has for some time been rendered useless. The military gentry, it is said, despise, or affect to despise, the Americans as cowards. They say, the Americans will never have courage to fight but will immediately disperse on the first appearance of regular troops. In this they may probably find themselves mistaken, to their cost. This single province can, upon occasion, bring more men, and those pretty well disciplined, into the field than the whole military establishment of Great Britain; and those that can be spared upon an emergency from other employments joined with those of the neighboring colonies will form an army which the general will not find it easy to subdue. They have no design of attacking the King's troops, but are determined, 19 in 20, I am told, upon the lowest computation, to stand upon their own defence, and the defence of their charter government, if attacked, and have prepared themselves accordingly. And indeed their ardor is such that it is found difficult to restrain it within due bounds. Consider, sir, what must be the feelings of men, descended from ancestors who fled hither as to a safe retreat from tyrannical power 150 years ago, while it was a perfect wilderness inhabited only by savages, and settled it at their own expence, without the least charge to the Crown or nation, and whose descendents have ever since been employed, with immense toil and danger, in turning this wilderness into a fruitful field, and the present generation possessed of fair inheritances, when they see themselves treated like a parcel of slaves on a plantation, who are to work just as they are ordered by their masters, and the profit of whose labors is to be appropriated just as their masters please, and then judge whether it be likely that such men will give up every thing dear and valuable to them without a struggle. What the event will be, can be known with certainty only by Him who seeth all things from the beginning to the end. We trust, we have a righteous cause, and we can cheerfully commit our cause to Him who judgeth righteously. We know that we are not the aggressors and that we are only striving to maintain our just rights. And I humbly hope, sir, that we shall be remembered in your addresses to the throne of grace. May a gracious God avert these dreadful evils! But whatever the events of war may be, they must prove ruinous to Great Britain as well as to the Colonies. A horrid carnage is the first thing to be expected, and if it once begins, it may continue for a length of time, till the Colonies are so exhausted and impoverished, that they will not have the ability, even if it could be supposed they would have the inclination, to purchase British manufactures. What then will become of the American trade? Will it be any compensation to the nation for the loss of this trade, that the ministry are in possession of a few fortified towns on the seacoast, where garrisons must be constantly maintained at a vast expence? But you, sir, have already anticipated the consequences, and had reason to say that their conduct is little short of insanity.

As soon as I had received your letter I went to deliver your respects to Dr. Chauncy and to inquire whether he had received yours of the 18th of October. He told me he had, and desired me to present his respects to you, and inform you that he had written an answer and sent with it a large packet of papers which he thinks went from hence about the middle of February. I hope they are come to your hand before this time.

I have the happiness entirely to fall in with the sentiments of your letter, that this contest may prove beneficial in the event to one, if not both, countries and hope I shall be excused if I publish (with the proper cautions) some extracts from it. I should think myself wanting in my duty to my countrymen if I should confine within the narrow circle of my particular acquaintance what is so excellently fitted to direct them in the true line of conduct they ought to pursue. And I have Dr. Chauncy's authority, in a similar case, to justify me.

I write also by Mr. Dana to our excellent friend Dr. Franklin, the friend of liberty, of America and of mankind.

With my most ardent wishes for your happiness and long-continued usefulness, I am, with the highest respect, sir,

Your most humble servant,
John Winthrop

P.S. I must beg pardon for the interlineations. I have not time to transcribe it, the messenger being now waiting.

Chauncy to Price[1]

Medfield
July 18, 1775

Reverend and dear Sir,

Yours of April 29th I have received, and return you my hearty thanks for it. Yours also to Mr. Josiah Quincy is come into my hands, as he was gone from our world to be here no more. None of his relatives nor friends had the opportunity of seeing him, as the vessel he came in went into Cape Ann harbour, thirty miles from Boston, from whence he was put on shore, but died the next day. We are ready to wish God had spared his valuable life. He might have been of great service to us in these calamitous times; but we would meekly bear this public loss, as it comes from the all wise, righteous, and holy Governor of the world. Notwithstanding Mr. Quincy's desire, Mr. Bromfield, I believe, would be justified should he open the packets sent to him, and not return them to America, as they might contain some articles of important intelligence proper to be known in England.

The three generals you speak of have been in Boston a considerable time, with the reinforcements, but are, there is reason to think, both disappointed and disheartened. The goods and tea brought over in the King's ships will be of no service to any merchant either at home or here, nor will they be hurtful to us, as they must be stored for want of buyers. Not a shilling's worth of them will be sold except to the Tories in Boston, who have at present other things to mind than that of purchasing English commodities.

The account of a defection at New York was one of the many falsehoods the friends of government (as they call themselves) have endeavoured to propagate here as well as in England. The people in that colony are in general as firmly attached to the cause of liberty as in the other colonies which, I suppose, is well known in London by this time.

The hope of the ministry, and the dread of our friends, respecting the cooling of the hearts of people here, the increase of disunion, and the im-

---

1. MHSP (1903), pp. 294–300.

possibility of carrying our commercial plan into execution, have no solid basis. Our spirits continually rise in warmth, our union is daily growing in strength and vigor, and such care is taken throughout the Colonies to bring into event the commercial plan that, humanly speaking, there is not the least probability of a failure.

Your merchants, we believe, are very hollow. Had they acted like men sincerely concerned for the prosperity of their American friends, we should not have suffered to the degree we have done. They may be assured, the Colonies have no expectation from them, as thinking they would willingly see them all enslaved, if their private interest might thereby be promoted. Perhaps some of them (I could mention their names) will never more have the advantage of commercial dealing with any of the Colonies.

General Gage, we had heard, had orders sent him to seize some of our leading men, and he had often opportunities to do it, but dare not. His endeavouring to take possession of the magazines has been the more immediate occasion of the war that is now commenced between him and all the Colonies, who are united as one in carrying it on. Our generals are constituted by the Continental Congress, the style of our army is, the American Army, the expence is defrayed by the Colonies in common. The cause contended for is not looked upon as the cause of Boston or the Massachusetts Province, but of the whole American continent, who are as firmly united and determined as men ever were to risk both their fortunes and lives in defence of their rights and privileges.

I shall now, with as much brevity as I can, give you an account of facts as they have happened, previous to the present civil war and since it began to this day. And you may rely upon what I write as the real truth, notwithstanding you may probably have quite different accounts from those who are enemies to us, for they will, the most of them, speak falsely with as bold a face as though they declared the real truth.

Colonel Lesly, about the latter end of March, was ordered by the General to go with about an hundred men to Marblehead in a transport that had been provided for them, and to go secretly by night; and from Marblehead he was to go by land to Salem, about 4 miles, and to bring off a number of cannon our people had there. He went nearly to the place where the cannon lay but was obstructed in his passage by the drawing up of a bridge, made for the convenience of vessels passing through; and after about an hour's continuance at this pass was obliged to return to Marblehead and get his men into the transport that brought them as soon as he could. Had he attempted to take the cannon by force, he and his men would surely have been cut off.

You must have heard before this reaches you of the battle at Concord. It was wholly occasioned by those who are seeking our ruin. The night before the 19th of April about a thousand regulars were ordered, with as great secrecy as you can imagine, to go to Concord to seize or destroy our magazine there. They arrived at Lexington, six miles short of Concord, about sunrise, when our men, having had some previous notice of their coming, began to collect together in order to watch their motions. They found nearly an hundred of our people in arms and ordered them to disperse, which they accordingly did, but while they were dispersing, the King's troops fired upon them, killed six or seven upon the spot and wounded some others. They then steered their course towards Concord. It has been pretended that our people gave the first fire, and I suppose such an account has been sent home. But it is a notorious falsehood. Some scores of persons then and there present have given their affidavits under oath that the King's troops killed six or seven of our men, and wounded others, before a gun was fired on our side. The same troops began the fire at Concord, but were soon obliged to retreat, though attacked by not more than between two and three hundred of our men; for no more had as yet got together. When they had retreated as far back as Lexington, they were joined by Lord Percy with about 900 regulars sent by the General as a reinforcement. By this time our men were increased in number, from one and another of the neighbouring towns, and behaved with such resolution and fortitude that Lord Percy's troops in common with the others were speedily obliged to be upon the retreat, and on they went retreating till they got back to Charlestown. It may be worthy of note here in favor of the King's troops that two regiments from Salem, Marblehead, and some other towns that way, did not come soon enough by half an hour to fall upon them in the rear as they were retreating. Had they been able to do this, they must have been cut off or taken prisoners. We know that 240 of the King's troops were killed and wounded. How many more met with the like fate we cannot say with certainty but it is generally said and believed that the number was not less than 450. In less than 24 hours after this engagement many thousands of our men were got together at Cambridge and Roxbury and we have now an army in these places of twenty thousand, as likely, able men as you would desire to look upon, in readiness to engage in any enterprise in defence of our rights and liberties. By means of this army all communication between the King's troops and the country is cut off and, as no fresh provisions have from that time been permitted to go into Boston, the troops there are in suffering circumstances, and must continue to be so till they can make their way into the country, which they will find to be impracticable. The day after the Concord fight the passages from Boston into the country were by the General's order shut, insomuch that no person could go out of the town. What his special design in this was, we cannot with certainty say, but in a few days of his own mere motion he sent for the selectmen of Boston, and made this proposal to them, that if the inhabitants would consent to put their arms into their custody they should have liberty to get out of town with their effects. The town was called together upon this occasion, and for the sake of their wives and children, and that they might secure their effects, they consented to deliver up their arms and accordingly did it. But what followed hereupon? The Governor, who is also the General, proved himself to be void of all faith as well as honor. He broke through his own proposal in which he engaged to let the inhabitants go out of town with their effects. For a while he suffered the inhabitants to go, but not without a pass from him, which soon became so difficult to obtain that but few comparatively could get out; nor were any suffered to get out without being searched and sent back if there was found with them provisions of any kind, or any merchandise. The whole merchandise of the people in trade is to this day in Boston, for what end I cannot say. The merchants in England are hereby greatly injured, for it is impossible their debts should be paid, while the possessors of their goods can make no use of them in a way of sale. And it is probable they will soon be the plunder of the troops. Mr. Gage has rendered himself the object of universal hatred and contempt by his perfidy, cruelty, and oppressive conduct.

The 27th of May another battle came on between the King's troops and ours. About three hundred of our men were sent to take from Hog Island (about 3 miles from Boston) the sheep, lambs, and cattle which were there; upon which a sloop, a schooner, and it may be an hundred boats filled with men were ordered by the General or Admiral or both to counteract our people in their design. This brought on a terrible engagement. It lasted between two and three hours. The issue was, our taking the schooner, driving away the sloop and boats, and carrying off from the just mentioned island all the sheep, etc. It is acknowledged by the regulars themselves that a considerable number of their men were killed and wounded. We know not how many, but it is generally said and thought that they lost nearly as many as at the Concord fight. We did not lose a single man and had but three wounded, and neither of them mortally. I heard General Putnam say, who had the command of our detachment, that the most of the time he and his men were fighting there was nothing between them and the fire of the enemy but pure air. They stood upon Chelsea-shore within reach of the enemy's shot for some hours, and yet not a man of them was killed; though they killed a considerable number of those that came against them. This can't be accounted for but by recurring to a remarkable interposition of Providence. The regular officers themselves acknowledge this was a fair fight and that they were fairly defeated.

The night before the 17th of June about fifteen hundred of our men were sent to Bunker Hill, in Charlestown, to throw up a breastwork and dig an entrenchment there. They began the work between 10 and 11 at night. By the dawn of the next morning they were fired upon from a battery at Coops Hill in Boston, which had some time before been erected

304   Appendix Eight. Selected Correspondence

by the General, and the fire was perpetual till about three thousand troops
were landed from Boston on the north side of said Bunker's hill. Upon this
there ensued a most terrible combat between the King's troops and ours.
The King's troops retreated twice. The third time they came on much
against their inclination. In very truth, they would never have ventured
up the hill again had they not been urged to it by the swords of their officers
pricking them along. They now got over the breastwork, such as it was,
and our men retreated, and went down the hill on the south side. The loss
on our side was nearly 80 or 90 men killed, and it may be an hundred and
fifty wounded, not more than two or three mortally. By all accounts from
those who have come out of Boston since this battle, not less than a thousand of the King's troops were killed, and nearly five hundred wounded,
including officers with the privates. It is credibly said that not less than 92
commissioned officers were killed and wounded. When I relate to you some
facts you will be able to judge whether the account of the enemy's slain and
wounded is exagger[at]ed, as also whether our men are such dastardly
creatures as Lord Sandwich represented them to be in the House of Lords.
The poor were ordered out of the public almshouse in Boston by General
Gage, and sent into the country, to make way for his wounded soldiers. The
same was done by the people in the workhouse there. Both these houses will
contain four hundred people. Soon after the Bunker Hill battle orders
were dispatched by General Gage in a cutter to New York, commanding
all the troops that were coming there to proceed to Boston with all speed.
I suppose they are all there by this time. These facts are not to be accounted
for unless his loss had been nearly as has been represented. The circumstances under which our men fought will demonstrate that they are not
such cowards as they are said to be in England. Not more than 15 hundred
fought with three thousand and killed and wounded one half of the whole.
On the north side of the hill on which the combat was the regulars had a
number of floating batteries which continually fired on our men. On the
south side of the hill, and in coming to it, or going from it, they were
annoyed by a number of the King's ships who were so anchored as greatly
to endanger our men. In front of the hill there was Coops Hill battery
which kept up a continual fire. Besides all this, soon after the fight began
the regulars in an inhuman cruel manner set fire to the town of Charlestown, which they wholly burnt down, to the unspeakable loss of hundreds
of families there. Upon such circumstances did our men fight, and with not
more than half the number the enemy had. And after all, they would not
have retreated, but that they had spent their ammunition, though they
came out well stocked with it. Some of our people fired at the enemy twenty
times, some thirty, and some till their guns were so heated that they dared
not to charge them any more. The King's troops, both officers and privates,
now say that our men will fight like devils. So far as I can learn there is

universal dejection and discouragement among the troops at Boston. Our army wish they would come out but it is not probable they will, though they have a reinforcement from the troops designed for New York.

Our people in all the Colonies are firmly united and resolutely fixt to defend their rights whatever opposition they meet with. And instead of being disheartened by what is done against them they rise continually in the strength of their determination to die rather than live slaves. It is remarkable, notwithstanding the sufferings of the town of Boston, and other towns, and the general oppression all the colonies are groaning under, I have never heard one who was not a Tory, so much as lisp, "Let us submit to the parliamentary acts."

I could have easily enlarged but have been obliged to write what I have done in a great hurry, as I am this afternoon going from this place, which is twenty miles from Boston, about 16 or 18 miles upon some special business. And Mr. Green, whose vessel this comes in, is going to Dartmouth before I shall see him again, from whence the vessel is to sail for London. He promises me the letter shall be delivered by the master himself with his own hands.

Mr. Winthrop lives now at Andover, about 27 miles from Boston. I saw him last week at his new habitation. He is well and would have undoubtedly wrote you had he known of this opportunity.

Next Wednesday, agreeably to the advice of the Continental Congress, this province, having made choice of representatives, will meet in order to choose counsellors and to transact public business, the Council acting in the place of the Governor, as they are allowed to do by our charter when there is no governor nor lt. governor, as is apprehended to be the case at present. None of the colonies look upon Governor Gage or Lt. Governor Oliver as constitutional officers, and think we may constitutionally act without them.

The following day, which is Thursday, will be observed by all the colonies as a day of fasting and prayer on account of our present circumstances. It was recommended to be observed by the Continental Congress. I pray God it may be observed in a truly Christian manner and so as that it may be acceptable to heaven.

I shall add no more but that I am, with all due regards,

Your assured friend and humble servant.

[No signature.]

I know not when I shall be able to write to you again but should be glad you would write to me as often as you can. Direct your letters to me at Medfield and they will come safely.

I shall send a number of late newspapers to Mr. Hyslop, who will give you the reading of them should you desire it. Mr. Bromfield can inform you of him.

Franklin to Price[1]

Philadelphia
October 3, 1775

I wish ardently as you can do for peace and should rejoice exceedingly in cooperating with you to that end. But every ship from Britain brings some intelligence of new measures that tend more and more to exasperate, and it seems to me that until you have found by dear experience the reducing us by force impracticable, you will think of nothing fair and reasonable. We have as yet resolved only on defensive measures. If you would recall your forces and stay at home we should mediate nothing to injure you. A little time so given for cooling on both sides would have excellent effects. But you will goad and provoke us. You despise us too much, and you are insensible of the Italian adage that there is no little enemy. Our respect for them will proportionably diminish, and I see clearly we are on the high road to mutual hatred and destruction. A separation of course will be inevitable. 'Tis a million of pities so fair a plan as we have hitherto been engaged in for increasing strength and empire with public felicity should be destroyed by the mangling hands of a few ministers. It will not be destroyed, God will protect and prosper it. You will only exclude yourselves from any share in it. We hear that more ships and troops are coming out. We know you may do us a great deal of mischief but we are determined to bear it patiently as long as we can, but if you flatter yourselves with beating us into submission, you know neither the people nor the country.

The Congress is still sitting and will wait the result of their last petition.

[No signature.]

Price to James Bowdoin[1]

[December 12, 1775][2]

Dear Sir,

The ministry amidst all their violence and appearances of decision, are, it is believed, much embarrassed; and wish for some method of retreating.

---

1. This letter is included in the copies of the "Price Letters" which were presented to the Massachusetts Historical Society and provided the basis for their 1903 edition. They are now in the library of the American Philosophical Society in Philadelphia. Hereafter cited as "Price Letters."

1. James Bowdoin (1726–1790), graduated from Harvard College in 1745; first president of the American Academy of Arts and Sciences; governor of Massachusetts (1785–1787).

2. Although Price did not date this letter, his reference to "a bill passed yesterday by the House of Commons," the American Prohibitory Bill, dates it December 12, 1775. A copy is in the Bowdoin-Temple Collection in the Massachusetts Historical Society.

They must see, if not totally blind, the impossibility of succeeding in the war they have brought on, should the Colonies continue united and determined. This has been strongly urged by the opposition in both houses. The Duke of Grafton (Lord Privy Seal) mentioned in the debate on Thursday 20,000 or 30,000 men as the utmost land force we could send including foreign troops. Tho' last year with the ministry, he spoke warmly against the present measures, and proposed repealing all the acts relative to America which have been passed since 1763. General Conway did the same in the House of Commons.

The Colonies, therefore, should be upon their guard against insidious offers; and consider this as their time for securing for ever their liberties. Perseverance and activity, whatever present sufferings may attend them, cannot but make all end well. The stake is vast, and worth any temporary sufferings.

What can America, it is said, do without trade, money or resources? Trade never yet promoted the true interest of any state. Money is not necessary, and there are substitutes for it. And as to resources, this contest will do the Colonies infinite service by obliging them to find all their resources within themselves.

[No signature.]

Mr. B— may if he pleases transcribe this and give it as an account of the sentiments of one of Dr. Winthrop's correspondents who has lately writ to him.

The petition of the Congress to the King has been rejected by the Parliament as well as the King. A bill passed the House of Commons yesterday which cuts off the colonies from all intercourse with the rest of the world; confiscates all their ships wherever found and also all ships trading with them; and establishes a commission which is to be sent over to America to grant pardons and indemnities under particular limitations.

Arthur Lee to Price[1]

Paris
April 20th, 1777

Dear Sir,

I beg you will accept my thanks for the favour of your pamphlet, than which I never in my life read any thing with more satisfaction.[2]

But alas! the decree is gone forth, and we are one no more. Providence,

---

1. MHSP (1903), pp. 308–310.

2. "It was entitled 'Additional Observations on the Nature and Value of Civil Liberty and the War with America.'—Eds." MHSP (1903).

by inspiring the same hardness of heart that delivered the children of Israel from their oppressors, has delivered us. A series of the most undistinguishing and inhuman barbarities by the German and British soldiery, together with General Howe's order to put all persons to the sword who should be found in arms without an officer, have planted in the minds of all men an utter detestation of the British government.

Congress have appointed a committee to enquire into the cruelties that have been committed, that if there be any distinction among the perpetrators, the punishment may fall where it is most deserved. The 17th Regiment, which had behaved with remarkable cruelty, fought with such desperate valour at Princeton that they were almost entirely cut to pieces. And such was their brutal ferocity, that even during the action, which had various turns, if any American fell into their hands they murdered him with the most savage inhumanity. This was the fate of General Mercer, a very brave and worthy officer from the state to which I have the honour to belong.

These, sir, are the lamentable fruits of Scotch principles and politics. But the calamity which they meant solely for us has fallen heavy upon them and their adherents. Elevated with the first appearance of success, and unmindful of the lenity which had spared and protected them, they openly and in all parts began to agitate the ruin of the people. This at once produced a distinction and a necessity of expelling them, which was effected by proclamation, and with every degree of lenity which the nature of the thing will admit of. In Virginia they are allowed to sell their property and depart in peace. But where the war presses and the enemy is invading, the necessity of the situation would not admit of more indulgence than time to remove their families.

The new governments in the different states are well established and that of the Congress deeply rooted.

Amid these wonderful events, it is a source of infinite satisfaction to me, that I have the honour of being numbered with you and others as having earnestly and sincerely laboured to avert this calamity from England, and to persuade those in whose power it was to send forth the spirit of peace, and re-unite us upon terms of equal liberty.

If any one can save a nation so pressed within and threatened without it is our friend Lord Shelburne. At least he is the only man of his rank whom I have the honour of knowing, whose virtues and abilities seem equal to the arduous task of retrieving a public overwhelmed with so many evils as that of England now is. Indeed, in my opinion, it would require a people of more virtue than the world ever yet produced, or than human nature will admit of, to resist the contagion of Scotch principles, to be united with Scotland, and not be undone. I mean as to its morals and public principles. The conduct of these people after their emigration to America proves the inveteracy of their national character. They had fled from the tyranny and exactions of their chiefs. In America they found refuge and relief. Yet at the call of those very chiefs they took up arms to destroy their benefactors, or reduce them, and return themselves under that domination of which they had had such bitter experience. A striking instance how impossible it is to wean them from the principles of perfidy, slavery and ingratitude which are native to them and which mark them as a people, *hostis humani generis*.

To form a nation upon the principles of equal justice and permanent liberty is perhaps little less difficult than to retrieve one from its degeneracy. That task is ours. So many various spirits are put in motion during a civil war, so many opportunities offer to the daring and the vicious, the sweets of power and pre-eminence are so necessarily tasted by so many, that it must be fortunate indeed if some of them do not attempt to augment and extend the enjoyment of them beyond the limits prescribed by a system of equal liberty. But it may be well hoped that these attempts will be frustrated by the checks of so many republics and the vigilance of those who are aware of such consequences. Rome perished because the people mistook the spirit of faction for that of liberty, and because the collection of the whole into one head left no check, and rendered its corruption fatal to the whole.

May your lights and labours, sir, reform the degeneracy of the times, and re-inspire the spirit of liberty into the people of England. May the example of her children teach her how invincible that spirit is where it really operates! The unworthy conduct of the Scotch government, to which she has submitted, has not so utterly extinguished the love I bore her as to prevent me from wishing her most sincerely the full enjoyment of that liberty which she has at least contenanced the Scots in their base and brutal endeavours to wrest from us.

I must beg the favour of you to make my best respects to Lord Shelburne, Col. Barré, Dr. Priestly, and all those of our acquaintance who yet do me the honour of their remembrance, and remain unterrified and unseduced from the cause of truth and liberty.

I have the honour to be, with the most sincere respect and esteem, dear sir,

Your most obedient servant,
Arthur Lee.

Earl of Shelburne to Price[1]

Bowood Park
24 September, 1777

My dear Friend,

It's a long time since I have had the pleasure of hearing from you. It therefore gave me great satisfaction to find that you and Mrs. Price were well by your letter to Dr. Priestley. I should have been in London before now, if the indolence of my life here, where I sit under the shade of trees of my own planting, and the seat of government having little inviting in a time of such public calamity, had not insensibly detained me. I was inclined to write to you frequently, if I did not apprehend the fidelity of the conveyance, as long as you were at any distance of London. I wished to tell you of letters which I received from both armies, especially as those from Canada were quite necessary to form a right judgment of what had passed there, after the high colouring of the General of the King's troops. The most material particulars I find since in General St. Clair's letter published by the Congress; my accounts contain nothing more than that 50 Americans had not joined them by the 12th of July, 5 days after their boasted victory. I hear accounts of the same nature from General Howe's army, who have found the country universally hostile, nothing but women remaining in the houses, no intelligence to be had, at the same time that General Washington was instantly informed of every motion of the King's troops. That General Washington had not above 10,000 troops with him, how many other corps were afoot, and what numbers, they were ignorant, but wherever they turned they were sure to meet an enemy. These accounts made the army despond of conquering the country, and certain that nothing decisive would take place this campaign. I hear the avowed displeasure of administration towards General Carleton was his not employing the Indians sooner. In this state of things, America is safe, but, my dear friend, what will become of England? I just hear of some extraordinary orders given by government, which mark something more than common apprehensions, for arming more ships, etc. When I write to you my heart and pen go together. But as it may affect others, and we have all to deal with a wicked administration, I beg you'll not mention your authority for the above honest opinions from America, lest those who gave them should suffer for them.

I have read with great pleasure Lord Abingdon's pamphlet.[2] I hope all parties in the city will join in doing justice to his spirit, and to his sentiments.

---

1. MH*SP* (1903), pp. 312–313.
2. See footnote *c* to the *General Introduction*, p. 49.

I hope to be in London by Saturday sennight if not before, and shall not have more pleasure in anything, than in assuring you that I am,

Most truly yours.
Shelburne.

P.S. I beg my best compliments to Mrs. Price.

Price to Franklin[1]

[Newington Green]
May 10, [1778]

Dr. P_____ is very sorry the bearer of this has any reason for giving Dr. Franklin any farther trouble; but he doubts not but Dr. F_____n will receive him with his accustomed goodness.

Is there any truth in the stories propagated here that the Congress is divided; that General Washington is grown unpopular; that his army deserts in great numbers; and that the sufferings of the Americans are excessive? The commissioners are gone assured, that the terms they are impowered to offer by the conciliatory bills, tho' much short of independence will be accepted. Is there any reason to expect this? Any notice which Dr. F_____ may take of these questions to Mr. P_____r, or any intelligence which he can give with propriety, will be gratefully accepted by Dr. P_____ who indeed, in these sad times is extremely anxious.

He wishes his particular remembrances may be delivered to Mr. S_____ and Dr. B_____. Mr. Curteis and Mr. Webb are both broken and ruined. Many events of the same kind have lately happened; and there is reason to fear they are by the beginning of sorrows.

A family in which Dr. F_____ used to be very intimate and particularly the amiable Miss G_____a, are very inquisitive about him, and wish him to know they are all well, and that they always remember him with particular affection and regard. The Society of Whigs at the L_____ never forget him.

[No signature.]

---

1. "Price Letters."

Lee to Price[1]

Paris
December 8, 1778

Dear sir,

I cannot express the pleasure I felt at receiving the note which accompanies this. I am in the fullest hope that both your inclination and your circumstances will permit you to gratify our wishes.[2]

You are sensible how much the future happiness of a people depends upon the proper arrangement of their finances, how difficult it is to remedy original defects in all constitutions and therefore how much ill you will prevent, and how much good promote, by giving the assistance that is requested.

It seems that where you are your aid is not required. Those who conduct that government esteem themselves much abler than you can advise. And indeed considering how opposite their end is to ours, I think they are right. Their abilities are exactly shaped to their purpose, the ruin of the Empire.

Let me therefore beseech you to come where you will be welcome and be useful. It will be the noblest consolation for the calamities that must fall upon the old people, to promote the happiness of the new. As long as there was any hope of preventing those calamities, your utmost endeavors were not wanting. But the total prevalency of vice and corruption have not left a probability of amendment.

In this situation the pure and unambitious voice of Congress has desired your assistance in a manner that bears the most honorable testimony of your merit, and of their wishes to promote the permanent good of the people who have reposed in them the guardianship of their rights and interests.

It is the voice of wisdom which calls you to the noblest of all works—the assisting to form a government which means to make the principles of equal justice and the general rights the chief object of its attention. Generations yet unborn will bless the contributors to this inestimable work,

---

1. A copy of the letter is contained in the Bowdoin-Temple Collection in the Massachusetts Historical Society.

2. The wish was expressed in a "Directive to the American Commissioners; in Congress, October 6, 1778. Resolved: That the honorable Benjamin Franklin, Arthur Lee and John Adams, Esqrs., or any one of them, be directed forthwith to apply to Doctor Price and inform him that it is the desire of Congress to consider him as a citizen of the United States and to receive his assistance in regulating their finances; that if he shall think it expedient to remove with his family to America and afford such assistance a generous provision shall be made for requiting his services."

The three commissioners had extended the invitation and, at the time of this letter, Price was apparently considering it. In the end, however, he found he could not accept. He expressed his regrets to Adams, Franklin, and Lee in a letter dated January 18, 1779.

and among them I trust the name of Dr. Price will hold a distinguished place.

I am, with the sincerest respect and friendship, dear sir,

Your most obedient servant,

Arthur Lee

Price to Lee[1]

Newington Green
January, 1779

Dear Sir,

Your most kind and excellent letter, together with the letter conveying the resolution of Congress, has made the deepest impression on my mind. I entreat you to accept yourself and to deliver to Dr. Franklin and Mr. Adams my best acknowledgments. Though I cannot hesitate about the reply addressed to the honourable commissioners, and through them to Congress, which accompanies this letter, yet so flattering a testimony of the regard of an assembly which I consider the most respectable and important in the world cannot but give me the highest pleasure, and I shall always reckon it among the first honours of my life.

There is an indolence growing upon me as I grow older, which will probably prevent me forever from undertaking any public employment. When I am in my study and among my books, and have nothing to encumber me, I am happy; but so weak are my spirits that the smallest hurry and even the consciousness of having any thing to do which *must* be done, will sometimes distress and overpower me. What I have written on the subject of finances has been chiefly an amusement which I have pursued at my leisure, with some hope indeed, but very little expectation, of its being useful. Nothing can be more melancholy than to see so many European states depressed and crippled by heavy debts, which have been the growth of ages, and which in the end must ruin them, but which a small appropriation faithfully applied might have always kept within the bounds of safety. This is particularly true of this country. Here our debt must soon produce a shocking catastrophe. The new world will I hope take warning and profit by the follies and corruptions and miseries of the old.

My pamphlets on the principles of government and the American war were extorted from me by my judgment and my feelings. They have brought upon me a great deal of abuse; but abundant amends have been made me by the approbation of many of the best men here and abroad;

---

1. Richard Henry Lee, *Life of Arthur Lee, LL.D.* (Boston: Wells and Lilly, 1829), pp. 148–150.

and particularly by that vote of Congress to which I suppose they may have contributed. When you write to any of the members of that assembly be so good as to represent me as a zealous friend to liberty, who is anxiously attentive to the great struggle in which they are engaged, and who wishes earnestly for the sake of the world that British America may preserve its liberty, set an example of moderation and magnanimity, and establish such forms of government as may render it an asylum for the virtuous and the oppressed in other countries.

Tell Dr. Franklin that he is one of the friends in whom while in this country I always delighted, and for whom I must ever retain the greatest esteem and affection. We are now separated from one another never probably to meet again on this side of the grave. May he long be preserved as a blessing to his country. My connexions and state of health are such that I must stay in this country and wait its fate. I do this with a painful concern for the infatuation which has brought it into its present danger; but at the same time with indifference as far as my own personal interest is concerned, and a perfect complacency in the consciousness of having endeavoured to act the part of a good citizen, and serve the best of all causes. Will you further mention me particularly to Mr. Adams, and inform him that I greatly respect his character.

Some good friends of yours and mine are well, but I differ from them at present in opinion.

Under a grateful sense of your friendship and with great regard, and wishes of all possible happiness, I am, my dear sir, your obliged and very obedient humble servant,

Richard Price.

P.S. The interest of mankind depends so much on the forms of government established in America, that I have long thought it the duty of every man to contribute all he can towards improving them. I am possessed of some observations which have been made by a great man with this view, and I may some time or other take the liberty to communicate them with a few additional observations.

Chauncy to Price[1]

Boston
May 20th, 1779

Reverend and dear Sir,

As the honorable Mr. Temple is going to Holland, and may have it in his power to convey a letter to you with safety, I could not excuse myself

---

1. MHSP (1903), pp. 319–321.

from writing by so favorable an opportunity. What I have in view is to assure you, that the situation of our public affairs is not as has been represented by Governor Johnson and the commissioners sent with him to America. They were confined to Philadelphia and New York the whole time of their continuance here, and had, nor could have had, no other information respecting the Congress, or the circumstances of these states, than what they received from British officers, and refugees who had taken part with them. The ministry therefore could, by their accounts, have no true knowledge of the state of things in this part of the world and so far as they might be disposed to act upon principles grounded on these accounts, they must act upon the foot of misrepresentation, not to say direct falsehood. Governor Johnson by his conduct while here has proved himself to be nothing better than a ministerial tool, and is universally held in contempt. By his speeches in Parliament relative to America he appears to have known nothing of its real state, or to have given a notoriously wrong representation of it. A very great part of what he delivered there, as we have had it in the newspapers, is wholly beside the truth, and indisputably so. We pity the man, but much more the ministry in giving so much credit to his accounts as in any measure to govern their conduct by it. It is indeed acknowledged, our paper currency has sunk in its value to a great degree, which has occasioned the price of the necessaries of life to rise to an enormous height; but this has not been disadvantageous to us collectively considered. None have suffered on this account but salary men, those who depended on the value and interest of their money for a subsistence, and the poor among us. As to the rest, whether merchants, farmers, manufacturers, tradesmen, and day-laborers, the rise of their demands has all along been in proportion to the depreciation of the currency and the rise of the necessaries of life thereupon. It may seem strange, but it is a certain fact, that the American States, notwithstanding the vast depreciation of their paper currency and the excessive high price of provisions of all kinds are richer now in reality, and not in name only, than they ever were in any former period of time, and they are much better able to carry on the war than when they began it. One great fault they are justly chargeable with. It is this, they have almost universally been too attentive to the getting of gain, as there have been peculiar temptations hereto since the commencement of the present contest. They would otherwise, I have no doubt, have cleared the land of British troops long before this time; and nothing is now wanting (under the smiles of Providence) to effect this, but such exertions of the King's forces as would generally alarm the country. There would then appear a sufficiency of strength to do by them as was done by Burgoyne and his army. While they suffer themselves to be, as it were, imprisoned in New York and Rhode Island, and go not forth unless to steal sheep and oxen and plunder and burn the houses of poor innocent people by surprise, it makes no great noise here, whatever, by pompous exaggeration, it may do in London. Our people want only to be roused, it would then be seen what they could do. I may add here, our freeholders and farmers, by means of the plenty of paper money have cleared themselves of debts, and got their farms enlarged and stocked beyond what they could otherwise have done, and rather than give up their independency, or lose their liberties, would go forth to a man in defence of their country, and would do it like so many lions. The British administration hurt themselves more than they do us as a people by continuing the war, and they must bring it to a conclusion, or they will ruin themselves instead of us. The longer they protract the war the more difficult it will be to obtain such terms of peace as they might have had, and perhaps may still have. These states will soon lose that little confidence they may now place in the British ministry. None of the minority in Parliament have a worse opinion of them than is generally entertained here. A valuation of the Massachusetts State has lately been made in order to its being properly laid and it is found, notwithstanding the vast number of cattle which have been slain for the army, as well as inhabitants, that they are more numerous now than in any period of time since the settlement of the country. In the county of Worcester only, which within my remembrance had but a very few inhabitants, there appears to have been more than forty thousand head of cattle, and sheep in proportion. No longer ago than the year 1721 I rode through Worcester, now as well and largely inhabited a town as almost any in this state, and it was in as perfectly wilderness a condition as any spot between Boston and Canada, not an house or inhabitant to be seen there. I have mentioned this only to point out to you the internal source of provision we have, should the war be continued ever so long. But I may not enlarge.

Your good friend Mr. Professor Winthrop died about 12 days ago. I am also grown infirm as well as old, and very unable to write, for which reason you will excuse the blots, as well as almost illegible writing of the present letter, for I could not transcribe it to send it to you.

If I should live to see a settled state of things, I will, if I should have strength, write you very largely upon our affairs. I am with all due respect,

Your friend and humble servant.

[No signature.]

P.S. Congress are as firmly united as ever in their attachment to the liberties and independence of America, and the people place as entire confidence in them as from the beginning, notwithstanding all that Johnson and the other commissioners ridiculously (to me) endeavour to make people believe on your side the water. And notwithstanding the depreciation of our currency, and the high price of provisions, the people are more averse than ever to submission to Great Britain, and would rather die than come into it. Mr. Temple[2] has been from New York to Boston, and from Boston to Philadelphia, and from Philadelphia back again to Boston. He went through most of the more populous towns between these two places, and as he had opportunity of seeing and conversing with the first and best gentlemen we have in these states, he can, should he go to England, give you a more just and true account of our political affairs than you have yet had. And I believe you may depend upon his giving you an honest account of things among us.

Price to Franklin[1]

Newington Green
October 14, 1779

Dear Sir,

Will you be so good as to get the enclosed letter conveyed to Mr. A____r Lee, if he is near you and it can be done easily? If not, be so good as to burn it. Being obliged for particular reasons to avoid politics, it is a short acknowledgment of the favour he did me by a letter I received from him at the beginning of last summer, and contains nothing of much importance.

I received the greatest pleasure from the note which you sent me by Mr. J____s and Mr. P____se. They were much gratified by your kind notice of them. Dr. Priestley is well, and much engaged in prosecuting his experiments on air. Dr. Ingenhouz, by whose hands this is conveyed, has lately been warmly employed in the same pursuit. He will tell you what great success he has met with. The society of honest whigs which you used to honour with your company, are soon to renew their meetings for the winter and you will undoubtedly be one of the first subjects of our conversation. I spent in August some time with an amiable family near Winchester. The house in the garden that you used to frequent often brought you to our remembrance. You can scarcely imagine with what respect and affection you are talked of there. I have heard with particular concern of the death of Dr. Winthrop. To this we are all destined but the virtuous will be happy in better regions. The clouds gather frightfully over this country. I am waiting for the issue with anxiety but at the same time with much complacency in the reflexion that at this most important period I have endeavoured to act the part of a faithful and good citizen.

Accept, my dear friend, these lines as a testimony of my very affectionate remembrance. May heaven preserve you and grant you the best enjoyments. With great regard, I am ever yours

R. Price

---

2. "Afterward Sir John Temple, son-in-law of Governor Bowdoin.—Eds." MHS*P* (1903).
1. "Price Letters."

Franklin to Price[1]

February 6, 1780

Dear Sir,

Your writings after all the abuse you and they have met with begin to make serious impressions on those who at first rejected the counsels you gave and they will acquire new weight every day, and be in high esteem when the cavils against them are dead and forgotten. Please to present my affectionate respects to that honest, sensible, and intelligent society who did me so long the honour of admitting me to share in their instructive conversations. I never think of the hours I so happily spent in that company without regretting that they are never to be repeated, for I see no prospect of an end to this unhappy war in my time. Dr. Priestley you tell me continues his experiments with success. We make daily great improvement in natural, there is one I wish to see in moral, philosophy: the discovery of a plan that would induce and oblige nations to settle their disputes without first cutting one another's throats. When will human reason be sufficiently improved to see the advantage of this? When will men be convinced that even successful wars at length become misfortunes to those who unjustly commenced, and who triumphed blindly in their success, not seeing all its consequences? Your great comfort and mine in this war is that we honestly and faithfully did everything in our power to prevent it. Adieu, and believe me ever, my dear friend.

[No signature.]

Price to Francis Dana[1, 2]

Newington Green
September 26, 1780

Dear Sir,

Two of my friends are just setting out for Paris, and I cannot make myself easy without embracing the opportunity their journey offers me to convey to you a few lines to express my gratitude for a very kind letter with which you favoured me some time ago. I received particular pleasure from

---

1. "Price Letters."

1. Francis Dana (1743–1811), diplomat, jurist; graduated from Harvard College in 1762; member of the Sons of Liberty; secretary to the legation headed by John Adams in France to negotiate peace with Great Britain; commissioner to Russia; chief justice of the supreme court of Massachusetts.

2. Copy in the Bowdoin-Temple Collection.

the proof it gave me that I am remembered by you and have a place in your good opinion. I am a very anxious spectator of the struggle in which your country has been for some time engaged. The part I have taken in it, tho' it has brought upon me a vast deal of abuse and ill-will, I reflect upon with the greatest satisfaction. May God grant it a happy issue. The ardent wish of my heart is that every country under heaven may enjoy the blessings of liberty and independence. We are continually amused here with accounts of the disposition of the Americans to return to a connexion with this country, their sufferings, and their weariness of the war and of the government of Congress. These accounts are greedily swallowed, and since the taking of Charlestown the common expectation has been that America will soon be ours again.

But I must not enlarge. With this you will probably receive the second edition of a pamphlet which I published at the beginning of this summer. Tho' of little value I hope you will accept it as a testimony of the author's respect. May you, dear sir, enjoy every blessing that can make you happy. With great esteem I am your obliged and very obedient and humble servant,

R____ P____

Price to Franklin[1]

December 22, 1780

Dear Sir,

I have received with particular pleasure your letter by Dr. H____ and I cannot help returning by him a few lines to thank you for remembering me and to express the satisfaction with which I have heard, that you are recovered from a fit of the gout which you think has been of service to you. May your life be preserved to do good to the world, and to see the end of the present struggle. I cannot describe to you the feelings with which I view the progress of it. God grant that the issue may prove favourable to public liberty and the general rights of mankind.

You cannot imagine how much I have been lately abused and threatened. My enemies by their charges against me make me of much more consequence than I am. I feel easy. There is nothing in the conduct of my life that I reflect upon with more satisfaction than the part I have taken in the dispute with America, and the endeavours I have used to warn and serve my country, and to communicate right sentiments of government and civil and religious liberty. On the subject of toleration I have writ a good

1. "Price Letters."

deal, but the friend who told you that I had published on this subject was mistaken. When you see Mr. T_____t deliver my best respects to him and my thanks for a kind letter with which he has lately obliged and honoured me. Dr. P_____ lives at Bir_____m and has lately been invited to preach in the afternoon to a congregation there. His health is better, but he was last week alarmed by some symptoms of a return of his bilious disorder. He has just finished another volume upon air.

With the greatest respect and affection I am, my dear friend, ever yours.

[No signature.]

Dr. Frothergill is relapsed into the disorder (a suppression of urine) which brought him to the brink of the grave last winter, and lies now dangerously ill.

I shall take care of that the letter to M. I_____s be safely delivered. He is now in the country.

The war spreads. What will become of us?

Price to Benjamin Rush[1,2]

Newington Green
June 26, 1783

Sir,

I feel myself very happy in the approbation of my attempts to serve the cause of liberty which you express in the letter with which you have favoured me, and which has been delivered to me by Mr. John Vaughn. From a regard to the general rights of mankind and a conviction that all dominion of one country over another is usurpation and tyranny, I have always defended, as far as I have been able, the cause of America and opposed the late wicked war, and in doing this, I have gone through much abuse and some danger in this country. The struggle has been glorious on the part of America and it has now issued just as I wished it to issue, in the emancipation of the American states and the establishment of their independence. It is not possible for me to express to you the satisfaction this has given me. I think it one of the most important revolutions that has ever taken place in the world. It makes a new opening in human affairs which may prove an introduction to times of more light and liberty and

---

1. Benjamin Rush (1745–1813), physician, patriot, humanitarian; graduated from the College of New Jersey (now Princeton) in 1760; studied medicine in Edinburgh and London where he met Franklin; professor of chemistry in the College of Philadelphia; staff member of the Pennsylvania Hospital from 1783 until 1813; worked for medical and social reform and the abolition of slavery.

2. Library Company of Philadelphia, Yi–2–7260–F, 43:105–109.

virtue than have been yet known. This must be the consequence, if the United States can avoid the infection of European vices and establish forms of government and a plan of political union that shall be perfectly favourable to universal liberty, and prevent future wars among themselves. Should this happen, they will without doubt be the refuge of mankind, and a great part of the world will endeavour to participate in their happiness. I wish I was capable of advising and assisting them. Were I to attempt this what I should recommend, with particular earnestness, would be a total separation of religion from state policy and allowing an open field for improvement by the free discussion of all speculative points, and an equal protection, not only of all Christians, but of all honest men of all opinions and religions. I see, with the greatest pleasure, that the new forms of government are in this respect liable to but few objections. From what I have said you must conclude that I cannot but be deeply interested in all that is now passing in America and that, therefore, it will be highly agreeable to me to be informed of any transactions there. Any information of this kind will be gratefully received but I cannot promise much in return. There is more in this country to be avoided than imitated by America.

This letter is to be conveyed to you by Mr. Vaughn. I have long had a particular respect for him and for good Mrs. Vaughn and the rest of the family. May they be ever prosperous and happy.

With many thanks to you for your letter and the best wishes, I am, sir,

Your very obedient and humble servant,
Richard Price

Price to Franklin[1]

Newington Green
April 6, 1784

My dear friend,

I have been long intending to write to you and I feel ashamed that I have not done it sooner. Your letter which was brought me by Mr. Bingham gave me great pleasure. It enclosed a case for an air balloon and a print which in conformity to your desire I delivered to the president of the Royal Society. Soon after Mr. Bingham's arrival, Mr. Daggs brought me your paper on a mathematical prize question proposed by the Royal Academy of B____. I conveyed this to Dr. Priestley, and we have been entertained with the pleasantry of it and the ridicule it contains. The dis-

1. "Price Letters."

covery of air balloons seems to make the present time a new epoch and the last year will, I suppose, be always distinguished as the year in which mankind began to fly in France. Nothing has yet been done here in this way of any consequence.

In the Royal Society a great part of the winter has been employed in a manner very unworthy of philosophers. An opposition has been formed to the president. Motions for censuring him have been repeatedly made at our weekly meetings, and supported by Dr. Horseley, the Astronomer Royal, Mr. Masenes, Mr. Maty, etc., etc. and these motions have produced long and warm debates. Lately there has been a suspension of these debates, but there is now some danger that they may be revived again, for Mr. Maty has just resigned his place of secretary in resentment.

In your letter you have intimated that you then entertained some thought of visiting London in the spring. This is much wished for by your friends here and particularly by the club at the London Coffee-House which you have so often made happy by your company. Dr. Priestley intends coming to London from Birmingham in about a fortnight but could he reckon up the pleasure of meeting you in London at any time he would contrive to come up at that time. He has, I find, been chosen a member of the Royal Academy of Sciences at Paris. This is indeed a singular honour and it must give him particular pleasure.

I can scarcely tell you with what emotions of concern I have heard that you have for some time been suffering under symptoms of the stone. What a sad calamity it is to be visited in the last stage of life by so dreadful a distemper? Dreadful I know it is to be from experience. I have, however, been so happy as to discharge the stone and my only present trouble is the sad state of health into which my wife is fallen. About a month ago she was struck a third time with paralytic symptoms. She is extremely debilitated and I live in a constant state of painful apprehension about her. She hopes you will accept her best respects.

Political affairs in this country are at present in great confusion. The King, after dismissing from his service the leaders of the late odious condition, and appointing other ministers in their room to the great joy of the kingdom, has at last found it necessary, in order to maintain the new ministers in power and to carry on the public business, to dissolve the Parliament. We are, therefore, now in the midst of the heat and commotion of a general election and such is the influence of government on elections and also the present temper of the people that probably this new minister will have a great majority in their favour in the new Parliament. The more wise and virtuous part of the nation are struggling hard to gain a parliamentary reform and think, with great reason, that while representation continues such a mockery as it is, no change of ministers can do us much good. But an equal representation is a blessing which probably we shall never obtain till a convulsion comes which will disssolve all government and give an opportunity for erecting a new frame.

In America there is, I hope, an opening for a better state of human affairs. Indeed I look upon the revolution there as one of the most important events in the history of the world. Wishing, for the sake of mankind, that the United States may improve properly the advantages of their situation, I have been lately employing myself in writing sentiments of caution and advice which I mean to convey to them as a last offering of my good-will. I know I am by no means qualified for such a work, nor can I expect that any advice I can give will carry much weight with it or be much worth their acceptance. I cannot however satisfy my own mind without offering it such as it is.

I always think of your friendship with particular satisfaction, and consider it as one of the honours and blessings of my life. You have attained an eminence of credit and usefulness in the world to which few can aspire. That it may be continued as long as the course of nature will allow, and that you may enjoy every comfort that can make you most happy is, dear sir, the sincere wish of yours most affectionately

Richard Price

Should Mr. Jay or Mr. Adams be at Paris, be so good as to deliver my respectful remembrances to them when you see them. You probably well remember Mr. Paradise, a friend of Dr. William Jones and a very worthy man, who has considerable property in Virginia and to whom you have been kind. He has lately been in great trouble. The folly, temper, and extravagance of his wife produced for some weeks a separation between him and her and made him one of the most unhappy men I ever saw. But they are now come together again.

Price to Franklin[1]

Newington Green
July 12, 1784

Dear Sir,

I request your acceptance of the pamphlet which accompanies this letter. It is intended entirely for America and you are one of the first persons to whom it has been communicated. Most of the few copies which I have

---

1. "Price Letters."

printed will be conveyed to America and I hope the United States will forgive my presumption in supposing myself qualified to advise them. Indeed I almost feel myself ashamed of what I have done but the consciousness which I have that it is well intended and that my address to them is the effusion of a heart that wishes to serve the best interest of society helps to reconcile me to myself in this instance and it will, I hope, engage the candour of others.

The letter from M. Turgot which you will receive with this stands at present in the press, and will stand there till I shall be made acquainted with your opinion concerning the propriety of making it public by conveying it to the United States with my own pamphlet. The reason of my doubts about this is the charge of secrecy with which it concludes, and which you will find written in the margin. In compliance with this charge I have hitherto kept this letter private but lately I have considered that probably it was only some apprehension of personal inconvenience that led him to give this charge and that consequently the obligation to comply with it ceased with his life. Dreading, however, everything that might be reckoned a breach of confidence, my scruples are continually returning upon me, and I feel them the more, when I think that possibly he may have left a family which may suffer in France when it appears there that he was so much a friend to liberty as this letter will show him to be. In this state of mind I cannot make myself easy in any other way than by determining to request the favour of your judgment and to abide by it. Should you think that no ill consequences can result from publishing this letter to any family that M. Turgot may have left, and that his death has freed me from any obligation to keep it secret, I will order it to be printed off and send it to America with my pamphlet. Should you think the contrary, it shall be suppressed and I shall depend on your being so good as to destroy the copy now sent you. You will add much to the obligation I am under to you for all your friendship by giving me a few lines on this subject as soon as may be convenient to you. Should you think it improper to write by the post, a letter or any parcel you may wish to convey to London, may be sent by Miss Wilkes who is on a visit with the Duchess de la Valliere at Paris and will return the 2d of August.

I writ to you by the post about three months ago and hope you received my letter. I have heard lately with pleasure that you are pretty well. May your health and life and usefulness be continued as long as the course of nature will admit. Are we never to have the satisfaction of seeing you again in London? I have lately been at Birmingham to visit Dr. Priestley. He is very happy there and going on successfully with his experiment.

Mrs. Price desires to be respectfully remembered to you. She is in a very weak and low state but not worse than she has been for some time. We are thinking of spending the next month at Brighthelmston. Wishing you every blessing, I am, my dear friend, with the greatest regard,

Ever yours,

Richard Price

Perhaps some passages may occur to you in M. Turgot's letter which might be best omitted should you approve of publishing it. I have marked one in p. 91 and another in 102.

Jefferson to Price[1]

Paris

February 1, 1785

Sir,

The copy of your *Observations on the American Revolution* which you were so kind as to direct to me came duly to hand and I should sooner have acknowledged the receipt of it but that I awaited a private conveyance for my letter, having experienced much delay and uncertainty in the posts between this place and London. I have read it with very great pleasure as have done many others to whom I have communicated it. The spirit which it breathes is as affectionate as the observations themselves are wise and just. I have no doubt it will be reprinted in America and produce much good there. The want of power in the federal head was early perceived, and foreseen to be the flaw in our constitution which might endanger its destruction. I have the pleasure to inform you that when I left America in July the people were becoming universally sensible of this, and a spirit to enlarge the powers of Congress was becoming general. Letters and other information recently received show that this has continued to increase, and that they are likely to remedy this evil effectually. The happiness of governments like ours, wherein the people are truly the mainspring, is that they are never to be despaired of. When an evil becomes so glaring as to strike them generally, they arouse themselves, and it is redressed. He only is then the popular man and can get into office who shows the best dispositions to reform the evil. This truth was obvious on several occasions during the late war, and this character in our governments saved us. Calamity was our best physician. Since the peace it was observed that some nations of Europe, counting on the weakness of Congress and the little probability

---

1. MHSP (1903), pp. 325–326. See also Julian P. Byrd, ed., *The Papers of Thomas Jefferson* (Princeton, N.J.: Princeton University Press, 1950), pp. 630–631. Hereafter cited as *Jefferson Papers*.

of a union in measure among the states, were proposing to grasp at unequal advantages in our commerce. The people are become sensible of this and you may be assured that this evil will be immediately redressed, and redressed radically. I doubt still whether in this moment they will enlarge those powers in Congress which are necessary to keep the peace among the states. I think it possible that this may be suffered to lie till some two states commit hostilities on each other, but in that moment the hand of the union will be lifted up and interposed, and the people will themselves demand a general concession to Congress of means to prevent similar mischiefs. Our motto is truly *"nil desperandum."* The apprehensions you express of danger from the want of powers in Congress, led me to note to you this character in our governments which, since the retreat behind the Delaware, and the capture of Charlestown, has kept my mind in perfect quiet as to the ultimate fate of our union; and I am sure, from the spirit which breathes through your book, that whatever promises permanence to that will be a comfort to your mind. I have the honour to be, with very sincere esteem and respect, sir,

Your most obedient and most humble servant.
Th: Jefferson

Price to Jefferson[1]

Newington Green
March 21, 1785

Dear Sir,

I received with peculiar pleasure the favour of your letter by Dr. Bancroft, and I return you my best thanks for it. Your favourable reception of the pamphlet which I desired Dr. Franklin to present to you cannot but make me happy and I am willing to infer from it that this effusion of my zeal will not be ill received in America. The eyes of the friends of liberty and humanity are now fixed on that country. The United States have an open field before them, and advantages for establishing a plan favourable to the improvement of the world which no people ever had in an equal degree. Amidst the accounts of distress and confusion among them which we are often receiving in London, the information which you and Dr. Franklin have communicated to me comforts and encourages me, and determines me to maintain my hopes with respect to them.

Such an enlargement of the powers of Congress as shall, without hazard-

---

1. *Jefferson Papers*, 7:52–54.

ing too much public liberty, make it capable of preserving peace and of properly conducting and maintaining the union, is an essential point and the right settlement of it requires the greatest wisdom. You have gratified me much by acquainting me that a sense of this is becoming general in America and by pointing out to me that character of the confederated governments which is likely to preserve and improve them. The character, however, of popular governments depending on the character of the people, if the people deviate from simplicity of manners into luxury, the love of show, and extravagance, the governments must become corrupt and tyrannical. Such a deviation has, I am afraid, taken place along the sea coast of America and in some of the principal towns, and nothing can be more threatening. It is promoted by a rage for foreign trade and there is danger, if some calamity does not give a salutary check, that it will spread among the body of the people till the infection becomes general and the new governments are rendered images of our European governments.

There is, I fancy, no probability that Britain can be brought to consent to that reciprocity in trade which the United States expect. This is sad policy in Britain but it may turn out to be best for America; and should the issue be our exclusion from the American ports we may be ruined, but I do not see that America would suffer in its true interest. The fixed conviction, however, among us is that such an exclusion cannot take place and that we are able to supply America on so much better terms than any other country that, do what we will, we must have its trade. But, dear sir, I ask your pardon for detaining you by entering on a subject of which probably I am not a competent judge. I meant by these lines, when I begun them, only to make my grateful acknowledgments to you for the kind notice you have taken of me by your letter, a notice the agreeableness of which is much increased by the high opinion I have been led to entertain of your character and merit. With great respect and every good wish, I am, sir, your most obedient and humble servant,

Richard Price

I have desired Dr. Franklin to convey to you a copy of an edition of my *Observations* etc. which has been just published here. You will find that I have made considerable additions by inserting a translation of Mr. Turgot's letter and also a translation of a French tract conveyed to me by Dr. Franklin. The *Observations* are the very same except two or three corrections of no particular consequence, and an additional note in the section on the dangers to which the American states are exposed.

John Adams to Price[1]

Auteuil
April 8, 1785

Dear Sir,

Some time since I received from Dr. Franklin a copy of the first edition of your *Observations on the Importance of the American Revolution*, and lately a copy of the second. I am much obliged to you, sir, for your kind attention to me and for these valuable presents.

I think it may be said in praise of the citizens of the United States that they are sincere inquirers after truth in matters of government and commerce; at least that there are among them as many, in proportion, of this liberal character as any other country possesses. They cannot, therefore, but be obliged to you, and any other writers capable of throwing light upon these objects [subjects?], who will take the pains to give them advice.

I am happy to find myself perfectly agreed with you, that we should begin by setting conscience free. When all men of all religions consistent with morals and property, shall enjoy equal liberty, equal property, or rather security of property, and an equal chance for honors and powers, and when government shall be considered as having in it nothing more mysterious or divine than other arts or sciences, we may expect that improvements will be made in the human character and the state of society. But at what an immense distance is that period! Notwithstanding all that has been written by Sidney and Locke down to Dr. Price and the Abbé de Mably, all Europe still believes sovereignty to be a divine right, except a few men of letters. Even in Holland their sovereignty, which resides in more than four thousand persons, is all divine.

But I did not intend to enter into details. If you will permit, I should be glad to communicate with you concerning these things.

John Adams

Price to Franklin[1]

Newington Green
June 3, 1785

My dear friend,

An affair which interests my compassion a good deal obliges me to send you this letter by the post. A person of the name of Bourne in considerable

---

1. Charles Francis Adams, ed., *The Works of John Adams, Second President of the United States* . . . (Boston: Little Brown and Company, 1852), 8:232–233.
1. "Price Letters."

business as a broker absconded suddenly from London four years ago leaving behind him, to shift for themselves, a wife and four small children. During all this time he has not once sent any account of himself to his wife or any of his friends, nor probably would they have heard any thing of him if Mr. Bingham had not told me some time ago that he had heard of such a person and seen him at Philadelphia. Mr. Bingham now says that he saw him lately at Paris and, in compliance with the earnest desire of his wife, has writ to Mr. Cranford who pointed him out to him for farther information. With the same view, I take the liberty to write to you and to request that, if any opportunity offers, you would have the goodness to acquaint him with the great distress of his wife and her wishes that he would take some notice of her and give her some account of himself. I will only add that she is an agreeable and worthy woman with whom he was happy and that his conduct in this instance is reckoned very unaccountable. It is with pain I make thus free with you fearing I may put you to too much trouble but I have in some measure been induced to it by the consideration that what I have said of Mr. Bourne may prove a direction to you should he, as it is suspected he will, make applications to you and resolve to return to America.

I writ to you and Mr. Jefferson a few weeks ago and sent you some copies of the edition lately published here of my pamphlet on the American Revolution. Mr. Williams has given me much pleasure by calling upon me and bringing me a letter from you. I have, according to your desire, furnished him with a list of such books on religion and government as I think some of the best, and added a present to the parish that is to bear your name of such of my own publications as I think may not be unsuitable. Should this be the commencement of parochial libraries in the states it will do great good. Mr. Williams tells me that you have obtained permission to resign, and that you are likely soon to return to America there to finish your life, a life which, without doubt, will be one of the most distinguished in future annals. Indeed I cannot wonder that, after being so long tossed on the sea of politics and seeing your country, partly under your guidance, carried through hard contest, and a most important revolution established, you should wish to withdraw into rest and tranquility. May the best blessings of heaven attend you, and the sad malady under which you are suffering be rendered as tolerable to you as possible. You are going to the new world. I must stay in this but I trust there is a world beyond the grave where we shall be happier than ever. I shall be always following you with my good wishes, and remain, with unalterable respect and affection,

Yours,
Richard Price

Deliver my respects to Mr. Franklin, your grandson if at Paris. I wish also to be respectfully remembered to Mr. Jefferson, and the Abbé Morellet.

Mr. Adams is arrived in London, but I have not yet seen him. The Bishop of St. Asaph and his family are just gone to Twyford to stay till Christmas. Mrs. Price, sadly broken by the palsy, sends you her respects and wishes.

Price to Jefferson[1]

Newington Green
July 2, 1785

Dear Sir,

This letter will probably be delivered to you by Dr. D'Ivernois, lately a citizen of Geneva, and the author of an interesting work lately published and entitled *An Historical and Political View of the Constitution and Revolutions of Geneva in the 18th Century.*[2] He wishes to be introduced to you and I doubt not but the respectableness of his character and abilities and the active part he has taken in defending the liberties of a republic once happy but now ruined, will recommend him to your notice and esteem. His habits and principles carry his views to America and should he remove thither will make a very valuable addition to the number of virtuous and enlightened citizens in the United States.

Accept my best thanks for the account of Virginia which you were so good as to send me by Mr. Adams. This has been, indeed, a most acceptable present to me, and you may depend on my performing the condition upon which you have honoured me with it. I have read it with singular pleasure and a warm admiration of your sentiments and character. How happy would the United States be were all of them under the direction of such wisdom and liberality as yours? But this is not the case.

I have lately been discouraged by an account which I have received from Mr. Laurens in South Carolina. Mr. Grimkey, the speaker of the House of Representatives, and Mr. Izard have agreed in reprobating my pamphlet on the American Revolution because it recommends measures for preventing too great an inequality of property and for gradually abolishing the negro trade and slavery, these being measures which (as the former says in a letter to Mr. Laurens) will never find encouragement in that state. And it appears that Mr. Grimkey thought himself almost affronted by having the pamphlet presented to him by Mr. Laurens. Should such a disposition prevail in the other united states, I shall have reason to fear that I have made myself ridiculous by speaking of the American Revolution in the

---

1. *Jefferson Papers*, 8:258–259.
2. Francois d'Ivernois (1757–1842), *An Historical and Political View of the Constitutions and Revolutions of Geneva in the Eighteenth Century*, trans. John Farell (Dublin: Printed by W. Wilson, 1784).

manner I have done; it will appear that the people who have been struggling so earnestly to save themselves from slavery are very ready to enslave others; the friends of liberty and humanity in Europe will be mortified, and an event which had raised their hopes will prove only an introduction to a new scene of aristocratic tyranny and human debasement.

I am very happy in the acquaintaince of Mr. Adams and Col. Smith. I wish them success in their mission, but I have reason to fear that this country is still under a cloud with respect to America which threatens it with farther calamities. With the greatest respect, I am, sir,

Your very obedient and humble servant,
Richard Price

Should Dr. Franklin be still at Paris deliver to him my best remembrances.

Price to Rush[1]

Newington Green
July 22, 1785

Dear Sir,

The letter which I have just received from you, together with the considerations addressed to the legislature of Pennsylvania, have given me a good deal of pain by the account they have brought me. Before I received them I knew nothing of the test law in Pennsylvania, and I am truly sorry that such a law is maintained there[2] contrary to every principle of justice and good policy. The reasonings upon this subject in the pamphlet you have sent me do the writer great honour and appear to me scarcely capable of being resisted by unprejudiced and disinterested men. That is a miserable legislature which relies much on the use of tests for in general they bind only honest men. This test is expressed so strongly that real friends to the American cause and particularly Quakers might very well scruple taking it when first proposed; but to continue *now* the disfranchisement it occasioned, and thus to deprive two fifths of the inhabitants of the rights of citizens while any foreigner may entitle himself to these rights, is an act of oppression which I should have hardly thought possible to take place in Pennsylvania.[3] The credit of the United States would have been much higher had this been done, as far as it could be done without too much

1. Library Company of Philadelphia, Yi–2–7260–F, 43:61–64.

2. ("chiefly it seems by the Presbyterians)" scored out.

3. "I doubt not however but the majority of those who refused this test were influenced by very improper motives; but this should be now forgotten, and the magnanimity of forgiveness should be exercised" scored out.

danger. Indeed, sir, I have, since the publication of my *Observations on the American Revolution,* heard so much that I do not like, that I have been sometimes afraid of having made myself ridiculous by what I have said of the importance of this revolution. One of my correspondents in America who has been all along zealously attached to the American cause assures me that nothing can be more utopian that the expectations I have formed and he informs me of facts which, if true, have a considerable tendency to lower my hopes. From South Carolina I learn, that my pamphlet will by no means suit that state and that some of the leading men there are offended by the recommendation it contains of measures for abolishing the negro slavery and preventing too great an inequality of property. I will, however, still hope that the American Revolution will prove an introduction to a better state of human affairs and that in time the United States will become those seats of liberty, peace, and virtue which the enlightened and liberal part of Europe are ardently willing to see them.

This letter will be conveyed to you by Dr. Franklin. He is leaving for ever this part of the world. May God grant him a prosperous voyage. His excellency, Mr. Adams, in whose acquaintance I am very happy, desires me to present his compliments to you. Your tract on spirituous liquors I have not yet read. A friend took it from me soon after I received it but it will be sent back in a day or two and I doubt not but I shall read it with pleasure. I thank you for it and also for sending me the Pennsylvania newspapers. With great regard and every good wish, I am, dear sir,

Your very obedient and humble servant,
Richard Price

Jefferson to Price[1]

Paris
August 7, 1785

Sir,

Your favour of July 2nd came duly to hand. The concern you therein express as to the effect of your pamphlet in America induces me to trouble you with some observations on that subject from my acquaintance with that country. I think I am able to judge with some degree of certainty of the manner in which it will have been received. Southward of the Chesa-

---

1. *Jefferson Papers,* 8:356–357.

peake it will find but few readers concurring with it in sentiment on the subject of slavery. From the mouth to the head of the Chesapeake, the bulk of the people will approve it in theory, and it will find a respectable minority ready to adopt it in practice, a minority which for weight and worth of character preponderates against the greater number who have not the courage to divest their families of a property which however keeps their consciences inquiet. Northward of the Chesapeake you may find here and there an opponent of your doctrine as you may find there a robber and a murderer, but in no great number. In that part of America, there being but few slaves, they can easily disencumber themselves of them, and any emancipation is put into such a train that in a few years there will be no slaves northward of Maryland. In Maryland I do not find such a disposition to begin the redress of this enormity as in Virginia. This is the next state to which we may turn our eyes for the interesting spectacle of justice in conflict with avarice and oppression, a conflict wherein the sacred side is gaining daily recruits from the influx into office of young men grown and growing up. These have sucked in the principles of liberty as it were with their mother's milk and it is to them I look with anxiety to turn the fate of this question. Be not therefore discouraged. What you have written will do a great deal of good and could you still trouble yourself with our welfare, no man is more able to give aid to the labouring side. The College of William and Mary in Williamsburg, since the remodelling of its plan, is the place where are collected together all the young men of Virginia under preparation for public life. They are there under the direction (most of them) of a Mr. Wythe, one of the most virtuous of character, and whose sentiments on the subject of slavery are unequivocal. I am satisfied if you could resolve to address an exhortation to those young men, with all that eloquence of which you are master, that its influence on the future decision of this important question would be great, perhaps decisive. Thus you see that, so far from thinking you have cause to repent of what you have done, I wish you to do more and wish it on an assurance of its effect. The information I have received from America of the reception of your pamphlet in the different states agrees with the expectations I have formed. Our country is getting into a ferment against yours, or rather have caught it from yours. God knows how this will end but assuredly in one extreme or the other there can be no medium between those who have loved so much. I think the decision is in your power as yet, but will not be so long.

I pray you to be assured of the sincerity of the esteem and respect with which I have the honour to be, sir,

Your most obedient, humble servant,

T. Jefferson

P.S. I thank you for making me acquainted with Monsr. D'Ivernois.

Price to Jefferson[1]

Newington Green
October 24, 1785

Dear Sir,

Dr. Rogers, the bearer of this, is the son of Dr. Rogers of New York. He has been for some time in this country studying physic and he intends, I find, to spend this winter at Paris with a view to farther improvement. I cannot help taking the opportunity which he offers me to convey to you a few lines to acknowledge the receipt of the letter with which I was favoured in August last and to return you my thanks for it. The account you give of the prevailing sentiments in the United States with respect to the negro slavery, and of the probability of its abolition in all the states except the Carolinas and Georgia, has comforted me much. It agrees with an account which I have had from Mr. Laurens, who at the same time tells me that in his own state he has the whole country against him. You do me much honour by the wish you express that I would address an exhortation on this subject to the young persons under preparation for public life in the College of William and Mary at Williamsburg. But I cannot think of writing again on any political subject. What I have done in this way has been a deviation from the line of my profession to which I was drawn by the American war. Divinity and morals will probably occupy me entirely during the remainder of a life now pretty far spent. My heart is impressed with a conviction of the importance of the sentiments I have addressed to the United States but I must now leave these sentiments to make their way for themselves, and to be approved or rejected just as events and the judgments of those who may consider them shall determine. It is a very happy circumstance for Virginia that its young men are under the tuition of so wise and virtuous a man as you say Mr. Wythe is. Young men are the hope of every state and nothing can be of so much consequence to a state as the principles they imbibe and the direction they are under. Able and liberal and virtuous tutors in all the colleges of America would infallibly make it in time such a seat of liberty, peace, and science as I wish to see it.

I find myself very happy in the conversation and friendship of Mr. Adams. I have lately managed for him the assurance of Mr. Houdon's life, but of this he will himself give you an account.

I see with pain the disagreeable turn which affairs are likely to take between this country and yours. I am grieved for the prejudices by which we are governed. From an opinion of the necessity of maintaining our navigation laws against America, and that its interest together with the weakness of the federal government will always secure the admission of our

---

1. *Jefferson Papers*, 8:667–669.

exports, we are taking the way to lose the friendship and the trade of a world rapidly increasing and to throw its whole weight into the scale of France. Such is our policy. I have given my opinion of it but without the hope of being regarded. The United States, however, may be gainers by this policy if it puts them upon strengthening their federal government and if also it should check their rage for trade, detach them from their slavery to foreign tinsel, and render them more independent by causing them to seek all they want within themselves.

We are, at present, much encouraged here by the rapid rise of our stocks and the influx of money occasioned by a turn of exchange in our favour which has hardly been ever known in an equal degree.

Accept, sir, of the repetition of my assurances that I am with all the best wishes and particular respect, your obliged and very obedient and humble servant.

Richard Price

Dr. Rogers will be made happy by any notice you may take of him.

Price to Franklin[1]

Newington Green
November 5, 1785

Dear Friend,

I send you with this a pamphlet at the end of which you will find an account of a remedy which has been lately tried with success in the sad malady with which you are troubled. I have been led to this by the remarkable relief which it has lately given in this malady to a gentleman among my acquaintances. This gentleman is Mr. Barnett, brother-in-law to Mr. Hollis in Great Ormond Street. After going through more misery than can be expressed and being long confined, he now enjoys a considerable degree of ease and is able to go about in a carriage. Knowing this fact I could not make myself easy without communicating it to you together with an account of the remedy.

I heard a few days ago with particular pleasure of your safe arrival at Philadelphia and of the joy with which you were received there. We had been alarmed here by accounts in the public papers of your being taken by an Algerine pirate and carried into slavery. I was so foolish as to believe this account when I first read it but a little enquiry and consideration soon convinced me that the distress it gave me was groundless. May you still live to be happy in the respect and gratitude of your country and to bless

1. "Price Letters."

it by your counsel. It was a mortification to me that I could not make one of the friends who had the pleasure of being with you at Southampton. I return you many thanks for the kind lines you sent me from them. They gave me great pleasure.

I received some time ago from Mr. Vaughn a diploma constituting me a member of the Philosophical Society at Philadelphia. Will you be so good as to convey to the president and other members of the society, in whatever manner you may think proper, my very grateful acknowledgments? I cannot but be impressed by the honour they have done me and I hope they will accept my wishes of their increasing credit and prosperity to which, were it in my power, I should be glad to contribute.

I am sorry for the hostile aspect of affairs between this country and yours. The general cry during the war was that the colonies were too important to be given up and that our essential interests depended on keeping them. It seems now to be discovered among us that they are of no use to us and the issue may be that we shall lose the trade and friendship of an increasing world and throw it into the scale of France. Our restraint, however, will do good to the United States should their effect be to oblige them to strengthen their federal government, to check their rage for trade, and to render them more independent by causing them to find all they want within themselves. Should you happen to see Mr. Vaughn or any of his family deliver my kind compliments to them. With every respectful sentiment and the most affectionate regard I am ever yours,

Richard Price

Mrs. Price sends her respects. She continues sadly depressed and crippled by the palsy.

Price to Rush[1]

Newington Green
July 30, 1786

Dear Sir,

I have lately received two very agreeable letters from you, one dated in April and the other in May. I cannot enough thank you for the information in these letters and also for your oration, and the plan for establishing public schools and the diffusion of knowledge in Pennsylvania. The observation on which your oration is grounded cannot be denied. You have

---

1. Library Company of Philadelphia, Yi–2–7260–F, 43:117–121.

strongly illustrated it and a due attention to it would teach us more candour and charity to one another than we are apt to entertain. I am persuaded that the irregularities which shock us in the characters and conduct of some men not thought to be insane, ought to be ascribed to a derangement of this kind, in the intellectual and consequently in the moral faculties, produced by bodily disorders and physical causes. You have also in your other pamphlet inculcated with much ability the importance of education in general and the proper mode of education in a republican state. Nothing, certainly, can be of more importance and I heartily wish you success in all your attempts to instruct and enlighten your fellow citizens.

You flatter me much by exhorting me to address the United States and Congress and by encouraging me to it by telling me that probably I should be attended to. But, dear sir, you do not know how slow a writer I am, and how much I am pressed by a variety of necessary business. Sometimes, indeed, I am disposed to think it hard that at a time of life when my powers are declining fast, and when tranquility is becoming every day more necessary for me, and when for this reason I am continually thinking of withdrawing from the world, my engagements should increase. This however is at present my condition. I am by no means a Franklin who, at 80, preserves so wonderfully his abilities and vigour, but a poor weak creature who, at 63, finds himself under the necessity of considering the working time of his life almost over. My pamphlet on the American Revolution I have addressed to the United States as the last testimony of my good will to them. It contains the best advice I am capable of giving them on education and other subjects and having thus contributed my mite towards making them happy among themselves and a benefit to mankind, I must now leave others to advise them and refer the issue to that Providence which orders all events.

You observe that in writing to the citizens of America it would be necessary that I should be silent about the disputed doctrines of Christianity, and particularly the Trinity. I am afraid that were I to write again, I should find this a hard restraint. I am likely soon, in consequence of a petition from the congregation to which I preach, to publish in this country a free discussion of these doctrines and I hope your countrymen will learn not only to bear but to encourage such discussions. It is only vice and error that can suffer by them.

I am sorry that the convention of Episcopalians which met last year at Philadelphia did not carry their reformation of the church articles and service farther. If that improvement takes place among them which must be the consequence of free discussion they must in time see reason for doing this. I am informed that another convention was to meet in June last and I wish to know what it has done. Should another application be made to this country for a bishop it will probably succeed; for a bill has lately been brought into our Parliament by our bishops and passed, for enabling them to consecrate bishops for any foreign states. The bishops, before they applied to the King for leave to bring in this bill, met for the purpose of holding a consultation about the petition from the convention at Philadelphia; and it was asserted at this meeting, that this petition was owing to some management of the Jesuits who, it was said, had got in great numbers into the United States and were doing great mischief there by promoting popery. This objection, however, was overruled and the result was the resolution which I have just mentioned to apply to the King. How strange is it, that the same people who have discarded the nonsense of the hereditary right of kings should retain the greater nonsense of the heredi-tary right (or uninterrupted succession) of bishops, and for this reason scruple to make their own bishops.

Virginia, I find, has given a noble example of legislative wisdom and liberality. I am indeed delighted with the act passed there at the beginning of this year for establishing intellectual and religious freedom. It is the first of the kind that was ever passed. It does that state infinite honour and is a happy omen of the benefit to mankind that may arise from the Ameri-can Revolution.

Your information that a convention of delegates from the United States is to meet at Annapolis in September for the purpose of enlarging the powers of Congress has given me particular pleasure. All that is valuable to the states depends on a just settlement of the federal government. A jeal-ousy of power is necessary to check the tendency of all government to despotism; but it may be carried so far as to defeat its own end and to in-troduce evils equal to those of despotism. Of this, I fear, there is some dan-ger in America; but you say at the conclusion of your first letter concerning property, the good sense, and wisdom of America are now coming forth and taking the direction of public affairs. This is charming news. There are, I know, in the United States some of the wisest men in the world. May it appear in this convention that they are indeed come forth and have ob-tained the lead.

I rejoice to find that Dr. Franklin continues to enjoy tolerable health and spirits. His counsels and influence must be a blessing to the states over which he presides. I writ to him at the beginning at last winter and sent him a book containing an account of a remedy for his malady which had been remarkably successful in a deplorable case of the same kind which has happened to fall under my notice.

Very unfavourable impressions are made here by the false accounts which are often appearing in our newspapers of American affairs. An account drawn up by Dr. Franklin of a contrary tendency has been lately circulated with good effect. I am thinking of sending to the paper a few extracts from your letters.

Under a grateful sense of your kind attention I am, sir,

Your obliged and very humble servant,

Richard Price

Mr. Peters when in London last winter told me that you had sent me a letter by him but that he had lost it.

John Adams to Price[1]

Grosvenor Square
February 4, 1787

Dear Sir,

I am happy to learn, by your obliging letter of the second of this month, that you have found some amusement in the volume I left with you and that I may entertain a hope of its doing any good.[2] It is but a humble tho' laborious office to collect together so many opinions and examples but it may point out to my young countrymen the genuine sources of information upon a subject more interesting to them if possible than to the rest of the world. A work might be formed upon that plan which would be worthy of the pen and the talents of a Hume, a Gibbon, a Price or a Priestley, and I cannot but think that the two former would have employed their whole lives in forming into one system and view all the governments that exist, or are recorded, more beneficially to mankind than in attacking all the principles of human knowledge, or in painting the ruins of the Roman Empire, instead of leaving such an enterprise to the temerity of an American demagogue worn out with the cares and vexations of a turbulent life.

There is no proposition of which I am more fully satisfied than in the necessity of placing the whole executive authority in one. This I know will make me unpopular with a number of persons in every American state, but this is no new thing. Before even the government of Virginia was erected and before the convention that formed it met, which was several months

---

1. MHSP (1903), pp. 364–365.

2. "The first volume of Mr. Adams's 'Defence of the Constitutions of Government of the United States of America, against the Attack of M. Turgot.' This volume was published in London in 1787, as a complete work and was immediately reprinted in America in three editions, at Boston, New York, and Philadelphia. The second and third volumes were published in the following year.—Eds." MHSP (1903).

John Adams, *A Defence of the Constitutions of Government of the United States of America, against the Attack of M. Turgot in his Letter to Doctor Price Dated the Twenty-Second of March 1778*, 3 vols. (London: Printed for C. Dilly, 1787–1788).

before the convention which made the constitution of Pennsylvania, in the beginning of 1776, I wrote at the desire of several gentlemen in Congress, a short sketch of a government which they caused to be printed under the title of *Thoughts on Government in a Letter from a Gentleman to his Friend*,[3] in which three independent branches were insisted on. This pamphlet was scattered through the states and was known to be mine. Afterwards in 1779 in the convention of Massachusetts I supported to the utmost of my power the same system in public debates in convention, as well as in the grand committee and sub-committee, and drew up the plan of their constitution with a negative to the governor. So that my opinion, such as it is, has always been generally known, and I am not apprehensive of any uncandid reflections in consequence of the late publication. On the contrary, it is well known that Mr. Turgot's crude idea is really a personal attack upon me, whether he knew it or not, and therefore very proper that the defence should come from me.

Your favourable sentiments of it oblige me very much. I have great reason to lament the hurry in which it was done, having neither put pen to paper nor begun to collect the materials till after my return from Holland in September. Such a work too ought to have been grounded wholly upon original authorities, whereas I have made use of any popular publication that happened to fall in my way. If apologies were not always suspected, I should have made one.

Mrs. Adams and the children desire me to make you their affectionate respects. With the highest esteem, I am, dear sir, your most obedient servant,

John Adams

Price to Franklin[1]

Hackney
September 26, 1787

My dear friend,

I am very happy when I think of the encouragement which you have given me to address you under this appellation. Your friendship I reckon indeed one of the distinctions of my life. I frequently receive great pleasure from the accounts of you which Dr. Rush and Mr. Vaughn send me. But I

---

3. *Thoughts on Government: Applicable to the Present State of the American Colonies. In a Letter from a Gentleman to his Friend* [George Wythe of Virginia] (Philadelphia: Printed in Boston, reprinted by John Gill, 1776).
   1. "Price Letters."

receive much greater pleasure from seeing your own hand. I have lately been favoured with two letters which have given me this pleasure, the last of which acquaints me that my name has been added to the number of the corresponding members of the Pennsylvania Society for abolishing the negro slavery, of which you are president, and also brought me a pamphlet containing the constitution and the laws of Pennsylvania which relate to the subject of the society. I hope you and the society will accept my thanks and believe that I am truly sensible of the honour done me. As for any services I can do they are indeed but small for I find that (far from possessing in the decline of life your vigour of body and mind) every kind of business is becoming more and more an encumberance to me. At the same time the calls of business increase upon me as you will learn in some measure from the report at the end of the discourse which you will receive with this letter.

A similar institution to yours for abolishing the negro slavery is just formed in London and I have been desired to make one of the acting committee but I have begged to be excused. I have sent you some of their papers. I need not say how earnestly I wish success to such institutions. Something perhaps will be done with this view by the convention of delegates. This convention consisting of many of the first in respect of wisdom and influence in the United States must be a most august and venerable assembly. May God guide their deliberations. The happiness of the world depends in some degree on their result. I am waiting with impatience for an account of it.

In this part of the world there is a spirit which must in time produce great effects. I refer principally to what is now passing in Holland, Brabant, and France. This spirit originated in America, and should it appear that it has there terminated in a state of society more favourable to peace, virtue, science, and liberty (and consequently to human happiness and dignity) than has ever yet been known, infinite good will be done. Indeed a general fermentation seems to be taking place through Europe. In consequence of the attention created by the American war and the dissemination of writing explaining the nature and end of civil government, the minds of men are becoming more enlightened and the silly despots of the world are likely to be forced to respect human rights and to take care not to govern too much lest they should not govern at all.

You are acquainted with Mr. Paradise. He is sailed with his family for Virginia where he is the proprietor of a good estate. His accomplishments as a scholar and his excellent principles as a citizen must make him useful there, and I hope also happy.

During the course of last spring and summer I was frequently fearing that my health was declining. In order to recover it I have spent near two months in seabathing and dissipation at East-Bourn in Sussex and I hope that I have gained some recruit of spirits for another winter. Be so good as to deliver my kind respects to Mr. Vaughn when you see him. I am much in his debt for two agreeable letters and I hope soon to write to him. He is, I doubt not, useful where he is but, as we have Mrs. Vaughn with us, we are in hopes he will not be long absent.

Last night the *Gazette* told us that Turkey has declared war against Russia. It has also told us that the King of Prussia having entered Holland with his army and taken possession of Utrecht and many other towns, has reinstated the stadholder in all his honours and powers. But at the same time our preparations for war by pressing sailors, filling regiments, creating admirals, etc. show that our ministers expect that the French will interpose and that they are determined to join the King of Prussia in supporting the stadholder against his constituents.

With all the best wishes I am most affectionately and respectfully,

Yours,
Richard Price

Index

advice for, 323, 324; and improvement of world, 326; citizens of, sincere inquirers into truth, 328; develops friction with England, 333, 334, 336; false accounts of, in England, 338; convention of delegates of, at Annapolis, 338
Utilitarianism, 28

Vandals, 239n
Vaughn, John, 321, 336, 340, 342
Virgin Mary, 190
Virginia, 330, 338
Virtue: no one totally lacks, 153; danger of degeneration of, 208; proper motive to practice of, 276; private and public, and religion, 279; decline of, 281
Virtuous course: as action in accordance with imperative of liberty, 37; importance of weighing relevant factors, 38
Virtuous men: nature of, 278–280; dependence of states upon, 280–281
Voltaire, 278n

Wallace, Robert, 208
Walpole, Robert, first Earl of Orford, 56n, 59n

War with America: headings for enquiry into, 82; justice of, 82–90; issue of taxation and legislation in, 87; and justification, by principles of constitution, 90–91; a contest for power only, 92–95; financial effects of, 107–110; effect upon honor of, 110–114; dsgrace of, 112–113; will help check vices, 119; consequences of, 162–164; as inexcusable, 163; by laws as well as arms, 266; must be abandoned, 268; origins of, in Parliament, 270; prospect of horrors of, 298; as ruinous to Britain and colonies, 299
Washington, George, 10, 11, 310, 311
Watson, Richard, 145n
Wesley, John, 133n, 246, 228
Wilkes, John, 50n, 160n
Willard, Joseph, 14
Winthrop, John, 288, 296, 297, 305, 307, 316, 317
Wythe, George, 333, 334, 340n

York, Lord Archbishop of (William Markham), 51–55, 133n, 228, 261, 283n

Zubly, John Joachim, 114n

ADDITIONAL OBSERVATIONS

On the NATURE and VALUE of

CIVIL LIBERTY,

AND THE

WAR WITH AMERICA:

ALSO

OBSERVATIONS on Schemes for raising Money
by PUBLIC LOANS;

An Hiftorical Deduction and Analyfis of the
NATIONAL DEBT;

And a brief Account of the DEBTS and RESOURCES
of FRANCE.

Should the morals of the Englifh be perverted by luxury;—
fhould they lofe their Colonies by reftraining them, &c.—
they will be enflaved ; they will become infignificant and
contemptible ; and *Europe* will not be able to fhew the
world one nation in which fhe can pride herfelf.

ABBE' RAYNAL.

By RICHARD PRICE, D.D. F.R.S.

LONDON:

Printed for T. CADELL, in the STRAND.

M.DCC.LXXVII.

[Price Two Shillings and Six-pence.]